# THE ONE-PARTY PRESIDENTIAL CONTEST

## ADAMS, JACKSON, AND 1824's FIVE-HORSE RACE

### DONALD RATCLIFFE

UNIVERSITY PRESS OF KANSAS

Published
by the
University
Press of Kansas
(Lawrence,
Kansas 66045),
which was
organized by the
Kansas Board of
Regents and is
operated and
funded by
Emporia State
University,
Fort Hays State
University,
Kansas State
University,
Pittsburg State
University,
the University
of Kansas, and
Wichita State
University

Library of Congress Cataloging-in-Publication Data

Ratcliffe, Donald J. (Donald John), 1942–
The one-party presidential contest : Adams, Jackson, and 1824's
five-horse race / Donald Ratcliffe.
pages cm. — (American presidential elections)
Includes bibliographical references and index.
ISBN 978-0-7006-2130-9 (cloth : alk. paper)
ISBN 978-0-7006-3247-3 (paperback)
ISBN 978-0-7006-2159-0 (ebook)
1. Presidents—United States—Election—1824. 2. Adams, John
Quincy, 1767–1848. 3. Jackson, Andrew, 1767–1845. 4. United
States—Politics and government—1817–1825. I. Title.
E375.R38 2015
324.973'54—dc23
                                        2015017659

British Library Cataloguing-in-Publication Data is available.

Printed in the United States of America

10 9 8 7 6 5 4 3 2 1

*For Ruth and Alison,*

*and all who helped*

Late in 1824 David Claypoole Johnston, a Boston engraver and illustrator, drew one of the earliest cartoons illustrating a presidential election, which he conceived of as a "foot-race." This detail focuses on the three leading runners in a race that onlookers consider "not slow." John Quincy Adams is shown leading, just ahead of William H. Crawford but with Andrew Jackson coming up fast on the side nearest the viewer. The large figure in the crowd behind the two leaders is former president John Adams, who is cheering on "our son Jack"—unlike the Westerner (with powder horn and musket) next to him who shouts, "Hurrah for our Jack-son." Crawford is described as "the inner track fellow" who "must have got the better of the bots [?]," but a coachman (with whip) doubts whether he can "get the better of the QUINSY," whom others describe as the "bald filly" with "fine bottom." One "stupid NINNY" has hurt himself "trying to stop" one of the leaders, a reference to Ninian Edwards's self-defeating attack on Crawford in the A. B. Plot, which did much damage to Edwards's "honor." One gentleman of the turf thinks Jackson "has the best bone," and according to a bystander outside of this frame, "if he once gets upon ALL FOURS, he'll devilish quick take the lead of the whole PACK." Though watching a foot race, much of the crowd's commentary is drawn from horse racing. Detail from "Crackfardi" [David Claypoole Johnston], "A Foot-Race" (1824). Courtesy: American Antiquarian Society.

# CONTENTS

Old interpretations, like old habits, die hard. Of these, few have been more conspicuously long-lived than the conventional wisdom concerning the presidential election of 1824.

We know, or think we know, the story. A five-way race (that becomes a four-way race) for the presidency decisively ends the "era of good feeling" and slays "King Caucus." A four-way race becomes a two-way race as the Electoral College is deadlocked. Candidates three and four (William Crawford, by then disabled, and Henry Clay, eliminated) hold the key to whether candidate one or two shall be chosen by the Congress. General Andrew Jackson, hero of the battle of New Orleans, has won a plurality but not a majority of either the popular or the electoral vote. Secretary of State John Quincy Adams, occupying what up until 1824 has been the Cabinet stepping-stone to the presidency, has come in a close second.

Both candidates attempt to persuade Clay and his supporters. In the end, a "corrupt bargain," in which Clay ("the Judas of the West" in a colorful Jacksonian formulation) gains the secretaryship of state in return for supporting Adams, almost immediately launches the campaign of 1828 and renders the New Englander, like his father before him, a one-term president.

All very exciting—and all so appealing to those historians of a Jacksonian persuasion, and others besides, who too often shape their understanding of what comes before by their knowledge of what comes after. In this reading, 1824 takes on meaning as a prelude to 1828 and what one historian has called Andrew Jackson's "search for vindication." Exciting and appealing, but—as George Gershwin once wrote, and as Donald Ratcliffe's stunning reexamination of the election of 1824 clearly demonstrates, it "ain't necessarily so."

Beginning with an introductory essay that is, by itself, a gem, Ratcliffe tells us why this election is significant, explains how it has so often been either overlooked or misunderstood, and prepares readers for the narrative to follow. That narrative is at once succinct, comprehensive, and provocative. It is also persuasive in its fresh and fundamentally different take on the "corrupt bargain." This interpretation ought in time to find its way into textbooks, course lectures, and subsequent studies of the emergence of the Second Party System. In cautioning us, as we need so often to be cautioned, not to read our knowledge of the future back into the past, Ratcliffe takes these men and issues as they were and for what they said and did, and not for what they would in time become. So simple to say. So hard to do.

At the same time, we get a clear sense of character and temperament, of setting and color. Ratcliffe makes us feel as though we are there, even as he systematically demolishes the conventional wisdom. That this reconsideration has been so long overdue adds to its value. With this volume, Donald Ratcliffe invites readers on a journey of twists and turns, and of surprises aplenty. There could not be a more congenial, or credible, guide.

## ACKNOWLEDGMENTS

I was first introduced to the 1824 presidential election fifty years ago. Charles Sellers asked me the pertinent question: how did an election that historians conventionally typified as a purely personal contest lead on to a party system that became as issue-oriented as the Second Party System had by the early 1840s? The immediate result was an essay on the 1824 election in Ohio that appeared in the *Journal of American History* in 1973. Though my work became increasingly obsessed with medium-term political development in Ohio—among a variety of other things—my interest in this election has never dimmed, and I must acknowledge my gratitude both to Sellers for his lasting intellectual stimulus and to Kenneth Stampp for godfathering that invaluable year of graduate study at Berkeley. Inevitably the long gestation of this book means that I have acquired so many debts over half a century that this brief note cannot possibly express my gratitude to all who deserve it.

The University of Durham provided consistent support throughout a full career there, culminating in a Christopherson Research Fellowship. The university's financial assistance was generously and decisively reinforced at critical moments by the American Council of Learned Societies, the American Antiquarian Society, and the British Academy and its grant-making successor, the Humanities Research Council. Ohio State University gave me employment for a year in 1980, and the friends I made there continued to provide hospitality and stimulus over many years following. I have spelled out my gratitude in two previous books on the political history of Ohio, and I continue to benefit from the aftereffects of their kindness.

The American Antiquarian Society has been an important source for my research ever since I was awarded a short-term fellowship in 1984. Its excellent staff have for over a generation been an unfailing source of advice and assistance on a number of research trips. In particular I have benefited from many conversations with Philip Lampi, whose amazing collection of voting returns (now available at http://elections.lib.tufts .edu) and extraordinary detailed grasp of their significance have been far more important in developing my understanding of 1824 than may appear from the text and notes.

In 2004 the University of Oxford appointed me to a departmental lectureship that led on, in retirement, to a fellowship at the Rothermere American Institute. This good fortune transformed my research and publication through the combination of the stimulus of an excellent set of colleagues, the support of the institute under Nigel Bowles, the wonderful resources of the Bodleian's Vere Harmsworth Library, which the institute houses, and the commendable helpfulness and advice of the library staff. I could not have written this book without Oxford's resources—or, indeed, without its many visiting American historians. Chief among them must be Joel Silbey, who suggested the first sentence of this book, though he may not approve of the direction in which I have taken it.

Some material and ideas in this book have appeared previously in articles in the *Journal of American History*, the *Journal of the Early Republic*, and *Ohio History*, as well as in my *The Politics of Long Division, 1818–1828*. For encouragement to reuse some of that material, I am grateful to the *Journal of American History* and the Organization of American Historians, to the Society for Historians of the Early American Republic and the University of Pennsylvania Press, to the Ohio Historical Society, and to the Ohio State University Press. In the course of my long preparation, I have run up some important intellectual debts, notably to John Ashworth, Daniel Feller, Ronald Formisano, Howell Harris, Michael Heale, Michael Holt, Daniel Walker Howe, Philip Lampi, Peter Onuf, Daniel Peart, Daniel Preston, Andrew Robertson, William Shade, and David Waldstreicher, as well as to many other friends in BrANCH and SHEAR and to numerous anonymous critics. This present work has been read for me by several good friends who blessed me with constructive criticisms, for which I am deeply grateful: Richard Carwardine and Jay Sexton in Oxford, Daniel Peart, who has been most generous with his time and his research, and the ever pertinent, independent, and vigorous Daniel Feller.

I must in particular also thank the staff of the University Press of Kansas for making the process of production so comparatively swift and painless. I am grateful for the professionalism and thoughtful help of Larisa Martin, my production editor; the copy editor, Karen Hellekson; Marketing Director Michael R. Kehoe and Art Director Karl Janssen (who designed the dust jacket); Sara Henderson White; and no doubt countless others. But above all I must thank Director Emeritus Fred Woodward and the two editors of the series, John McCardell and Michael Nelson, for showing the most extraordinary patience and humanity in enticing me along to the completion of the project through difficult and, I hope, unusual circumstances.

Halfway through writing this book, I was laid low by a mental illness that for more than a year submerged me in a world of paranoia, hallucination, and nightmare. The people who helped me get through that slough of despond contributed more than they can know to the completion of this book. I owe most to my wife and my sister, to whom in particular I dedicate this book; to my children and their partners; to village friends and distant relations; to my family doctor and psychiatrist (both of them dedicated professionals freely provided by our National Health Service); and to many friendly souls scattered from the University Press of Kansas to Durham University. Much support came from within the American history community: from colleagues in Oxford, notably Nigel Bowles, Richard Carwardine, Gareth Davies, Jay Sexton, and, by affiliation, Michael Heale and David Turley; from partners in BrANCH, especially Martin Crawford and Dan Peart; from many friends in SHEAR, including Dan Feller, Craig Hammond, Dan Howe, Matt Mason, Andy Robertson, and Stacey Robertson; and no doubt others whom I cannot, regretfully, bring to mind at this moment. All of them in some measure contributed to my restoration, to my rediscovery of confidence, of memory, of critical faculty, of my pen. I hope they think it was worth it.

*Donald Ratcliffe*
Hook Norton, Oxfordshire

# 1

## MYTH AND REALITY

So at last it had come to this. Stephen Van Rensselaer knew how he acted in the next few minutes would determine not just the sixth president of the United States, but whether there would be a safe and sure transition to a new administration. For only the second time in American history, the result of a presidential election had to be decided by the House of Representatives; on the previous occasion, in 1801, much uncertainty had surrounded a prolonged contest, threatening chaos. A result on the first ballot this time depended on how the New York delegation voted, and that now depended on Van Rensselaer. The silver-haired Patroon bowed his head in prayer, seeking guidance. When he opened his eyes, he saw a ticket lying at his feet. It bore the name of John Quincy Adams. Seizing on what he took to be a sign from God, the devout Van Rensselaer slipped it into the ballot box. In so doing, he determined that Adams, and not Andrew Jackson, would be the next president of the United States.[1]

This well-known story offers useful reminders as well as important warnings. This was the one occasion since George Washington retired when the presidential election worked the way the Founding Fathers had envisaged. Because they assumed that there would normally be more than two candidates, they did not expect that any candidate would usually win a majority in the Electoral College, because only one ballot was held by the Electoral College's various branches in each state; therefore, the final decision would normally be taken by a "contingent election" in the House of Representatives, with each state delegation casting a single vote.[2] Only if one candidate stood head and shoulders over his rivals—as Washington did in 1788 and 1792—would the Electoral College normally be able to make the decision. The Founding Fathers had not anticipated the emergence of two national party formations in the 1790s that effectively reduced the number of candidates to two in election after election between 1796 and 1816, and so guaranteed that (barring a tie) one of them would have a majority in the Electoral College. The 1800–1801 election had gone into the House because at that time, the presidential and vice presidential candidates competed on the same ballot and the two Democratic Republican candidates had tied in the Electoral College. That quirk could not be repeated after the Twelfth Amendment of 1804 separated the two elections.

The presidential election of 1824–1825 thus stands as a warning of what might happen if ever a third candidate were to win enough Electoral College votes to prevent a decision on the first round. In 1948, 1968, and 1992 commentators openly debated what would happen if the intervention of Strom Thurmond, George Wallace, or Ross Perot forced the election into the House. They saw that it could extend the election far longer than the disputed Bush–Gore election would in 2000. Today, if the contingent election extends beyond the date prescribed for the retirement of the existing head of state, the newly elected vice president acts as president until one is properly elected. Even if the House election produces a speedy result, the rules governing it would, as in 1824–1825, enhance the power of the small states—every state, regardless of size, has in this instance only one vote—and place the final outcome in the hands of critically situated individuals, like Stephen Van Rensselaer.[3]

The story of divine intervention in February 1825 also warns us that much myth surrounds the accepted understanding of this confused election. According to New York's master politician, Martin Van Buren, Van Rensselaer had promised to vote for Van Buren's favored candidate, William Harris Crawford of Georgia. After the event, the Patroon told Van Buren his tale of divine guidance as an explanation for his change of mind. Van Buren did not repeat the story until "a long time afterwards" and first recorded it in the autobiography that he wrote in the 1850s. Quite apart from the egregious factual error it contains (see chapter 10), the story looks suspiciously like Van Buren's effort to emphasize that in 1825 the election was stolen from General Jackson, though the "theft" (as one modern historian calls it) succeeded only because of Van Rensselaer's spur-of-the-moment decision. Thus Van Buren emphasized that Adams was elected by chance, in denial of the popular mandate that Jackson had won, and so justified the subsequent Jacksonian campaign against the Adams administration.[4]

In fact, the greatest myth surrounding this election is the belief that General Jackson was the most popular candidate across the twenty-four states of 1824. It is true that he won a plurality of the popular vote cast in eighteen states, but what of the other six states where members of the Electoral College were chosen by the state legislature? While two of them were indecipherable but too small to make much difference, in the other four states the voters made it amply clear in the elections to the legislature which presidential candidate they expected their representatives to vote for. One of those states was New York, which in 1824 contained one-seventh of the nation's population and cast more votes in its state election in November than even the most successful candidate had won in the popular-vote states. All the indications are that Adams had the backing of about 40 percent of the votes cast in New York, while Jackson had failed to register any significant popular support there at all. That is sufficient to have given Adams a nationwide lead of at least 34,000 votes. In no way was Jackson the clear choice of the people in 1824.[5]

The election out of which this final competition between Jackson and Adams arose has gained the reputation, in historian Roy F. Nichols's words, as being "formless, unorganized, chaotic, and confusing." Others have seen it in terms of premodern politics; as Morton Keller has told us, "From 1788 to 1824, presidential selection was steeped in the deferential political world of the eighteenth century." Thus choices were essentially made by insiders, who were absorbed by the personal aspect of political advancement. Edward Stanwood in 1884 thought "all the arguments used [in the election] . . . were purely personal, and added nothing to political history"; it was, according to a historian writing ninety years later, "the personalist election beyond compare." This stress on personality is sustained by the continuing popularity of political biographies, which often disappoint in their weak sense of the political circumstances that dictated so much of their protagonists' careers.[6]

At the same time, historians have perceived that the mold of the old aristocratic republic was cracking. They tell how a newly enfranchised electorate was beginning to assert itself as a new breed of professional politicians strove to devise popular appeals and invent partisan techniques appropriate to the newly emerging democratic political culture. Thus 1824, for two political scientists writing in 1998, became the "watershed election in American history," marking "a break between elite-driven politics and the modern era of mass electorates." For H. W. Brands in 2005, it sounded "The Death Rattle of the Old Regime." Fifty years earlier, George Dangerfield had seen it as "the beginnings of the invasion of American history by 'the people,' not as rebels but as voters," in an election "devoted to the overthrow of an old and oppressive political structure." In General Jackson they found the ideal candidate, one who came from nowhere to win the popular vote. This view tells how the old elite of political insiders in the House of Representatives decided they knew what was best for the republic (and themselves) and cheated Jackson out of the election. The 1824 contest gave the Jacksonians the grievance they used to rouse the public and finally gain victory for the people in 1828.[7]

This is the tale told in many modern accounts of the election, including some of the most impressive works on the Jacksonian period.[8] It recurs in the many brief accounts that have appeared in anthologies and encyclopedias devoted to presidential elections or in broad surveys of political development or in brief biographies; too often, these summaries are tainted by gross factual errors by writers who should do better.[9] A fresh look not only confirms that Jackson's extraordinary popular appeal was restricted in its reach in 1824 but also hints at other, perhaps surprising, perspectives.

First, while the 1824 election was certainly "the first contested presidential election to be decided largely by popular vote," democracy was far from being a new phenomenon in the early 1820s. Popular votes among white men had long decided the course of American political life, and for at least twenty years, politicians had been mastering the arts of mobilizing a mass electorate. Through the Jeffersonian era, politicians had been campaigning for votes among an aroused electorate in most states, and they had at some periods roused high levels of voter turnout. Already a strong "electoral connection" existed between politicians and voters, who punished representatives who betrayed their promises. The right of the people to vote and determine government policy was not at issue in 1824—at least, not outside New York.[10]

Second, the arguments in 1824 were not about democratic rights but about the role of political parties in a democracy. For a quarter of a century, national politics had been dominated by the division of the electorate into two party formations, Federalist and Democratic Republican. Since 1815, partisan passions and popular interest had declined, replaced by sharp differences of opinion as to whether party processes were inherently beneficial to the republic's democracy or deeply corrupting and destructive of the people's will. Traditionally, the Democratic Republican presidential candidate had been nominated in a meeting, or caucus, of the party's elected representatives in Washington. In the run-up to the 1824 election, the practice was widely condemned as an aristocratic device for depriving the people of their right to choose a president, but it was defended at the time—as it well might be in a modern parliamentary system—as a democratic means of agreeing on the party's nominee. Indeed, its advocates justified it as the best means, in the circumstances of 1824, of ensuring the triumph of the popular will.[11]

Third, coming in the wake of a many-sided and deeply divisive crisis, the election revealed the fracture lines within the young republic. The most tangible were those created by the Panic of 1819 and Missouri's application for admission to the Union as a slave state. The South's growing anxiety over retaining and controlling its slave population was matched by a similar concern on the side of New Englanders to reduce the South's command of national politics. Equally, the eager support for positive national economic policies by people in Western and Middle Atlantic states confronted the determination of many Southerners and their allies to reinforce the traditional protection of states' rights and strict construction ideology. Complicating these cleavages lay the discontents and grievances of the lower classes in the great commercial cities and their hinterlands—grievances often expressed in terms of ethnic tensions or ideological differences. The Jackson campaign exploited those grievances, but they cross-cut each other to an extent that prevented an all-commanding popular movement.

Fourth, the attitude of the candidates on these issues was not quite what many historians have assumed. The heightened ideological issues of the Second Party System after 1837 cannot be read back into the early 1820s. Andrew Jackson did not stand for states' rights or the destruction of strong federal institutions and economic policies. John Quincy Adams was not "the most centralizing of the presidential candidates"[12] or an uncritical enthusiast for Henry Clay's American System. Attitudes to the major issues of the day were not yet rigidly set, and those of political leaders and voters would be formed essentially by the force of events, of which the 1824 election itself would prove one of the more decisive.

Fifth, the need to win votes without the support of an established party forced most candidates in many states to develop campaign techniques not previously seen in a presidential election. The election of 1828 is often seen as a moment of great innovation, the first occasion when politicians tried to excite a mass electorate about the election of chief executive. However, historians who have looked more comparatively have found 1824 to be the moment when innovation began, ranging from campaign biographies to straw polls and statewide delegate nominating conventions. Even the practice of selling political cartoons celebrating the candidates began in this election.[13]

Sixth, complex lines of division and a multiplicity of candidates ensured that no one emerged with an absolute majority in the Electoral College. The resulting election in the House of Representatives encouraged those dissatisfied by the result to shout "bargain and corruption!" with great effect, but that cry has effectively obscured what actually happened. By the end of January 1825, most observers believed that Adams would probably emerge as the winner, and the real issue became the nature of the coalition that elected him. According to veteran Federalist Rufus King, the bitterness of Crawford leaders after Adams's election derived not from his election but from their disappointment at not being the ones to elect him. Objecting to Adams's policies, they would in time concentrate on seducing Jackson to their viewpoint as the only possible hope for preventing Adams's reelection. Thus the maneuvers behind the House election helped determine the ideological shape of the future party division.[14]

Finally, the election of 1824 marked the beginnings of the process by which a new and lasting system of two-party conflict would be created in the United States. Although the so-called First Party System had generated deep popular roots before 1815, after the events of 1824–1825 the old distinction between Federalists and Democratic Republicans disappeared, and new political persuasions and voter commitments slowly evolved into what became the bodies of support for the Democratic and Whig parties. The political confusion that marked the 1824 election was the essential first stage in the most complete voter realignment in United States political history, even if initially it had the appearance of just a contest of fascinating characters.

## ENTRANTS IN THE RACE

All the candidates who won votes for president in the Electoral College were celebrities of considerable political appeal. All could point to significant public achievements that made them deserving of the highest honors; all attracted admiration, if in some cases reluctant admiration. In July 1823 one Tennessee newspaper published an anonymous article comparing the presidential election to a horse race—"a splendid political sweepstakes"—and each of the candidates was characterized in equine terms. Entrance to the race was free, it announced, and open to "any horse or gelding, mares being excepted." The weights to be carried were to be "nothing more than the obloquy which the respective riders of each could throw upon the nags of the others." The "magnificence" of the prize "produced great interest and excitement" and rather more horses were expected than "the five nags which were entered."[15]

The "horse of horses," according to his friends, was the JACKSON, "a tall slim horse . . . 'of mighty bone and bold emprise' . . . exceedingly spirited and high mettled," famous for his "splendid *victory* . . . over the noted British horse the PACKENHAM on ORLEANS TURF." According to his backers, "he was always at the service of the Jocky Club; . . . he required no keeping; and . . . he was always ready if the people should think fit to start him"; and he "came upon the ground full and rough—relying on his native strength, unaided by the skill of the jockies [*sic*]." Jackson's victory over the bloody British at the battle of New Orleans in January 1815 had indeed made him a national hero and a popular icon. As the first presidential candidate since Washington to arise from outside the ranks of established national politicians, he would achieve in 1824 some extraordinary popular successes that overthrew the expectations of most seasoned political participants. But Jackson was not taken seriously by most observers, at least not before February 1824, and many believed the election of a military hero could be fatal to the future of the republic.[16]

The ADAMS was treated less kindly by our horse-racing expert. Though "a horse of illustrious ancestry," he was "an obese, stout buttocked animal . . . much addicted to *bolting*." Born in Massachusetts, he was "*trained in Europe* . . . under the guidance of some royal grooms." Since then he had been frequently sent back to Europe "by the American jockies," but "the expenses attending the *outfits*, etc., always amounted to more than the winnings." John Quincy Adams would not have enjoyed the parody: the verdict of history is that he was a humorless, stiff-necked, distant patrician; he described himself as "reserved, cold, austere, and forbidding."[17] Yet he was also widely admired for his uprightness, his grasp of complex issues, his experience, and his dogged determination. His career was one of unequalled distinction, as U.S. senator for five years under Jefferson, as minister to various European courts under Madison and negotiator of peace in 1814, and as secretary of state through Monroe's two terms. Despite his Federalist origins, he was widely regarded as a committed Democratic Republican who had risked infamy in Massachusetts to support Jefferson's embargo in 1807. His national stature was undeniable, and in 1824 the sixty-year-old Adams was the only candidate to win votes in every state in which there was a popular election.

Equally respected was William Harris Crawford. In 1816 many politicians had considered him a better candidate for the presidency than Secretary of State James Monroe, but Crawford refused to split the party and supported Monroe's candidacy. As Monroe's secretary of the treasury, Crawford had worked effectively to restore the financial system after the War of 1812 and struggled to protect the nation's credit as the economy crashed after 1818. In the process he had built up a core of political support across the nation. Our horse-racing expert saw the CRAWFORD as a "tall, majestic figure, with wonderful bone, muscle, and sinew. His tread was *firm* and indicative of great strength and activity." He chose this horse, in July 1823, to win the race.

Sadly, in September this formidable candidate would suffer a dreadful illness at the age of fifty-one. Possibly because of inappropriate medication, probably because of a stroke, he became "practically blind, hands and feet paralyzed, tongue thickened, and speech thickened and nearly inarticulate." After twenty-three bleedings in three weeks, he improved only slowly. Though he recovered sufficiently to return to his office, he was never the same man again, suffering speech difficulties and bouts of incapacity. The fact that his protagonists continued to canvass his claims shows the depths of personal loyalty and admiration they felt for him. Even more, it demonstrates that important political interests of various kinds had become committed to his candidacy and could not be easily transferred to a rival candidate.[18]

The fourth horse in the race was the CLAY, "an airy supple-jointed fellow, of bright and cheerful countenance." At forty-seven, Prince Hal was considered the most popular candidate in his manners and accessibility. While Jackson was a retired military man and Adams and Crawford hardworking public servants, Henry Clay was the Great Commoner. In frontier Kentucky he had learned the arts of stump speaking and public appeal; he was the man who after the War of 1812 introduced into the United States the British practice of political dinners, with after-dinner speeches as well as the traditional toasts. He had deliberately stood apart from the Monroe administration, exercising his influence from the speaker's chair in the House of Representatives and taking up popular causes ignored by the administration. As 1824 approached, many believed that his appeal to Westerners would enable him to sweep at least nine states; then, if the election had to be decided in the House, his personal influence as speaker would ensure victory.

Other figures, of course, were influential. The fifth entrant, John C. Calhoun—"a mere colt, scarcely bridle-wise"—was not yet the extremist spokesman for the slave South, and his efficiency as Monroe's secretary of war made him a prominent candidate in the early stages of the presidential campaign. In the end he would be elected vice president with little effective opposition. In addition, as the horse-racing expert explained, "The *Dewitt Clinton,* of New York, a steed of no small celebrity, would have also *entered,* had not some Jockies of that state, last year, wilfully *lamed him.*" Clinton would hover in the background as the majestic (if unpleasant) candidate whose sudden intervention might yet upset all calculations. His rival in New York, chief jockey Martin Van Buren, risked his command of the largest state to elect his own preferred candidate, provoked public wrath, and lost control of both his state and its congressional delegation. This was not an election to be determined by managers.[19]

All the candidates had to be aware of the circumstances in which the election was held, and their success depended on being able to identify with significant political, economic, and cultural outlooks. All had to recognize that their personal campaign had to pay lip service to the tradition of the "mute tribune," which frowned on candidates campaigning for themselves.[20] All had to understand three critical realities that most historians of the election have overlooked or underestimated: the context of past political experience, the dire recent economic experience, and the immediate issues that concerned voters as they chose among the celebrated personalities before them.

## POLITICAL REALITIES

The rowdy scenes at the White House after President Jackson's inauguration in 1829 are traditionally seen as symbolizing the triumph of democracy. But eight years earlier, the man sometimes credited with organizing those scenes, Senator John Eaton of Tennessee, had himself complained of the "mobocratic collections," the "pressure through an immense crowd," at the second "coronation" of James Monroe.[21] So can the United States of 1824 realistically be described as an aristocratic republic, dominated by an elite and isolated from the people?

The republic had already long become, in most states, a functioning democracy, at least for white men. By 1792, state-imposed property tests on their right to vote had either been removed or made meaningless by inflation, while tax-paying qualifications meant little when a county road tax paid by labor on the roads could satisfy the requirement. The growth of two-party competition in the 1790s increased the numbers who actually voted, as partisans whipped up popular involvement and tried to drag every potential supporter to the polls. Fierce two-party conflict in state elections in the states north of the Potomac after 1807 encouraged statewide turnouts that in some states commonly passed 60 percent, even 80 percent, of white men. The powerful urge to vote made any suffrage restrictions meaningless, as the polls were swamped by force of numbers and sly manipulation of the rules; thus, constitutional reform in the North between 1815 and 1821 did little more than regularize what had become common practice. Though by 1824 only eight states out of twenty-four had adopted the principle of universal manhood suffrage (for whites), in practice every state except Virginia, Rhode Island, and Louisiana allowed almost all white men to vote for state legislature representatives and congressmen.[22]

These developments transformed the relationship between voters and representatives. Traditionally, voters had often chosen to vote for their social superiors and established office holders, except in moments of public crisis. However, between 1799 and 1815 vigorous party action encouraged partisans to invade localities dominated by their opponents and challenge the hold of local notables by using issues to rouse popular support for the outside party. The decline of habitual deference was furthered in the Middle Atlantic states and Ohio before 1810 by the introduction of local delegate nominating conventions to reassure voters that the candidates they voted for were indeed the people's choice. The growing power of constituency pressures forced the repeal of Jefferson's embargo in 1809 and the declaration of war in 1812, and in 1816 punished congressmen who increased their own wages in an outpouring of popular wrath that returned fewer than one in five for the next session.[23]

The Missouri crisis of 1819–1821 then demonstrated that most congressmen were unwilling to fly in the face of local public opinion, despite their better judgment. Any notion that the congresses of the early 1820s were divorced from the people they represented is entirely misleading.

In presidential elections, the final choice was more removed from the people, but haphazardly. Allowed by the Constitution to decide for themselves how to select their members of the Electoral College, half the states allowed their electorates to choose in 1796, 1804, and 1808. Those two Jeffersonian elections were probably the first in which a majority of white men had the opportunity to participate in a presidential election. The legislative method survived (and was occasionally restored, notably in 1800 and 1812) in states deeply divided by internal party conflict, because a legislative election could guarantee that the dominant party won all the state's Electoral College votes. Such maneuvers were accepted by partisan voters as long as defeating the other party was a popular priority, but with the decline of party hostilities after 1815, all but six legislatures had surrendered the choice of electors to the people by the time the 1824 election took place.[24]

The Era of Good Feelings saw the Federalist Party drop its formal opposition to the national administration and accept James Monroe's almost unanimous reelection in 1820. However, old party loyalties continued to dictate the outcome of state and local elections in many places where voters on both sides retained their sense of partisan identity. One Federalist insisted that Good Feelings were "distressing and odious to the subalterns" of the Democratic Republican Party, who remained "as full of fight and fury as ever." On the other side, a respected New York Republican remembered that "the federalists as a party were neither disbanded nor annihilated. It is true, the glitter and blaze of their watch fires were not visible, but they were smothered, not extinguished. The embers remained, and there were not wanting many who . . . were ready to fan them into a flame." As the Baltimore *Niles' Weekly Register* put it in 1823, "All are federalists, all republicans, when gathered at Washington, whatever persons may be at home."[25]

In 1823 the *Albany Argus* explained that, whereas old-style factions sooner or later disappeared, great parties like those of 1796–1816 took greater root. "Though they originate in a single point of difference . . . they outlive the causes of their commencement, and those who constitute them are led to opposite sides upon all questions which may arise in the progress of public transactions." Their supporters "are bound together by a thousand affinities and antipathies; real or fancied persecutions rivet the bonds of union; the succession of generations renders them more enduring, and the transmissions of sentiments and feelings of the father to the son is generally regular and unbroken." As a result, despite "the change of interests and of name, the same individuals and families have been found after the lapse of years, acting in concert on all questions of a public nature." In 1824 the old radical William Duane believed that in Philadelphia "the votes are given in the same way as twenty years ago," even if both parties now accepted the basic principles of democracy.[26]

In the early 1820s old party labels were still used in some congressional elections, and until 1825 newspapers still measured the balance of power between the old parties after congressional elections. At the local level, the old party nominating machinery was routinely mobilized in many places as an essential means of promoting party candidacies. At the state level, Republican nominations for governor and president were normally made by the legislature, but by 1815 the idea of a specially convened nominating convention made up of specially elected delegates was spreading. In Pennsylvania in 1808 and 1817 and New York in 1817, the party chose its gubernatorial candidate by holding a state nominating convention made up of both legislators and specially elected delegates. Such devices reflected an ideological shift: as Van Buren observed, by 1820 the party label "Democratic" was largely replacing that of "Republican."[27]

Opposing the regular Democrats stood an amalgam of dissidents. Federalists had to recognize that the persistence of party sensitivities doomed them to a perpetual minority, and their hope of influence and office depended on attracting the support of dissident Republicans. In most states some Republicans thought that party managers monopolized office, pursued the interests only of those who supported them, and prevented the proper pursuit of the common good. These dissidents were willing to work with Federalists, and for a decade at least, politics in many states had been a contest between Republican regulars and a shifting coalition of opponents. This independent approach appealed to many younger voters, at a time when about 45 percent of white males over the age of twenty were in their twenties and outnumbered all those aged over forty. According to one young Federalist, "Since the war a race of men have grown up, animated with love of country, unaccustomed to party discipline, and uninterested in those questions which have in an eminent degree sustained and nourished it." They were unwilling to blindly follow party nominations and, as "the active and most efficient body of voters," could not fail to give an impulse to public opinion in reference to the presidential question.[28]

These independents used vigorous democratic arguments to counter the regulars' attempts to guide voters by prior nominations. Federalists and dissident Republicans had long argued that party nominations interfered with the right of suffrage, kept power in the hands of the leading men of the dominant party, and so risked creating an aristocracy. It made little difference whether the nomination was made by a caucus or a delegate convention; indeed, many contemporaries did not make a distinction but referred to both modes as caucuses or committees. This accusation of aristocracy could be applied in particular to the Democratic Republican Party's practice of nominating its presidential candidate at a congressional caucus, which inevitably attracted all the criticisms of party dictation expressed over the last decade by Federalists and independent Republicans.

The Democratic Republican Party was not irretrievably committed to the congressional caucus. In 1816 some radicals, notably William Duane and his admirers, had suggested the party's presidential nomination should more properly be made by a set of delegates specifically chosen by the people for the task. Party leaders dismissed the proposal as impractical because transportation difficulties would prevent a full attendance at a special national convention and so deprive the nomination of its authority among the voters. The precise mode of nomination did not matter, they said, but it must effectively unite the party's support to prevent a Federalist resurgence. The party thought of itself as the "Democracy," and therefore by definition embodied the popular will.

Thus the political principles at stake in the presidential election did not concern egalitarianism or democracy but the continuing use of partisan techniques; it did not concern the overthrow of an old aristocratic ways of doing things but the legitimacy of any party structure that persisted after the issues that originally justified it had passed away. Men on both sides of that question accepted the same democratic values but disagreed over their practical implementation. The election must therefore be judged in terms of the democratic and partisan structures that contemporaries had known for over twenty years, not the future conflicts that they were unknowingly in the process of generating. The past tells us more about its past than it does about its future.

## CREDIT CRUNCH

Times were hard in 1820. According to contemporary calculations, half a million men were unemployed in the country as a whole—and that in a nation of only two million free men, a large proportion of whom were farmers who owned their own land. In many cities soup stations fed the indigent, and newspapers appealed for gifts of old clothes and shoes. In New York City one in ten of a population of 120,000 was receiving poor relief. In Cincinnati, an observer lamented, "All things are changed, the rich have become poor, and the poor distrust, one universal state of embarrassment exists; 'tis want, and fear and prosecution and suspicion and terror and dismay and bankruptcy and pauperism on all sides and on all hands."[29]

This economic abyss provided the inescapable background to the presidential election of 1824. The postwar speculative boom had collapsed in 1818–1819; economic distress struck everywhere in 1820–1821; and the depression dragged on for years in many places. While New England was less severely affected than other parts of the country and economic indices showed improvement from 1821 onward, in many parts of the West and South signs of economic revival were not evident until after 1824. This first nationwide economic downturn bears close resemblance to that which began in 2007: recessions that follow a banking crisis, resulting from irresponsible lending to an overblown property sector and excessive private indebtedness, always prove the hardest to recover from.

Looking back, most contemporaries had no doubt where the blame should lie. The boom had been underwritten by a great monetary expansion, fostered by those who thought they had discovered new, infallible ways to wealth. Since 1811 state legislatures had chartered an unprecedented number of small local banks, which printed their own banknotes and loaned them to private individuals, often on subprime terms. The borrowers used them to service purchases of landed property made on credit, often from the federal government. Banks were laxly regulated and, outside New England, based on unsound practices. They had weak, sometimes near-fraudulent, capital backing; the banks issued notes in quantities far beyond their power to redeem, confident that many notes would not be returned for redemption. In an age that believed only gold and silver had permanent value, the notes of most banks depreciated, making them worth less than the loans they had furnished.

Worst of all, the new Bank of the United States (BUS) that Congress had chartered in 1816 had not restrained the system, as intended, but had acted as "a mighty brokers' office," hurrying to make quick profits. When in 1818 the BUS found its own notes falling to a discount and its specie reserves draining away, it called on state banks to redeem their debts to the BUS, including the piles of state banknotes that it had accumulated. This contraction forced the state banks to call in their loans, often from those without the means of redemption. In a single year some 85 banks, out of a total of 392, were forced close their doors. The consequence was a wave of bankruptcies and defaults and a rapid sell-off of stocks of goods at sacrifice prices as men tried to rebuild their cash position. Property values collapsed as credit and purchasers disappeared; the means of exchange diminished, making it difficult for even wealthy men to pay off their debts.[30]

The monetary contraction was compounded by the reduction in European demand for American agricultural produce in 1819–1820. Prices collapsed, and the value of domestic exports fell by over two-thirds. This decline could not be compensated by domestic demand: the United States remained overwhelmingly rural, with only 28 percent of its labor force in nonagricultural work, and most of that in construction. The small-scale industry that had grown up in the period of trade restraint before 1815, mostly based in households and serving local markets, had been undermined by the massive influx of British goods after the war, and most industry—outside the very few textile factories in southern New England—already faced depression before the Panic. The few large urban centers—containing only 7 percent of the population—were not primarily industrial but existed to service the agricultural and trading sectors, and they accordingly suffered along with their customers.

By 1821, according to historian Murray N. Rothbard, "the painful process of debt liquidation was over, and equally painful process of monetary contraction had subsided." However, the collapse had medium-term effects that made economic recovery difficult. In some Western areas, almost all the instruments of credit that had existed in 1818 had been destroyed, and such banknotes as existed did not regain parity for many years. Many market-oriented rural areas retreated to a more subsistence basis and retracted from commercial activity. Some artisans and urban dwellers withdrew to the countryside in order to survive. Local trading continued, but often on a barter basis. The public's hard-earned mistrust of banks, credit, and paper money was itself a major inhibition of economic recovery.[31]

During this economic disaster, men looked to government for assistance, with success mainly (but not exclusively) in the West. Nine state governments passed stay laws, which postponed execution of a judgment, usually for two years. Five states passed minimum-appraisal laws to ensure that no property was sold for execution of debts below a certain minimum price, usually set by a board of neighbors. Four states established new state-owned banks to issue legal-tender notes, which soon depreciated rapidly and ceased to circulate. Other states, mainly in the South, allowed banks that had suspended specie payments to continue issuing notes they did not have to redeem. Among the seaboard states, only Virginia, New York, and New England were largely free from agitation to expand the money supply.

Debates over these measures aroused considerable bitterness and social conflict in the early 1820s. Merchants were accused of pursuing humble debtors while finding legal devices to avoid paying their own debts. Bankers were indicted of growing rich on paper wealth and illicitly retaining their shabbily gotten gains despite the crash: with the suspension of specie payments, they could carry on charging interest and expect repayment of loans they had made, yet refuse to redeem the paper money and promissory notes they had lent out. By contrast, ordinary farmers and artisans needed immediate relief, but many of them thought the future required the restoration of decent business habits in a world freed from the artificial stimulus of banks and paper instruments. Significantly, some of those whom historians have traditionally associated with lower-class interests, such as the radical William Duane in Philadelphia or Andrew Jackson in Tennessee, called for an end to stay laws and monetary issues, an abandonment of excessive debt, and a return to industry and economy.[32]

The evident class resentment turned against established politicians and embittered many elections in 1821 and 1822. In some jurisdictions local revolutions overthrew county and city elites and gave power to reformers keen to cut debt and expenditure. By 1824, however, these struggles had largely passed away, and in most states the relief acts had been repealed. The crisis had generated neither clear-cut lines of division nor a political movement that might dictate how men would align themselves in the presidential election. Local movements that described themselves as "democratic" or "popular" appeared before 1823, but they never directly correlated with the parties that competed in 1824 or (outside Kentucky) in 1828.[33]

The economic downturn had, however, created cultural attitudes that persisted. As early as 1818, commentators had blamed the excesses of the speculative boom on the moral decline of the citizenry, and into the 1820s men still demanded reformation. Yet this generalized sentiment had no immediate practical program beyond the demand that government waste be eradicated. Though the Bank of the United States was unpopular, attempts to reform or reduce it found little coherent support. The practical issues that invigorated politics in the states in the early 1820s were simply beyond the jurisdiction of the federal government. The class conflict that marked some elections in the early 1820s was confined to particular places and situations. But what did exist was a mood of discontent that might find expression in many varied ways. As John C. Calhoun said in 1820, "There has been within these two years an immense revolution of fortunes in every part of the Union; enormous numbers of persons utterly ruined; multitudes in deep distress; and a general mass of disaffection to the Government, not concentrated in any particular direction, but ready to seize upon any event and looking out anywhere for a leader."[34] But who should that leader be? Can it be possible that any of this experience connects with, and may even explain, the presidential election?

## MATTERS OF GREAT MOMENT

The presidential election of 1824 undeniably arose in a context of momentous and troubling events. Quite apart from the Panic and economic depression, the Union was shaken to its core by the Missouri crisis of 1819–1821, and bitter sectional disputes arose over internal improvements and protective tariffs. The balance of power within the nation changed with the "rise of the New West," the filling out of the Middle Atlantic states, the development of infant industries, and the expansion of the great seaboard commercial centers. New tensions expressed themselves in religious disputes, race riots, and industrial strikes. National security seemed threatened by the uncertainties surrounding the future of Florida, Cuba, and the new nations of Latin America. For a time it seemed that a French expeditionary force might carry a large Spanish army to the very flanks of the United States, prompting the president's declaration of what became known as the Monroe Doctrine. Could these events and developments really have had no impact on the forthcoming presidential election?

Federal policy could do little to help with most issues arising from the economic collapse. Though the Bank of the United States had been a major villain, prompting and aggravating the crisis, the assault on it was largely confined to the federal courts, and its future scarcely became an issue in the presidential campaign. The one thing the federal government could do was ease the difficulties of those buying federal land on credit, many of whom were on the point of losing their lands and improvements. Initially in 1819–1820 land policy tended to divide the newer Western states from more easterly ones. However, beginning in 1821, Congress helped its debtors secure part of their lands and control their debts, which greatly benefited most Western states but not Kentucky and Tennessee, where the land had never belonged to the federal government. For most others, this issue had in effect been solved before the election campaign was properly under way.[35]

In many states, ongoing arguments over local economic problems were overwhelmed by the large degree of internal agreement about the positive policies that the federal government should pursue to revive and strengthen the economy. These issues tended to pit the half of the population that lived within reach of Atlantic water (excluding those in the Middle States) against the half that looked to the development of the continental interior for their prosperity. The most prominent issue in the early 1820s concerned plans to use federal money to improve communications, with a view to binding the country more closely together and encouraging internal trade. Resolutions in the House in March 1818 revealed that the country was evenly divided on whether the federal government had the constitutional authority to adopt such a policy. By 1822, the demand for federal internal improvements was overwhelming in the West and the Mid-Atlantic states, while dominant groups in New England and the South Atlantic states were vehemently opposed. In spite of their resistance, it was a common opinion, according to Rufus King, that no one could be elected president in 1824 who opposed the power to finance the building of roads and canals.[36]

Transportation improvements were logically bound together with protective tariffs in what Henry Clay christened in 1824 the American System. Continuing dependence on imports of cheap, high-quality British manufactures had undermined effective national defense in the war against Britain, and it continued to undercut attempts to establish industries within the United States. In 1816 and 1818 a broad-based majority in Congress had accepted that the manufacture of items essential for national defense must be encouraged, and many would argue that the coming of the depression demonstrated that higher duties were necessary.[37] This demand did not come solely from industrial interests. Farmers appreciated that, given the collapse of foreign demand, the sale of their surplus crops depended on the creation of a home market by expanding the industrial sector. However, Southern planters who found their market in Europe, and Eastern merchants who serviced the Atlantic trade, opposed the raising of tariff barriers that might impede a vigorous commercial interchange with Europe. The contest over the tariff did not divide the country along the same lines as internal improvements but revealed a more North–South division, though with major exceptions.

Cutting across these economic alignments came the shock of the Missouri crisis. In its heat, men had threatened a dissolution of the Union; a fire had been kindled that, in the words of one Southern congressman, "all the waters of the ocean cannot put out, which seas of blood can only extinguish." Though enough votes were found to pass a compromise, the prolonged crisis proved a major polarizing experience for politically aware Americans. Many Southerners now looked for the means of sectional protection, though this would not become universally true south of the Border states until after 1825. Many Northerners saw the 1820 compromise as a Southern triumph that demonstrated that slavery had gained too powerful a political hold on the republic; like Rufus King, they wanted to break this "black strap," and to that end they advocated the election of a nonslaveholder as president. As Jefferson wrote, "A geographical line, coinciding with a marked principle, moral and political," had been "held up to the angry passions of men . . . and every new irritation will mark it deeper and deeper." A process of political reorientation had begun that would deeply affect the 1824 election.[38]

Of course, there were also many current distractions that, on the face of things, had little to do with politics. Local religious revivals preoccupied many folk. In many places this was a time of great sickness and mortality, with malarial fevers sweeping parts of the West. Even in Washington the socialite Margaret Bayard Smith observed in 1822 that conversation was dominated by illness and religion as well as the presidential election, and the city was just as sickly in September 1823. Then from August 1824 onward, the visit of General Lafayette became the excuse for a great patriotic party, as the nation's press followed his trip in huge, enjoyable detail as he journeyed along the East Coast from Boston to Washington in the weeks before and during polling. Yet these ostensibly nonpartisan events contributed importantly to the context of

A FOOT·RACE

*A Foot Race. David Claypoole Johnston's full cartoon takes a retrospective view of the election because it was not known until mid-December 1824 that Clay would come fourth in the Electoral College and so be excluded from the House election. Typical of its age in its concentration on the spoken word, the cartoon illustrates the active interest in the election taken by a broad cross section of the community, including the poor, immigrants, free blacks, and, in the background, women. Courtesy: American Antiquarian Society.*

the election. Illness and plague were a punishment for the immorality of the nation, seduced by easy material gain and attracted to immoral European fashions; a recall to traditional republican ways seemed all the more urgent. Lafayette's visit reemphasized the importance of the public sphere and the debt the nation owed to men who had sacrificed themselves for its establishment. All had electoral implications, however indirect, as the contest for presidency raised questions about the character of the republic, its health, and its purposes.[39]

The many issues and concerns underlying the politics of the early 1820s could scarcely fail to influence the way politicians and voters thought about the coming contest, but the popular election never became a simple referendum on future policy. The issues were so complex, so cross-cutting, that no candidate seeking national success could afford to take a clear-cut stand on every issue. The exceptions, Clay and Calhoun, failed to come in the top three candidates. Ambiguity was essential if the object was to build a national coalition. For that reason it was difficult to pin down just where the leading candidates stood on a particular issue, as they responded to a political situation in which each region possessed its own peculiar mix of interest, outlook, and desired outcome.

That regional bias explains one paradox of the election. According to almost all contemporary observers, the protracted campaign aroused "the most intensive political excitement throughout the country." As the most famous cartoon published during the election suggests, ordinary people of many kinds, including women and children, blacks and immigrants, took an interest, took sides, and expressed commitment in terms that revealed the particular ethnic, regional, and familial concerns that were of interest to them. Yet the overall level of turnout in the election was low, prompting many historians to describe the election as arousing little public interest. Certainly turnout in state elections between 1820 and 1825 was much higher: in eight out of the twenty-four states, it averaged over 64 percent of eligible voters, compared with 29 percent in the presidential election. The reason was that in most states, the outcome in the latter was already fairly clear, and voting did not seem a priority. Only half a dozen states experienced a real popular contest: in the Old Northwest, in New Jersey and Maryland, and in North Carolina. In these states, turnout in the presidential election rose to over 40 percent, compared with less than 24 percent in the ten other states that held a popular election. Remember the reluctance of voters at other periods to vote when traditional party lines are blurred; remember the customarily lower level of voter turnout in presidential elections before 1824; remember that the presidential election was commonly held on a different day from the general election for state and congressional offices at a time when voting could mean giving up a day's work in rural areas; remember that by polling day would-be voters knew that the final decision would be taken by a House of Representatives already elected—and then, all considered, 40 percent becomes a rather impressive turnout.[40]

The sectionalized character of the election of 1824 ensured that it consisted of different regional contests. By the time of voting, the issue in New England was between Adams and Crawford, and in New York between Adams, Crawford, and Clay. In the four Atlantic states from New Jersey through Maryland, Jackson, Adams, and Crawford competed with each other. In the Southeast, Crawford fought first Calhoun and then Jackson. In the Old Northwest and Louisiana, Clay battled against Jackson and Adams, but in Kentucky and Missouri against Jackson alone; in most of the Southwest, Jackson was opposed mainly by Adams.

In an effort to understand this complex situation, part 1 introduces the four major candidates and three minor ones, and considers the political interests and grassroots situations that dictated their progress up to the early months of 1824. Then part 2 examines the dynamic of the election campaign through February 1825 in its various critical locations—in Washington, in the battleground states, in some state legislatures, and finally in the House of Representatives, where, sadly, the Patroon plays a somewhat less critical part than he does in legend.

# PART I

## CANDIDATES AND CONSTITUENTS

# 2

## THE VIRGINIA CANDIDATE

The man to beat in 1824 was William Harris Crawford. Though surrounded by rivals we now consider political heavyweights, he was regarded by them as their most formidable opponent. A giant of a man, at six foot three and well over 200 pounds, he had a striking, handsome face and a powerful voice. Born in the Blue Ridge country of Virginia, he grew up in the rough-and-tumble of the Georgia frontier; his physical bravery was never in doubt, though he gave up dueling after 1806. As a local lawyer, he spoke forcefully and cogently, habitually presenting a case to judge or jury in thirty minutes or less. Even in Washington he showed signs of his frontier origins: unaffected in manner and dress, fond of his toddy and "boon companionship," sometimes awkward and lacking in some social graces, he could be witty and highly affable, swapping anecdotes and laughing uproariously. His physical presence made him impossible to ignore.[1]

His reputation had grown with some powerful performances in the U.S. Senate after 1807. His speeches demonstrated a power of clear and logical exposition, with sharp comment and penetrating observation. Firm and composed in debate, he became in 1812 the first president pro tem of the Senate to be elected on a continuing (and salaried) basis. After two critical years as minister plenipotentiary in Napoleon's Paris, he served as a reforming secretary for war and came within eleven votes of defeating James Monroe's nomination for the 1816 presidential election.

*William H. Crawford. Engraving by Stephen H. Gimber from a painting by John Wesley Jarvis, published in J. E. D. Shipp,* Giant Days: The Life and Times of William H. Crawford *(Americus, Ga.: Southern Printers, 1909), frontispiece.*

In October 1816 Crawford took over the treasury at Madison's request; he continued there throughout Monroe's two terms. He effectively reorganized the nation's finances after the war, restored specie payments by the banks, and helped establish the Second Bank of the United States. When the economy crashed and the presidential succession loomed, Crawford's management became a matter of controversy, but his handling of the national finances won admiration from those who knew. A former long-serving treasurer, Albert Gallatin, came to see Crawford as the one man fit to take on Jefferson's mantle. In his opinion, Crawford "united to a powerful mind a most correct judgment and an inflexible integrity—which last quality, not sufficiently tempered by indulgence and civility, has prevented his acquiring general popularity."[2]

Inevitably, Crawford was seen as the treasury candidate for the presidency. He built a corps of support for the succession, especially among men of influence who could manage the congressional caucus. Early in 1822 the South Carolina politician William Lowndes claimed that Crawford stood the best chance because he was "the only Candidate who had an *Organized Party.*" His rivals jealously ascribed this success to the huge patronage he commanded at the treasury, which won him support from officeholders in land offices and customs houses across the nation. Washington politicians claimed that the Tenure of Office Act passed in 1820 was deliberately designed to strengthen Crawford's hold by making all officeholders who handled money subject to reappointment every four years. With such a web of support by self-interested agents, Crawford became the candidate whom all the others feared—the man suspected of deliberately contriving his own election. Such "policy" defied the long-standing republican convention that candidates did not seek their own election.[3]

We know little of Crawford's true purposes because little of his personal correspondence survives. However, his closest students believe that he was not the conniving, maneuvering self-seeker that his rivals branded him. The Tenure of Office Act was not introduced at Crawford's behest; its main purpose was to strengthen federal control without necessarily casting a shadow on any officeholder who failed to be reappointed. In practice, almost all those whose terms ended between 1820 and 1824 were reappointed, if only because President Monroe kept firm control of all appointments. Crawford seems to have positively disliked giving out federal jobs, and he avoided merely partisan considerations. On his death in 1834, one obituarist claimed that Crawford's "unconcealed disdain of every thing like pretence, subterfuge, or the ordinary arts and tricks of mere party-men" probably earned him "more respect and general regard" than any other quality.[4]

Whatever the truth, deep traditions in contemporary political culture ensured his reputation as a manipulator. Being the treasury candidate made him vulnerable to traditional suspicions of power and corruption. Since the early eighteenth century Robert Walpole had been remembered as the British prime minister who held onto power for nearly twenty years by the adroit use of treasury patronage to maintain majorities in the House of Commons. The Country Party ideology that developed from that time warned that men with power would use it to corrupt those who were supposed to check them. That ideology had helped mobilize the Revolutionary fathers in the 1760s and 1770s and the Jeffersonians in the 1790s: republican liberty would be threatened if the secretary of the treasury was ever allowed to corrupt Congress. Jackson put it bluntly in December 1821: "I would support the Devil first."[5]

Besides making him an easy target, Crawford's post at the treasury also affected his political stance on the issues of the day. After 1815 Crawford had used the postwar revival to boost federal income, control the debt, and finance the ambitious government programs of the Monroe administration. After 1818, however, the collapse of government revenue—from near $50 million in 1816 to $15 million in 1821[6]—created a mounting national debt, and Crawford took the traditional position of the treasury in such circumstances: the nation's credit must be preserved by curtailing government expenditure. The so-called Radicals in Congress began to cut back appropriations for government schemes, and Crawford became identified with them.

In effect, Crawford became the leader of the opposition to the signature policies of the Monroe presidency. "The whole system of his conduct," according to one opponent in 1821, "is war in disguise." By the summer of 1822 he and Monroe were at loggerheads. The president thought of firing Crawford, but they patched things up. Monroe tried to stand above the electoral fray: his object, he insisted, was to allow his senior cabinet officers an equal chance to win the succession. Crawford's stance ensured the combined hostility of all his rivals, but it also guaranteed that he would receive significant support in the Southeastern states.[7]

## THE ANTIFEDERALIST REVIVAL

Under Presidents Jefferson and Madison the Old South had become increasingly content with its place in the Union. Confident in the nation's political leadership, the Southern states had supported strong national policies: the acquisition of Louisiana, Jefferson's embargo, the war against Britain, and the nationalist economic legislation of 1816. Throughout, however, a small group of conservative Southerners, sometimes called the Old Republicans but less confusingly referred to as neo-Antifederalists, warned of the dangers implicit in encouraging the federal government to pursue policies that not only favored commercial and financial interests but also stretched the restrictions on federal power at the heart of the United States Constitution.[8]

These anxieties first gained wider expression in Virginia in 1817 in the wake of the internal-improvement debates in Congress. Troubled by the low prices and declining yields suffered by growers of tobacco and wheat, planters in the Tidewater and Piedmont appreciated that federal financing of internal improvements threatened to add to their financial burdens while increasing the competition they faced from new lands in the West. These concerns prompted a shift toward a more particularist viewpoint by the leaders of Virginia's Republican party, the group sometimes called the Richmond Club or the Richmond Party (but not yet the Richmond Junto).[9] This narrow set of Republican political leaders, drawn from eastern Virginia, took a line distinct from the national party and became the focal point of the neo-Antifederalist reaction. The key figures were Spencer Roane, a jurist, and Thomas Ritchie, editor of the long-influential *Richmond Enquirer,* but the best known of their national spokesmen were Nathaniel Macon of North Carolina and John Randolph of Virginia, together with some young congressmen elected after 1817, notably Philip Barbour, John Floyd, and John Tyler.

Behind the renewed emphasis on strict construction lay their awareness that the South no longer possessed the strength within the national government it had enjoyed under Washington and Jefferson. In 1790 Virginia had been the most populous state—twice the size of New York—and the South had dominated Congress. Since the reapportionment of 1812, however, Congress contained fewer Southern congressmen than Northern, and Southern Republicans no longer outnumbered Northern Republicans. The census of 1820 confirmed that voting power was about to shift even further from the South's grasp, and a federal government that could not be controlled must have its wings clipped.[10]

This simple truth had special meaning for a slave-owning minority. The seaboard states of the Upper South still represented the main center of slavery in the United States since more than half the slaves in the Union in 1820 lived in Maryland, Virginia, and North Carolina. In these states the economic decline of Tidewater agriculture was assuaged by the export of surplus slaves to the rapidly developing New South. Conscious of the need to control their crowded black population, the eastern counties were especially wary of outside interference and recognized the importance of written protections against unsympathetic majorities in Washington. As early as the spring of 1818, Macon warned that "if Congress can make canals they can with more propriety emancipate." This was a sentiment that would be much repeated in the early 1820s.[11]

This particularist outlook lacked broader influence until the events of 1819–1821 created a new appreciation of economic and political realities. The collapse of credit, banks, and agricultural prices made nationalist economic policies prejudicial: higher tariffs would raise the price of imported goods and thereby impose a greater tax burden on those dependent on selling their produce overseas. In 1820 and 1821 congressmen from the southeast voted against attempts to give further protection to the North's infant industries, with the Lower South frankly basing its opposition entirely on expediency and interest. Not until January 1823 did the neo-Antifederalists openly say in Congress that protective tariffs were unconstitutional.[12]

More significantly, Southeastern planters began to appreciate the wisdom of their warnings about the constitutional defenses of slavery. During the Missouri controversy the South found itself deserted by most of its Northern Republican allies and outvoted in the House of Representatives. The verbal assaults on slavery stung Southerners and revealed the depth and breadth of antislavery feeling in the North and Northwest. More importantly, James Tallmadge's attempt to prevent a would-be new state from choosing slavery for itself represented an implicit challenge to the fundamental assumption that each state had a right to determine its own domestic institutions. For if, at the moment of translation to statehood, Congress could insist on the abolition of slavery in Missouri, what price the Southern states' constitutional right to retain slavery free of external control? On this point the slaveholding states stood together: they insisted on statehood for Missouri without restriction, even though they divided on whether Congress could prohibit slavery in the northern part of the Louisiana Purchase. For the neo-Antifederalists, Congress had no power to exclude slavery from any territories; roughly half the South's congressmen, mainly from the eastern counties, refused to vote for the Thomas amendment, the 1820 compromise's concession to antislavery sentiment. Already the ability to expand territorially was regarded by the Virginia school as critical to the South's defenses, and they saw future safety in the strictest regard to the precise words of the Constitution.

But if the survival of Southern domestic institutions depended on the provisions of the United States Constitution, was the meaning of the Constitution certain? Under Chief Justice John Marshall, the Supreme Court had begun to deliver interpretations that favored the nation rather than states' rights. In *McCulloch v. Maryland* (1819), it even upheld the national bank's constitutionality in words borrowed from Alexander Hamilton, thus accepting both the principle of broad construction and a moneyed institution that the Republican Party had originally regarded as anathema. In the 1821 *Cohens* case, Virginia itself was sued in the Supreme Court "as a party in her sovereign capacity as a State, notwithstanding the provision of the Constitution that no state shall be sued."[13]

All these dissatisfactions came to a head early in 1821. According to William Plumer, Southerners, particularly the Virginians, "talk coolly & deliberately of a separation of the States, or at least of an attempt to deprive the General Government of some portion of its powers. . . . They say that the General Government is every year setting up new claims & pretensions." At stake was the sanctity of statehood: Virginians insisted not only that a new state could not be prevented from choosing its own domestic arrangements for itself but also that a state came into existence when it, not Congress, chose—hence the "defiance and rage" of some Virginia congressmen when Congress failed to accept Missouri's Electoral College vote in February 1821 on the grounds that Missouri had not yet been accepted as a state. Had not Missouri become a state, with the privileges of a state, the moment its people had chosen a republican constitution for themselves?[14]

By the early 1820s the neo-Antifederalists found their region catching up with them. A backlash against nationalist policies had begun, especially among the planters of the Atlantic seaboard, from Delaware to Georgia. It was most powerful among those political groups that had traditionally been most influential in the politics of the Democratic Republican Party, and it ably exploited the "Radical" sentiment for retrenchment in other parts of the nation. In December 1821 they secured the election of a Virginia conservative, Philip Barbour, as Speaker of the

House of Representatives, in place of the antislavery John Taylor of New York. This victory, repeated twelve months later, gave Southern conservatives control of the House committee system for the first time since 1807 and ensured that the federal government would enact no constructive national legislation in 1822 and 1823.

The neo-Antifederalists equally recognized the importance of controlling the presidency. In 1820 Virginia's leaders had been skeptical of Monroe's political stance, forcing his friends to work hard to achieve his renomination. In March 1822 Thomas Jefferson's family physician assured Jackson that there was no chance that Virginia would support Monroe for a third term: "There is, in his native state, a powerful party as yet without a head, or in array—silently but decidedly disapproving the aberration (from the old republican principles) which has manifested itself for the last five or six years."[15] Some leading Virginians wanted the arch strict-constructionist Spencer Roane as their candidate, but his death in September 1822 frustrated that somewhat unrealistic plan. They had to look elsewhere for a new "Virginia candidate," and gradually most turned to Crawford.

Crawford, however, was not necessarily the most obvious candidate for Virginia's states' rights men. He was embarrassed by past evidence of a "dubious creed"—on the national bank, internal improvements, and the tariff.[16] During the Missouri crisis his position had been essentially that of Monroe, who had opposed executive interference in Congress's decision. In contrast, Adams was highly regarded by some prominent states' rights men, notably the thoughtful agrarian conservative, John Taylor of Caroline; Taylor disliked Crawford's association with moneyed monopoly and party manipulation, "with paper and patronage," and warned of the dangers to republicanism of sinister financial forces. Though Adams came from a hostile section, Taylor believed his record of conciliatory nationalism was less harmful than Clay's far-reaching federal programs.[17] In the end, most Virginia conservatives came to favor Crawford because he seemed less heterodox than other candidates. Even the unpredictable John Randolph would come out for him publicly in May 1824.

Long before then, however, in the course of 1822, the Richmond leaders had made their choice, following the lead of men they venerated. Nathaniel Macon, known as Father Macon in Washington, had already made clear his preference; Jefferson, who had expressed neo-Antifederalist sentiments since at least 1819, by 1822 was praising Crawford as "a Republican of the old school, and a friend to the barrier of State rights."[18] Ritchie at the *Richmond Enquirer* began explaining away Crawford's occasional lapses from strict-construction orthodoxy. That he would be the choice of the neo-Antifederalists was obvious to many observers, even before candidacies were openly canvassed. But would ambitious colleagues allow him a clear run at the great prize?

## PREEMPTIVE STRIKE

As Monroe's second term opened, most observers assumed that Crawford's chief rival would be the secretary of state, John Quincy Adams, with Clay as the most likely outside contender. Though it was said that seventeen names had been mentioned as possible candidates, through almost the whole of 1821 not one name was formally announced. Adams assumed that rivals within the Cabinet had been covertly at work for years, and some newspapers "lashed the heads of departments [including Adams] for their electioneering tours" in 1820. Men already complained that their maneuvering ensured there was "little concord, harmony, or concert in the cabinet." However, when Congress met in December, there were still no declared candidates. One observer thought that "the Presidential question . . . is troubling the waters below and causing many undercurrents to set in different directions," although "nothing appears on the surface." Then late in December it was announced that the secretary of war, John C. Calhoun, had accepted the invitation of a group of congressmen to stand as president.[19]

Of striking appearance, with piercing eyes and thick black hair that he brushed back defiantly, even his enemies conceded that Calhoun was "a man of fine genius, of much promise, and of great address." Clay found him "a most captivating man"; De Witt Clinton thought him "unquestionably the only great man in the cabinet." Contrary to his later career as Southern sectionalist, he was admired at this period for his nationalism: Adams famously described him in 1821 as "above all sectional and factious prejudices." As a congressman, he had fathered the tariff of 1816, the second national bank, and the abortive bonus bill of 1817 designed to finance federal internal improvements. As Monroe's secretary of war, Calhoun strengthened the institutional basis of the army, constructed forts for defense against the Indians, and built strategically important roads. If the Monroe administration's national program were to be driven forward, he was the man to do it.[20]

*John C. Calhoun. Engraving by Archibald L. Dick based on a miniature by W. S. Blanchard, ca. 1834, published in [R. M. T. Hunter,]* Life of John C. Calhoun . . . 1811–1843 *(New York: Harper & Brothers, 1843), frontispiece.*

By 1821 Calhoun and his friends in South Carolina had developed an intense personal hostility to Crawford and his ambitions. When anonymous articles appeared in a Georgia newspaper accusing the Monroe administration of betraying Republican principles, Calhounites in South Carolina responded by claiming that the articles were prompted by a "certain magician" in Washington who "moves you by wires." A Georgia Crawfordite threw down a challenge to the author of the response, and Calhoun's friend George McDuffie took it up. The result was three duels, one of them bizarre, a "war of newspaper ribaldry," and, for McDuffie, a bullet lodged permanently and painfully in his spine. This affair was followed in Washington with great interest: as Congressman Plumer of New Hampshire told his father in December 1821, "This opposition of views between the two Southern secretaries does not much look like Crawford's being next President."[21]

Behind the personal hostility lay a deep difference over policy. When the economy collapsed in 1819, Crawford insisted that the country could not afford Calhoun's ambitious defense program. Backed by dissident congressmen who favored a return to "the Republican simplicity of former days," by January 1821 "reform & economy" had become "powerful words before which army, navy, fortifications, magazines, salaries and improvements of all sorts are to bow." In that session Congress slashed the army's appropriation by 40 percent, reducing it from 10,000 to 6,000 men, and drastically cut back the appropriation for coastal fortifications. These economy measures won support from all over the Union, as traditional suspicions of a standing army coincided with growing financial constraints; Westerners in particular thought federal money could be better spent improving communications. However, Congress's failure to pass similar proposed reductions in the civil list suggested to some that a prime purpose of the economy drive was to cut the secretary of war down to size in advance of the presidential election.[22]

Certainly Calhoun saw the treasury secretary as an unscrupulous pretender to the throne whose election would corrupt republican politics and undermine the nation-strengthening program of the Monroe presidency. No man, he said, "with abilities so ordinary, with services so slender, and so thoroughly corrupt" had ever tried to be president before.[23] Calhoun claimed to prefer Adams but feared that he could not defeat Crawford in the Southern and Middle states; it therefore fell to Calhoun to challenge the assumption that Crawford was the favorite of the Southeast. The duty to defend the administration and stop Crawford and the Radicals became for Calhoun the essential justification for his ambitious and premature bid to become president himself.

Rumors that Calhoun would run were dismissed in January 1821, "as he is still a young man & so many are visibly before him in the race." In March Calhoun said he had "no views to himself for the next presidency."[24] However, Calhoun, still under forty, was a young man in a hurry. Already he was traveling widely, cultivating old college friends and political associates in New England, New York, and Pennsylvania, including many currently inactive Federalists and army officers he had worked with through the War Department before their dismissal or demotion in 1821 in the wake of the army cutbacks. Overestimating his popularity, Calhoun believed that he could build a solid core of support by appealing to the economic interests of the two most powerful states, New York and Pennsylvania, and by consolidating his home base in the Southeast.

In particular, Calhoun looked toward the second most populous state, Pennsylvania, which wanted to buttress its infant industries and improve its transportation links. There were signs that its grand old men who had figured high in national politics favored Crawford. Calhoun cultivated relations with their rivals, a group of aspiring young Republican politicians in Philadelphia known as the Family Party—including George Mifflin Dallas, son of Madison's secretary of the treasury, Samuel Ingham, and Richard Bache—which opposed the conservatism of the traditional leaders of the state's Republican Party. They not only admired Calhoun's commitment to positive economic policies but also appreciated that his Scotch-Irish origins could be an electoral asset in Pennsylvania. In December he was apparently nominated by his friends in Philadelphia, and late in the month a group of congressmen, mainly from Pennsylvania, called on him in Washington and formally invited him to become a candidate. After "some hesitation," he assented.[25]

The invitation had come just in time, and perhaps not entirely fortuitously so: Calhoun may have spotted the need to get his name into the race quickly. On December 18, 1821, the South Carolina general assembly met in caucus and made the first legislative nomination of the 1824 campaign, naming not Calhoun but the much-respected William Lowndes. Though less brilliant than Calhoun, Lowndes was considered less hasty and more balanced. His judgment was generally trusted; in Congress he had defended Southern interests while maintaining a moderate, conciliatory note. The legislature specifically named him as "the

*William Lowndes. This affectionate caricature is based on a sketch in the Lowndes family collections, published in Harriott Horry Ravenel,* Life and Times of William Lowndes of South Carolina, 1782–1822 *(New York: Houghton Mifflin, 1901), frontispiece.*

*National candidate"* who could unite the "confidence, respect and esteem" of all the sections. Had that nomination come first, Calhoun would
have been seriously embarrassed; he needed an outside nomination
before his own state nominated someone else. In any case, Lowndes's
diffidence inclined him to defer to his friend Calhoun; the two men
continued to take daily walks together in Washington and unreservedly
agreed that each should stay in the field, especially as Lowndes was already a very sick man.[26]

Calhoun's surprise move prompted much excitement in Washington
in the early months of 1822. At first his candidacy met with some ac-
claim, but "the knowing ones were astonished at the rashness of his
keepers" in placing such "a mere colt . . . in competition with such
tried speed and bottom" as Crawford and Adams possessed. Van Buren
thought Calhoun had allowed himself "to be made a dupe and victim
of a few noisy clamorous members of Congress, without influence at
home." The warfare between two Southern secretaries injured both, as
"the competition . . . creates jealousies and divisions in the proceedings
of Congress." The session finished "leaving the Candidates in the situation in which it found them." In general, politicians and editors were
reluctant to commit themselves publicly with two years to go before the
election. Uncommitted now, they could interfere with effect later.[27]

The Calhoun campaign concentrated during 1822 on developing
newspaper support. In Philadelphia, the Family Party's *Franklin Gazette*
came out for Calhoun "with great tone." Through the spring and early
summer it published what amounted to the first-ever campaign biography, a memoir presenting Calhoun as the towering statesman of the
age.[28] In Washington, Calhoun recognized the advantage that Crawford
gained from having a supportive newspaper, the *City Gazette,* to which
he gave the treasury's advertising. Believing that establishing "an able
and active paper" in Washington was "almost everything in fact in the
coming contest," Calhoun and his friends (and possibly his money) established the *Washington Republican* during the summer, an evening
paper under the editorship of Thomas L. McKenney. To increase its circulation, Calhoun pressed his friends around the nation to subscribe,
and it was regularly sent to many who were not subscribers. The paper attacked Crawford and condemned "the madness of retrenchment,"
which threatened an "amputation . . . which would leave the government
a limbless and desolate trunk." The Calhounites distinctly pitched their
appeal on policy as much as personality.[29]

By the time Congress met again, in December 1822, Calhoun's campaign was showing a second wind. The death of Lowndes in October had removed one embarrassment; in December the South Carolina legislature at last transferred its nomination to Calhoun, by a near-unanimous vote. He particularly cultivated ambitious Federalists, privately whispering that he approved of Alexander Hamilton's policies, though their support risked being counterproductive; his key man in New England was Daniel Webster, though Calhoun was not considered a serious candidate there. In the first half of 1823 new Calhounite newspapers appeared in Richmond, Virginia; Salisbury, North Carolina; and New York City, with Calhoun urging his friends to write for them. Between January and April a series of letters appeared in the *Washington Republican* accusing Crawford of misappropriation, corruption, and mismanagement. These so-called A. B. Letters, penned anonymously by Ninian Edwards of Illinois, probably with Calhoun's knowledge, prompted a congressional investigation that was inevitably deeply embarrassing to Crawford.[30]

Behind the scenes, the supposedly impartial president now appeared to pull strings for Calhoun, whom Adams had long suspected he favored. The president granted significant official appointments to Calhounites, making Samuel Southard of New Jersey secretary of the navy and John McLean of Ohio postmaster general. McLean in particular used his new position to Calhoun's advantage, whisking away well-connected visitors to meet the secretary of war, who lived "next door . . . across the lawn." To greater purpose, McLean could place friendly men in key post offices: because mail was paid for by recipients, they had to collect their mail from post offices, where a sympathetic postmaster might hand out political leaflets or partisan newspapers to those he thought susceptible and influential.[31]

Yet despite these advantages, Calhoun's campaign did not progress. As the *Richmond Enquirer* said, "The enthusiasm of [army] officers; the zeal of personal friends; panegyrics in the newspapers and the puffs of letter writers" could not in themselves produce popular support.[32] Calhoun had some strongly attached personal friends who would keep him in the field, but as early as February 1823 Rufus King thought his chances diminishing. Whereas initially Calhoun had calculated that Adams's friends would come over to him, King now conjectured that it would be the other way round. Calhoun's campaign depended on "the army [and] the people of Pennsylvania, as well as South Carolina," but Pennsylvania's preference depended on his winning substantial support in other states, which increasingly seemed less likely. Crawford remained the favorite of a majority in Congress, as Crawford increasingly benefited from the support of the major organized political force in the nation.[33]

## THE GRAND OLD PARTY

Crawford's great advantage in fighting off Calhoun was his established position as the favorite, even outside the Southeast, of many leading spokesmen for the Democratic Republican Party. Throughout the nation, many well-known figures privately expressed their support for him both on personal grounds and because he seemed most likely to carry the grand old party's banner in the election. Many supported Crawford from the beginning, seeing his restraint in 1816 as deserving the gratitude of the party; as Adams said, Crawford's policy was the "Democratic party."[34] Most of his proponents initially believed that an official party nomination would give the nominee a tremendous advantage, even in states where the candidate's sectional origin gave him little appeal. Though in the end the official nomination proved incapable of overcoming local preferences and prejudices, for a long time it appeared that the dominant political forces would carry the election for whoever was earmarked by the national party as its official candidate.

Powerful voices in the old Democratic Party constantly warned that the Era of Good Feelings was a sham. Jefferson scorned people who claimed that "there are now no longer parties among us; that they are all now amalgamated. . . . Do not believe a word of it. The same parties exist now as ever did." Not, he agreed, under the old names, because since the battle of New Orleans the Federalists had rallied behind a "consolidated government." As he told Van Buren in 1824, Good Feelings represented "an amalgamation of name but not of principle. Tories are tories still, by whatever name they may be called."[35] Mahlon Dickerson, the prestigious senator from New Jersey, was a long-tried "old republican" who in 1799 had gone "arm in arm" with Thomas Cooper to jail for his principles. In December 1823 he told the Senate, "The same array of parties which for many years distracted our country may not again take place; but if not the same, certainly a different one, probably more violent, more sectional, more geographical, more clannish, more inveterate, more dangerous." He therefore remained committed to the old Democratic Party and to Crawford's claims, even though he was also a strong advocate of high tariffs and federal internal improvements.[36] Pennsylvania's senior U.S. senator, Jonathan Roberts, had become a Democratic Republican in the 1790s when "political feeling was very violent," and had entered Congress in 1811 at a time when, he recalled, "party feeling" had "a stronger hold on men's minds" than at any other time. He had constantly worked to keep the party together through trying times, and he feared that the threat of dangerous economic pressures and irresponsible demagoguism meant that the republic could be preserved only by maintaining the distinctive character of a united Democratic Republican Party.[37]

The resistance to party amalgamation ensured that President Monroe could take only limited steps to assuage party feeling. Though the Federalists had withdrawn their opposition to the national administration in 1817, he made no serious attempt to appoint Federalists to federal office in his first term. Then, after his reelection, the Cabinet decided that a few Federalists could be safely appointed because, in the words of Attorney General William Wirt, "there was no longer any politics."[38] In January 1822 the administration duly appointed Federalists as marshal of the western district of Pennsylvania and as postmaster at Albany, New York. Those appointments were a red rag to Democrats who regretted the blurring of party lines. Elected only one year before but already highly regarded within Washington, Senator Van Buren of New York seized on this challenge to the supremacy of his state party as "the proper moment to commence the work of a general resuscitation of the old democratic party."[39]

Van Buren roused the senior New York Democrats in Washington to protest on behalf of "the Democratic party" in "a language" that Van Buren said had become obsolete at the capital but "must again come in fashion." Insisting that "all good democrats have who understand the matter sympathized with us," he asked his state legislature to protest and so satisfy "the great republican party of the Union." Though it failed to change the postmaster general's mind, Van Buren believed the campaign helped to redraw the lines of party: it met "the approbation of all my old political friends; their feelings on the subject are very strong & universally the same." Democratic Republican newspapers "in every part of the Union came out loudly in our favor, the spirit which animates them is felt here [in Washington]." Though the president continued to insist that "a great object of his administration" remained to "mitigate the asperities of party spirit," he recognized that he could go only as far as "public sentiment would support him"; he would not again risk "losing the confidence of his own party" by appointing a Federalist to a prominent office. Significantly, "the aspirants for public favour" in the presidential election who (like Calhoun) had looked in heterodox corners for political support now began to emphasize once more "their political stability & fidelity" to the party.[40]

Old Republicans all agreed that the presidential election opened the way to Federalist infiltration and even a return to power, making it essential that the Democratic Republican Party hold together to elect a sound man. Van Buren and Roberts were convinced that popular loyalty to the party could carry New York and Pennsylvania, and each was willing to take a bold stand to ensure that it did so. Roberts's Pennsylvania colleagues serving in London and Paris, Albert Gallatin and Richard Rush, fully agreed; they firmly believed it "best to act and think with the party whose essential principles we feel to be our own."[41]

The appeal of old party principle and connection ensured Crawford the support of some of the oldest established newspapers in the land. The Washington *City Gazette* came out openly for him in August 1822. The *National Intelligencer* of Joseph Gales and William Seaton had been the voice of the administration since Jefferson's day, but Clay had used his influence as speaker to make public printing contracts dependent on Congress. That move had destroyed its commitment to the executive and made it more eager to propitiate whoever might emerge as the rising power; despite its official character, its editors soon decided Crawford was the man. When Calhoun's papers attacked the idea of deferring to party leadership, the *National Advocate* in New York, the *Boston Statesman,* and the *Richmond Enquirer* raised their voices in disagreement. The *Advocate* in particular, under the editorship of Mordecai Noah, throughout 1823 stressed the danger of a Federalist revival and the need to accept whichever candidate the congressional caucus named, following the traditional process of the party.

These papers agreed that the caucus was "the only mode of preserving the harmony, inviolability and predominance of the Great National Party whose interests and character have hitherto been promoted through it."[42] Admittedly "party spirit can sometimes lead to . . . excesses," but "the essence and foundation of [our] party . . . is nothing but adherence to a set of principles . . . essential, in our opinion, to the maintenance of our free institutions" and "the happiness of the people." Fail to give a firm a lead, and the country would be ripped apart by, in Gallatin's phrase, "the disordinate ambition of individuals," which could prove "the greatest danger to our free institutions." Without that guidance, the people could be misled into choosing some man of insufficient principle.[43]

In recent times it has been easy for historians to assume that a congressional caucus could now have little influence because the First Party System had collapsed long before 1824. Leading politicians of the time knew otherwise; even the Federalist Rufus King recognized "the Reluctance [of voters] to vote ag[ainst] the regular nomination."[44] The Philadelphia publicist Mathew Carey disapproved of old party ties but acknowledged in October 1822, "Although it might puzzle sensible men of all sections to explain the present meaning of party words—*the charm* remains, and some men of sense, as well as blockheads, believe it is unsafe to vote independently of party."[45] In August 1823 Crawford was authoritatively assured by Governor William King of strong support among the people of Maine, but he must not count on it unless he won the nomination. "If there is a caucus, and . . . if [you are] successful, they may be counted upon in the electoral vote."[46] Others told him that he could scarcely win 2,000 votes in Pennsylvania on his own account, but with a congressional nomination he could well carry the state. The Pittsburgh congressman Henry Baldwin was eager to promote Jackson early in 1823, but apparently he was warned off on the grounds that the people of Pennsylvania might like Jackson but they also obeyed congressional nominations, and Jackson could not win in caucus.[47]

The confidence of party regulars arose from everyday observation. Voter loyalty patently persisted in places where the old party contest continued at the state and local levels, as in New England. In New Hampshire, for example, Federalists continued to elect members to the House of Representatives and contested state senate and council elections in districts where they had some chance of electing their candidates. Rhode Island's legislative elections saw close party competition between 1821 and 1823. Most strikingly, in Massachusetts the Federalists had been revitalized by the departure of heavily Republican Maine. Between 1820 and 1824 gubernatorial elections ranged Federalists against Republicans, with each party concentrating on a single candidate in closely competitive contests, with few scattering votes. According to one outside observer in 1823, "In old Massachusetts, the old party distinctions are still alive and were, perhaps, never adhered to with more zeal than at present."[48]

South of New England, the great states of New York and Pennsylvania were marked by complex internal political alignments caused by factional divisions among the Republican majority. Yet in each the Federalists remained a separately identifiable force: in New York they were themselves internally divided, but in the Philadelphia area they acted as a distinctive voting bloc. Contests in these two states took on more of a party character after 1820 than they had a few years earlier. By contrast, elections to the New Jersey general assembly tended to reflect a breakdown of party discipline, but in some counties in 1823 two party tickets faced off, attracting fairly consistent ticket voting on both sides. In the Border states, candidates for Maryland's governorship were identified by party in both 1821 and 1824, though only the Republicans managed to concentrate their votes on a single man. In Delaware gubernatorial elections were fought on strict two-party lines in 1822 and 1823, as were the county elections for the state house of representatives in 1824, when the Federalists as a party yet again won control of both legislature and governorship. Further South, the overwhelming dominance of the Republican Party ensured that internal state politics would be riven by factions, but in parts of Virginia congressional elections were still fought on old party lines, even in 1824.

Throughout the middle region—from New York to Maryland, and west to Ohio—delegate conventions continued to be held at the local and district level, ostensibly as a means of choosing candidates who were acceptable to the party's grass roots. In New York City, for example, the Democrats routinely assembled in ward meetings to choose the committee that would nominate the county's candidates for the assembly. In 1823 regular party men credited such "concert in action" through the various counties with securing "the triumph of the democratic party" in New York. They bragged that "this state and the state of Pennsylvania are united in favour of the old and regular systems of the party, and who shall oppose this united power?"[49]

How effective party management would prove could only be discovered in the voting. All the early maneuverings of 1822–1823 were essentially movements of politicians, with their assumptions of influence among the voters; as the campaign progressed, many of them would change their minds or rue their early commitment to candidates who could not carry their state. No doubt many prominent and experienced politicians were moved by loyalty to the man most likely to win the party's official nomination, but in the current political climate, would the voters follow suit? In particular, would they in states where the party leadership and Crawford cause were identified with the special interests of an alien section of the country? However, the first reality check, for both Crawford and Calhoun, came not in distant states but on their home turf, in a section far from alien to them.

## SOUTH ATLANTIC REALITIES

The Southeastern states did not form a solid bloc in the early 1820s. Still the main center of slaveholding, the Upper South showed a greater sensitivity to the threat of overly strong national government while neo-Antifederalism proved less strong in the Lower South. More significant was the cleavage in outlook between the seaboard and inland sections that ran from the Mason-Dixon Line to the Florida border and largely dictated the politics of each state. The seaboard was more heavily involved in producing staple crops for export, possessed higher concentrations of slaves, worried more about threatening congressional action—and tended to favor Crawford. The interior was more isolated, more economically diverse, less dependent on staple crops and slave labor, more interested in securing federal internal improvements, and more prone to Calhoun's blandishments.

In Virginia, an entrenched conservative tidewater dominated state politics to the disadvantage of the piedmont, the Great Valley, and modern West Virginia. Westerners resented the unfair system of apportionment that gave eastern interests political control. The assembly's failure to make sufficient appropriations to improve communications in the west and along the Potomac prompted numerous mass meetings in the northwestern and Potomac counties to call for a federal program of internal improvements, a proposal fiercely opposed in eastern Virginia. Many leading Virginia spokesmen for federal action, however, like the Federalist congressman Charles Fenton Mercer, opposed protective tariffs.[50]

Because the presidential election would be decided by popular statewide vote, the rapidly populating west would count for more than in a state election, though the state's property requirement restricted the vote to only about 60 percent of the state's adult white men. Calhoun, however, found little support even in western Virginia: this border area preferred other opposition candidates, initially Adams but also Clay and then Jackson. In the political climate of Virginia, Calhoun was simply too latitudinarian even for those wanting federal aid. As a newspaper correspondent remarked in February 1822, Calhoun "has no friends in

Virginia who will rally to the hustings in any of her districts. . . . No considerate Virginian who values the constitution of his country will lend himself to the care of an ultra politician of the federal school." Overall, Crawford's allies were too powerful: Calhoun's Richmond newspaper, the *Daily Virginia Times,* closed in August 1823 after only six months' operation, and Calhoun complained he could find none "to do [him] justice" in Virginia. Even former Federalists saw the force of Crawford's campaign: Mercer ran for reelection in 1824 as a Crawford Republican.[51]

North Carolina had traditionally followed Virginia's lead, but in this case, the state's established Republican leadership took the initiative in supporting Crawford. The main source of its strength lay in the area of tobacco, rice, and cotton plantations that stretched through the middle section of the coastal plain—the "Middle East"—from the Roanoke Valley in the north to the lower Cape Fear in the south. This was the main slaveholding area of the state, with slaves making up more than half the population. Its representatives resisted the nationalist program and generally opposed proposals for state-financed internal improvements.[52]

Other areas of the state saw government activism in a more positive light. The mountainous western third of the state remained in a frontier condition, its isolated farmers scarce able to sustain trade with distant markets. Small farms predominated too in the fertile and arable Piedmont area in the center of the state, though the spread of tobacco in the north and cotton in the south was slowly bringing it in tune with the more prosperous parts of the coastal plain. These interior areas resented seaboard political predominance, and together with disadvantaged eastern areas, they demanded a vigorous state internal-improvement program. In Salisbury, Charles Fisher's *Western Carolinian* directed this body of opinion toward Calhoun and his policies, especially his proposal for a new National Road across the Piedmont. East of the mountains, these counties also included the old Federalist areas of the state where a strong vestigial loyalty persisted to which Calhoun deliberately appealed.[53]

Partisans on both sides saw that the state elections of August 1823 could be critical. The legislators elected then would probably appoint the Republicans' statewide Electoral College ticket, and the congressmen would decide the final outcome if the election entered the House. As Calhoun urged in June, "We have reached the moment to act, and concert and activity are required." The Crawford party brought out "as many of Mr. Crawford's partizans as possible," without necessarily naming them as such. The Calhounites also nominated friendly candidates, and in a few districts the presidential question became the pivotal issue. Although overall it was subordinated to personal and local issues, the Crawford men gained the dominant position in the legislature, winning certainly a plurality and probably a narrow majority of the members. Almost all the congressmen elected were friendly to him, though in at least three districts they had declared that in a House election they would vote for the man favored by their constituents.[54] Though Calhoun, backed by six of the state's twelve newspapers, was Crawford's main rival, a significant constituency called for Adams, and Calhoun needed "a concert of action" among all Crawford's opponents if he was to challenge the Georgian's supremacy.[55]

The tension between states' rights Easterners and western nationalists did not operate as powerfully in the Lower South, mainly because of the attraction of favorite-son candidates. Georgia displayed a modified east–west split that underlay a fierce internal feud between Republican factions: the seaboard faction, headed by George M. Troup, was particularly strong in south Georgia and among the Virginia element in the uplands, and increasingly spoke for the expanding cotton interest, while the faction led by John Clarke expressed the outlook of ordinary farmers, especially in the interior, who were not accumulating land and slaves. Crawford himself was a former leader of the Troup faction and had fought a duel with Clarke; his presidential claims thus suffered when Clarke was reelected governor in 1821. In 1822 Crawford spent four months in the state campaigning for his candidates for state and federal office, but the legislature was still closely divided. The legislative election of governor in fall 1823 produced a "violent struggle" that lasted three days, which Troup narrowly won. According to a report from Milledgeville, "the direct bearing which the result of this election was admitted to have on that of the President of the United States, has produced the defeat of the most popular man in the state of the Clark [sic] party." Apparently no more than twenty members of the legislature opposed Crawford's presidential claims, and thereafter it was assumed that the favorite son had Georgia's Electoral College votes sown up.[56]

South Carolina did not give its adhesion to Calhoun as easily as this favorite-son logic might suggest. The state had a long tradition of favoring nationalist policies, but in 1820 its two serving U.S. senators, William Smith and John Gaillard, were neo-Antifederalists who had already decided in favor of Crawford. The assembly snubbed their extreme states' rights views and nominated Lowndes in December 1821 specifically as an opponent of excessive "State sovereignty" and "unrelenting economy." Inheriting Lowndes's nomination almost unanimously, Calhoun engineered Smith's narrow defeat for reelection to the Senate in December 1822; Smith responded by leading an active but limited Old Republican opposition to Calhoun in 1823–1824. The state remained in the hands of the nationalists, but not without challenge.[57]

By January 1824, one Northern congressman could observe that "the south now appears to have (except S. Carolina) a fixed and warm opposition" to Calhoun that would not be removed even if Crawford died.[58] Calhoun had failed to persuade the other Southeastern states to reject strict construction, neo-Antifederalism, and Crawford. That failure marked a distinct stage in the development of Southern political attitudes: in the years soon to come, Calhoun himself would adopt the sectionalist outlook that, writ large, would mark the South's progress to secession over thirty years later. For the moment, though, his continuing hopes for Pennsylvania kept him in the current national contest, but Crawford remained the man to beat.

# 3

## A NORTHERN MAN

Charles Hammond was an acute observer of American politics who would become the first great journalist of the Old Northwest. A Federalist by upbringing and persuasion, a careful articulator of ideas and argument, his legal talent impressed both Thomas Jefferson and John Marshall and would lead John Quincy Adams to think of him as a future Supreme Court justice. In February 1820 Hammond was thoroughly aroused by the Missouri crisis and thought it "fraught with important consequences. A new state of parties must grow out of it—Give me a Northern President, whether J.Q. Adams or D. Clinton—or anybody rather than things should remain as they are."[1]

Hammond was not alone. In 1820 some attempts were made to organize an opposition to Monroe's reelection, and tickets favoring De Witt Clinton attracted votes in New York, Pennsylvania, New Jersey, and Ohio. Overall, the election of 1820 came too closely on the heels of the controversy for Northerners to decide on a standard-bearer. New Hampshire congressman William Plumer Jr. appreciated that those best fitted to mount a challenge would "be candidates after the next term—& they know that any present attempt would destroy their future hopes." Looking to 1824, Adams privately told Plumer, "The question of Slavery in the new states—a President from the slave or the free states—would in his opinion, be the great rallying point at the next election, &, of course render it a struggle between the north and the south."[2]

Behind this prognostication lay a recognition of the impact of the Missouri crisis on Northern opinion. One opponent of slavery's expansion declared, after traveling extensively in the North, that "on this question, there appears to be no difference of opinion, all wishing to prevent by all the means in their power the further extention [sic] of that crying Evil, alike inhuman and disgraceful in a country like ours." Northern congressmen agreed, voting—with extraordinary cohesion in the face of Southern cries of fury and threats of secession—to admit Missouri as a state only if it agreed to ban the future admission of slaves. Some Northern representatives recognized that such a restriction could not pass the Senate and so a compromise was necessary, but the pressure of opinion back home obliged them to maintain their stand—almost unanimously, up to the final votes. When eighteen "doughfaces" (as John Randolph famously called them) at last voted to admit Missouri without restriction, they duly paid the price: only five survived the scrutiny of the 1820–1821 elections.[3]

Undeniably, the strength of feeling in the North resulted partly from jealousy of the political power that Southerners exercised in the republic. New England Federalists had long grumbled that the Constitution's three-fifths rule gave the slave states an unfair political advantage, which they had used to impose disastrous foreign and commercial policies. Some Northern Democratic Republicans resented Southern control of their party, as New Yorkers made clear in the Clintonian campaigns of 1808 and 1812. This discontent was certainly reinforced by the dissatisfaction of Northern commercial and manufacturing classes with Virginia's unsympathetic leadership. Yet underlying all these jealousies lay a deep objection to the immoral nature of the institution that gave the South its economic and political power.

The antislavery attitudes created in the Revolutionary era had weakened in the South but still retained much force in the North. Despite the enervating effect of gradualist assumptions and racist attitudes, after 1815 Northerners expressed great anxiety over Southerners' demands relating to the illegal importation of slaves, the rendition of runaways, the kidnapping of free blacks, and the status of slavery in the Old Northwest. From the point of view of Northern antislavery sentiment, the attempt to admit Missouri as a slave state looked like another step in the Southern campaign to entwine slavery even more tightly in the fabric of the republic. Its success in 1820 was interpreted by many as a Southern triumph which demonstrated that slavery had gained too powerful a political hold on the republic.[4]

But would a confection of antislavery and anti-Southernism provide a sufficient base upon which to build a presidential candidacy? Any candidate supported on those grounds would have to write off the South, as Adams's protagonists well recognized. True, victory was possible on the basis of Northern votes alone. True, many Northerners initially wished to break the South's monopoly of the presidency. However, only certain religious groups, most notably the Quakers, prized their antislavery commitment above all other considerations. Other Northerners, including Charles Hammond, gradually fell away from the anti-Southern standard and came to regard other concerns as more important in the 1824 election. For many reasons, they hesitated about sustaining a sectional confrontation.

### LIMITS OF ANTISLAVERY

A heightened antislavery sentiment threatened to become a significant political force in the aftermath of the Missouri crisis. Some newspapers in the free states that fringed the South began to refuse to print advertisements for the recapture of fugitive slaves. From 1821 on, petitions circulated annually demanding the abolition of slavery in the District of Columbia, where ostensibly Congress had full discretion to act. Within Congress, Southern attempts to pass a new fugitive slave bill in March 1822 were criticized for threatening to "excite afresh those angry feelings which are hardly yet subsided" and were defeated by a two-thirds margin.[5] Then in February 1824 the Ohio general assembly passed resolutions calling on the federal government to pass a law—with the consent of the slaveholding states—freeing at the age of 21, and then colonizing, all slaves born after the passage of the act. The resolutions declared that because "the evil of slavery is a national one," the people of all the states should share the costs. Seven other Northern states plus Delaware rapidly endorsed the proposal.[6]

Persisting antislavery sentiment even affected General Lafayette's visit to the United States in 1824–1825. The Revolutionary hero was celebrated in much same terms of republican enthusiasm wherever he went around the country. However, in parts of the North, specific reference was also made to his record as a friend of slave emancipation. In

*Kicking Black Freedmen. This detail from Johnston's cartoon "A Foot-Race" (1824) shows a black youth aping white dandies and being kicked by another dandy. The words of the casual assailant, who speaks with a foreign accent, can be seen outside this frame: "Ah hah! Now, Neddy, I tink dat kick on de back of you side as worse den have no dinner de fourt of July." This could be a reference to the spread of black celebrations of the national anniversary after 1820, and it suggests the antagonism of European immigrants to free blacks even in 1824. Courtesy: American Antiquarian Society.*

New York in September, Lafayette visited the "Free school for young Africans, directed by the Abolition Society," and was unanimously elected a member of the society, along with two renowned English abolitionists. "This election agreed well with his . . . declared opinions relative to negro slavery, and appeared to excite in him considerable feeling," for he had always insisted that "all men without exception" have a right to liberty. When he reached Boston in October, the old Federalist paper, the *Columbian Centinel,* published a poem written from the perspective of slaves. Declaring that slavery was incompatible with the ideals of the Revolution, the anonymous poet called on Lafayette to tell the South "To take off our fetters with wisdom and grace, / To treat us as brothers—tho' sable our race." Northern antislavery could still embrace the genuinely liberal attitudes of the late eighteenth century, when reformers had been willing to consider that perhaps Africans were not innately different from white Americans.[7]

Since the 1790s, however, Northern attitudes had been shifting to the view that Negroes were inevitably alien and inferior, and as freemen would corrupt the societies they lived in. Such hesitations were perhaps understandable in the five coastal states from Pennsylvania to Rhode Island, where some 20,000 black Americans were still enslaved in 1820. In these states, the process of gradual emancipation was still unwinding, and the white population faced the psychological problem of absorbing people who had long been held in chains. Formally, for the most part, Northeastern freed men were treated reasonably: when in 1821 the proposed Missouri constitution threw doubt on whether African Americans could become citizens, its representatives could reasonably object that freedmen still retained civil and even political rights in most older Northern states. In 1824 skin color in itself would not debar a black man from voting in Pennsylvania, New York, and four New England states.

The new Northwestern states, by contrast, had relatively small black populations but feared an influx of newly freed slaves from the South. Though relations with existing black populations remained relatively harmonious, many Northerners, in both East and West, thought improvident, barely civilized former slaves would bring with them poverty and vice. Between 1807 and 1822 free blacks were disfranchised in New Jersey, Connecticut, Rhode Island, and partially in New York as well as in the Old Northwest, while there were clear signs that discrimination and de facto segregation were increasing and race relations deteriorating throughout the North. In October 1824 a white mob in Providence,

Rhode Island, destroyed at least seven houses belonging to black residents in the Hard Scrabble area of the city; the seven whites arrested for disturbing the peace and destroying property were found not guilty. This began a sequence of race riots that would disgrace Northern cities from Boston to Cincinnati in the 1820s, marking a deterioration in race relations that by 1824 was already affecting political differences over slavery.[8]

As the presidential campaign proceeded toward its climax, racial concerns began to intrude on the debate, even in the North. Crawford was especially vulnerable to racial slurs because during his brief spell at the War Department in 1815–1816 he had written a report suggesting that the Indian population should be assimilated by encouraging interracial marriage. This "odious and repulsive proposition" was roundly denounced in 1816 by Thomas Cooper in a set of "strictures" that were reprinted in Philadelphia in 1824 in an effort to destroy any lingering loyalty to the Democratic Party's leading man. One cartoon published in the city late in the campaign contained, in one corner, a side reference to the dispute (see opposite): it labeled the U.S. Treasury the "Amalgamation-Tool Department" and showed Crawford telling a woman that it was better to "marry our wild Indians than Foreigners Good or bad." Such racial slights were incidental in the 1824 campaign, but their occasional surfacing revealed how some Northerners feared the implications that the South's racial problems might have for Northern society.[9]

White racial fears were quite compatible with hostility to the expansion of slavery into the West. People could dislike slavery on grounds of high-minded moral and political principle even when prejudiced against African Americans: in 1819–1820 Northerners sometimes argued that the new homeland for whites in the Louisiana Purchase must be kept clear not just of slavery but of a "slave population." In the wake of the crisis, such sentiments recurred more frequently. Some newspaper editors in Ohio continued to accept fugitive slave advertisements because they wished to discourage settlement by black "nuisances to society, destroying our peace and quiet." Runaway "negroes," one warned, created "great danger [to] our property and the mortifying prospect of one day having our posterity mingled with black blood." Racist attitudes, ranging from virulent hatred to intellectual disapproval, undoubtedly helped to weaken the power of anti-Southernism.[10]

This growing emphasis on racial differences chimed neatly with the views of politicians who wished to restore sectional goodwill. Like Van Buren in New York, they believed that the blurring of national party dis-

*A Pappoose President. This detail is taken from a cartoon by James Akin entitled "Caucus Curs in Full Yell, Or a War-Whoop, to Saddle on the People, a Pappoose President," which was published in 1824, probably in Philadelphia. In one corner it shows a building marked "Uncle Sam's Treasury Pap House / Amalgamation-Tool Department." The term* pap *was at the time commonly used to refer to the patronage, subsidies, and payments that the treasury was suspected of using to buy political support for Secretary Crawford. However, the reference is also to Crawford's controversial proposal in 1816 that whites and Native Americans should intermarry in order to solve the Indian problem. The cartoon shows Crawford offering a bowl of dollars to a fashionable lady, saying, "Here's a bowl of solid pappoose meat, that's a good Girl, better marry our wild Indians than Foreigners good or bad." The woman tells her baby, "Treasury pap is better than rum." The Crawford character's insult to Pennsylvania's immigrants is obvious. Courtesy: Library of Congress Prints and Photographs Division.*

tinctions had produced the recent popular "clamour against Southern Influence and African Slavery" in the North, and they suspected that some restrictionists had cynically encouraged the agitation in order to revive the fortunes of the Federalist Party. The solution was to revitalize the old party, but first Democrats needed to go along with the antislavery tide until it slackened. Some Massachusetts representatives publicly took a strong stand over Missouri in Washington, but then, "having saved themselves at home," privately asked state leaders to ensure that the legislature expressed no opinion on the subject so as to open the way for retreat. They sensed a growing weariness with the arguments over the Missouri constitution in 1821, both in Washington and among their constituents, and at least thirty congressmen who had supported restriction in 1820 gave up the cause in 1821, thus allowing Clay's compromise over the Missouri constitution to carry the day.[11]

Democratic Republican leaders in New England were especially aware of their interconnection with the rest of the national party. Ohio congressman John Sloane observed that "certain eastern democrats who have grown up under the care of Madison's & Monroe's administration are too much the creatures of courtly power to be depended on." King himself declared, "The inveteracy of party feelings in the Eastern states, the hopes of influence and distinction by taking part in favor of the slave States . . . will keep alive and sustain a body considerable numerous" who will "preserve to the slave States their disproportionate influence." Some of these Northerners had ambitions at Washington, which proved "a deadly Poison operating on all our political men, in regard to everything national, and more especially on this question of Slavery." This reluctance by New England's representatives, according to one old Federalist, undermined the whole Northern political effort.[12]

As a result, political leaders in New England throughout the crisis of 1820 had proved "much below the People themselves" in their adherence to antislavery principle.[13] Many Yankee Republican politicians had wanted to secure prompt statehood for Maine, which the South was blocking until it secured a slave Missouri. Others, notably John Holmes of New Hampshire, insisted the excitement over Missouri was a plot to work some politically unreliable Northerner such as Clinton into the White House. Though New Hampshire had initially shown great unity against slavery in 1819, its leading Republican spokesmen soon changed their minds. Isaac Hill, the influential editor of the *New Hampshire Patriot,* hated "reviving sectional prejudices" in consequence of the deliberate creation of "a Northern and a Southern interest . . . for sinister party purposes." As early as April 1820 the paper had dropped its opposition to slavery in Missouri.[14]

In effect, the Missouri crisis had persuaded many Republicans that the survival of the republic depended on preserving the old party. They accepted that some Northern politicians had been sincere in their resistance to the expansion of slavery into Missouri, but they suspected the motives of others and determined to hound out those who had undermined party feeling by supporting the restrictionist cause. In Pennsylvania, Connecticut, and New York, the regulars began serious efforts to put down anyone associated with the restriction of slavery: in December 1821 they joined in defeating the reelection as Speaker of John W. Taylor of New York, who had taken over leadership of the antislavery forces in Congress from James Tallmadge in December 1819.[15]

Even some Federalist leaders from Massachusetts proved unwilling to take a stance likely to upset the South. Harrison Gray Otis, for one, had long expressed sympathy for the rights and needs of the slave South, and Federalists have been seen as early authors of a proslavery outlook. Massachusetts Federalists were also reluctant to do anything that might alienate the national administration and prevent Congress from agreeing to pay the state's claims for its wartime expenditure. They were blasted for their complaisance by other, more sectionally conscious, Federalists through the early 1820s.[16]

Elsewhere in the free states, some folk were troubled in 1822 and 1823 by some early indications that men might choose their next president "on northern and southern grounds." One Ohio editor argued fiercely that this was "a distinction that should never be made by anyone who makes the least pretensions of friendship for his country or who wishes a continuance of its union." He far preferred that the contest take place "between the friends and *enemies* of roads, canals and domestic manufactures," but he hoped that the West, while pressing the claims of its favorite candidate, would accept the decision of the congressional caucus: "This is the plain old republican path, and a deviation from it may be dangerous to the party and to the interests of the nation." If the official nominee be not accepted, "it will tend to dismember and weaken" the Republican party and open "a wide door for the admission of its opponents."[17]

Ironically, Adams himself reflected Northern hesitations about a firm sectional stance. He deeply disliked slavery and thought that it ought to die; some of his private comments to Calhoun during the Missouri crisis were surprisingly absolute in their moral condemnation. However, Adams had not been as committed to the cause of ending slavery in Missouri as outsiders assumed. He doubted not only Congress's constitutional power to impose restriction but also the practicality of trying to impose abolition, however gradual, on Missouri. As secretary of state he insisted on compensation for slaves carried off by the British in 1815, and he opposed signing a treaty with Britain to suppress the international slave trade if it included the right of mutual search of each others' ships at sea. Such a concession would betray the cause for which the United States had fought in 1812: determined to assert American rights against Britain, he refused to assist pirated black slaves if it meant making white Americans slaves. Adams's nationalism implied a greater willingness to make concessions to the South than many contemporaries perceived.[18]

The Northern states were marked, then, by a lack of internal unity that made a lasting coherent stand more than unlikely. The consistent antislavery of the Quakers and of some Presbyterian and Methodist groups was at odds with the more qualified attitudes of other churches. In 1820 there was no lasting sense of Northernness and no sense that free states had a common regional identity, such as they would have in 1860. They simply constituted the states in which slavery was either dead or dying, and men commonly distinguished between the Northern and the Middle states. The term "North" was used uncertainly at the time, mainly to mean New England (also often called the "East"), sometimes New England plus New York, and only occasionally to mean the free states as a whole. In the end, New England was the only northern region to show any degree of unanimity in 1824, and it came to that conclusion more fitfully and hesitantly than might be imagined.

### THE NORTHERN MAN

In the 1824 election John Quincy Adams would carry all New England's Electoral College votes, worth nearly 20 percent of the whole. In the five New England states that allowed a popular election of their electors, Adams won nearly 83 percent of the vote—that is, 62,378 votes compared with the 12,847 cast for rival tickets, mainly supporting Crawford. This result seems in retrospect almost inevitable; from 1821 onward, many people had assumed that New England would be unanimous for him. Yet in the past New England had rarely agreed on national politics, and as late as January 1823 Adams himself denied that the region would "unitedly" bring him out as a candidate. "Q." was a divisive figure, and many Yankee politicians initially regarded him as most unsuitable and looked around for alternatives.[19]

Few observers denied that Adams was the most distinguished candidate in the field. According to Rufus King, "The opinion of his integrity and of his superiority as a learned statesman is not disputed by anyone. . . . He is above all controversy the best informed, & some persons believe the best qualified, of the Candidates." As the campaign threw up accusations against him, Adams replied with thoughtful and substantive newspaper essays. These were highly regarded and were considered well judged to influence whatever latitude they were aimed at. However, as King remarked in March 1823, while Adams's newspaper interventions raised his reputation in Washington, they did not increase his chances of election.[20]

Adams was considered an inevitable candidate because in both 1808 and 1816 the presidency had gone to the current secretary of state. Well aware of these precedents, President Monroe in 1817 saw that whomever he appointed to the State Department would probably be regarded as heir apparent. He would have given the post to Crawford if Clay had been willing and vice versa, but neither would concede to the other. Not wishing to give either an advantage, Monroe gave it to Adams, on the grounds, he said, that "it was impossible he should ever be president"![21]

This view reflected Adams's evident personal limitations. In 1817 William Henry Harrison, fresh from his military triumphs, described him as "coarse, dirty, and clownish in address and dress, and stiff and abstracted in his opinions." His negligence of dress became a minor election issue: in August 1822 a Philadelphia newspaper complained that Adams wore "neither waistcoat nor cravat, and sometimes go[es] to church barefoot." His wife was "much concerned" by the charge, however exaggerated. One Maryland congressman complained that the secretary of state's "head Glistened too much like a Sun Dial—He had neither the manners nor the appearance of a Gentleman—He could not make a bow, and had not learned to Dance when he was young &c." Others found his eye affliction off-putting: according to one politician from western Massachusetts, "The Professor has too much *water in his Eyes* to see common things—and I doubt much whether he gets his own state."[22]

More serious was his awkwardness in personal relationships. One

*John Quincy Adams. This engraving by Asher Brown Durand, based on a portrait of the new president by Thomas Sully, was published in Philadelphia in October 1826. The maps emphasize Adams's success as secretary of state in expanding the territorial boundaries of the United States. Courtesy: Library of Congress Prints and Photographs Division.*

close supporter thought Adams needed to develop greater "acquaintance with the temper & disposition of those around him, manners more accommodating, & and a readiness to yield small points that he may carry great ones." According to Supreme Court justice Joseph Story, an admirer, "The great objection to him is that he is retiring and unobtrusive, studious, cool, and reflecting; that he does nothing to excite attention, or to gain friendships." This "want of those properties which produce and maintain personal attachments" created "a disinclination towards him that it will be found difficult to overcome." James Buchanan, then a young congressman, considered "Adams out of the question. . . . His manners are so distant and anti-republican and his nature so austere that upon personal acquaintance he loses all the friends whom at a distance his political reputation has acquired."[23]

Adams's personal failings were aggravated by his old-fashioned attitude to the harsh realities of political competition. He believed that the best man should be elected—the man who had truly earned the reward—and that his own services made it clear who that man should be. Therefore any opposition must be malicious, must be focused on destroying the good character he held before the American people. When criticized for his dress, he decided not to smarten up but to remember "the perpetual and malignant watchfulness with which I am observed . . . with the deliberate purpose of exposing me to public obloquy or public ridicule." In paranoid fashion, he believed the whole campaign through 1821 and 1822 centered on an effort by his enemies to undermine his character before the country by a barrage of "ribaldry and invective." Hence he devoted much time to defending his record, rebutting newspaper charges, almost regardless of whether his intervention would advance his election or not.[24]

He was determined not to be an active candidate or to maneuver to promote his own election. Admittedly, he was accused of delivering an excessively anti-British July Fourth oration in Washington in 1821 to promote his own advancement. However, he insisted that if the presidency was "the prize of cabal and intrigue, of purchasing newspapers, bribing by appointments, or bargaining with foreign missions, I had no ticket in that lottery." It was almost a matter of pride, in August 1822, that while Crawford and Calhoun had newspapers in Washington, he had nothing. Curiously, Adams's policy was based on a touching trust in popular good sense: whereas Monroe feared "mere popular prejudices," Adams believed in publicly confronting "the newspaper scavengers and scapegibbets" because he trusted "the good sense of the people to see through their sophistry and their motives."[25]

By early 1823 supporters complained that Adams was "too fastidious and reserved" on matters where "his friends and his country have a right to certain degree of cooperation from him." He had to recognize, they said, that presidents were now made by politicians and newspapers, and not simply by merit. His "indifference" simply served "to chill and depress the kind feeling and fair exertions of his friends." Robert Walsh was turning the Philadelphia *National Gazette* into "a decided influence" for Adams, but he felt that Adams was inclined "to check and discourage his exertions in the cause. It is an ungracious and weary task to serve another against his will, and no zeal and devotion can continue it long." As his son, Charles Francis, later remarked, "The friends of Mr. Adams were numerous and influential in the Northern Atlantic states, but they lacked organization, and complained of . . . his neglect to use certain means of advancing his cause, resorted to with little hesitation by most politicians in place who are ambitious of higher promotion."[26]

Rather than suffer such a leader, many of Adams's potential supporters looked for an alternative Northern candidate. Usually, as Plumer said, the South rallied round a single name while the North failed "to unite upon some one man among themselves," but in 1824 the situation turned the other way round. All the possible Northern alternatives to Adams proved impossible. Rufus King was too old and also unwilling. Vice President Daniel Tompkins was "obviously out of the question": quite apart from his excessive drinking and his financial irregularities, Tompkins had failed to defeat Clinton in the New York gubernatorial election of spring 1820, partly because of his perceived reluctance to support the restriction of slavery. Even the secretary of the navy, Smith Thompson, thought his own New York birth and location might make him available; he held off accepting a seat on the U.S. Supreme Court for eight months before being persuaded that he stood no chance of the presidency. The only alternative therefore appeared to be Clinton, who had an undoubted appeal as a conspicuous Northern man in 1812 and 1820. However, he suffered from the memory of his past involvements with Federalists, and in any case by 1822 it was clear that he had self-destructed at home in New York—helped, as we shall see, by the subtle hand of Mr. Van Buren. This left Adams as the only Northern candidate against five slave state candidates, which Calhoun thought gave Adams huge advantages—"if he knew how to improve them."[27]

Even then, New England politicians were desperately reluctant to settle on Adams. One Massachusetts congressman said, in May 1822, that "there is no doubt the New England States would prefer a *man of their own*—But he did not think it possible to unite them in support of Adams." In December a Kentucky congressman explained, "Hereon lies the indecision of the North—they want the next President—they can't unite on Mr. A and they are sounding to see if any other will do." This evident unpopularity among New England's representatives gave Calhoun's friends hope. A Maryland politician learned that they calculated "that when Mr. Adams is sensible he must fail, he & his friends will go over to Calhoun," on the grounds that he was the most Northern of the Southern candidates.[28]

For his part, Adams had no desire to run as the New England candidate. He "doubted the correctness of the principle upon which it was supposed I should be supported by that section of the Union and opposed by another." He had always served the nation as a whole, in an independent spirit that roused the opposition of both sectionalism and party spirit. When he was attacked by a Virginia congressman, General Alexander Smyth, Adams produced a "very skillful" newspaper reply in December 1822 that was, "as the Virginians admit, well calculated for the meridian of the antient Dominion, but I apprehend he cannot become acceptable to the peculiar faith which does & must control the opinions of this region."[29]

Adams's hopes for nationwide support were indeed doomed by the way in which other people saw his candidacy. Rufus King commented in 1823 that "as between Adams and any one of the Candidates from the slave States, the most powerful argument which could be used would be that which constitutes the Missouri Question." In the course of 1823, King's son, Charles, at the *New-York American* started to make "bitter denunciations . . . against the south, against the slaveholding population, and southern interests generally" and demanded the election of Adams as the Northern man. As a result of this onslaught, according to the New York *National Advocate*, Mr. Adams's "prospects in the south have been blighted, I may say annihilated. . . . They have united all parties against what Mr. King calls the 'northern man.'" Sectional hostility on both sides guaranteed that Adams would be forced back on to his potential base in New England.[30]

## WINNING NEW ENGLAND

In January 1823 Adams himself doubted whether "even New England would unitedly offer me as a candidate." Federalists could not forget his desertion in 1807, and in Massachusetts they were still the majority party early in 1823. By contrast, Democratic Republicans saw him as a patriotic statesman but showed little affection for an "apostate": Adams thought them "lukewarm and distrustful of [his] success." The "independence of party" that Adams prided himself on meant that he would always be vulnerable to misunderstanding, as party spirit worked against him through "misrepresentation and slander." Regional Republican leaders were far from convinced that they should pander to the popular urge for a Northern candidate: as a former congressman said of Massachusetts in February 1823, "There is a sort of undefined attachment toward a native—but you know how far this goes with politicians."[31]

The Republican establishments of New England showed little enthusiasm for Adams. The party press in Boston said not a word against Crawford in 1822; they treated Adams as an unreconstructed version of his father. In February 1823 Maine's first governor, William King, thought Adams unelectable and had no doubt that in the end the state would prefer Crawford. In Massachusetts, some Federalists and a few nationalistic Republicans flirted with Calhoun and gave him unrealistic hope. Republican business leaders favored Adams, but the party's regional political leaders doubted whether early indications of popular favor for Adams would be sustained, suspecting that loyalty to the congressional caucus would ultimately ensure a Crawford victory in the state. Hence early in 1823 the legislatures of both Massachusetts and Maine—the two most populous New England states—stated a preference for Adams but insisted that the need for party harmony nationwide meant that it was too early to make a formal nomination. As the old Federalist Charles Gore commented, these hesitations paralleled the earlier "disgraceful" hesitations over the Missouri crisis: "Massachusetts failed to do her duty, and Maine and Rhode Island were divided. Had they done their duty on that occasion, the support of Adams would have been certain" because Virginia's control would already have been broken.[32]

In the end, the hesitations of Republican leaders were overwhelmed by the growing evidence that ordinary voters were willing to vote out those who ignored them. The most famous political overturn came in Boston where a series of arguments over municipal affairs, beginning in 1820, resulted in the emergence of the "Middling Interest," a group of artisans and tradesmen who objected to the tight control of the Federalist "Junta" in municipal affairs. In the elections of April 1822, the Middling Interest inflicted "a total overthrow" on the city's ruling party. In state and national affairs, the insurgents reunited with the Federalists, but observers saw that "their Power . . . [could] be used for any other purpose." Though the presidential question had little impact on municipal and state politics in Massachusetts, by June Charles Gore could see that "Our politics here are rapidly changing, and we only want some call on the Passions of the People to produce a change in the rulers of the state."[33]

In New Hampshire the acknowledged leader of the Democratic Republican Party, Isaac Hill, showed from the start a settled commitment against regional candidates and for a congressional nomination. In the spring elections of 1823 Hill's control was challenged by Levi Woodbury and Republicans from the coast, who accused Hill of favoring the interests of the interior. Woodbury's campaign also argued that the state must have a governor who would ensure that the state's electoral votes were cast as the people wished, and that meant a Northern man: "In the approaching contest for President we don't want any of Mr. Randolph's 'dough faces' for leaders—we want a man in the Presidential as well as in the gubernatorial chair able to vindicate the cause of the free States, against the spread and contamination of the moral pestilence that darkens the face of the southern states." This appeal attracted the support of those already committed to Adams and gave Woodbury victory over Hill's machine by 4,000 votes. According to the Federalist Ezekiel Webster, this "most unexpected" result had "not killed Democracy (who could?), but we have penetrated its solid columns" and "broken its line of march." Though Hill would quickly restore his position in state politics, he clearly could no longer hope to carry the state for Crawford against the wishes of the majority of the people. In June 1824 the legislature would nominate Adams, with 5 dissenting votes out of 166.[34]

Even Federalists who deeply despised him came to agree with the Democrats that Adams was the man to support for president. Ezekiel Webster had told his brother, Dan, that he had never liked Adams and would prefer "fifty others" first. However, he soon conceded that New Hampshire folk will "have a Northern man for President," though they would probably have preferred Clinton if he stood a chance: "There is among us a pretty strong local feeling, something like a very general wish that the next President should be from the North. There is a kind of presentiment that after this election we may give up all expectation." Adams "may not be very popular, yet it seems to be in some degree a matter of necessity to side with him—if any man is to be taken from the land of the *Pilgrims*."[35]

By the beginning of 1823 most political observers believed that Adams would carry New England easily. In February the chief justice of Massachusetts reported that Adams was "fast gaining in the affections of the people—hardly an opposing Voice in the quarter." As a result, the politicians found their self-seeking hesitations and doubts overwhelmed by popular sentiment that crossed party lines. In one district in Maine, for example, the Republicans divided in 1823 between two congressional candidates; the Independent Federalists then decided the issue by persuading enough of their fellows to vote for the Republican who was "an avowed and unequivocal friend" of Adams rather than the one "wedded to the interests of a southern slave-holder."[36]

Some Democratic politicians continued to hope that a caucus nomination would open the way for Crawford in New England but were soon disillusioned. In Rhode Island, the "State Junta" committed itself early in 1824 to supporting the caucus candidate but quickly became aware of "their total inability to change public opinion from Mr. Adams." They therefore refrained from pressing Crawford for fear of defeating their state ticket. Connecticut too had been dominated since 1818 by Democratic politicians who were "neither manly nor moral" and "were in a good measure for Sale." Early in 1824 these party men tried to whip up newspaper support for "Mr. Crawford and Democracy," but they were dampened when the members of the legislature nominated Adams with 124 out of 147 votes. As Rufus King had predicted without enthusiasm a year earlier, Adams had gained the preference of New England because he was the only viable Northern candidate.[37]

### LAND OF THE PILGRIMS

The rallying of New England opinion behind John Quincy Adams's presidential aspirations might be explained as a simple act of loyalty to a fellow New Englander, even one as unprepossessing as Adams. Yet historically that sense of Yankee identity had not often translated into regional political solidarity: the unanimity for the New England candidate in 1824 was a new phenomenon that ran at odds with the deep internal divisions that in reality marked New England life.

Economically, the issues of the American System divided New England just as they did the South. Those parts that had already built their own roads and canals out of their own pockets scarcely enthused over federal support for internal improvements. Manufacturing had not yet become all powerful in the region; it was essentially confined to parts of southern New England. Although between 1808 and 1815 the Boston Associates had famously started to invest in manufacturing, notably at Lowell, the real wealth was still primarily involved in overseas commerce. In votes on raising tariff duties to more protective levels after 1815, most New England congressmen voted nay, as Daniel Webster famously did in 1824. This resistance represented the interests not just of State Street but also of small ports along the coast. The only representatives to vote for the tariff bills of 1820 and 1824 were those representing Vermont grain farmers and the small-scale manufacturing interests of Connecticut and Rhode Island.[38]

Nor did New England express a common Puritan outlook on national affairs, as the region was deeply divided along religious lines. Rhode Island had always been a center of religious dissidence, but the old established Congregationalist Church had also recently lost its established position in every state except Massachusetts. In Connecticut the old Standing Order had fallen before a coalition of dissenters and Jeffersonians in 1818, and Methodists and Baptists continued to expand even in areas where the Congregationalist revivals of the New Divinity had once held sway. The new state of Maine disestablished its church as soon as it had the power. In Vermont a broad movement of moral and humanitarian reform was, by the 1820s, creating a new conservative and Christian consensus that has been equated with a new political consensus, but in most places the old sectarian divisions continued to embarrass common action, especially in southern New England.[39]

In Massachusetts, the cleavage between Unitarians and Calvinists within the established Congregational Church divided many communities and disrupted the unity of the Federalist Party. The Dedham decision in the state supreme court in 1821 turned a theological dispute within the established church into a struggle for control of churches and church property: now Unitarian minorities in local churches began to unite with the secularist majority in the parish to overthrow traditional Calvinist control of the church's ministry. This undermining of the Standing Order encouraged traditional Trinitarian Congregationalists to oppose the Unitarian Harrison Gray Otis in the April 1823 gubernatorial election, even though it meant voting against the Federalist Party. The hold of the established church was further undermined by the Religious Liberty Act of 1824, which strengthened the position of all dissenting congregations. Thus the internal political conflict of 1823–1824 was religious as much as partisan and social; yet despite Adams's clear identification with the Unitarians, religious differences did nothing to reduce his general acceptability to most Massachusetts voters.[40]

Ironically, in view of the disruptions to the Federalist world, a closely defined group of Federalist intellectuals was responsible for creating New England's collective identity as a distinctive region. The picture of a land of steady habits, of white-painted villages, of a literate, hardworking, God-fearing people whose enterprise created a prosperous, stable, and just society, emerged after the Revolution from the popular geographical works of Jedidiah Morse and the travel writings of Timothy Dwight. They heightened this identification of New Englanders as the archetypal American republicans by contrasting other parts of the Union, which they claimed scarcely qualified for inclusion in the ideal American community. As James Sabine said in 1820, New England was "distinct from the character of all other nations on the face of the earth." In retrospect, this attempt to advance an essentially "sectional nationalism" may look like a form of cultural imperialism designed to "Yankify" the republic, but before 1825 it was essentially defensive in its motivation.[41]

These writers were all distinguished Federalists who regretted their party's loss of power in 1801, which they blamed on the Constitution's bias in favor of slave owners. Significantly, however, the ideal New England described by these writers excluded those parts of New England that did not fit their picture. Rhode Island they dismissed as a den of libertarianism and licentiousness, while northern New England had not yet reached the pitch of republican civilization that it was clearly destined to achieve. The Federalist creators of a collective New England identity could find no place in their picture for the very elements in New England society that, by 1824, had displaced them politically, even at home.[42]

The Adams campaign in New England represented not these old Federalists but rather the dominant forces in the region's politics. Though many Federalists accepted him as the regional candidate, Adams insisted that his nomination in Massachusetts be restricted to the Republican legislative caucus, which in January 1824 duly named a pledged ticket made up of strictly Republican electors. He also publicly answered Old Federalists when they began to question his father's good name and his own political behavior during Jefferson's presidency. The total effect was to separate Adams from extreme High Federalists and underline his loyalty to Republican administrations since 1808. Some partisan Republican die-hards who were committed to the congressional caucus nomination opposed his candidacy, but indisputably Adams ran as the state's Republican candidate.[43]

As a result, the old irreconcilable Federalists provided implacable (and self-contradictory) opposition to his hegemony. In 1823 and 1824 the Boston-based Federalist elite deliberately nominated the High Federalist Harrison Gray Otis as governor and thereby reopened "the breach between the two parties" that had been mollified under the previous mild and compromising Federalist administration. Otis then revived old controversies by attempting to defend the Hartford Convention against Republican accusations of disloyalty, which hung "like a Millstone round the neck of Otis." In that spirit, the highest of High Federalists, Timothy Pickering, wrote a letter in 1823 preferring Crawford to Adams. Crawford, he said, was "always a *faithful democrat,* and Mr. A—is a *dishonest apostate.*" Even the young Massachusetts Federalist William Lloyd Garrison advocated Crawford in 1824; he even thought Jackson less dangerous than Adams. In practical terms, this personal hostility resulted in the effort to build an "Unpledged" or "Opposition" electoral ticket made up of both "high-toned federalists and radical democrats." In reality uniting on Crawford, "these queer ingredients," according to one New York newspaper, represented "an amalgamation of all the ultra notions that have at any time marked the politics of the country."[44]

Thus the political triumph that was the most tangible evidence of the sectional nationalism that now swayed New England was in no way the work of either the old Federalist elite or, at this stage, of cultural sectionalists. The most conservative among them were the most unwilling to reconcile themselves to the younger Adams, and some pandered to Calhoun's ambitions. More moderate Federalists took Daniel Webster's advice to hold aloof from the presidential campaign; only after the results of the presidential election nationwide were known did New England Federalists, including Webster, begin to draw close to Adams, in search for party advantage. This would open the way to the creation of a Union party in Massachusetts—but after 1825.

New England Republicans shared the sense of regional identity but expressed it within a broader nationalist Americanism. Yankee Jeffersonians liked to think of themselves as archetypal Americans, establishing the ways upon which the true republican nation could be built. One sign was the growing approval for Calhoun late in 1823, who was seen as the most national of the non-Northern candidates; hence it was entirely appropriate that the Adams campaign finally adopted him as its vice-presidential candidate, and the pair be hailed in the regional press as the "NATIONAL CANDIDATES." Adams, according to one New York country paper, would act on "broad, national principles, having in view the true object of lawful government: the greatest good of the greatest number." That same appeal was even used on his behalf in some Southern states. As the Norfolk, Virginia, newspaper said, if the South was sincere in "its anti-sectional pretensions," it was bound to let the Northern or Middle states choose the next president. The South would be safe with Adams, and his election would promote "the annihilation of sectional prejudices and animosities, the *only* rock which can sever our federative system." The adoption of Adams as the leading opposition candidate in parts of the Upper South and the Old Southwest would in time be one of the more surprising features of the campaign.[45]

Yet New England Republicans were now willing to cooperate with the South only on their own terms. The consciousness that New England possessed a superior but neglected version of the national ideals was heightened by its awareness of the immorality of the South's peculiar institution and its realization that Southerners now ruled the nation in their own interest. In other words, this sectional nationalism derived from a widespread distaste for chattel slavery, even if their antislavery sentiments were crippled by unappealing racial sensitivities and a desire not to jeopardize national unity; and the only persuasive explanation for its emergence at this precise moment lies in the shock that the South's triumph in the Missouri crisis had given to Yankee sensibilities.

Because its antislavery had no political program, New England's indignation could be expressed only in terms of regional rivalry. As the *Boston Centinel* said, "All minor political controversies, all interior distinctions, are absolved in this great national question between *Virginia* and the *Northern* states." From an early stage, Clay's correspondents warned him that nothing would drive New Englanders together more quickly behind Adams than an effort to elect a Southern man. Their reaction to the threat of continuing Southern dominance might impose a regrettable North–South division on American politics, but politicians like the Republican William Plumer thought that might be necessary "to restore to the northern states their due weight in the councils of the Union."[46]

In November 1822 the Philadelphia editor Robert Walsh explained why the Crawfordite appeal for Republican support in New England could not succeed. The people of New England, he predicted, would recognize the hostility of the "Virginia race" to Eastern men and would be "true to themselves." As a consequence, Mr. Adams "will be the candidate of *all New England*—of the universal Yankee nation wherever dispersed throughout the Union."[47] Walsh was recognizing not just New Englanders' sense of cultural identity but also the fact that since 1800 many of them had migrated into the New West, especially into western New York State. Wherever they went, they retained the same sense of themselves as special Americans, as Yankees who had created the model republican society that the United States as a whole should emulate. That sense of identity worked for Adams in New England; the question was, would it also work in the weighty and critical state of New York?

# 4 THE DREAD OF APOLLO

The elephant in the room in 1824 was De Witt Clinton. A tall, handsome figure, Clinton was regarded by many (including himself) as "the greatest man in America." Born in 1769, this Magnus Apollo gained renown for his literary and scientific accomplishments, his cultural and philanthropic foundations, and his independent political course. By 1801 he was a leader of the Democratic Republican Party in New York State and was helping to develop a spoils system designed to keep power in the hands of his partisans. With the backing of his uncle, George Clinton, longtime governor of New York and Jefferson's second vice president, De Witt by 1805 had served in both houses of the state legislature and in the U.S. Senate, and had been appointed mayor of New York City. For all his attainments, he was at bottom a professional politician dependent on office for his living.[1]

But then Clinton had diverged from strict partisan loyalty. Concerned to defend the state's agricultural and commercial interests against the Jeffersonian trade restrictions, he supported Uncle George's attempt to block Madison's succession to the presidency in 1808. In 1812 De Witt himself accepted a presidential nomination by the New York legislative caucus in defiance of the congressional party. Securing the support of the Federalists, Clinton carried enough Northern states to come within one state—Pennsylvania—of defeating Madison's reelection. He then compounded disloyalty in time of war by opposing the reelection of the regularly nominated war governor, Daniel Tompkins. As a result, Clinton lost the support of regular Republicans in New York City, and the state party in 1813 dismissed him as mayor. Few prominent Republicans sympathized: "He is the victim of ambition, treachery & rage; but he must never be forgiven."[2]

Extraordinarily, by 1817 Clinton had restored his position. When the war ended, he campaigned for the building of a great canal to connect Lake Erie with the Hudson and won broad support, especially in the western counties. He successfully submitted his claims to become governor to the Republican Party's state nominating convention in 1817, the first ever held in New York. The Federalist Party also supported Clinton's election, and his many projects for educational, cultural, scientific, and economic improvement were largely adopted by the state assembly. Symbolizing both positive government and the decline of party spirit, he seemed a preeminent candidate to succeed Monroe.

Clinton also identified himself with the restrictionist cause in Missouri in 1820, favorable "to the rights of man, to the perpetuity of this union, and to the just balance of political power."[3] If an alternative Northern candidate were needed, Clinton was the man. Besides New York, Clinton had vocal and influential friends in the large states of Pennsylvania and Ohio, and he was particularly admired by the other apparently undisciplined great men in the nation, Jackson and Calhoun. Interestingly, in 1822–1824 there would be a degree of interchangeability among their supporters, and Clinton saw the others as stalking horses for himself.

However powerful the appeal of independent candidates elsewhere, Clinton's presidential ambitions depended entirely on his ability to command New York. Its population had quadrupled over the last thirty years, making it the largest state, with far more Electoral College votes than any other. However, beneath the surface unanimity of New York in 1817 lay an ill will and mistrust that would soon generate a "reformed democratic party" and destroy his next presidential candidacy before it was launched.[4] Even then, he remained a looming absence whose possible entry into the race dictated the strategy of others. He continued to receive nominations in other states, and late in 1823 his opponents foresaw scenarios whereby he might yet become a serious player. He would indeed make an extraordinary comeback in 1824, reclaiming New York, but not for the presidency.

Clinton's triumph in the 1824 gubernatorial election is often represented as the triumph of democracy in New York. A newly enfran-

*De Witt Clinton. Lithograph by F. Michelin based on a portrait by Charles Cromwell Ingham, ca. 1824, published in William W. Campbell,* Life and Writings of De Witt Clinton *(New York: Baker & Scribner, 1849), frontispiece.*

chised electorate, we are told, resented the control of New York's affairs by a political elite. In 1824 a People's Party organized, resurrected the martyred Clinton, and punished the governing party. Because among its grievances was the assembly's refusal to allow the people to vote directly for president, the People's Party's triumph had a major effect on the presidential election and destroyed the hopes of the Crawford campaign. However, this interpretation puts things the wrong way round: New York had already undergone its democratic revolution as part of the process that by 1822 had destroyed Clinton's political standing in the state. It was the presidential election itself that was responsible for stimulating the popular protest that resulted in the triumph of the People's Party in 1824.

## DEMOCRATIC TRIUMPH

By 1820 New York City had grown from the small port of 1776 to the major commercial and financial center in North America. Its population of 123,000 had overtaken Philadelphia and had reached twice the size of Baltimore and almost three times that of Boston. Since 1787 Federalism had been powerful in the city, but skillful electoral organization and the mobilizing of the more radically minded artisans, professional men, and immigrants had made its Democratic Republican Party formidable by 1800. Control of the city party lay with its General Committee, which consisted of the locally elected three-man ward committees. From 1812 on, the committee met in the newly built Tammany Hall, itself owned by the once deeply partisan Tammany Society. Since 1808 Tammany's influence had been hostile to Clinton: as the society's Matthew L. Davis said, we "have learned sufficiently to know the folly of connecting our political destiny with that of any Individual; and more especially when the wishes and conduct of that Individual is not in unison with the wishes and expectations of the party."[5]

Tammany did not always see eye to eye with the up-country leaders of the party, but on this subject their views were echoed by the group of Democratic Republicans who would later become known as the Albany Regency. They too acknowledged that Clinton had great virtues, but they feared that his ambition meant the end of the Republican Party. He had not only ignored the decisions of the party but arrogantly believed that "he was in himself the party" and favored only those who showed "personal devotion to him." As governor, he showed little interest in conciliating former critics within the party, as he vindictively concentrated his considerable patronage on old friends. In any case, his "cold and haughty selfishness" did not make reconciliation easy. As the *Albany Argus* would say, "Notwithstanding his capacity, his manners are too repulsive, his temper too capricious and imperious, his deportment too dictatorial and tyrannical to acquire the affections or retain the confidence of any party."[6]

Moreover, old anxieties remained as it became clear in 1819 that Federalism had not died. In some counties where the Federalists retained a majority, they were nominating and supporting "candidates who had uniformly belonged to that party." In other counties, they voted for Clintonian candidates and thus revived the old suspicion that Clinton was "improperly but secretly united with the old federal party." The New York Republican Party now divided irrevocably into two separate political formations, the Clintonians and the Bucktails. According to the closest historian of these events, Jabez Hammond, writing twenty years or so later, after the spring of 1819 the two factions never again "attempted to caucus together as political friends" and "were now known as two distinct parties."[7]

The thirty-seven-year-old leader of the Bucktails could not have been more of a contrast with Clinton. Martin Van Buren was a man of "splendid talents," as the Clintonian Jabez Hammond acknowledged, already a renowned lawyer and usually a skillful public speaker. He was also a man of immense personal charm, refined and affable, easy and suave, soon to be renowned for his "extraordinary tact, address and persevering industry." He entirely lacked Clinton's mean spirit and scathing view of his opponents. As a political tactician and conciliator of waverers, Van Buren became "the life and soul" of his party. Singing the praises of partisan virtue and discipline, he and his colleagues worked closely with "the hot bed of Tammany Hall" and readily accepted the traditional symbol of the Tammany Society, the bucktail, as their nickname and title.[8]

No issue of policy divided the two state parties once the evident success and popularity of the canal had removed initial doubts about the project. However, their attitude to partisanship differed fundamentally. Clinton thought that for the sake of national improvement, the time had come for a new politics. "The odium attached to the name of Federalist has become a millstone around the neck of true policy," he said. "Names in politics as science are matters of substance," and the need was to abolish "the old names as well as the old lines of party." Van Buren be-

*Martin Van Buren. Portrait by an unidentified painter, about 1822.
Courtesy: Kinderhook Memorial Library.*

lieved that only the principles of the old Democratic Party could preserve the republic and its values; sacrifices of individual interest and opinion must be made for the sake of holding the party together. He conceded that it would be easy to interpret the party conflict as a mere contest for place and office, but he insisted it involved "differences of opinion and principle . . . of the greatest character," dating back to the 1790s. As a result, parties had developed "cohesive influences and innate qualities" that made it naive to think they could simply die away.[9]

Van Buren needed to ensure that his faction was identified as the true Republican Party because, as Hammond acknowledged, "If names and forms, on any occasion, are things, they emphatically were so at that time." The Bucktail leader faced the real difficulty that the governor was nominally the head of the regular state party whom loyal members would not oppose. However, the Clintonians destroyed their own claims to legitimacy: they criticized the Monroe administration, fired Democrats from state office and appointed prominent Federalists, and in the assembly supported a Federalist for speaker even though he had been rejected by the Republican legislative caucus in which they had voluntarily taken part. Both Hammond and Van Buren believed that this "violation of plighted faith" in 1819 was "the cause of [the Clintonians'] prostration and ruin as a party." As a result, by 1820 the Bucktails could fairly be denominated "*the* republican party," representing the mass of traditional Republican voters, in opposition to a Clintonian party that depended heavily on Federalist votes.[10]

Ironically, Van Buren was not averse to exploiting a split within the Federalist Party. Whereas the majority of Federalist voters backed Clinton, a minority did not. Stronger in talent than numbers, many of these "high-minded" dissidents had supported the War of 1812 once declared, objected to excessive state bank charters, and disapproved of Clinton's failure in 1817 to heal old political wounds. In January 1820 Van Buren persuaded the Bucktails to decide a hung election for U.S. senator by voting to reelect the hero of the Federalist dissidents, Rufus King. In April, fifty renowned Federalists publicly declared that their old party was dead, that Clinton's cynical building of a personal party of sycophants was "disgusting to the feelings of all truly high-minded and honorable men," and that they would henceforth unite with "the great republican party of the state and union." Despite prejudices against these "federal tammanies" among Republican veterans, Van Buren insisted that they must receive a share of state patronage. In effect, they had joined a "reformed democratic party," and even Rufus King accepted a nomination in 1821 "as a democrat."[11]

In "a period of party excitement almost unparalleled," the new expanded Democratic Party immediately exploited its electoral dominance. Taking advantage of the existing antiquated system of central appointment in New York, it removed opponents from office at all levels "with greater rigor" than ever seen before. It also passed a law calling a constitutional convention to reform the state constitution. When the state's Council of Revision vetoed the bill on Governor Clinton's casting vote, his supporters insisted on a referendum, which the Democrats won with 82 percent of the total vote on a franchise specially expanded for the occasion. Winning an even higher proportion of seats in the convention, the Democrats destroyed the ancient Councils of Appointment and Revision, and substantially opened local government and public office to popular control. The suffrage was widened to something close to universal white manhood suffrage, restrictions on voting for governor and state senators disappeared, and the results of elections became less vulnerable to fraud. Overwhelmingly approved by the voters in January 1822, New York at last acquired a virtually democratic frame of government (for white men) such as almost all Northern states had long enjoyed.[12]

Branded as a self-seeking apostate from Republicanism and an opponent of democratic reform, Clinton found his term as governor prematurely ended by the new constitution. He was now too weak electorally to compete in the subsequent election in November 1822: there was "scarce any opposition" to the Democratic state ticket, and no more than a dozen Clintonians were elected to the lower house. Needing to staff the new structure of government, Governor Joseph Yates and the assembly placed good Democrats in almost every office; accepting the recommendations of county meetings composed of delegates chosen in each town, they approved them in caucus and imposed strict party unity in the assembly. Faced by this Democratic machine, Clinton had no hope of winning New York in the presidential election, and without it, he could scarcely be regarded as a viable candidate. His prospects also declined when his nemesis won election to the U.S. Senate in February 1821. Within a few months of taking his seat in December, Washington observers would recognize Van Buren as "perhaps the greatest manager here."[13]

## THE KINGMAKER

In Washington, Van Buren's focus shifted to the presidential race. Initially attracted toward Calhoun, he was soon disillusioned when Calhoun in private conversation revealed his "Federalist" views of national power. Adams was suspect because he thought party was not an appropriate criterion for appointments to office—and in any case, was it prudent to elect a Northern man at that moment? Worried by the challenge to the Union evident in the Missouri crisis, Van Buren believed that the restoration of Mr. Jefferson's party—the "combination," as he would later call it, of "the planters of the South and the plain Republicans of the North"—was the best way of avoiding the geographical divisions that most threatened the survival of the great experiment.[14]

The republic had been weakened, he believed, by the Monroe administration's willingness to preach reconciliation with Federalism, an amalgamationist policy that undermined party morale nationally and could sap party loyalty in New York. He particularly feared that a Clinton or a Calhoun might leap to the presidential chair and govern without proper partisan commitment or principles. As he wrote from Washington in January 1822, "The disjointed state of parties here, the distractions which are produced by the approaching contest for the president, and the general conviction in the minds of honest but prudent men that a radical reform in the political feelings of this place has become necessary, render this the proper moment to commence the work of a general resuscitation of the old democratic party."[15]

That work partly involved the proper use of federal patronage, in New York and elsewhere. Recognizing that major post offices played a critical role in aiding the free circulation of party communications, in 1820 Van Buren persuaded the postmaster general, Return Jonathan Meigs Jr., to fire politically unsafe postmasters in New York and replace them with Bucktails. This made particularly shocking the decision of the postmaster general in January 1822 to appoint the renowned Federalist military hero Solomon Van Rensselaer, cousin of the Patroon and a considerable power in Albany County, as postmaster for Albany. Placing a long-standing political opponent in charge of "the principal distributing office in the State" was not only a practical blow against the regular party's political control in New York, but it also rebuked the deliberate partisanship of the state's Democrats. Van Buren's campaign to reverse the decision failed, but it successfully reinforced awareness of the Federalist threat.[16]

Van Buren also wished to assuage the destructive passions generated by the Missouri controversy. The Bucktail leaders had bowed before the antislavery wind in 1820, but, as Adams saw, the behavior of the Bucktails amply showed that "their leaning was to the south." Van Buren himself believed that the Democratic Party was too important to be jeopardized by unnecessarily agitating the South, even though well-intentioned Northerners were well within their rights to press for the ending of slavery in Missouri. Whereas most of the New York congressional delegation had been independent of party control during the crisis, the Bucktails among them voted with the South to replace the prorestriction Speaker of the House, John W. Taylor, with Philip Barbour of Virginia. They then opposed Taylor's reelection to Congress, along with that of other outspoken antislavery men.[17]

Virginia's speakership triumph with the aid of Northern votes persuaded Van Buren that the antislavery passions of 1819–1821 had been a passing phase. An official Republican candidate could carry the forthcoming presidential election; old party loyalty was more firmly rooted than antislavery. Northerners in 1822 may still talk of the need to elect a Northern man, but in the long run, the regular candidate would pick up votes if key legislatures could be prevented from making premature nominations. Thus, in the winter of 1822, the Bucktail leaders persuaded the New York legislature to defer all consideration of the presidential election; Rufus King considered this to be the same policy that they had pursued in 1819–1820 to prevent any legislative expression on Missouri question that might embarrass their representatives in Washington. The backlash against Missouri's admission was still powerful, as Taylor demonstrated when he secured his reelection to Congress in the fall elections of 1822. However, Van Buren was confident that time was on his side: as he said in March 1823, "In the West & East, there are men ready, if they have opportunity, to join Crawford, in case the case of Clay or Adams becomes dubious."[18]

From that point of view, the coming presidential election had to be decided by the authority of the national party's nomination—and that meant close cooperation between Virginia and New York. He possessed an "absolute certainty that the presidential question will be settled in caucus." Hard upon his first arrival in Washington, Van Buren reached out to the neo-Antifederalists. At an early point, he made friends with John Randolph. In March 1822 he traveled to the South to promote the resuscitation of the Republican Party, finding common ground with Spencer Roane and winning commendations from Thomas Ritchie at the *Richmond Enquirer,* "the political barometer of the State of Virginia." He also sniffed briefly around Henry Clay as a possible party candidate in the winter of 1822.[19]

Though Van Buren still kept his views "dark," by February 1823 Rufus King was certain that his fellow New York senator "*au fond* is for Crawford." In April Van Buren had long discussions with Crawford in Washington and left him in no doubt as to his choice. The critical consideration, Van Buren later recalled, was that Crawford's friends "seemed more anxious to preserve the unity of the Republican party." In the same month the Republican caucus in the New York legislature accepted a set of resolutions written by Van Buren, proposing that the national party yet again make a nomination in a congressional caucus and the state's Republicans accept that candidate, whosoever it might be.[20]

Van Buren calculated this strategy could carry the election for an old-party candidate. A union of Virginia, its satellite North Carolina, and New York would mean 75 votes out of the 131 needed to win in the Electoral College. He believed that traditional Republican voters elsewhere would in the end turn to Crawford, after all the huffing and puffing. Men might now criticize the caucus and insist that the voters should be allowed a free choice, but they would soon recognize that the net effect of a multitude of state nominations would be to throw the election into the House of Representatives, where it would be in the hands of politicians capable of all sorts of skullduggery. The strongest argument for allowing a congressional caucus to focus the party's attention on one man was that it would avoid a corrupt House election, and so prevent insider dealing from perverting the people's will.[21]

Leading New York Democrats understood that the nominee in question would be Crawford, and they "correctly judged that a majority of the leading and influential Democrats in the union concurred."[22] They also knew that traditionally New York's presidential electors had been chosen by the state legislature, which they now safely controlled. But could they really sell Crawford, however elected, to the newly empowered citizens of New York?

## UNIVERSAL YANKEE NATION

Rufus King was convinced that "if what Mr. Walsh calls the Universal Yankee Nation should unite in his [Adams's] favor, it would produce effect, particularly in New York." If it did, it could destroy Van Buren's strategy and make Adams the preponderant candidate. For more than the last thirty years, settlers from New England had settled mainly in the central and western counties of New York, shifting the state's center of gravity. Whereas in 1777 two-thirds of the state's population lived south of Albany, by 1820 only one-third did. Yankees dominated the western counties, which, according to the 1820 census, had doubled their population—and therefore future representation—in the last ten years. The state was now fairly evenly divided between Yankees and the longer-established Yorkers of Dutch extraction; the two rarely saw eye to eye.[23]

The settlers from New England were distinctive in their religious character and enterprising attitude. Religiously, they often came from dissenting traditions rather than the established order, but had not yet been burned by the flames of evangelical revival, as they famously would be after 1825. As farmers, most preferred open lands and looked toward rapid development. According to the writer Timothy Flint, they showed "the independence, self-scrutiny, self-respect, and the sturdy, unshrinkable self-reliance of the northern character." Politically, many of them—especially in the western counties—had been attracted to Clinton's plans for improving transportation, but they still regarded themselves as committed Democratic Republicans. By 1821 they accepted that Clinton no longer represented the good old party and that, to all appearances, his political prospects were dead. However, though willing to follow party guidance, the choice of Crawford flew in the face of their sensibilities and preferences.[24]

Anti-Southernism was common not only among New York's Yankees. According to Jabez Hammond, many Republicans in general "were tired . . . of defending themselves against the charge of supporting southern men, to the prejudice of the northern section of the union, and they were anxious to be relieved from that reproach." Hence they would hesitate before following their party south; indeed, Hammond thought it "not improbable that a majority of the democratic party [in New York] were at heart in favor of Mr. Adams." He commanded the respect, an old Democrat assured him, of "the old Jeffersonians, the middle class of the republicans & the yeomanry," and his nomination would prevent a Northern party clustering round the treacherous Clinton. According to Hammond, this difference of opinion over the next president "was not confined to politicians, or to the leaders of the democratic party in the state of New York. It existed among the people, and particularly among those who belonged to the democratic party."[25]

The reluctance of New York Republicans to commit themselves to Crawford compelled Van Buren to play his cards carefully. Bucktail spokesmen through 1822 avoided mentioning candidates by name, stressed the need to preserve the "Democratic party," and concentrated on getting loyal men elected to Congress for the sessions that ran from 1823 to 1825. Van Buren avoided revealing his personal preference until April 1823, when the party caucus in New York issued its call for a caucus nomination in Washington. Insisting that "he never engaged in anything which he could not see his way through," Van Buren felt convinced that party loyalty would ultimately prove itself a stronger force than his opponents believed.[26]

On this point, the High-Minded Federalists, who since 1820 had shown such a willingness to behave as Democrats in state politics, parted company with Van Buren. In February 1822 their leading newspaper, the *New-York American,* came out for Adams; a year later it objected to the legislature's resolutions and predicted that the coming fall's assembly elections would produce "a large majority of men favorable to a northern candidate." By then, Rufus King had frankly agreed to differ with Van Buren on the presidential question: he preferred Adams not from any personal partiality but because he could see no other viable Northern candidate. He recommended his political friends to observe a "discreet reserve" for the moment: "The question must assume in the end a sectional character—and the public feelings may reach such a tone as may prove quite embarrassing for those who early & actively support a distant candidate." The important thing was to rouse the public "against longer submission to a Southern master," to the "black strap" that bound the federal government.[27]

King was convinced that Van Buren's only hope was to "rally . . . the old democratic spirit against all other opinions." The editors of the *New-York American* thought the attempt would fail because "the leaders have less power over the Party . . . than formerly." However, King felt sure the regular Republican leaders would retain much influence with the voters because of "the antiquity of their faith" and the association of the Adams cause with former Federalists in New York. Partisan appeals were not "mere shadows—or if they are, shadows are substances to defective vision."[28]

In New York City, however, leading Republicans were on the verge of rebelling against Van Buren's schemes. According to Calhoun, by April 1823 "three-fourth[s] of the general Republican Committee of the city" had decided to start a new newspaper as the party organ in rivalry with Mordecai Noah's Van Burenite *National Advocate;* the new paper, the *New-York Patriot,* duly appeared in May, "with a majority of the Republicans of the city in its favour." The paper focused initially on opposing the Regency, but it was firmly under the influence of Calhoun advocates, such as Samuel L. Gouvernour, the president's son-in-law; Henry Wheaton, the distinguished reporter of the U.S. Supreme Court; and acolytes of Clinton like Charles G. Haines, his personal secretary. By September the *Patriot* was "out for Calhoun as large as life," as both the leading advocate of the administration's policies and the most Northern of the Southern candidates. Wheaton was "astonished at the rapid progress we have made since April."[29]

Not all Crawford's opponents in the state approved of Calhoun. One elderly observer prophesied that "the Yankee interest, governed by their prejudices in favour of an Eastern man, would give Mr. Adams a majority." Westerners, led by Peter B. Porter, preferred Clay. Others, notably the die-hard Federalists, looked around for alternative Northern candidates. However, these various anti-Crawford elements could all agree on one point: the choice of electors should not be left to the state legislature but must be given to the New York electorate at large. If Crawford could win popular support, so be it, but let the candidates fight it out in public. By the summer of 1823, this was the cry of both the Adamsonian *New-York American* and the Calhounite *New-York Patriot.*[30]

By September observers noted that "recently an astonishing change has taken place in the mind of the community." In the "ferment," most voters had turned against Van Buren's effort "to barter this State, for the purpose of furthering his own views." Crawford had become unelectable in the city, with three-quarters of its voters "arrayed in hostility to him." One well-regarded New York Republican reported that "this burst of public feeling has been mainly brought about by the friends of Mr. Adams," but, he thought, Adams would not be the main beneficiary. By then, however, Clay had been persuaded by his correspondents that Adams would win a popular vote in New York State.[31]

All recognized that the 1823 fall elections could decide who would secure New York's Electoral College vote. If they were conducted in the usual way, allowing the process of party nomination to control the election, the next legislature would be guided by the Albany Regency and cast the state's Electoral College votes for Crawford. The friends of the other candidates, however, were willing to fight the elections on the presidential issue, "regardless of local questions." As early as April 1823 the opposition had taken "strong ground" in favor of an electoral bill that would let the people choose the presidential electors. The Clintonians, internally divided and ostensibly maintaining a neutral attitude on the presidential question, declared themselves willing to support any candidate for the legislature who would avow himself in favor of that change. According to one regular Democrat, the electoral proposal was a "universal Yankee notion" that "will take out of the Republican ranks so many . . . [that] the Federalists, Clintonians & dissatisfied will unite & together make a majority."[32]

## PEOPLE'S MEN

In the fall of 1823 New York City's sixth ward, which ranged from Broadway to the Bowery, saw a furious tussle over nominations for the election. A ward selection meeting had to be held on October 3 to choose delegates to attend the party's nominating convention in Tammany Hall. Though the ward meeting was organized by the regulars, its chairman could not muzzle the repeated demands from the audience for resolutions demanding an electoral law, and so he left the chair. As his replacement, those present named a Clay supporter who was a former grand sachem of Tammany. Some of the regulars then dethroned him by force, while others broke lamps and snuffed out the candles. Dispossessed, the rebels duly reconvened at Dooley's Tavern, where they resolved to support only candidates committed to the popular election of presidential electors. Other ward meetings held the same day also experienced "a total disruption of all political organization," with the result that of seventy-two ward representatives elected, thirty-nine were anticaucus men.[33]

Both regulars and dissidents recognized the advantage of securing the official party nomination. At the citywide delegate convention at Tammany Hall on October 27, the regulars organized the meeting and proposed a ticket but faced a hostile audience variously estimated at between 2,000 and 3,000 men. The regular chairman lost control, tried to adjourn the meeting, and then fled. The opposition took charge, but the regulars tried to "dissolve the meeting in riot and confusion, according to the usual Crawford tactics." Amid turbulent scenes, the regulars brought crashing down both the dissenters' chairman and the table on which he was standing, but he managed to put the names of their alternative ticket to the vote. The *Advocate* claimed that the regulars had carried their ticket before disorder triumphed, but all the other newspapers agreed that it had been rejected by "a very large majority of the people present" in Tammany Hall. The dissidents had the better of the argument, and Calhoun—who never knowingly understated his prospects—claimed that most of those named on the ticket were his supporters.[34]

At this point the dissidents began to call themselves "the *people's* men." The label referred in 1823 not to Clintonians but to those Bucktail Republicans who rejected a party leadership that tried to override the strongly held presidential views of many of its usual supporters. In the months that followed, the dissidents increasingly branded the regular leadership as the "Albany Regency," thus identifying it with the monarchical habits of reactionary Europe. Clintonians were largely unrepresented in this dissident movement, but Clinton himself well appreciated the significance of the cleavage within the Bucktails. "The reign of King Caucus is at an end," he declared, "and the people have taken their concerns into their own hands. In a change of politics, the people leave the leaders and effect the change."[35]

The People's Party now made formal nominations in opposition to the regular Democratic candidates in those rural counties where they thought they could win. All together, they contested four Senate districts (of the ten up for election) and won two. In the House, they won thirty-four out of 128 seats, twenty-five in the eastern Mohawk and Hudson valleys. They did particularly well on Long Island and in New York City, where, according to the *Philadelphia Sentinel,* the "ancient landmarks" of "the democratic party" were overwhelmed. In a number of counties the People's Party candidates won by margins so large that they averaged 16.5 percent more of the vote across the state than the Bucktail ticket. "Great is your victory," acclaimed Calhoun. The Bucktails still won control of the legislature, however, with the Clintonians reduced to being the third party, with only seventeen seats.[36]

As far as the electoral bill was concerned, things were less clear-cut. In many counties, the People's Party men had questioned candidates to great effect. According to Jabez Hammond, "The proposition was so well and favorably received by the people, that no candidate, however regularly nominated by a democratic caucus, dare avow his opposition to the measure." The *Cherry Valley Gazette* claimed that seventy-five of those elected to the assembly, including some Regency men, had pledged themselves to vote for the new electoral law, and some new senators who had not been elected as People's Party men subsequently acted with that party.[37]

What inspired this rebellion against a party that seemed to be riding so high in state politics? The People's Party in New York City undoubtedly expressed the outlook of manufacturing and economic enterprise, which on the whole disapproved of negative government. The People's Party men everywhere tended to be lawyers, merchants, and industrialists, and were less likely than the regulars to be farmers. They particularly objected to the law passed by the legislature in 1823 to tax personal property, including bank stocks. Outside the southeastern counties, People's Party tickets did well where manufacturing was developing, but their tickets were also made up—unlike the regulars—of men of strong religious commitment, including many pious Yankees.[38]

Beyond local economic issues, the People's Party protest revealed a concern about the presidential election. In the city the *National Advocate* had said that the Democratic ticket would be formed without reference to presidential tests: "Old Democrats will be chosen who will go with the party on the great question." The editor associated "an Adams ticket" with "the *American* and the federal committees," though in fact the successful dissident ticket in the city included Adams, Calhoun, and even Crawford men. In Suffolk County, covering the eastern (and New England–settled) part of Long Island, some county meetings urged voters to vote only for candidates who were pledged to Adams.[39]

More widely, according to the *Portland Argus,* "The presidential canvass has mingled more or less in the contest throughout the State. In some of the counties the elections turned on predilections and prejudices for and against particular candidates for the presidency." According to the *Philadelphia Sentinel,* "The friends of Mr. Crawford, although comprising . . . a very large majority of democrats, were not quite a match for the Federalists and Clintonians, united to the friends of Mr. Adams and Mr. Calhoun to be found among the democrats." Regulars later claimed that Crawford's supporters won "a very decided majority" in the new legislature, while Adams had only twenty-six "decided friends" out of 128 members. However, there were also some "successful caucus candidates" who were "either known or supposed to be partial to Mr. Adams," especially from the northern and western counties where the regular nomination prevailed because its candidates made whatever pledges were necessary in a Yankee constituency.[40]

In this rallying toward Adams, the issue of slavery played a significant role. Dutchess County elected General Tallmadge their state representative with 52.9 percent of the vote, "after the most contested election we have ever had." Though regarded as unreliable (and not entirely selfless) by those who knew him, he continued to be identified as an antislavery spokesman: best known for his famous amendment to the Missouri bill in 1819, he had also made a loud effort in the constitutional convention of 1821 to bring about the immediate emancipation of New York's slaves. In 1823 he placed the grounds of his dissent on economic issues, but slavery still figured strongly in the contest. According to the *Cherry Valley Gazette,* the opposition ticket succeeded mainly because the idea was

> so illustriously circulated at the polls, in the towns of the interior, that the persons composing it would support Mr. Crawford for the Presidency, and withhold from the people the right of choosing the Electors. Indeed, one ticket was stigmatized as being for "Crawford and Slavery," and the other for "Adams and Liberty!" This produced such an effect that many of our old and substantial republicans voted the "people's ticket," because they preferred a northern President.

The pressure forced the regular candidates to accommodate to the popular will. Two of those on the regular ticket publicly declared their preference for Adams, a third was said to be friendly to him, and all were committed to giving the choice of electors to the people. A Clintonian who was elected in this usually strongly anti-Clintonian county "undoubtedly owed his election," according to Hammond, "to the hostility of a majority of that county to Mr. Crawford as a candidate for the presidency." According to another observer, in forty-six out of fifty-four counties, "to arouse the prejudices of the people the more successfully the tickets were headed [by the opposition] 'Crawford and Slavery' [and] 'Adams and Liberty.'"[41]

The slavery issue still loomed large in 1823 because of a new threat that slavery might be introduced into Illinois. Rufus King insisted in July that because the slave states were always quick to complain about Northern interference, Northerners must reciprocate by complaining whenever Southerners invaded freedom; they should not stand by to see slavery admitted to states where it had never existed: "This project of Illinois is the most barefaced and infamous that has ever disgraced any part of the United States, and if it prevails, the spirit and principles of freedom in this country are dead."[42]

King's personal response reflected a public controversy through the summer. In August, the *New-York American,* edited by his son, Charles, condemned the cherished party loyalty of Noah and the regulars as a device to conceal a plot to betray the people of the North: in order to win treasury support, New York's "cabal of politicians" were joining a plot to change Illinois's constitution, making slavery legal there in violation of the spirit of the Northwest Ordinance. Only the popular election of presidential electors could defeat them. The *National Advocate* responded that the dangerous and unsettling attacks on Southern slaveholding launched by Adams's supporters jeopardized the Union and looked toward a "Northern Confederacy." These themes were given a new twist at the widely reported celebration of the passage of the first boat from the Erie Canal into the Hudson River in October 1823. Some of the speakers pointed out that the canal would tie the Northwest closer to New York, and its example of republicanism, enterprise, and freedom would affect the great struggle that was taking place for the future of the West and therefore the republic.[43]

Later Van Buren would claim that the 1823 election had been a test on the presidential question and that Crawford had won, thus settling the assembly's decision for it. Yet surely the election had shown that it was folly for Van Buren and the Regency to cling to Crawford and the caucus. Many believed that Adams was the only candidate with supporters spread throughout the state; if the election came soon, he would probably win it, though not with an absolute majority. In the circumstances, many thought Van Buren should give up Crawford because it was now clear that his chances in New York depended entirely on "the necessity of *party discipline.*" Any refusal to pass the electoral bill, they were warned, could kill the Democratic Republican Party in New York for a decade, but the Regency soon showed it was determined to put the national issue before local pragmatism.[44]

### APOLLO AWAKES

The election of 1823 had changed the whole aspect of the presidential election in New York. It made clear that Crawford's best hope of winning the state's electoral vote was to keep the election in the assembly's hands. Even then, the outcome would be far from certain, because many members of the Democratic Republican majority in the lower house were "so hampered by premature commitments, and many of them so goaded by their constituents." In addition, Calhoun retained some firm supporters, including eight out of ten city members, while Clay had done well in the western counties and had at least fourteen committed supporters. Adams was generally regarded as the leading candidate, but his support lacked unity and was considered soft: he did not attract the personal commitment that Calhoun and Clay men showed. According to Henry Wheaton, many members were still "in the market," and there was not "much pertinacity for A." In this volatile situation, the Regency had two assets: the Bucktails retained a majority in the Senate, where most of their members had been chosen in 1822 without reference to the presidential question; and many of those in the House who opposed Crawford feared that a popular election might provide the means for Clinton to make a comeback. Conceivably the former governor might attract enough popular support, especially from those wanting a Northern president, to carry a much-divided state by a plurality vote.[45]

Clinton may once have seemed down and out, but he himself had never given up hope of a resurrection. According to John Bigelow, Clinton so suffered from "presidential rabies" that he was the last person to abandon his own cause. Scornful of the known candidates, he continued to dream whether "in this crisis *may not some other person bear away the palm?*" Since leaving the governorship in January 1823, he had produced a series of speeches and pamphlets in which he developed an ideology of economic, civic, and moral improvement. In effect, he was sketching out what would become the political culture of the later Whig Party, in contrast with the small-government ideology of the New York Democrats. By November Webster was astonished to discover that Clinton's popularity had "experienced a sudden and most extraordinary revival; so much so as to inspire unlimited expectations." This revival Webster ascribed to the triumphant opening of the Erie Canal into the Hudson at Albany the previous month.[46]

In the circumstances, Clinton was rumored to be reconsidering his position. In December he was nominated by two public meetings in Ohio, at Cincinnati and Steubenville. His friends were involved in the campaigns of Calhoun and Jackson in Pennsylvania and New York, and he himself backed Jackson during 1823. He may well have seen the Jackson movement in its earliest stages as unlikely to get anywhere but representing an urge for an independent leader that might later turn to his own advantage. Though weak in the New York legislature, he retained support outside; and in the event of a popular election, he might draw heavily from the ranks of those who currently favored Calhoun, Clay, or Adams.[47]

The distant threat of Clinton helped to determine events in the legislature. Most of those elected in opposition to the regularly nominated tickets still regarded themselves as Democratic Republicans. In January, the evening before the session opened, most of them voluntarily entered the Republican caucus, where they voted for Tallmadge for speaker. When he was defeated by large majority, the People's Party men accepted the result of the caucus and did not oppose the successful nominee. As the Calhounites had feared, Clinton's revival had "the effect of reuniting the fragments of the old Republican party."[48]

When the assembly considered the electoral law in January, the regulars ostensibly embraced the principle of popular election. However, in committee, they added an amendment requiring the successful candidate to win an absolute majority of the votes, which in the circumstances of 1824 was unlikely to happen. Because there would be insufficient time to arrange a rerun, the result would be to disfranchise the whole state. Clay's supporters (and some of Adams) were so afraid of Clinton winning on a popular plurality that they voted with the Bucktails to pass this unsatisfactory measure in February 1824.[49]

That device opened the way for the Senate to reject the bill. They could argue that it was necessary to unite the state's strength, at least until Congress approved a promised constitutional amendment establishing a uniform district system. In its absence, only a legislative election could give the state its full weight. On these grounds, seventeen members of the Senate justified killing the electoral bill and so ensured that the election would remain in the hands of the legislature. The consequence was popular opprobrium, as newspapers published lists of the "immortal seventeen," lining the list with the black border suitable for a death announcement.[50]

The rejection of the electoral law was the decisive turning point. A further attempt to pass the measure would be made at a special session in August, but the Regency had already shown how its command of the state senate made the move pointless. The February decision effectively killed off Clinton's lingering presidential chances, and it forced those in Ohio who hoped for a Clinton candidacy to look elsewhere. If Clinton were out of the running, then Adams's position as the only viable Northern candidate was consolidated, in spite of the general lack of enthusiasm for him personally. His fate in New York would be determined in smoke-filled rooms during the sitting of the state legislature in Albany late in 1824—but those indoor events would still be mightily affected by electoral politics out of doors in the remaining months of 1824.

# 5 THE WESTERN INTEREST

As early as 1817 the forty-year-old Henry Clay thought of himself as a future president. His distinguished career—as War Hawk congressman, Speaker of the House, and peacemaker at Ghent—gave him a standing that prevented President Monroe from appointing Crawford secretary of state in 1817, on the grounds that it would put Clay at an unfair disadvantage in a future presidential race. Preferring to remain outside the administration and build an independent political position, Clay pressed for policies that would promote Latin American independence and strengthen the economic independence of the United States. His oratory won him many admirers, including the English radical Fanny Wright. Hearing him speak in 1820, she praised his "ardour of feeling and expression" and pronounced his voice "without exception the most masterly . . . that I ever remembered to have heard." According to Jabez Hammond, "Few men ever lived who possessed, by dint of personal address, greater power over the human mind than Henry Clay; and it was probably more owing to his social qualities than to his great and unrivalled powers as an orator, that so many of his old congressional associates and acquaintance adhered to him."[1]

In 1820 his long experience as Speaker of the House had made him critical in engineering the Missouri Compromise. In the dispute whether Missouri's vote should be counted in the presidential election, he decisively overrode attempts to block the declaration of a result and, in Plumer's words, brought "the election to a close in peace, if not tranquility." Clay had himself angled for the vice presidential nomination in 1820 as a stepping-stone to higher things but was vetoed in the caucus by the friends of potential rivals. Adams thought Clay had "disclosed his designs too soon" before uniting his supporters and thus alienated Crawford's friends in the South. No one doubted that Clay would be a candidate in four years' time, though he had learned to bide his time and not leap into the contest in the early months of 1822. After all the froth generated by the early scrapping, the egregious Thomas Hart Benton, Clay's leading advocate in Missouri, privately gave Clay an equal chance with Crawford, with Adams a poor third.[2]

Clay also had serious claims on traditional party men. He possessed great standing as a consistent and loyal *"Republican of the old school,"* with strong party attachments. As a native Virginian who had moved to Kentucky, he enjoyed, in Adams's phrase, "that clannish preference which Virginia has always given to her sons." He had been recognized as a stout defender of states' rights through the Missouri crisis, and he could speak persuasively of maintaining the federal balance. He had distanced himself from Monroe's desire to mitigate old party antagonisms and, as Speaker, did not himself "venture to disregard the old lines of distinction." Even in 1824 Clay and Crawford could be seen as the "democratic candidates" and were repeatedly rumored to be close to a deal to produce a party ticket. However, Clay's views on national policy guaranteed that he would never be acceptable to the neo-Antifederalists.[3]

Clay possessed an honorable record of articulating in public arenas the argument for positive national economic policies. In the congressional debates of 1818 over internal improvements, he had descended from the Speaker's chair to deliver a burning defense of the constitutional power to build a much-needed communication system. In 1820 he promulgated a classic defense of protective tariffs, insisting that the staple produce of the country needed home markets, which would develop only slowly and painfully in the absence of positive government action. Otherwise the United States would continue to rely on British markets and manufactures: the country would continue to be "a sort of independent colonies of England—politically free, commercially slaves." No other candidate so publicly committed himself to the package of policies that Clay himself would soon call the American System.[4]

These were policies that appealed strongly in what Clay naturally saw as his heartland. Since 1815 the New West had grown rapidly, especially in the Ohio Valley, and had developed a distinctive sense of regional

*Henry Clay. Clay is portrayed following his temporary retirement from Congress in 1821, proudly displaying the resolution that he proposed that year as Speaker of the House, calling on the United States government to recognize the independence of Spain's rebellious colonies in Latin America. This engraving by Peter Maverick of New York was based on a painting by Charles Bird King and published in Washington, D.C., by Benjamin O. Tyler in 1822. Courtesy: Library of Congress Prints and Photographs Division.*

identity. Regarding themselves as representing the future of the nation, Westerners believed that their views on both foreign and domestic policies should be more fully appreciated in Washington. As Benton pronounced in his *St Louis Enquirer* in 1819, *"It is time that western men had some share in the destinies of this Republic."* Adams soon noted that Clay "is evidently their first man. . . . They must therefore unite for him or abandon for the present the idea of giving a President to the Union."[5]

All counted, the Western states together had only one Electoral College vote more than New York and Pennsylvania, but they did number nine states out of the twenty-four in the Union. If the multiplicity of candidates threw the presidential election into the House, the Western candidate would probably command the largest bloc of states there. Clay's personal standing as the long-serving and much-respected Speaker would give him the extraordinary opportunity to seduce the delegations of four more states—some consisting of a single congressman—and so gain an overall majority in the House.

This scenario was troubling enough for Clay's rivals to develop arguments that a House election would be intrinsically undemocratic and probably corrupt. Crawford's protagonists in particular argued that it would ignore the opinion of popular majorities in the large states, whose interests were best expressed through the Electoral College. The best way of ensuring that the most populous states made their numbers felt was by uniting on a single candidate through the traditional mechanisms of the Democratic Republican Party. In other words, the congressional caucus was the essential defender of democracy, ensuring that a president would be elected who was acceptable to a majority of the people. If Clay could win that nomination, well and good; but otherwise he ought not to be allowed to win the presidency as the representative of a minority interest.[6]

## RISE OF THE NEW WEST

The trans-Appalachian West developed a pronounced sense of itself as a distinctive section mainly because its settlers had special needs that were neglected by Washington. After 1815 Western farmers increasingly acknowledged that the region's adverse balance of trade, its shortage of money, and its slow rate of settlement could all be quickly put right if transportation routes were improved and demand for its produce increased in the East. In Missouri, Benton's *Enquirer* argued that the state needed national roads to Washington, New Orleans, and Louisville; post roads throughout the Territory; and canal links to Lake Michigan and Lake Superior. Only the federal government could command the resources to build these improvements. With missionary zeal, the governor of Ohio, Ethan Allen Brown, urged fellow citizens to follow the example of New York: if the Ohio River were connected with Lake Erie, Ohio's farmers would gain access to the markets of New York and the East for their surplus crops. To strengthen those markets, protection must be given to industrial producers.[7]

These hopes achieved little success before 1824. Congress agreed in 1820 to locate the route of the National Road from Wheeling, Virginia, to Indianapolis, but no money was forthcoming to build it. Congress even refused to vote money to repair the Eastern sections of the road: when in 1822 it passed a bill authorizing the erection of tollgates on the road to pay for repairs, President Monroe vetoed it on constitutional grounds. Then in December 1822 the Speaker of the House, Philip Barbour of Virginia, appointed a House committee on the National Road that was overwhelmingly hostile to the project, with not a single member from Maryland and Ohio, "the states principally interested."[8]

Westerners could conclude only that they were seriously disadvantaged by Eastern political control. Western states suffered the financial disadvantage of not being able to tax federal lands either before purchase or for five years after. They claimed that if land sales were revenue, the West was more highly taxed by the federal government than the East, though federal money was spent almost totally in the East. Congress happily provided lighthouses and anchor buoys on the Atlantic coast, but not on the Great Lakes. The West even found itself shortchanged in the provision of federal circuit courts. One of the seven circuits that had existed since 1807 covered Ohio, Kentucky, and Tennessee, but the six newer states had to make do with district courts. Efforts since 1816 to create extra circuits in the West had all been frustrated by Congress's reluctance to increase the size of the Supreme Court.[9]

Westerners blamed this antipathy on New England and the Southeast, which together uniformly voted down any measure calculated to promote Western interests. The summit of sectional pettiness came in 1821 when the Maryland legislature resolved that sales of public land in the West should be used to support schools in the older states. Western states riposted strongly that new states needed extra help in establishing educational institutions from scratch, which was why Congress had made its far from generous grant of school lands to them in the first place. Eastern newspapers replied that federal resources should be distributed according to numbers and not need, and ten seaboard legislatures formally approved the Maryland proposals. The question, it was expected, would raise "much excitement of sectional feeling" in Congress, but it fizzled out after neo-Antifederalists and others expressed doubts about the constitutionality of Maryland's proposal.[10]

In Ohio, most spectacularly, the hostility of Congress drove popular opinion to embrace a drastic plan to solve the state's transportation problems. Persuaded that roads and canals were absolutely essential but refused a land grant by Congress, the state turned to the New York money market, where Clinton himself assured them they could find the necessary capital. The essential thing was to pledge the faith of the state and establish specific funds to pay interest and capital, based on a fair and effective taxation of landed property. A public works scheme was devised to build two canals from Lake Erie to the Ohio River, paid for by the taxpayer, and then carried into the state elections of 1824. An unprecedented turnout produced a political revolution that gave the canal scheme 85 percent of the votes in the new state legislature.

The decision to rely on local resources did not mark a turning away from federal action. Ohioans still hoped for grants of public lands to help with the canal burden. They looked for the building of the National Road from Wheeling across Ohio, the route for which had been laid out in 1822. They hoped too for river and harbor improvements, not least the building of a canal around the Louisville Falls, which had been argued for since 1804. Both voters and politicians had learned that positive government programs offered them the only way of transforming their situation, ending their economic isolation, and at last climbing out of debt and depression. The lesson had large implications because, as historian Richard L. McCormick has suggested, "changing expectations for government . . . helped call forth the transformation in politics" that was about to overtake the nation.[11]

Public programs required a change of heart at Washington, but at least the recent influx of settlers into the West promised that change must come soon. Western politicians prophesied in 1820 that their strength was "growing too mighty to be treated with contempt" because "the next census shall have given us our full share in the national government." The census demonstrated that Kentucky now had almost as many people as Massachusetts, the largest New England state. Remarkably, Ohio since 1810 had doubled its population, to over half a million. As a result, the decennial reapportionment of 1822 gave the state fourteen congressmen and sixteen Electoral College votes—more than Massachusetts, and fewer only than New York, Pennsylvania, and Virginia. Westerners everywhere were determined to use their enhanced political power to gain a more sympathetic government in Washington. That included capturing the presidency: Madison and Monroe had shown, in 1817 and 1822, how deadly an executive veto could be to the best-laid plans.[12]

## THE WESTERN CAMPAIGN

The West's commitment to the American System ensured the unpopularity of the candidate from Virginia. Some leading politicians were attracted by Crawford's command of patronage and his approval by the Richmond Junto, but they found it heavy work to attract broader support. The old-party appeal worked less well in the West, where Federalists were few and most of those had rallied to the flag during the war. Crawford's supporters insisted that privately he favored internal improvements and protective tariffs, but, as one Ohio newspaper said, "The violent hostility which many of his most zealous friends have manifested against the tariff and internal improvements have conspired to keep him almost entirely out of view in this quarter."[13]

Early in 1822 the widespread approval of Clay as the Western candidate embraced all the southwestern states. Missouri and Kentucky enthused over the American System, and Clay could boast substantial support in Alabama, Mississippi, and even Tennessee. From New Orleans Clay heard in April 1822 that "in Louisiana, our bales of Cotton & hogsheads of sugar absorb all other considerations. . . . You are the only Candidate for the P[residency] known here, and the only one having warm personal friends." In comparison, the other candidates had done little to further the interests of the West, and they certainly had not put their political lives on the line as Clay had. As a result, throughout much of the West, congressmen and local politicians from all the old factions and parties began to make clear their preference for the Kentucky candidate.[14]

Clay's campaign proved capable even of overwhelming the serious divisions inflicted on Western society and politics by the Panic and subsequent depression. Disputes over how best to tackle the severe difficulties in which people found themselves generated contentious elections that drew unprecedented numbers of voters to the polls. Kentucky, for example, had been divided by the triumph, since 1819, of forces favoring debtor relief. In particular, they restricted the ability of creditors to recover money owed they had lent, unless they were willing to accept the rapidly depreciating notes of a new state bank. These measures were naturally opposed by those businessmen who could not pay their own bills because of legalized defaulting on the part of their debtors, by those wanting to revive economic activity, and by a legal profession that objected to the interference with the sanctity of contract. In 1821 a state judge declared key parts of this legislation unconstitutional and thereby initiated an internal political struggle that would polarize Kentucky politics for most of the decade.[15]

In this internecine conflict, Clay was identified with the more conservative view. As his then ally Amos Kendall reported, the relief party leaders were privately "very jealous" of Clay. Some politicians in Washington presumed, therefore, that he could not rely on the united support even of his own state. Hence, his unanimous nomination by the state legislature in November 1822, at a time when the relief forces held the majority, was a decisive demonstration of his popularity in Kentucky. The offending replevin laws were replaced in January 1824 by a less provocative measure, but the dispute over the powers of the state judiciary would become more intense. In August 1824 the state elections resulted in an overwhelming popular endorsement for the relief party, but despite the intense passions roused by the internal contest, Clay's hold remained firm on Kentucky's popular vote for president.[16]

Kentucky was united in its attitude not only to federal economic policy, but also to the federal judiciary. U.S. circuit courts pronounced unconstitutional not only Kentucky's debtor laws but also the state's occupying-claimant laws, which protected the interests of actual settlers against those who claimed title to their land. In *Green vs. Biddle* in 1823, the U.S. Supreme Court sustained the circuit court's condemnation, thereby provoking great hostility to federal judicial interference and calls for repeal of the 1789 federal judiciary act. However, the protest against outside interference came not just from debtors but from their antirelief opponents in Kentucky; privately, Clay himself was disappointed by the verdict, though he could not support Governor Adair's threat to resist it. Hostility to the East and its tyrannous ignoring of Kentucky's interests had the effect of uniting the state in national elections. As one ally said, the force of public opinion was too strong to resist, at least in Kentucky.[17]

Clay had hoped to demonstrate the West's unanimity by securing nominations from other state legislatures, but he faced practical difficulties. His campaign depended on his own energizing influence, but severe illness between October 1822 and November 1823 affected his ability to correspond, coordinate, prompt, and enthuse as Calhoun did. Kentucky's example was not itself sufficient stimulus for Indiana politicians because Kentucky newspapers were not generally taken in the state, and late in 1822 efforts had to be made first to encourage a more vigorous exchange between editors. Further disappointment had come when the Tennessee legislature nominated Jackson in July 1822, creating a tactical quandary. Many observers thought this a local enthusiasm that would prove only a passing phase, and they presumed that Jackson would soon withdraw from the race. Clay's supporters therefore chose not to attack him while he was vulnerable because they believed his supporters in the Southwest would sooner or later turn to Clay.

Elsewhere, legislatures did publicly announce for Clay. In November, frontier Missouri—acting at Benton's prompting—anticipated Kentucky. Ohio, the great prize, proved more difficult than expected, but in January 1823 a meeting of Ohio legislators approved resolutions naming Clay. These early nominations, it was hoped, would create an irresistible tide that would sweep on to some major seaboard states: "The West once united, the current will flow easily."[18]

In particular, strategists believed that Clay would begin to pick up support in the Middle states. They assumed that the West and the Middle states had a common interest in the American System, which would encourage them to unite behind one candidate. As Clay recognized, the union of either of the two largest Middle states with the West would "present a stronger mass of solid interest" than any other candidate could claim, especially as New Jersey, Maryland, and Delaware would probably follow suit. "If the *West* be true to themselves—and some partial support can be had from the middle states," Clay had been assured, "your election might be calculated on with confidence."[19] But would any Middle Atlantic state see Clay as the best American System candidate?

## THE MIDDLE INTEREST

By 1820 the Middle states, unlike their neighbors to the north and south, had largely rejected their traditional Atlantic orientation. Clay himself remarked that if the West and the states from New York through

Maryland "constituted an Independent Nation, it would immediately protect" the "Home market." Rufus King observed in February 1823 that Pennsylvania and New York were "all burning with the canal fevers" and, together with New Jersey, were "up in favor of Manufactures." Hence, he thought they would be "unwilling to create a President whom they may believe to be opposed" to federal support for internal improvement or home industry.[20]

The consonance of interest with the West reflected the geographical situation of the Middle states. Parts of both Pennsylvania and New York lay west of the Appalachians. The great seaport cities saw that their commercial futures depended on tapping the trade of the interior. New York had seized the initiative with the Erie Canal, and both Philadelphia and Baltimore were desperate to find some means of competing. Unfortunately, each suffered from much greater challenges than New York. For Philadelphia, the mountain barrier in Pennsylvania was much more difficult to negotiate; a cross-state canal to Pittsburgh would face formidable physical obstacles and be hugely expensive. Just as awkwardly, the main drainage of central Pennsylvania ran due south along the Susquehanna, drawing central Pennsylvania's exports and commerce into the Chesapeake, away from Philadelphia and into the hands of Baltimore.

In turn, Baltimore suffered from Maryland's lack of natural routes to the West. It shared the promising Potomac route with Virginia, a state that was willing to support improvements but not to commit itself realistically to interstate cooperation or large governmental involvement. In any case, a successful Potomac canal would likely benefit Alexandria (then in the District of Columbia) rather than Baltimore. Baltimore's most attractive bet in the early 1820s was to encourage the clearing of the lower Susquehanna River to draw Pennsylvania farm produce to itself, but that depended on Pennsylvania's cooperation.

The price Pennsylvania had extracted long before was Maryland's support for a canal connecting the Chesapeake and Delaware estuaries across the neck of the Delmarva Peninsula. This project would enable Philadelphia to extend its hinterland and itself tap Susquehanna exports, but it required Delaware's permission for a development that was not necessarily to the advantage of key groups in that state. In 1821–1822 the energetic campaigning of the publisher and publicist Mathew Carey raised enough subscription money in Philadelphia to reorganize an earlier company that had ground to a halt in 1805. Involving three states directly and creating a secure water route between two major Atlantic inlets, this project was undoubtedly of national importance, and all concerned saw the need for congressional help of the sort that the current ruling groups in Washington were unwilling to provide.[21]

Clay might reasonably be expected to prosper in this situation. In places that benefited from internal improvement projects with which Clay was associated—notably along the National Road in Maryland and western Virginia—he won early support. In New York, as the 1823 election loomed, Clay anticipated that "views of general and State policy . . . obviously indicate the expediency of her looking Westwardly." The main problem, he was advised from New York, was to prevent public support from the Clintonians, which would "prostrate all your hopes here." Clay thought his chances there equal to anyone's, but things were never quite so simple in New York.[22]

For one thing, the state's attitude to the American System was not entirely straightforward. Admittedly, the successful opening of parts of the Erie Canal enthused the canaling spirit, but some people were already wondering whether it was in the state's interests to advocate federal aid for internal improvements when that would enable other states to build rivals to New York's great ditch. Some portions of the state—along the southern tier, on Lake Ontario, and on Long Island—felt excluded from the state program but could be attracted toward federal projects more attuned to their needs. There was also huge enthusiasm for protecting manufactures, and the state assembly passed resolutions in favor of the policy in 1823. However, some leading canal men, like Clinton's ally Charles G. Haines, saw the main virtue of the Erie Canal as increasing the hinterland for New York City's imports and so were not enthused by the tariff cause. For many New Yorkers, these were fine hairs that could not override their support for both internal improvements and manufactures.

However, enthusiasm for the American System did not necessarily translate into support for Clay. Many of those most committed to internal improvements still hankered after Clinton and hoped he might yet come out of retirement as a candidate for the presidency. In New York City Calhoun had captured much support, notably from Henry Wheaton and the *Patriot* newspaper, though there was "no asperity" between the Calhoun and Clay camps. In the revulsion against Crawford in the late summer of 1823, Clay began to receive more visible support, especially in the western part of the state, where at least five newspapers came out in his favor. Some saw the main contest in New York as looming between Clay as the Democratic Republican candidate and Adams, who was vociferously backed by old Federalist and Clintonian newspapers.[23]

When the People's Party revolt came in November 1823, a number of its activists favored tariff protection and Henry Clay. Fourteen committed Clay men were elected to the House, and they hoped to attract Calhounite support when the South Carolinian's cause faltered. However, Clay's strong appeal to firm Democratic Republicans was also a source of weakness. Some of them hoped that Van Buren might yet shift from the unelectable Crawford to Clay as the only other "democratic" candidate, and as a result they felt unwilling to act independently. Early in 1824 some significant advocates, including those planning a Clay newspaper, were seduced by Van Buren back into the regular ranks. Fearing a renascent Clinton, the Clay men supported the Bucktail insistence that a popular election for electors must be decided by an absolute majority. In effect, early in 1824 they were acknowledging that Clay's best bet was to win a handful of New York's electoral votes by playing the Bucktail game.[24]

Similarly, in Pennsylvania Clay's hopes gained strength from the widespread commitment to the American System but suffered from its arcane factional state contests. Unlike New Yorkers, most Pennsylvanians did not allow the presidential race to distract their attention from unrelated local concerns until after the gubernatorial election of fall 1823. Here too Calhoun's early strike had enabled him to take the forward ground in Pennsylvania as Crawford's leading competitor, though many felt his support would ultimately go to a stronger American System candidate. Clay had his early pockets of popularity, but still in November 1822 Langdon Cheves thought Clay did not have "any party in the state." He also suffered from resentment that the National Road had been built through Maryland rather Pennsylvania. However, Clay's main worry in late 1822 was to find newspaper support "to express and enlighten public sentiment there" in a fashion that would prepare the way for Crawford's opponents to rally on the Western candidate. The failure to secure the "earnest" support of an influential *"democratic"* newspaper in either New York or Philadelphia remained a continuing weakness for Clay's cause; Clay explained that he disapproved of corrupting the press—but then he lacked both the money and the patronage his secretarial opponents enjoyed.[25]

As 1823 wore on, Clay remained the second choice of those in Pennsylvania who for the moment preferred other candidates. Unfortunately, the others did not fade as expected. Clay considered Calhoun's cause hopeless, but his support among established politicians and newspapers in the East remained firm. Adams proved surprisingly powerful, especially among the Federalists of the Philadelphia area, who were "still a strong party here." Crawford was considered the most unpopular, but he possessed the patronage to hold his key supporters in place. Then there was Jackson, who began to rouse popular support in Pennsylvania during the spring. This "disorder" prevented Clay from making "much headway" because Jackson appealed to "exactly that school of politicians who would otherwise have been decidedly and unanimously" for Clay. The Jackson enthusiasm was expected to prove temporary, but in the meantime, it undeniably took the wind from Clay's sails.[26]

Clay also suffered from the eagerness with which Calhoun used the War Department as a means of encouraging internal improvements. In 1823 he permitted two officers of the Corps of Engineers to survey first the proposed route of the Chesapeake and Delaware Canal, and then that of the Delaware and Hudson Canal across northern New Jersey. Their reports approving the routes were publicly acclaimed as signs of the federal government's "approbation and countenance." When advocates of the proposed Chesapeake and Ohio Canal met in Washington in December, Calhoun spent "three whole days . . . canvassing with these delegates." Who then, after Clinton, was the nation's foremost champion of "canal navigation"?[27]

The backwardness in pressing Clay's claims in the Middle states arose partly from the desire of his partisans not to alienate the supporters of rival candidates who might later on be tempted to take up Clay. That tactic rested on two assumptions: first, that a common interest in the American System would ultimately force its supporters into one camp, regardless of other pressures and considerations; and second, that Clay would be the one to survive because of his sound base in the West. However, as Langdon Cheves told him in November 1822, his chances in the Middle states depended on "an Unanimous *western demonstration.*" To that end, Western papers needed to be active and noisy on his behalf. The question therefore remained: was the West as united as Clay and his friends insisted, or was it "too much divided," as Calhoun thought? Were the states north and south of Kentucky equally enthusiastic? Was the West really one section, or was it divided into subregions like the seaboard?[28]

## ANTISLAVERY CHALLENGE

Elisha Whittlesey was a sober young Ohio congressman in his first session in Washington. Returning home by stage early in 1824, he stayed with fellow lawyers at an Ohio tavern where the guests were invited to mark the register with their presidential preference. This was a growing fashion in 1823–1824, as voters looked for indications of how an unpredictable election might go. Whittlesey at first refused. When severely pressed, he wrote in the register, "The next President; may he look well to the interests of the West." Immediately his local rivals reported back home on the Western Reserve that he was in favor of Clay and therefore of the interests of slavery. This accusation deeply troubled Whittlesey, who had been well advised not "to break with your good friends the Adamsites," not even "for the finest *Clay,*" because his constituents were divided. Through the election Whittlesey never stated his personal preference publicly, answered "measures not men" to all enquiries, and refused to "mingle in the presidential contest," leaving the question "to the people unshackled."[29]

This congressman's embarrassment demonstrates the main weakness Clay suffered northwest of the Ohio River. Many settlers there had strong objections to voting for a man who lived in a slave state, owned slaves, and was responsible for the compromises that had allowed slavery to expand into the Louisiana Purchase. "Had the vote of Ohio been taken at the heels of the Missouri business," claimed the speaker of the Ohio house of representatives, "he could not have recd. fifty votes." As elsewhere, this resentment diminished with time, but still some Ohioans looked for a candidate "free from the *political sin of slavery.*" Rufus King's son in Chillicothe thought that if the New England states raised the cry of "No Slavery," the Western free States would probably abandon Clay and "unite in this policy."[30]

In both Ohio and Indiana a strong sense of identity had developed that included a dislike of slavery at its core. Both states had experience of fighting off attempts to introduce slavery that tried to override the restrictions of the Northwest Ordinance and their state constitutions. In Ohio a suspected further proslavery effort in 1818 aroused public awareness and inspired the state's vigorous response to the Missouri controversies. In Indiana antislavery had triumphed at statehood in 1818, but by 1822 had detected an alarming new campaign to legalize slavery through a revision of the state constitution. These alarms ensured an "opposition to southern politicians" that, as one of Clay's key Ohio advocates observed, was "not the work of any political association of men who impose their notions on the people, but . . . the spontaneous effusion of public sentiment."[31]

Illinois seemed rather different because of the long-standing influence of those wishing to introduce slavery there. During the Missouri crisis, its U.S. senators had behaved as though Illinois was essentially a slave state in outlook and attitude. Soon thereafter, the campaign to legalize slavery by revising the state constitution revived with apparently every prospect of success. Yet antislavery sentiment proved stronger than assumed. The voters deliberately elected an antislavery man, Daniel Cook, as their sole congressman in 1820 and 1822. By July 1823 Jesse B. Thomas, the leading Crawford man, acknowledged that "a revolution of feeling has taken place, and the people have determined . . . to withstand any effort" to legalize slavery.[32]

The persisting core of hostility to slavery was strongest in the Old Northwest among some small religious sects. The Quakers, be they in their major center in eastern Ohio or the smaller communities found in southwestern Ohio and Indiana, were said to "nauseate so greatly at slavery in Clay." Some Presbyterian and Baptist communities of Southern and Pennsylvanian origin generated a radical antislavery commitment and consistently looked for a nonslaveholding president. However, the main demand for a Northern man came from the many New England settlers, especially in Ohio, where they were most numerous, as in Whittlesey's district. Their anti-Southern outlook may have been based on an ethnocultural self-identity, but they expressed themselves with more open reference to the slavery issue than was true in the seaboard states.[33]

From their point of view, the obvious Northern candidate was Adams. He suffered, however, from a major objection: he was identified as an Eastern man unsympathetic to the West. Early in the campaign he was mischievously accused—by Clay's friend William Russell—of having been willing, in the peace negotiations of 1814, to allow Britain the right to sail its warships on the Mississippi in return for preserving New England's fishing interests. More critically, before the summer of 1824 Adams never publicly disassociated himself from New England's continuing opposition to federal internal improvements. He may privately have favored federal action in principle, but in his days in the Senate he had voted against specific projects helpful to the West, including the National Road. On the tariff, Adams was thought to be at heart favorably disposed but unwilling to offend Eastern merchants. His continuing silence on these subjects was a great liability in the Old Northwest.

Clinton, by contrast, united Northern residence with a distinguished record in internal improvements. In December 1822 state legislators in Ohio hesitated to commit themselves publicly to Clay because they feared Clinton might come forward and out-trump Clay. Support for him continued to raise its head in Ohio, and his supporters "hurled the question of Slavery" at Clay's backers, even into the early months of 1824. When the failure of the electoral bill in New York made Clinton unviable, Clay was "relieved from all collision with him in Ohio, where he would have given me trouble."[34]

As many had seen from an early point, Adams was the only available Northern candidate: however unappealing he was on Western issues, he still appealed to a key element in the minds of many Westerners. As in New York and parts of New England, Adams's friends in Ohio and Indiana attempted to discover in advance the presidential allegiances of candidates for the state legislature in 1823 and publish them in their newspapers, with a view to influencing the coming state legislature. In this situation, the famous Ohio resolutions on slavery were passed overwhelmingly in January 1824: Ohio's legislators wished to demonstrate that they favored emancipation even if they supported a slaveholder for the presidency. Clay himself believed the Northwestern states in general will "vote for me because of other & chiefly local considerations outweighing the Slave objection."[35]

Thus the first great challenge to Henry Clay in the Old Northwest came from those who insisted on the overwhelming need to reject the influence of slavery in national affairs and assert non-Southern values, even if it meant electing a man whose position on the American System was far from certain. In effect, the choice between Adams and Clay required the region's citizens to decide how they perceived themselves. Were they Northerners, identified by their distance from slavery and their distinctiveness from the South, or were they Westerners, committed to the development of their new country and the creation of a strong internal economy? There was also a second question, however: if the Western interest was more important that Northern identity, was Clay the most desirable exponent of Western interests?

Clay suffered from the extra disadvantage faced in this election by all candidates well favored by prominent politicians. The chronic economic difficulties of recent years, which still lingered on, were widely blamed on politicians too eager to grant special privileges to bankers and men with power. Thus, to be hailed as the presidential choice of local political leaders was not necessarily an advantage. Crawford suffered wherever he was the choice of officeholders. Calhoun suffered from relying on the advocacy of self-interested city politicians and army officers. Clay suffered from the early and very public backing of the leading men in Western communities.

Curiously, the Adams campaign tended to avoid this disadvantage. In New England areas, Adams benefited because he was not initially the choice of any state ruling party, whether Republican or Federalist, and his name was forced on politicians by popular demand in 1823. In many parts of Ohio, Adams's supporters insisted that their campaign was hostile to the "aristocratic" tendencies evident in the Crawford and Clay national and state campaigns, and they portrayed Adams as the people's candidate. Adams, they claimed, would be "a real democratic republican president" who would encourage "the growth and advancement of the middling and lower order of the people." This populist theme was particularly emphasized in the Old Northwest in counties where dissident politicians latched on to Adams partly as a means of embarrassing dominant local leaders who backed Clay.[36]

The Kentuckian was particularly vulnerable to this line of attack. In 1820 Clay's personal finances were undermined when friends defaulted on loans that he had personally guaranteed. To restore his position, he accepted appointment as legal agent for the Bank of the United States in the West and gave up his congressional seat. He took the lead in the bank's case against the state of Ohio, which had forcibly collected a tax from the BUS's branches in the state; the case, *Osborn v. Bank of the United States,* would be finally argued before the United States Supreme Court and decided, adversely to the state, in March 1824. More embarrassing was Clay's "painful" duty to pursue debtors of the BUS through the law courts, often himself acting as prosecutor at a time when the people in the West had been "goaded almost to desperation by pecuniary embarrassments." In choosing to work for the national bank, Clay damned his political prospects for 1824.[37]

Clay's damnation was most apparent in the major cities on the Ohio

River, from Pittsburgh to Louisville. These metropolises had huge sway over their agricultural hinterlands, which suffered from the waves of distress, bankruptcy, and ruin that emanated from the local commercial center. Of them all, none suffered more dramatically from the Bank of the United States and its agents than Cincinnati. The influence of the Queen City radiated outward over a metropolitan area that included highly populous southwestern Ohio, an area of northern Kentucky, and southeastern Indiana.

Between 1812 and 1818 Cincinnati had enjoyed a huge boom, attracting over 10,000 people and becoming the largest town in the West apart from New Orleans. By 1820 the city, according to one resident, presented "a scene of bankruptcy ensued unparalleled perhaps in the history of any trading town." The recent hothouse expansion had been financed by the irresponsible credit policies of the city's banks, encouraged by the local BUS branch. Then the parent BUS office in Philadelphia cracked down on the branch, forcing the local banks to call in their loans and mortgages, closing the Cincinnati branch, and beginning the long process of hauling its debtors through the courts. Almost inevitably, Clay was blamed—unjustly—for recommending "the rash, impolitic and barbarous step of indiscriminately suing all the debtors to the Branch Bank." Those injured were recommended, *"whenever in their power, to remunerate the author of this mischief with a coat of Tar and Feathers!"*[38]

Through these difficult times, severe internal antagonisms racked the city. The inhabitants had suffered real distress through 1820 and 1821, and recovery did not come into sight until 1823. Municipal elections were rowdy, near-violent affairs, and even the congressional election of 1822 reflected a deep antagonism between the "Big Bugs" and those who excoriated men in privileged positions. Beyond such arguments, however, Cincinnati's politicians, businessmen, and editors agreed that the city needed the implementation of sensible, pragmatic policies to bring about full economic recovery. The restoration of decent banking facilities required the reopening of the BUS branch. The rebuilding and extension of local industry depended on enhanced tariff protection, while the city needed better communications both with its hinterland in the Miami Valley and with the lower Mississippi. Commitment to the American System made Henry Clay the natural presidential candidate for Cincinnati—except for the small objection that he was unelectable locally.

The problem was to find an alternative candidate who was committed to American System policies. In 1822 and 1823 attempts were made to run, in turn, Calhoun, Clinton, and Jackson, but none was taken seriously. One of the newspapers that pressed Jackson's claims collapsed in 1823. In December 1823 Jacksonians tried to take over a grand mass meeting in Cincinnati, but they were outvoted by a Clintonian movement that represented all sides of Cincinnati politics. In particular, Clinton appealed to the town's substantial New England community, which comprised about 30 percent of the population. These self-conscious Yankees wanted "to mount the stalking horse slavery," and so opposed all Southern candidates. However, many local politicians simply wished to wait and see how things developed and whom it would be politically safe to support.[39]

The hope of finding a viable American System alternative to Clay was fading in the early months of 1824. In Cincinnati the leading Clintonians and Calhounites gave up their man in response to events elsewhere in February and March. With both men removed from the competition, locals had to choose between a Western slave owner and an Eastern non–slave owner. Some "Yankee lawyers" opted for Adams, starting a hard-hitting Adams newspaper and building a ward organization. Others finally resigned themselves to Clay, despite his unpopularity locally. Yet others saw that there remained one controversial substitute: another Western candidate, the one with an impressive military reputation, whom the Southwestern states had already taken up: Andrew Jackson.

# 6

## ENTER THE GENERAL

Andrew Jackson's victory at New Orleans in January 1815 came at a critical moment in the war against Britain. The downfall of Napoleon had allowed Britain to turn part of its huge military machine against the United States. The Royal Navy dominated the approaches to the United States and ranged along the Atlantic seaboard. Washington had been sacked, Baltimore threatened. Failures of finance and supply undermined the American war effort; even Detroit might have to be abandoned, yielding the fruits of hard-won victories in the Northwest. A British squadron in the Gulf of Mexico launched an invasion by battle-hardened regulars to seize New Orleans and the lower Mississippi Valley. At that moment of maximum danger for the young republic, Jackson saved the day, with a sensational victory over Wellington's regulars.

No matter that peace had already been signed at Ghent; news did not arrive until after the battle, and the treaty seemed a response to Jackson's victory. The nation celebrated the victory and honored "the immortal Jackson" as the military savior the new nation had sorely needed:

> Genl. Andrew Jackson. The Mirror of Washington.
> A Chief in All the Ways of Battle Skill'd,
> Great in Council, Mighty in the Field.

In the fall, military friends urged him to consider running for president, largely on the grounds that the republic

needed decisive leadership while affairs in Europe remained dangerous.[1]

As celebrations of Jackson's achievement spread throughout America, some citizens spelled out the political danger. Napoleon Bonaparte's
subversion of the French republic had given fresh warning of what could
happen if a military chieftain arose, Caesarlike, to translate military victory into dictatorial regime. Federalist newspapers in particular pointed
to Jackson's recent arbitrary rule in Louisiana and feared that military
despotism might be introduced through unscrupulous use of the army.
The same concern raised its head after Jackson and his troops chased
warring Seminole Creeks into Spanish Florida in 1818, seized Pensacola,
and executed two British subjects. On both occasions, Jackson showed
scant regard for the civil authorities, asserting the superiority of his personal judgment as commander on the spot. When Congress decided
to investigate Jackson's behavior in 1818–1819, numerous junior army
officers—"his suite"—turned up in Washington, thuggishly announcing
their presence in the streets. One Democratic Republican representative
was reminded of the *dragonnades* in France, when an overweening military presence close at hand had deliberately pressed people to change
their beliefs.[2]

Behind these anxieties lay an awareness that Jackson would make
a formidable presidential candidate. In 1818–1819 his name was again
mentioned for the highest office; Adams thought Crawford and Clay in-
stigated the congressional debate over his Florida campaign in order to
weaken him as potential candidate. Jackson came to Washington for the
proceedings, greeted en route by a proud display of popular approval.
Even so, according to Mrs. Adams, he was depressed by the proceedings
in the Senate, which were managed so as to leave the nation with the
sense that he had behaved improperly. "Even American Generals," said
one Ohioan, "must submit to the laws of Nations, however flushed with
victory."[3]

Jackson himself refused to take any action that might be seen as seeking office, insisting that he was tired of public life. He refused to take
talk of the presidency seriously; apparently in 1821 he angrily declared,
"I can command a body of men in a rough way; but I am not fit to be
President." Many believed his behavior as governor of Florida in 1821
proved the point: President Monroe privately thought Jackson had "executed the Spanish powers too much in the Spanish way." Again Congress investigated and exonerated him, but the attorney general, William

*Andrew Jackson. Jackson's figure had been much reproduced since 1815 in prints and on material objects commemorating his victory at New Orleans. He was commonly depicted as a dashing Napoleonic hero, as in this engraving by Henry Bryan Hall, which is based on a portrait by John Vanderlyn painted soon after 1815. Reproduced in James Parton,* Life of Andrew Jackson, *3 vols. (New York: Mason Bros., 1861), vol. 2, frontispiece.*

Wirt, claimed "it will require all his popularity to gild this pill." Many people had developed a negative view and had come to see him as a potential destroyer of the republic. Such criticism hurt Jackson, who retired to private life in the winter of 1822, determined to spend his latter days on his farm.[4]

Given Jackson's standing as an authentic American hero, it is difficult to imagine how his name could be kept out of the coming presidential campaign: politicians of many different stripes were just too eager to find advantage through promotion of a popular candidate. As early as August 1821, prominent Pennsylvania politicians were exploring the prospects for a Jackson campaign, and in January 1822 the *Nashville Gazette* touted his name as a possible successor to Monroe. Even Randolph said that Jackson would be the next president. The sole doubt was whether Jackson himself would agree to run. Only his sense of public duty could press him to accept. As with Adams, nothing would engage the General's commitment more fully than criticism, however mild and respectful, of his past conduct from those who feared his competition.[5]

### SOUTHWESTERN ORIGINS

The criticisms of Jackson's hot-headedness and apparent lack of political judgment ensured that in the early stages of the 1824 campaign, he was not regarded as a likely presidential runner. Even on his home turf, in the Old Southwest, the contest shaped up initially as between Crawford and Clay. As elsewhere, Crawford's support came from "those who *have* been considered capable of wielding the political sentiments of this country," while those aware of the wishes of the great body of the people favored Clay. Even in Tennessee some of Jackson's personal friends and political allies pressed Clay to run: Judge John Overton, for one, insisted that Clay's candidacy was "much desired in this Country" and would succeed easily against any candidate except Jackson. Overton believed, on "good authority," that it was "almost certain" Jackson would not "suffer himself to be run for that office."[6]

In this situation, the General's entry into the race appears almost accidental. Some close personal friends, notably Major William B. Lewis and U.S. senator John H. Eaton, had been pressing him to run, but the pressure was ineffective until important allies in Tennessee saw a need to use Jackson's name to restore their local political standing. Traditionally the state's politics had been dominated by a group of land speculators and bankers led first by William Blount and then by John Overton, in opposition to the faction led by Jackson's bitter personal enemy, Andrew Erwin. The Overton group had begun to lose control after the Panic roused popular discontents, and demands for relief gained satisfaction in the state legislature under the leadership of the independent Felix Grundy. Then in 1821 the Erwin group secured the election, by an overwhelming margin, of its gubernatorial candidate, William Carroll, who established a reforming regime based on hostility to private banks and paper money.

In response, the Blount–Overton faction decided to use Jackson's popularity to revive their standing in Tennessee. They believed his name would help them elect a governor and a legislature more favorable to their views and interests, and gain more sympathetic representatives in Washington. With the backing of Grundy and other influential figures, the Overton group used a special session of the legislature to secure a unanimous nomination of Jackson in July 1822. Jackson had been asked if he had any objection and had replied with resigned acceptance. The Erwin group was unenthusiastic but in no position to oppose Jackson publicly. One of Jackson's oldest friends, Hugh Lawson White, complained that "scoundrels" were using Jackson's name "to effect their dishonest or dishonorable purposes. . . . They have no more notion of trying to make him president than of making me."[7]

Some observers interpreted Jackson's nomination in Tennessee as deliberate maneuvering to weaken Clay. Benton learned from his Tennessee contacts that "hardly anyone" thinks Jackson "has any chance nationally, and many see in his offering nothing but a diversion in favor of Adams." The object, according to White, was "to use the name of Gen. Jackson, only for the purpose of electing Mr. Adams, by dividing the western vote." Informed politicians assumed in 1822 and even 1823 that when the lack of support elsewhere became clear, Jackson would gracefully withdraw. However, they ignored the weight of local opinion.[8]

Jackson's name aroused popular feelings of both "state pride" and gratitude to the man who had removed the Indian menace from Tennessee. Many politicians who privately preferred Clay found they could not oppose the old Indian fighter. To counter persisting rumors that Jackson could not carry Tennessee, his supporters organized "a drumbeat of county meetings" throughout the state between April and July 1823 to demonstrate his popularity. However, Overton and other reluctant sponsors apparently doubted Jackson's reliability because since 1820 he had openly opposed relief measures and supported Carroll's antibank reforms. They therefore backed the reelection as U.S. senator of Jackson's old enemy, John Williams, a Crawford man from east Tennessee, who gained promises of support from a majority of state legislators elected in August 1823. Because the election of Williams would effectively undermine claims that Jackson commanded Tennessee's affections, his closest friends, Lewis and Eaton, felt they had no alternative but to defy Jackson's personal wishes and nominate him for the Senate seat. The nomination swung sixteen votes to defeat the Crawford man, 35–25.[9]

Already Jackson's cause had begun to spread through Tennessee's neighbors to the South, and for reasons that came close to home. The Southwest had long been vulnerable to hostile Indian tribes, and they applauded Jackson for his crushing victories over the Creek and Seminole. His de facto destruction of Spanish power in Florida removed what was perceived as a foreign base for terrorist invasion and opened the way for the 1819 Transcontinental Treaty that gave the Southwest full command of the rivers flowing into the Gulf. His treaties with the tribes had imposed the surrender of tribal land to the federal government, which in due course would open millions of acres to white settlement. Even so, the Creek, Cherokee, Chickasaw, and Choctaw retained title to wide acres in the Southwest, amounting in 1820 to one-third of Alabama and two-thirds of Mississippi. A president who knew how to deal with Indians had an obvious appeal to all who eyed this fertile land.

Clay's early supporters in these states were well aware of the situation. In September 1822 Thomas B. Reed, from Natchez, warned Clay that "nothing in this state opposes itself to your interests, in this State, but the part you took upon the Question growing out of the Seminole war," when Clay had criticized Jackson's behavior. It was thus no surprise when the "contagion" that had begun to infect Tennessee spread to parts of Alabama in the course of 1823; by September a "large majority of the people" in Alabama were said to favor Jackson. As Clay was told, "A majority of the most intelligent are strongly your friends, yet such is the influence of public opinion many of them conceal or abstain from an expression of their preference." The disputes arising from the Panic—debtor relief, monetary expansion, bank paper—had produced massive turnouts in local elections in recent years and taught state politicians to have a healthy respect for public opinion.[10]

Yet at first the General's popularity did not sweep all before it in the Southwest. In Alabama, the presidential election "thrust itself" into a legislative election to the U.S. Senate in January 1823: the Jackson feeling was credited with blocking the election of a Crawford man but did not prove strong enough to carry a legislative nomination. The state elections of September 1823 were dominated by supporters of Crawford and Adams because too many Alabama politicians believed that Jackson could not win nationally. Jackson himself kept a close eye on the state's complex politics and advised on the newspaper campaign to improve the situation. In Mississippi, Adams had been the leading candidate before Jackson's entry into the race, apparently because he had championed Jackson after the Seminole campaign and had acquired the Gulf Coast in 1819. As late as January 1824 a caucus in the Mississippi legislature divided evenly between Adams and Jackson, with the speaker breaking the tie in Adams's favor; meanwhile, the state's congressional delegation was said to favor Clay. In Louisiana, where the local Indians had been expropriated long before, the Jackson cause was even slower to take off.[11]

As with Clay, Jackson's eventual success depended entirely on his ability to break out of his own backyard. Certainly he was seen as a potential threat, and President Monroe tried in February 1823 to remove the complication by offering him the ministry to Mexico; seen by some as the equivalent of sending him to Siberia, Jackson graciously refused the honor. The heartening thing from Jackson's point of view was the grassroots movement in his favor that was taking shape in Pennsylvania, a state with so many Electoral College votes that it could transform him into a major candidate.

## JACKSON'S KEYSTONE

Simon Cameron would long remember the scene. Abraham Lincoln's first secretary of war had begun his long career as a Democratic journalist when he attended the Harrisburg convention of 1824, the first state party convention anywhere called to nominate a presidential candidate "singly and alone." The popular wind blew irresistibly toward Jackson, who was nominated by 124 votes to 1. However, that one man had stood out like a gnarled old oak before the Jackson hurricane. Committed through his career to preserving the unity of the Democratic Republican Party, Jonathan Roberts found it "not a pleasant scene to encounter such a host of enthusiasts" at the Harrisburg convention. Half the delegates he thought "giddy young men," "boys of a day's growth," who behaved with indecorum in their "moon-struck madness" for Jackson. The "good men" present were "panic struck" with "fears of losing popular favor," and so "when it came to the pinch every man went over" to Jackson but himself.[12]

The tide of enthusiasm that carried the Harrisburg nomination of March 4, 1824, and ensured the final result in Pennsylvania, was widely appreciated as resulting from popular passion. Yet it is an oversimplification to conclude, as did William Plumer in Washington, that "the movement in Pennsylvania was made by the people altogether & not by the politicians." Jackson's stupendous success resulted from the interaction of two factors: first, the extraordinary fissiparous complexity of the state's politics, which ultimately made the various factions eager to gain the advantage of a popular presidential candidate; and second, the unusual grassroots excitement that Jackson's candidacy excited among certain sections of Pennsylvania's ethnically diverse and socially divided population.[13]

Like New York, Pennsylvania's state politics had long been marked by pronounced factionalism within the predominant Democratic Party, as it increasingly called itself. Since 1808 the advantage lay with the regular Democrats, who had backed the Madison administration, the war, and positive national legislation. While retaining the loyalty of the "Old Pennsylvania Democracy," they increasingly approved the encouragement of commercial and business advance and became known as the New School Democrats; in 1817 they successfully elected William Findlay as governor. Thereafter, though, older political leaders like Albert Gallatin, John Binns, and Richard Rush found their control of the regular party increasingly contested by a group of younger politicians known as the Family Party, who commanded the Philadelphia branch of the regular party.[14]

Opposed to these New School Democrats stood an Independent Republican coalition, made up of apparently contradictory groups. The Federalists were divided between the "ultras" in the city of Philadelphia, where they remained strong and unaccommodating, and the "liberal" wing outside, which was willing to cooperate with antiparty Democrats. In Philadelphia the dissident Democrats called themselves the Old School because they rejected the economic modernism of the New School. Initially led by the radicals William Duane and Michael Leib, they preached legislative supremacy over judicial review, opposed bank charters, and objected to the congressional caucus in 1816. They repeatedly challenged the regular party at the polls, even though this meant "dividing the democratic family" and allowing the Federalists to win in the city. The Old School enjoyed effective newspaper support from Duane's venerable, if malignant, newspaper, the Philadelphia *Aurora,* as well as strong voter support in southeastern Pennsylvania.[15]

In 1820 this coalition of moderate Federalists and Old School Democrats defeated the reelection of the New School's Governor Findlay. The election focused on personalities and concerns arising from the Panic, but the distribution of votes closely echoed that of 1817. Each state party was itself factionalized; when the new governor, Joseph Heister, alienated many politicians on the Independent side by trying to reform the state administrative and patronage system, he threw the factional game into further disarray. As a consequence, Pennsylvania politicians sought a new, clearer dividing principle. In historian Philip Klein's words, at first they tried reviving "the hereditary fears and local prejudices of the old Federal and Democratic names," and then they "tossed their antes on the board of the great national guessing game at the national capital"—in other words, the presidential election.[16]

The sense of commitment to the Democratic Party increased partly because the gubernatorial election of 1820 had shown that the Federalists were far from dead. New School Democrats like the young Simon Cameron determined to prevent the election in 1823 of any governor to whom "the federal party shall again cling." In both 1820 and 1823 the counties east of the Susquehanna divided evenly, while the "Clodhoppers" in the west proved overwhelmingly Democratic, just as in the old two-party system. The press reported that the 1823 elections produced twenty-three Democrats to ten Federalists in the senate and eighty Democrats to twenty Federalists in the house, as well as the election of the regular Democratic gubernatorial candidate, John Andrew Schulze. This triumph encouraged older Pennsylvania Democrats like Jonathan Roberts and Albert Gallatin to hope that old party loyalty, reinforced by official patronage, could yet carry the state for a presidential candidate named by the congressional caucus.[17]

Others thought differently. The Family Party, led by George Mifflin Dallas and Samuel D. Ingham, turned instead to Calhoun—young, dynamic, and nationalist—who won early endorsements but failed to excite popular enthusiasm. The Federalists of eastern Pennsylvania by the end of 1822 regarded Adams as the only respectable choice. The Old School Democrats had backed Clinton in 1816 and 1820 and initially looked toward him as their savior for 1824. When Clinton became unviable, the Old School looked elsewhere for an independent presidential candidate likely to prove more popular in Pennsylvania than the New School's Calhoun.

### JACKSONIAN EFFERVESCENCE

When the Old School's leading spokesman in Philadelphia, William Duane, retired in 1822, a new newspaper, the *Columbian Observer,* appeared in place of the old flagship *Aurora.* The new editor, Stephen Simpson, had volunteered for military service during the war and found himself at the "Siege of New Orleans" in 1815. He later regarded the "honour and glory" of serving under Jackson an experience he would "ever remember with pride & exultation, both as an *American* & a *Man.*" In the political conditions of the early 1820s, Simpson saw Jackson (in historian Kim Phillips's words) as "a political messiah come to save the soul of America," though his reasoning would not become fully clear until later. In May 1822 Simpson's *Columbian Observer* became the first paper in Pennsylvania to back Jackson, only weeks after the first agitation in Tennessee, and he was soon in contact with the Jackson committee in Nashville.[18]

Other Independent Republicans elsewhere followed suit. In western Pennsylvania, a meeting in Greensburg, Westmoreland County, established a committee of correspondence in December 1822 to organize a Jackson campaign in the state. Next month the Pittsburgh Independent leader Henry Baldwin asked Jackson if he would agree to stand, though a public meeting was not held in Pittsburgh until August. At the state capital, a county meeting in January endorsed Jackson, ordered 10,000 copies of its public address, and informed the General of their choice. Published in the independent Harrisburg *Commonwealth,* his reply was his first public expression of his willingness to accept nomination for the presidency.[19]

This announcement encouraged an attempted coup at the regular state nominating convention in Harrisburg in March 1823. Though it had been called to nominate a gubernatorial candidate, the Family Party also planned to nominate Calhoun, mainly in order to boost his cause in other states. At the convention, however, Jacksonians from Westmoreland County beat them to the draw, and the Family Party men had to fight off the attempt to name Jackson by arguing that a nomination would be premature! Calhoun claimed that two-thirds of the delegates favored him but were wary of acting beyond the convention's brief. According to a Kentucky Jacksonian paper, however, three-fourths of the delegates had favored Jackson.[20]

Jackson's growing appeal, in defiance of the Family Party's preference, offered the state's Federalists a tactical advantage that they seized eagerly in the fall gubernatorial election of 1823. Their newspapers linked Jackson's name with the campaign to elect the Independents' gubernatorial nominee, Andrew Gregg, hoping to excite an "effervescence" to affect the election. One New School regular blamed the whole Jackson phenomenon on them: "The artful Federalists & Gregg men, knowing the General's popularity, as a patriotic warrior, have started his name for the Presidency, as I believe, for the purpose of sowing dissentions in the Democratic party, & elevating themselves into some degree of consequence." If so, the ploy worked: by Christmas Jonathan Roberts expressed his surprise at "how the public, the uninformed part at least, are carried away with Jackson."[21]

The alignment of Federalists with Jackson persuaded his leading partisans at the start of 1824 that they would have to run him in opposition to the regular state Democratic nomination. They planned to hold a separate state convention at Huntingdon to nominate Jackson, in opposition to whichever Democratic candidate triumphed at the Harrisburg convention in March. If they did so, Jonathan Roberts believed, the Jackson ticket would clearly be "the federal ticket" in Pennsylvania, and in that case, the argument for preferring the official Democratic national nomination would be considerably strengthened.[22]

Events soon showed, however, that the Jacksonians could themselves win the state's Democratic nomination. Between November and January his supporters began to carry the "primary assemblies" of the Democratic Party called to select regular delegates for Harrisburg. Though a number of county meetings left their delegates uninstructed, in some places meetings called to support other candidates nominated Jackson, sometimes unanimously. By the first week of February the Jacksonians had dropped their plans for an independent convention, confident that they could carry the regular Democratic convention.

The critical victories came in Philadelphia, where Simpson, operating through the "Hickory Clubs" directed at young, uncommitted voters, mobilized popular support and muscle to seize control of the Democratic Party's machinery. In January the Jacksonians, with "violence and audacity," took over a special town meeting called by Crawfordites and prevented it from endorsing a call for a congressional caucus. They then contested the party's elections to choose ward delegates, overthrowing Family Party control and winning ten of the fourteen wards. That made them masters of the party's general ward meeting in February, which selected the city's delegates to the party convention. In Philadelphia the Family Party leader George Mifflin Dallas had initially dismissed Jackson's "excessive popularity" as "an effervescence that can accomplish nothing," but by early February he was privately warning Calhoun that "the cause was lost in Pennsylvania."[23]

By then even Washington politicians recognized that "the course of events in Pennsa" made it "inevitable" that "Mr. Calhoun will be dropt in a few days," as his supporters in Pennsylvania "drooped beneath the outcry in favor of Jackson."[24] On February 18, at a public meeting in Philadelphia, Dallas announced that he and his friends were transferring their support to General Jackson. They claimed that the dangerous Crawford might yet carry a divided Pennsylvania, and Jackson was best placed to stop him; Calhoun would be held in reserve as the vice presidential candidate. Thus Jackson gained the eleventh-hour support of the regular New School Democrats, who were significantly more numerous than his Old School supporters, and so guaranteed an overwhelming majority at the Harrisburg convention. The two Jacksonian factions were soon disputing the party ticket for the 1824 local and state elections.

Once Jackson had won the regular nomination in March, his victory in Pennsylvania was virtually assured. The Old Democrats who favored Crawford disliked the General's victory but were reduced to arguing that Jackson was not a sound Democrat. Accordingly, they made great play with the revelation made by the influential regular Pennsylvania Democrat Walter Lowrie that in 1816 Jackson had written to incoming President Monroe urging him to appoint two Federalists to high office. That argument failed to gain traction in Pennsylvania, partly because the Philadelphia Federalists campaigned against Jackson and for Adams. In any case, the popular presumption was in favor of the man who had fought for the republic in its hour of direst danger; in effect, active support for the War of 1812 had become the touchstone of true loyalty to the Democratic Republican Party. Jackson's war record made him fireproof against claims of disloyalty, especially for those groups inherently attracted toward his cause.[25]

## HICKORY MEN

Calhoun's friend George McDuffie dismissed the movements for Jackson in Pennsylvania as "made by the grog-shop politicians of villages & the rabble of Philadelphia and Pittsburgh."[26] If so, Jackson's capture of the state Democratic Party's nomination within little more than a year of announcing his candidacy demonstrated that lower-level politicians had known something, not least that the rabble had votes. The extraordinary groundswell of popular support was not a generalized phenomenon, but arose among specific identifiable social and ethnic groups in the state's heterogeneous "rabble." Not only did their inclinations prompt the initial suggestion of Jackson's name but also their critical location within Pennsylvania's balance of electoral power proved decisive in ensuring his triumph at Harrisburg.

The wellspring of Jackson's popularity in the western counties was the presence of large numbers of Scotch-Irish people, the descendants of Protestant Ulstermen who had migrated from northern Ireland before the Revolution. "Of the Presbyterian faith in religion, very democratic in politics, and kindly to whisky," they animated a distinctive cultural region that had spread from Pennsylvania's western counties south into Virginia's Great Valley and west into Ohio. Their attraction to Jackson reflected more than common ethnicity; they never forgot Britain's maltreatment of Ireland, including the Protestant North. From their point of view, Jackson had been "the instrument under Providence of their salvation" from British invasion in 1815. During Congress's investigation of the Florida invasion, one Scotch-Irish constituent warned his congressman that the people were "ready to Tare [*sic*] the Livers out of any member that would take part against Jackson." An elderly itinerant preacher named Edward Patchell, who in 1823 and 1824 widely canvassed Jackson's name through Pennsylvania's western counties, revered him as the man whom "my God, and your God, . . . hath raised . . . up for to be a Saviour and a deliverance for his people."[27]

This body of enthusiastic support proved decisive in swinging the state. Scotch-Irish voters regularly voted for the New School Democrats, giving that faction an advantage in western Pennsylvania that proved decisive statewide in 1817 and 1823. The Philadelphia-based Family Party had backed Calhoun partly in the hope that his family's Scotch-Irish origins would win approval in the western counties. When it became clear that these westerners preferred Jackson, the Independent Democrats seized the opportunity to outflank their rivals, in a maneuver that brought Federalists like the young James Buchanan into the Jackson ranks. It was the real threat of losing Scotch-Irish support in state politics that prodded Family Party leaders like Dallas to jump on the bandwagon at the eleventh hour.[28]

The other original source of Jacksonism arose in Philadelphia city and county, where the Democratic radicals Michael Leib and William Duane had built an Old School constituency based on mobilizing foreign-born voters and cultivating lower-class discontents. Duane's newspaper, the *Aurora,* had long carried attacks on the irresponsible and unjust practices associated with the speculative postwar boom in a city that by 1820 contained 121,497 people. Between 1818 and 1820 anonymous articles appeared that amounted to "bold, defying, scathing attacks" on the management of the national bank: under the pseudonym "Brutus," they revealed "the secrets of the directors' room" in Philadelphia and attacked the officers as "insidious and corrupt," in "a nervous, solid, and sarcastic style" of crushing vehemence. When the *Columbian Observer* appeared in 1822 in place of the "setting Aurora," the new editor, Stephen Simpson—son of a Philadelphia banker and himself a former employee of the national bank—was soon recognized as the author of the Brutus articles.[29]

In time, the respectably born Simpson would develop a critique of contemporary economic behavior that went beyond the criticisms of earlier Old School writers, and his Owenite protosocialism began to find a sympathetic audience in the Philadelphia of the 1820s. Already in 1822 he swore to defend the "just pretensions of the *productive and middle classes of society*" and to oppose all expressions of "aristocracy, English politicks, and family influence." He condemned men who had once been honest Democrats and had not considered "labour and industry a disgrace," but were then seduced by material success to cultivate more aristocratic friends. Like Duane, Simpson condemned relief measures for sustaining a corrupt financial system that benefited banks and bankers, those monsters of "corruption, fraud, and nobility"; he wanted to see economic transactions returned to a simpler basis of honest dealings and sound money. Though conservative in impulse, such doctrines threatened contemporary business practices. By 1824 his supposed allies in the Jackson party were publicly condemning Simpson as "*now a radical, a leveller,* a would-be destroyer of almost everything fixed, and stable, and valuable in our republican government."[30]

Simpson's radical critique found a following among Philadelphia's skilled workers. The development of a broad-based market economy had encouraged the rise of merchant capitalists who increasingly dictated how artisans worked. Ambitious artisans had formerly endeavored to compete by raising bank loans but were undermined by the banking crash. In the context of economic depression, they found themselves losing their independence and social esteem, and the writings of Simpson and his fellow radicals helped to politicize them. In the years to come, they would help to create Philadelphia's first labor movement, but in 1824 they would follow Simpson in seeking improvement through political reform managed by a new president.

These alienated working-class radicals were of critical importance in helping Jackson win control of the city's Democratic machine in the ward elections of February 1824, but their numbers should not be exaggerated. Old School success had also depended on winning the support of the German middling and lower classes and of Irish immigrants; indeed, Duane's radicalism had expressed the views of the United Irishmen who, like himself, had fled from Ireland in the 1790s and later because their political opposition and armed resistance roused the Anglo-Irish authorities against them. On election days they had brought out large numbers of foreign-born plebeians, especially in the Northern Liberties and Southwark wards, on the expanding edge of the city. Yet after 1807 they ceased to be a coherent political force: by 1823–1824 one former Irish radical, the publisher and economic improver Mathew Carey, supported Clay, while another, John Binns of the Philadelphia *Democratic Press,* backed the regulars and Crawford. Indeed, the Philadelphia attacks on Crawford in 1824 for having previously proposed intermarriage with the Indians focused almost entirely on the "spirit of aristocracy, bigotry and proscription" that his attitude revealed towards *"adopted citizens and foreigners by birth"*; this was a conspicuous effort to unite immigrant opinion and destroy Binns's attempts to identify Crawford with the Democratic party. Still disunited, however, the Democrats at large in 1824 were as usual outvoted by the city Federalist Party's plurality.[31]

In the statewide election the voting power of the rural Irish and of Pennsylvania Dutch farmers proved more decisive. The venerable John Adams once remarked that when the Irish and the Germans agreed in Pennsylvania, they gave majorities of 30,000. The overwhelming popular support that Jackson received from the Irish—mainly Protestant but not entirely—derived from a common folk reaction. When asked after the presidential election "how it happened that all the Irish voted for General Jackson," one Irishman (who does not sound to British ears like an Ulsterman) replied, "By the powers, for the best *rason* in the world, *becase* he beat the English at Orleans, my darling [*sic*]."[32]

Equally striking was Jackson's amazing popularity among the German farmers of southeastern Pennsylvania, who contributed overwhelmingly to Jackson's 25,000 majority in the election. A young British traveler (who would later become prime minister) noted in 1824 how in all Pennsylvania elections, including that for president, "the German party seems to consider itself as an interest distinct from the rest of the community." These self-conscious agrarians persistently preferred self-sufficiency to commercial farming, feared debt, and "did not readily become reconciled to a flimsy substitute for gold." With these long-held doubts about loans, banks, and paper money, they had long been attracted toward the Old School's criticism of modern entrepreneurial policies. Their point of view was thus broadly encapsulated in the Jacksonian persuasion that was developed by Stephen Simpson and others in the course of the campaign.[33]

## JACKSONIAN PERSUASION

The tidal wave for Jackson in Pennsylvania that broke with crushing power at the Harrisburg convention transformed his political fortunes nationally. Even in Tennessee and the Southwest his hand strengthened, while in New Jersey and Maryland it invigorated powerful currents already running his way. It forced the withdrawal from the race of Calhoun, who felt his disappointment deeply but resigned himself to running for the vice presidency. Jackson inherited Calhoun's strength in the Southeast, opening the way to a more united opposition to Crawford in North Carolina. Despite a brief flurry in New York, the General's chances did not strengthen north of Pennsylvania, but in parts of the Northwest, the burblings of discontent with Clay now found a realistic alternative. Jackson looked like a winner, and most politicians preferred to be on the winning side.

In the middle sections of the republic, rapidly growing cities and their immediate rural hinterlands showed great susceptibility to his appeal. As early as October 1823 the people of Baltimore were said—even by his opponents—to be "all alive for Jackson"; by January the city was "decidedly, and without doubt, in his favor." Urban centers in the Ohio Valley, from Pittsburgh to Louisville, showed early enthusiasm for the General; in the face of Kentucky's commitment to Clay, a public meeting in Louisville in May 1823 lined up the supporters of each candidate, counted them precisely, and Jackson won, though narrowly. In Cincinnati the friends of other candidates prevented Jacksonism from sweeping all before it, but when Clinton and Calhoun ceased to be viable alternatives, "the Jackson fever" began to rise "almost to *blood heat.*"[34]

Like Philadelphia and Pittsburgh, these urban centers had been the cutting edge of economic growth, either industrializing or becoming the centers for intensive frontier development, and all had suffered in the financial and economic collapse. Ordinary citizens had learned to mistrust regular politicians as they became more disillusioned with the current economic and social direction of the republic. Popular anxiety increased with the return of recession to Western cities early in 1824: in May laborers in Cincinnati could not find work; middlemen, auctioneers, and commission merchants found trading not worth the effort; shippers operated at a loss; and farmers coming to town with their produce received negligible prices.[35]

Why, though, in the context of economic uncertainty, turn to Jackson, whose views were scarcely known at all? Of course, his standing as military hero gave him ready name recognition and immediate appeal. In the early stages of the campaign a Maryland politician had remarked that "the gentlemen now up, Adams, Crawford, Clay, Calhoun, & Lowndes, tho' respectable, either from the want of occasion or want of power have never yet made so strong an impression upon the public sentiment as to meet with ardent favour as soon as presented to public view."[36] That could not now be said of Jackson: when he traveled to Washington in November 1823 to take up his Senate seat, crowds came out to see him, even in areas that would ultimately vote for someone else. When straw polls were taken at random, Jackson usually did well; straw polls at militia musters nearly always resulted in Jacksonian victories, except in his rivals' centers of overwhelming strength. Young men were qualifying to vote in the early 1820s who had never known a competitive presidential election, and they were by definition men whose formative public experiences had been the War of 1812 and its victorious culmination.

Jackson's military glory did more than just satisfy national pride. It placed him in a position to exploit a yearning that grew from the social experiences of recent years—economic distress, political bickering, sectional antagonism, a sense of moral decline. It gave him something of the aura George Washington had possessed in 1789, though Washington's moral eminence had been more universally acknowledged; he had the aura of a republican Patriot King, a man who stood above the petty fray and could provide a symbol of republican virtue. As early as January 1823 a pamphlet appeared in Washington advocating exactly this "Idea of a Patriot President"; the author did not name a particular candidate, at least not in the only surviving number, but his emphasis on "intellectual ability" and "great experience" would seem to exclude Jackson.[37]

In fact, a similar line of justification for Jackson's candidacy developed at an early stage in his campaign. It grew partly from his own perception that the great danger to the republic lay in Crawford's manipulation of the political system, using patronage as the lure to buy support and fix elections. The political class, on this view, had become too skilled at managing, and the republic needed a revitalizing release of popular power through public meetings. Many saw this. Clay, for example, had been advised in 1822 to stay out of Congress rather than lose the advantage of being a candidate from outside the halls of power. Jackson himself was reluctant to accept the Senate seat in 1823 because he feared it would make him look like another seeker after office and advantage. His friends did their best to spin his election as that of a patriot coming to the rescue of state and country by undertaking a commission he did not seek or welcome.[38]

The classic expression of the developing Jacksonian persuasion came in the *Letters of Wyoming*, written, initially without Jackson's knowledge, by his Tennessee friend and adviser, U.S. senator John Eaton, who had written a laudatory biography in 1817. Directed at the people of Pennsylvania, the Wyoming essays first appeared in mid-March 1823 in Simpson's *Columbian Observer*, and the first twelve papers were published in 1824 as a 104-page book. They were then widely reprinted and quoted in newspaper articles; indeed, some apparently local pieces supporting Jackson borrowed heavily from Wyoming, and they certainly used its general argument.[39]

Wyoming argued that American liberty was at risk because a trusting people had allowed "leading men" to acquire too much influence in the electoral process. Trust had rightly been put into the hands of the Founding Fathers, whose commitment to the general welfare was not in doubt. With the passage of time, however, they had been replaced by men skilled in managing power—men who could use party devices to dictate nominations and so keep office and patronage in the hands

# THE LETTERS

OF

# WYOMING,

TO THE

## PEOPLE OF THE UNITED STATES,

ON THE

### Presidential Election,

AND

## IN FAVOUR OF ANDREW JACKSON.

ORIGINALLY PUBLISHED IN

### THE COLUMBIAN OBSERVER.

---

'Midst the battle's commotion he rose on the view
Of his Country—to shield her, or perish there too.

"JACKSON, all hail! our Country's pride and boast,
Whose mind's a Council, and whose arm's a host!
Welcome blest chief! Accept our grateful lays,
Unbidden homage of our grateful praise.
Remembrance long shall keep alive thy fame,
And future ages venerate thy name."

*Life of Jackson.*

---

## PHILADELPHIA:

PUBLISHED BY S. SIMPSON & J. CONRAD.

---

1824.

*Letters of Wyoming.* The Letters of Wyoming, to the People of the United States, on the Presidential Election, and in Favour of Andrew Jackson, Originally Published in the Columbian Observer *(Philadelphia: S. Simpson & J. Conrad, 1824), title page. Courtesy: American Antiquarian Society* of their friends. Thus, popular carelessness was allowing power to drift from the people toward a professional political class that, in effect, was becoming a privileged aristocracy. This trend could undermine the democratic fabric of republican liberty because genuinely free popular elections were the ultimate guarantee of the people's freedom.

The only hope for rescue was to choose a man who stood apart from the political process and who had therefore not been corrupted by it. In Simpson's words, Washington needed "the pure eye of a Patriot stranger" to "discern abuses" and "correct and purge them." Jackson had demonstrated his devotion to the republic, risking his life in the republic's recent crisis. He had shown he was not interested in public office for its own sake by retiring from every office he had been given as soon his basic task had been completed. He was therefore exactly the man who would exercise power with integrity, ensuring that officeholders of all kinds were kept under control and restricted to their true functions. As a result, according to the *Columbian Observer*, "Jackson has rather too much honesty and integrity to find many warm and substantial friends amongst the hunters for office," and so would never be named by a congressional caucus.[40]

The desire for a Patriot King who stood above the pettiness of everyday politics could of course be applied to others besides Jackson. Calhoun presented himself as an independent reformer concerned to defeat "political gamblers" and reestablish "political virtue."[41] Clinton too was often portrayed as a superior statesman; some thought Simpson was likely to shift ultimately from Jackson to Clinton. According to Wyoming, Clinton's fall from popular grace was a result of the slanders of a petty-minded faction. Such arguments possessed a strong antiparty element, expressing objections to the way in which the established party loyalties of many voters were exploited by politicians who simply perpetuated the culture of a no longer relevant party division. That line of argument built on the criticisms that had been made of the regulars over previous years by independent Republicans and Federalists in many states.

A key part of the Jacksonian argument had to deal with the great objections to the General: he was too rash, too easily impassioned, and would not obey constitutional and legal restrictions on his power. Wyoming insisted that Jackson was in fact a man of thought and reflection, someone who pondered his decisions and then acted with sudden speed and energy. If the man could be trusted to make critical decisions on the battlefield, why assume that he could not be trusted in situations where he had more time to ponder and take informed advice? Jackson's record, Wyoming insisted, showed that he appreciated the wisdom of restraint, when possible, and could display great humanity. If Washington could save the republic in 1789, then this latter-day Cincinnatus could bring the same element of disinterested moral leadership. Military service was superior to political experience as a qualification simply because it gave the hero a standing above that of mere politicians.

It also allowed its possessor great latitude in his policy positions. In general, Jackson held conservative economic views, opposing paper money and favoring reduced governmental intervention in the economy. Wishing to return to old standards, he opposed relief measures, although this was not widely known. Contradictorily, however, he also supported positive national economic legislation: domestic manufactures should be protected and internal improvements financed in order to build up the republic's defensive capabilities. A high tariff also fitted the common desire to exclude European imports, in particular the fashions and luxuries that were becoming an outward symbol of growing class distinctions. Homespun clothing and grass hats were symbols of a moral simplicity, of modesty and a concern with real value that were the mark of a true republican. This association with old-fashioned morals combined with his publicized activities as an active Presbyterian persuaded some that Jackson "will come out more decidedly in favour of religion than any other of the candidates." Hence there could be no sense of contradiction when practicing Methodists, Baptists, and Presbyterians supported him in 1824, as in Maryland and Pennsylvania. Clearly a persuasion that incorporated nationalist programs and religious commitment differed from the Jacksonian creed as it would emerge a decade later after the polarizing events of General Jackson's presidency.[42]

The popular influenza that overwhelmed Pennsylvania and much of the West did not reach all parts of the United States in 1824. Now that Jackson seemed a serious candidate, the press stopped ignoring or patronizing him and began to examine his past record critically. A broad body of opinion thought it "a bad omen that mere military glory, for he has no reputation as a Statesman, should thus captivate the popular feeling, & throw the nation headlong into the arms of a military despot." Plumer noticed that "the fear of such an event has made Mr. Adams many friends," and in states like New Jersey, Delaware, and Maryland, the months that followed saw the campaign for Adams gain impetus as the most formidable statesman opposing Jackson.[43]

New Englanders as a whole proved quite immune to the General's appeal, whether in New England or other parts of the nation. Old Republicans, especially in Virginia and New York, could not accept great men who were superior to the good old party. New York possessed both groups, and in any case Jackson could make little popular headway there without a popular election. Above all, Jackson's cause everywhere depended on the support of politicians who were not already committed to some other candidate, and in some states such commitments had been made to others at an early stage. But in those places where ambitious and available leadership combined with grassroots enthusiasm, the General looked unstoppable.

# PART II

# CAMPAIGNS AND COALITIONS

# 7 A SEASON IN WASHINGTON

Toward the end of November 1823, 264 congressman and senators made their way to the nation's capital for the Eighteenth Congress, many arriving "earlier than usual."[1] As always, their arrival transformed Washington for a few months from a backward provincial town into the political center of the Union. The federal city was still not easy to get to, despite some road improvements, and it did not possess the same command over the nation's life that it would in later times. Already, however, it was the focus of political life during the session, which in 1824 would last till the end of May. That influence was transmitted mainly by widely quoted Washington newspapers, which were devoted to each of the three Cabinet candidates. The course of the presidential election was not determined in Washington, but it was considerably influenced by what happened within the formal and informal worlds of the capital.

Washington before 1828 has been famously characterized by the political scientist James Sterling Young as an isolated village built in the middle of a bog where no sensible person would have built a town, had it not been for the famous compromise of 1790 over the site of the federal capital. The architect L'Enfant's plans for the future metropolis had placed the executive and legislative branches at opposite ends of Pennsylvania Avenue, the constitutional separation of powers reinforced by the distance of a muddy mile. The difficulty of communication helped to reduce the influence of the president over Congress, and, Young argued, physical separation from the rest of country ensured that national government remained, in Alexander Hamilton's disapproving phrase, "at a distance and out of sight." Many students of the period have assumed that that is how things were before politics were democratized in the Age of Jackson: there were no structures to enable the effective use of power and its interrelation with the people.[2]

That picture held some truth in the early 1820s. Washington had some magnificent buildings and a population of about 15,000 people, making it the seventh largest city in the country, but it remained undeveloped. According to historian Constance McLaughlin Green, "Most of the Mall was a wasteland of swamps dotted with clusters of sheds along the canal. Vacant lots occupied much of the city of magnificent distances, and the streets connecting one village with others that together comprised the capital were still little more than rutted paths." At its heart lived an official community of executive officers, foreign diplomats, and about 300 federal employees; they stood socially apart from both ordinary residents and most of the congressional representatives who flooded in every December.[3]

However, structures did exist to provide communication between president and Congress. Under President Jefferson, the Democratic Republican Party had created important linkages, and Jefferson had exploited them successfully until almost the end of his second term. Thereafter disagreements within the party over the international menace of France and Britain had weakened his successor, James Madison, even during the war, and had given the renascent Federalists the opportunity to make mischief. After 1815 party linkages lost much of their effectiveness, sectional differences grew more extreme, and the political situation within Washington became more like the unstructured world described by Young—a world peculiar to the years 1818–1824, and not typical of the early republic as a whole.

Young found the main determinant of congressional voting behavior in the messes in which representatives lived, talked, and gambled. In these boardinghouses, congressmen segregated themselves "into mutually exclusive, closely knit voluntary associations, forming a segmented social structure of face-to-face peer groups." However, rather than giving cues that generated in-house agreement among messmates, the messes were themselves made up of like-minded men who had chosen to live together, and even highly sociable messes could be broken up by disagreements on substantive issues. When Solomon Van Rensselaer first went to Washington as a congressman in 1819, he joined a mess of nine other New Yorkers, including "Bucktails, Democrats, and Federalists; . . . all political discussions are prohibited." In 1822 the argument over the Albany postmaster caused great embarrassment in Van Buren's mess, where he was spoken to very bluntly; within a month, he and Rufus King left the mess and moved to Georgetown to join one made up of Federalists. The boardinghouse was scarcely an independent political unit, and voting in Congress was more influenced by the state delegations, which in some cases met together to agree on a common position on appointments and legislative measures.[4]

Social contacts and personal relationships mattered more in Washington once party lines had become looser and more complex. The comparative invisibility of decision making helps to explain why the outside world often felt that things happened in Washington that did not reflect the will of constituents, that Washington was a corrupt world in which decisions were made behind closed doors, to the advantage of those admitted to the carve-up. It was partly to destroy that impression that stalwarts of the Democratic Republican Party wanted to revive the old party to restore old disciplines and standards; independents shared that goal but thought that party discipline was part of the problem.

Washington's bad name was made worse by news of the gay social whirl that marked the political season—the European fashions, the parties, the resident official elite. During the congressional season, ladies of fashion and consequence held soirees and balls; crowds gathered at the White House for the president's levees and receptions. Some complained that the social round of dinners, evening parties, and drawing rooms was exhausting, but they could not avoid going to those given by the heads of departments and foreign ministers. The season had long assumed "something of the character of a Matrimonial mart," bringing people together from different places, and womenfolk showed themselves off to their best advantage. One Ohioan was captivated by the low-cut dresses not seen at home, while another was taken aback by the boldness of one lady he met at a White House party, who wanted him "to ride her so badly." As early as 1816 one Federalist paper had thought "the fashionable dissipation and extravagance of the city" were turning it into a "confectionery shop or brothel."[5]

Such descriptions partly arose from the presence of European diplomats, who inevitably introduced seductive European habits and fashions into the republic's heart. On this view, diplomatic experience was not a

*South Front of the White House, 1825. Ben: Perley Poore,* Perley's
Reminiscences of Sixty Years in the National Metropolis, *2 vols.
(Philadelphia: Hubbard Bros., 1886), 1:24.*

recommendation, and Wyoming made much of the fact that Jackson had never been exposed to foreign corruption. After 1817 James Monroe, personally formal and versed in Old World court ceremonial, introduced into Washington society much "affectation of European and princely etiquette, where the president if he chooses can so decidedly give a tone to manners."[6]

The character of public and social life at Washington fed a growing popular belief that the distant capital was the fount of corruption in the republic. Inevitably the capital attracted floods of office seekers, especially in the wake of the army cuts and the reduction of state governments. As the *National Intelligencer* commented in 1822, "Many come here with high-wrought hopes of office, emoluments and honors, and when disappointment comes, it is identified with the place." As the ultimate location of power and patronage, Washington's corruption was assumed to overwhelm all who went there: reforming congressmen who found little financial corruption and governmental extravagance to root out were regarded back home as having been sucked into the vortex. That popular belief explains the appeal of nonpolitical candidates: in Stephen Simpson's words, Washington needed "the pure eye of a Patriot stranger" to "discern abuses" and "correct and purge them."[7]

In this atmosphere, the activity and interest of national politicians in choosing the next president made many fear, in Wyoming's words, that "a *deep and fatal* [game] was playing at Washington with the liberties of the People." Politicians there were making decisions behind closed doors for rest of the country, and those decisions were influenced by unworthy, unrepublican motives. Yet the suspicion that Washington conducted its politics in blithe disregard of the people was at that time deeply mistaken. Representatives in both houses wrote to constituents, sending news and official publications, and constituents wrote expressing their own views and those of their neighbors. Congressmen never forgot that they had to run for reelection after less than one year of their current term, and they were reluctant to set themselves in the face of local opinion on any issue, including those surrounding the presidential election. Washington may have provided government at a distance, but never out of sight or out of mind.[8]

In December 1823 Mr. and Mrs. John Quincy Adams decided to hold a grand ball for General Jackson in celebration of his victory at New Orleans. More accurately, Louisa Catherine agreed to Quincy's suggestion, but with some reluctance because she would have to do the work—and quickly, because it must be held on the event's anniversary, January 8. Mrs. Adams used her considerable experience of European courts to choose a decor that her son thought created a "very beautiful" effect, and she selected dances to encourage group participation. Five hundred invitations were sent out, most delivered personally, and a thousand people attended. According to the refrain of a widely reprinted poem, "Belles and matrons, maids and madams, / All are gone to Mrs. Adams."[9] The ball attracted huge interest and excitement and was reported widely. According to early commentators, this occasion lifted Jackson "from the comparatively vulgar place of a meteor, in the atmosphere of earth, to the position of a fixed orb in the firmament above. *From that moment he began to be thought of as a candidate for the presidency.*"[10]

From the point of view of Washington opinion, this view was not entirely mistaken. At the time—before the coup in Pennsylvania—Jackson was still "not seriously considered,"[11] though he had begun to rehabilitate his reputation. Since his arrival in December, he had healed some long-lasting enmities, notably with Winfield Scott, Henry Clay, and, remarkably, Thomas Hart Benton, with whom he had exchanged shots ten years before during a brawl in Tennessee. "This has destroyed the stronghold of my enemies who denounced me as a man of revengefull [sic] Temper and of great rashness," Jackson preened. "I am told the opinion of those whose minds were prepared to see me with a Tomahawk in one hand, & a scalping knife in the other has greatly changed—and I am getting on very smoothly." As a man of considerable personal charm, many ladies fell for him. Even Daniel Webster conceded that "General Jackson's manners are more presidential than any of the other candidates. . . . My wife is for him decidedly."[12]

Inevitably Washington social occasions were seen as political occasions that might affect the presidential election. In 1823 Calhoun held court in the "splendid" house on the Georgetown heights now known as Dumbarton Oaks and dazzled with his brilliant conversation, but he attracted little new support. In the same session, Crawford held a "grand party," which, according to Senator Eaton, was "so crowded that no one had more than six inches to move on." A year later a New England lawyer

*Louisa Catherine Adams. Engraved by G. F. Storm, who flourished about 1834, from a portrait by Charles Robert Leslie painted in London in 1816. Published in Laura Carter Holloway,* The Ladies of the White House, or, In the Home of the Presidents *(Philadelphia: Bradley, Garretson, 1883), facing p. 238. Courtesy: Library of Congress Prints and Photographs Division.*

who attended one of Calhoun's parties found it "simple and Republican enough—simple as to the entertainment, for there was scarcely anything to eat, and republican as to the company, for everybody was there." Mrs. Adams's regular evening parties saw her drawing room equally crowded:

> The air almost irrespirable—servants elbowing thro' with waiters [i.e., trays or salvers] elevated over their heads to save them from the greedy grasp of hungry expectants for offices and refreshments . . . —all in motion . . . —shaking of hands—talking of tariff or presidency—many plotting in corners no doubt against the success of their host, who was standing all the time in one snug place, trying to be pleasant and sociable.[13]

Eaton told Jackson in 1823 that he wondered about the political effect of these entertainments. They might serve "perhaps to call back some doubting friends, & to secure firm ones more firmly; for it is hard, very hard you know, that any man's wine and cordials should be drank, and his Ice creams fed upon and still to say or think ought against him." Of course any candidate who gave a great social event was suspected of trying to win support. "Oh! It is too abominably bad, to see gentlemen electioneering for this high office; & seeking by parade and kindness to win for themselves patronage & favour," continued Eaton. "Time was when the virtue of the people would have laughed to scorn such attempts, and contemned to the man who would have practiced them; but times alas are altered."[14]

Secretary and Mrs. Adams were therefore smart to hold their January 8 ball in Jackson's honor. It was a magnanimous gesture, showing Adams to be above petty self-advancement. His republicanism revealed itself both in his respect for a national hero and in his personal dress: he was the only man present not in formal attire. It also conciliated Jackson and linked the two men's names at a time when the Adams campaign was thinking of inviting Jackson to take second spot on its ticket. It is, however, a mistake to think the ball actually strengthened Adams's prospects; he remained socially awkward, and there is no evidence that his political position was any stronger after the ball than before.

Rather than influence politics, social occasions were themselves sometimes spoiled by the presidential contest. In 1822 the election had already become one of the "animating principles at present in our city society," and by 1824 it increasingly divided the social world. The editor Samuel Smith and his socialite wife, Margaret Bayard Smith, were friendly with both Calhoun and Crawford but were forced to choose between them. Mrs. Smith remarked in June 1824 how "some have been estranged by differing and conflicting politics . . . you have no idea . . . of the embittered and violent spirit engendered by this presidential question." Yet the candidates themselves, except for the ill Crawford, continued to dine together and preserve a gentlemanly courtesy.[15]

These social occasions had far less influence on the election than the substantive matters decided in Washington, settled not at soirees but in the Cabinet, in caucus, and on the floor of Congress. In 1824 men in the federal city made three critical decisions. First, the relationship of the United States to the outside world was decided in a way that determined how far outside events would affect the election, and vice versa; second, the attempt by a substantial element in Congress to direct voter opinion in the presidential election stretched old party loyalties to the limit, and beyond; and third, decisive legislation was passed that sharpened awareness of the policy issues at stake in the election.

## MONROE DOCTRINE

Through 1823 the election campaign was fought against a background of distant international crisis that threatened to become armed foreground. In 1820 an uprising in Spain had introduced a constitution designed to rein in the restored Bourbon king, Ferdinand VII. The conservative monarchs of the Holy Alliance encouraged France to invade Spain in 1823 to crush the "democratical" forces and restore Ferdinand's authority. Some Americans, including Jackson, believed that, if successful, the French invasion would lead to an attempt to reconquer the newly independent Latin American republics and so threaten the security of the United States. A reimposed imperial regime might prove more menacing than that of old, and Florida, so recently acquired, might once more become a base for racial terrorists and foreign meddlers. If Spain transferred ownership of Cuba to Britain or France, the whole Gulf Coast would be threatened.[16]

Some electioneers claimed that these dangers made election of their candidate essential. The *Letters of Wyoming* suggested that Jackson's "capacity, bravery, and decision will prove a security more than equal to the little army the Radicals have left us." Others argued for Secretary of War Calhoun; Crawford's supporters said the threat was exaggerated and portrayed their man as the "peace" candidate. The secretary of state, John Quincy Adams, was the man in the hot seat in Washington, and his more considered response was expressed in President Monroe's famous statement of December 1823, which later generations have called the Monroe Doctrine.[17]

The distinguished diplomatic historian Ernest May has argued that Monroe's policy statement was designed primarily to advance Adams's presidential ambitions. In August and September 1823, the British foreign secretary, George Canning, secretly proposed that the United States and Britain should issue a joint declaration that they would oppose the restoration of Spanish rule in Latin America by force. Canning's proposal appealed to all those privately consulted but, according to May, raised a major difficulty for Adams: as a former Federalist seeking Republican support, he did not wish to appear too favorable to Britain. Adams had long been criticized for publicly exaggerating his Anglophobia, but May's interpretation both traduces Adams and provides a misleading picture of both the foreign crisis and domestic politics.[18]

Adams appreciated the dangers of the international situation but was well aware that Britain opposed the Holy Alliance and its plans as keenly as the United States did. The British government had already given private assurances that it opposed Cuba's transference to either itself or France, and it had publicly threatened war if either France created a permanent military presence in Spain or Spain tried to regain its former American possessions. By May the British minister in Washington told Canning that his policy was "making the English almost popular in the United States." When Adams learned of Canning's secret proposal for an alliance, he saw the advantages but suspected that there was more to the offer than met the eye. Why did Canning hesitate to recognize the new republics? Was he trying to seduce the American government into promising that it would never annex Cuba or Texas?[19]

Adams showed little apprehension that he would be damned by Republican voters if he was involved in creating an Anglo-American entente. In spite of his Federalist past, he had already established his position in New England as an undoubted Republican candidate. Far from fearing a hostile reaction if he appointed a Federalist to a diplomatic job, Adams suggested in cabinet in 1823 that, if it were decided to send a special envoy to Greece, the well-known Massachusetts Federalist Theodore Lyman was the man. Adams never rejected the British offer, keeping his options open right through 1824.[20]

Those who favored accepting the British offer all overestimated the severity of the crisis. Jefferson and Madison privately urged Monroe to accept Canning's offer because they recalled the importance of British support in the more serious French crisis of 1801–1803. Calhoun himself was "perfectly moonstruck" with anxiety, and for a time his apprehensions infected Monroe. As over slavery in later life, Calhoun overestimated the dangers from distant threats by those he categorized as ideologically different. To his eyes, Britain was the only possible liberal ally against the almighty Holy Alliance. "He is for plunging into a war," said Adams, "to prevent that which, if his opinion of it is correct, we are utterly unable to prevent."[21]

Adams himself was much cooler. The French faced strong resistance in parts of Spain and did not capture Cádiz—the main Spanish port for Latin America—until the end of September. That news reached the United States in early November. By then it was clear that Ferdinand's regime needed to keep troops in Spain, while the French hesitated to send a fleet across the Atlantic in the face of Britain's superior Royal Navy. Another keen student of Latin American affairs at this time, the nascent Jacksonian William Duane, was certain that the United States had little reason to fear a European intervention in Latin America.[22]

In any case, by November 16—just as the American press awoke to the crisis—Adams knew that Canning had become less keen on joint action. Adams suspected that Canning had received secret assurances from France that it would not transport a Spanish expeditionary force. The news that Canning had appointed consuls and vice consuls to the very Latin American countries that France and Spain were supposedly about to attack bespoke British confidence. Adams finally convinced the president and Cabinet colleagues that, for the time being, the United States could rely on the British man-of-war without appearing to travel in its wake.

The president agreed to make his midcrisis response through a public declaration of policy in his annual message rather than through diplomatic correspondence. At Adams's instigation, he announced that the United States would stand apart from European conflicts and expected Europe to refrain from colonial aggrandizement in the Americas. It would oppose Russia's expansionist claims in the Pacific Northwest and anyone else's in the Gulf of Mexico. It would oppose the reestablishment of European rule where it had already been thrown off. Adams knew that the American people believed themselves at peace, and the annual message deliberately did not use alarmist language. Even so, some thought the message rather "squints towards war" and looked for a hostile reaction from Europe.[23]

None came. At last in spring the publication in Washington of the Polignac Memorandum—the French promise not to send an expeditionary force across the Atlantic—revealed the secret maneuver back in October that, as Adams suspected, had removed the threat to the Latin republics. Even Clay, the longtime advocate of assisting the Latin Americans, recognized that the crisis had passed. Adams stood revealed as the master of the mysteries of European diplomacy, though he never claimed credit in 1824 for the nicely calculated statement of guiding principles. The international crisis had been taken off the election agenda, except for the message's recommendation that the United States government steer clear of any sort of involvement in European matters.[24]

The determination to stand aside from the Greece's struggle to throw off Ottoman rule gave a possible weapon to Adams's opponents. The policy ran against the great public enthusiasm for the Greek cause, widely expressed early in 1824 in public meetings that reflected devotion to the republican principles founded by the ancient Greeks. In 1823 both Crawford and Calhoun had supported Albert Gallatin's proposal that the U.S. Navy in the Mediterranean—one frigate, one schooner, and one corvette—be sent to Greece's aid. Adams regarded this pathetic gesture as an attempt to build "castles in the air of popularity," in defiance of the true policy of the United States.[25]

In January 1824 both Webster and Clay made widely publicized speeches in the House advocating the recognition of Greek independence. Webster soon fell quiet, acknowledging Adams's superior wisdom on such matters; though by no means friendly to Adams's aspirations, he deferred to the wisdom of a presidential candidate likely to carry Massachusetts overwhelmingly. Clay advocated the Greek cause as once he had the Latin American, but he faced severe criticism from some self-conscious Northerners who thought he pressed Greece's cause to distract attention from his defense of slavery at home. That charge, when made in the House, roused Clay's ire and almost led to a duel. Foreign policy provided no easy opportunity for electoral gain in 1824.[26]

In spite of supposed electoral considerations, Secretary Adams maintained his policy of settling outstanding difficulties with Britain. He removed his objections to an agreement with Britain over policing the Atlantic slave trade; this may have been in response to Monroe's concern, but it might also suggest that Adams saw no disadvantage in strengthening his antislavery credentials. The Crawfordites in the Senate, led by Van Buren and John Holmes of Maine, severely criticized Adams for accepting Britain's right to search foreign shipping, which the nation had resisted in the War of 1812, while Southerners advanced fears that Adams was too sympathetic to the abolitionist views expressed in the British Parliament. The Senate amended the treaty by exempting the American coast from the mutual right of search—an exception that was unacceptable to the British. The destruction of this attempt to end the theft of slaves from Africa scarcely undermined Adams's prestige as a master diplomat, but it did give the Crawfordites, as Rufus King said, a hobbyhorse to ride that could embarrass Adams's presidential campaign throughout the South.[27]

## TO CAUCUS OR NOT?

For the first ten weeks of the congressional session, the main topic of conversation in the capital was not the international crisis but the prospects for a presidential nominating caucus. The main advocates came from within the Crawford campaign, but the congressional caucus also had a broader appeal as an established party institution. It had not been popular in the past, but it had always successfully indicated the party favorite. On only one occasion had more than 75 percent of Democratic Republican representatives in Washington attended the nominating caucus. In 1816, when 119 attended, Monroe had won with only sixty-five votes; in 1820, the caucus to nominate a vice presidential candidate had been attended by only 46 out of 191 Republicans, and immediately adjourned.[28] Yet on every occasion the nominees had triumphed in the actual election by overwhelming margins. Nobody could be absolutely sure in advance that the caucus would not work again even in the 1824 situation.

Many of "the oldest and most substantial Republicans" in Washington had come to believe that the stability of the republic as well as the survival of the party depended on uniting over the presidential question. The senior senator from Ohio, Benjamin Ruggles, a close friend of Van Buren's, observed that almost every candidate seemed determined to "try his own bottom with the people in the first instance, and then measure strength in the House of Representatives. . . . It is a hazardous game to conscience—bad shuffling, foul play and downright corruption may be the consequence." Would an administration elected in such circumstances be "honorably sustained and supported"? Ruggles believed that "the partisan warfare that has been kept up so long in favor of each of the candidates, and the ill-blood and bitterness of feeling which it has created, has become painful and irksome to the great body of the people." They were now ready to unite on a distinguished candidate if presented in an acceptable fashion, and no method "appears less exceptionable than the *old-fashioned* and *long practiced* one now proposed."[29]

For all the talk about the need for a caucus as a matter of principle, everyone knew that the beneficiary would be Crawford. In spite of his illness, which still confined him at home, Crawford was considered the strongest presidential candidate at the opening of Congress. His health was apparently improving, sufficiently for him to start attending Cabinet meetings again in April, though he was still severely handicapped. He was believed to have more friends in Congress than other candidates, and they were arousing themselves in his cause.[30] Crawfordites, including Van Buren, were convinced that a caucus nomination could still carry considerable weight, especially in firm Democratic states such as Pennsylvania and New York. Together with Virginia, New Jersey, North Carolina, and Georgia, they would represent 120 out of the 131 votes needed to carry the Electoral College.[31]

Within the critical large states, many old-line Democrats still hoped that "the party can be harmonized about the Pres<sup>cy</sup>." In Pennsylvania, Jonathan Roberts claimed in late December that the caucus project "gains friends daily." Some local party meetings backed the congressional caucus because it was "consecrated by the usage of the party for a long time." Crawford himself believed that he might carry the state with a caucus nomination, whereas without it he wouldn't win 2,000 votes. Reports from New York insisted that members of that state legislature would go for a caucus candidate if there were one. Even out in frontier Illinois, a prominent politician declared his determination to support the caucus candidate, whoever the nominee, because "without a nomination," the Democratic Republicans "must all go . . . to the devil."[32]

There were, of course, strong reasons for thinking that the caucus might not work its magic this time round. A broad body of opinion disliked the way party nominations limited the people's choice and in effect dictated the result of the popular election. Without prior partisan nominations, said one New Yorker, the choices in elections would be "completely the people's without any forestalling or attempt at it." Inevitably

Crawford's rivals denounced the caucus as a device to cheat the people by keeping the choice of president in the hands of "active and *managing*" politicians. In 1822 Hezekiah Niles, in his widely circulated *Weekly Register,* launched his "final war" against the principle of nomination by congressional caucuses, repeating the arguments against party control used over the previous decade in state politics by Federalists and dissident Republicans. He emphasized that while a caucus could be justified if, "as formerly," it represented "a gathering into principle," there could be none when it amounted to a mere choice among men. Devoting even more space to the subject late in 1823, Niles delighted in pointing out that some current advocates of the caucus—notably the Washington *National Intelligencer* and Ritchie's *Richmond Enquirer*—had opposed the caucus in 1816. Even in 1824 some of Crawford's most prominent supporters refused to participate in a caucus.[33]

The strongest and most consistent opposition to the caucus came from the Jacksonians. They knew their man stood no chance of winning in caucus, but beyond that, they saw it as the symbol of the very manipulation by insiders that they objected to most. Accordingly, the most prominent formal protest came from the Tennessee legislature, which passed anticaucus resolutions in October 1823 and circulated them to fellow state assemblies. Jackson himself believed a congressional caucus would fly in the face of the people's legitimate democratic aspirations: "Such is the feelings of the nation that a recommendation by a congressional caucus would politically damn any name put forward by it [sic]."[34]

Yet despite the weighty campaign against the caucus and the popular support it attracted, many politicians were reluctant to oppose its meeting. The Tennessee resolutions won formal approval from only Maryland and one house of the South Carolina legislature, while Maine, New York, Virginia, and Georgia decided, "with great unanimity," in favor of the caucus. Five states (Rhode Island, Pennsylvania, North Carolina, Ohio, and Indiana) formally postponed their consideration of the resolutions, some indefinitely. The nine legislatures that deliberately withheld approval of the Tennessee protest possessed 146 out of 261 Electoral College votes, over 55 percent of the whole, while no sort of formal legislative action was taken over the resolutions in Jacksonian Alabama and Mississippi, in most of New England, and in Clay's presumed area of Kentucky, Missouri, and Illinois.[35]

In Pennsylvania the Calhounites showed great uncertainty. Early in 1824 some of his friends invited county meetings to consider the alternative of a Republican national delegate convention as the best means of meeting public expectations, but only one out of thirteen meetings approved. While none opposed the convention idea, seven meetings preferred a congressional caucus in the circumstances of 1824. In the state legislature, the Calhounites divided over the Tennessee resolutions, with many unwilling to discount the congressional caucus. Calhoun himself had been an early opponent, though by 1824 his opposition weakened, as long as it was not used as merely a device to benefit politicians. In the circumstances, his supporters in Washington refused to attend any nominating caucus.[36]

New England's Republican representatives in Washington retained a strong attraction to traditional party ways, and observers thought many Yankee Adams men would happily take Crawford as their second choice. In January Adams himself showed some sympathy with the idea of running for vice president on a Crawford ticket, but only at a time when the Crawford men in Congress showed welcome hostility to Webster's campaign for Greece. Once the Webster resolutions were clearly going to fail, Adams let it be known he would not accept nomination for any office from a congressional caucus, and he authorized his supporters to take whatever action necessary to discourage the meeting of a caucus.[37]

Many observers had long believed that ultimately the Crawford and Clay forces would coalesce, and some agreed with Wheaton that neither of them could "get on . . . with the people" without a caucus nomination. Although Clay had previously spoken out against the caucus, on the grounds that it gave too much power to central authority, by December 1823 he and his main advocates were having second thoughts. If a caucus representative of all views were called, Clay could afford to submit his name because there would, of necessity, be many ballots, and Clay believed he was generally acceptable as a second choice. However, he feared the effect of nomination by a poorly attended caucus, and he appreciated that most of his Western friends were opposed to any association with the Crawford campaign. In any case, if a credible caucus were not held, the election would go into the House, and his friends were confident of the result there.[38]

## ST. VALENTINE'S DAY

For a caucus nomination to carry weight, it must appear to reflect the views of the Republican Party at large. To that end, one congressman said, "Every art and stratagem is resorted to bring the members into this measure." Crawford's friends privately mentioned doubts about his health and hinted that his vice presidential candidate might well finish up as president. They suggested to Clay's supporters that if Mr. Crawford had to be withdrawn, his friends would turn to Clay. According to Plumer, "They have thrown out the same hint to some of Mr. Adams' friends, in hopes of drawing them also into a Caucus." The response to these approaches revealed that not all Crawford's rivals absolutely opposed the calling of a congressional caucus.[39]

At the beginning of the session, the Crawfordites supported Clay as Speaker of the House in the hope of enticing him on to a caucus-nominated ticket as vice president. Van Buren wanted an early caucus to boost Crawford's cause, but he found that no more than sixty representatives would agree to attend—less than a quarter of the Republican members in the two houses. The House debated whether to formally disapprove the system, but the Crawfordites warned Clay that any "overt" act against the caucus would prevent them from shifting to his support later. Clay duly advised his friends to head off the proposal, while Van Buren postponed the call to January or February.[40]

The great question was how many Republicans would turn up to the caucus. The Crawford target was to gain more votes in the caucus than Monroe had won in 1816—that is, more than sixty-five. Crawford was considered to have between 80 and 100 representatives from the two houses, and, in one view, 115 were likely to attend. However, a significant number of these supporters had principled objections to a caucus nomination and were unlikely to turn up. The key figure was Nathaniel Macon, who since 1800 had refused to attend a caucus because he objected to the rule that the minority was bound to accept the decision of the majority. His colleagues worked hard on Macon and thought his resistance was weakening. On the whole, New England Republicans had no such objection, and about twenty were thought to be willing to accept Crawford if they could not have Adams. In most delegations there were one or two representatives who, if left to themselves, were willing to attend the caucus.[41]

The progress made by the Crawford men forced the supporters of the other candidates—after "some subcaucusing"—to announce their agreement not to participate. As Ruggles pointed out, by this union, they confessed that none of them could beat Crawford in caucus. They did have an alternative choice—to attend the caucus and carry a motion to dissolve it—but, as Clay had prophesied, opposition candidates would not go into the caucus if they could not predict the outcome "because of the difficulty of ascertaining what the secondary combinations may be." Nor did they wish to have to support an undesirable nominee. Hence, in the *National Intelligencer*'s words, they decided not to attend and "kill the monster" but to "let it kill itself."[42]

In early February a majority of congressmen signed a public statement that they would not attend a nominating caucus. Several state delegations held meetings designed to prevent individual members from strengthening Crawford's hand by entering the caucus, even if they intended to vote against him. The Ohio delegation, for example, held two secret meetings at which each member expressed his own opinion and that of his constituency. When they established that eleven out of fourteen participants objected to the caucus, three older congressmen who were disposed to attend "concluded to conform to the wishes of a majority of their colleagues." Just one, Senator Ruggles, felt obliged to "meet his brethren in caucus, and harmonize with the great republican family."[43]

After a call addressed to members of the "democratic" party, the caucus finally met in the House of Representatives chamber in the evening of February 14. The galleries were crowded for the event, but not the floor of the House. Only sixty-six representatives attended, mainly from Virginia, North Carolina, Georgia, and New York; none came from ten states, including Pennsylvania. Many significant neo-Antifederalist Crawfordites with doubts about the principle of a caucus nomination absented themselves, notably Macon and Randolph. Other absentees were "afraid of their constituents."[44] Crawford won sixty-two votes, with only four given to other candidates. Albert Gallatin was named as the vice presidential candidate to "show their nomination to be that of the old Republican party." Ruggles, who chaired the caucus, then issued a national address justifying the nomination of Crawford as official candidate of the "republican party" and urging the need to maintain party unity in order to prevent a Federalist revival. As he told his friends, if "the candidates were all Washingtons, but one could be President, and it seems the duty of brethren of the same principle to cultivate friendly feelings, and not divide and waste their strength."[45]

The small attendance had, however, ruined that appeal. As one wag had remarked as the vote was announced, *"Sixty two / Won't do."* The caucus was too obviously a meeting of a special interest to successfully pass itself off as representative of the whole Democratic Republican Party; the refusal of other candidates' supporters to attend had ensured that. The whole proceeding had been conducted with a degree of formality that Gallatin insisted not only lacked historical precedent but "furnished a pretence to attach to the whole the odium of being an attempt to dictate to the people." In Pennsylvania, Simon Cameron condemned it as the work "of the friends of a single individual, held in utter disregard or defiance, of the known wishes of the democratic party in Congress and throughout the Union." By May Plumer thought two-thirds of the people had made their mind up against Crawford.[46]

Back at home, Ruggles discovered the futility of his efforts. As Congressman John Sloane prophesied, "In Ohio it will not do. . . . The idea that a few, *the very few,* friends Mr. Crawford has in that State can, by beating up for old fashioned democrats, be able to carry him . . . is all the result of an inveterate attachment to the man which will prompt some of them to recommend a game of this kind to the overthrow of all who engage in it." Ruggles found himself mocked locally: "The Caucus expired in pains and in struggles, / The birth was abortion, the Granny was Ruggles." He decided to shift to Clay's support. As the Ohio press made clear, the problem was not merely that congressional caucuses in general were considered undemocratic but that this particular one was unrepresentative and did not choose an acceptable candidate. In the words of one, it was "so singular, so contrary to the old principles of caucusing, and so impotent" in the current divided situation of the old Republican party.[47]

Overall, St. Valentine's Day proved no massacre, but it was a political liability. As one old Federalist gleefully announced eleven days after, "The Caucus folks begin to feel bad; they begin to see that *party, party, party* names have not their usual charm." The reason, said a Western observer, was that "The old party land-marks are broken down, and others driven and distinctly marked. The friends of internal improvements and domestic manufactures are one party, and should unite upon one of the present candidates for president as their rallying point." If they did, wrote another, "We should equally avoid the risk of having our interest prostrated by the mercantile and shipping interests of the North, or the anti-manufacturing spirit of the cotton-growers in the South." Differences over economic policy had overtaken the old party division.[48]

As members wrangled over the caucus, Congress turned its attention to the president's call for a program of improvement and internal strengthening. Those in favor of the policy were now stronger than in the previous session because the reapportionment of 1822 had shifted power away from New England and the Southeast. Yet the beneficiaries were far from united. The states south of Kentucky would vote with the South Atlantic states on a protective tariff but not on federal internal improvements, while New England and New York were divided. The total effect of the debates was to strengthen Southern resistance to such policies—essentially on economic grounds, but in 1824 some Southerners began to argue in Congress that protective tariffs as well as internal improvements were inherently unconstitutional. For the time being, though, they proved much more effective in resisting the American System in 1824 than historians usually allow.[49]

Internal improvements took the lead on the congressional schedule as on the political agenda. The critical issue was constitutional: did Congress have the power to vote money for roads and canals? Van Buren claimed to favor federal construction, but only if a new constitutional amendment gave the federal government the power; Clay eloquently argued that the power was implicit in the Constitution. In practical terms, the "Internal Improvements Party" (as Van Buren later called that interest) faced the difficulty that too many districts had proposals that were of direct interest to them. If the federal government could not afford all, how did it choose which to support? A congressman wanting favor for his own locality might well vote against a rival scheme. Thus the automatic opposition of confirmed neo-Antifederalist opinion could often be supported by the jealousies of the supporters, as in the case of the National Road.[50]

This project was hallowed by the approval of both Jefferson and Madison. It had started as a result of the Ohio Compact of 1803, whereby the exemption of federal lands in the Old Northwest from state taxation for five years after sale would be compensated by the building of a federal road from the Atlantic to and through the new states. In theory, states' rights objections did not apply because the federal government was acting as a landowner rather than as a government. Yet the further extension of the road was obstructed by Eastern interests that did not benefit. Pennsylvania opposed it not only because the terminus of the road lay in Maryland but also because it had built, at its own expense, an (inferior) turnpike from Philadelphia to Pittsburgh on a route parallel to the National Road. As a result, even this undoubtedly deserving project failed to win enough support in the Congress of 1824.

A proposal was needed that would unite all supporters of federal internal improvements and provide a means of determining which projects were national. In the previous Congress, a committee chaired by Joseph Hemphill of Pennsylvania had proposed employing United States Army engineers, who were being paid anyway, to undertake the survey of named projects that were of national interest. Though the president conceded the constitutionality of the proposal, the bill failed to pass the House in 1822 and 1823. It was revived in the new Congress, but now the president was to decide which projects should be surveyed. Speaker Clay insisted that the general principles of constitutionality and expediency must be discussed before minor details such as the size of the appropriation for the survey. After three weeks of exhausting discussion, this landmark legislation passed the House on February 10 by a vote of 113–86, and the Senate later by 25–21.

The voting alignment underlined the tensions between seaboard and interior evident so far in the presidential campaign. The opposition came primarily from Virginia and North Carolina, from New England, and from New York. Their solidarity broke in the House, where helpful votes were cast in the western counties of the Southeastern states and New York, and in Massachusetts and Rhode Island. The Western states—both south and north—produced only one negative vote in the House and two in the Senate, while Pennsylvania, New Jersey, Maryland, and Delaware were almost unanimous in their support. For its advocates, the presidential vetoes of 1817 and 1822 made the election of a president who was favorable to internal improvements a necessity in a way in which he was not for protective tariffs; transportation projects could always be vetoed, whereas a president was unlikely to veto a tariff measure essential for the financing of his government.[51]

Serious discussion of the tariff began the day the House approved the General Survey bill. Positive support for increased rates of import duty inevitably came from manufacturers who would directly benefit from specific protection against foreign competitors, but the broadest demand came from cereal growers, who looked more generally for a growing domestic market as industry of all kinds developed. Public meetings and state legislatures throughout the Northwestern and Middle Atlantic states had for years been asserting that national independence, a less adverse balance of trade, a vibrant internal market, and greater employment could be achieved only if the federal government enacted a policy of high protective tariffs. In his great speech at the end of March, Clay linked tariffs with federal internal improvements in a scheme of policy that he christened the American System to describe the grand principles of national independence, mutual interdependence, and economic interchange that held together his vision.[52]

In contrast to this insistence on a national economic policy, there was a more pragmatic view, favorable to protection but more acceptable to the South. In February 1823 the Pennsylvania Jacksonian James Buchanan argued in the House that it was necessary to raise import duties for financial reasons. Secretary Crawford in his treasury report had said so: though the annual budget would begin to run at a surplus in 1823, scheduled repayments of the national debt would throw it into serious deficit by the end of 1824. Why not, asked Buchanan, so arrange increased tariff schedules as to both raise more revenue and give incidental protection to those industries that were necessary for national defense or to ensure consumption? With care, Congress could avoid giving particular industries too much protection or raising duties so high that import duties produced less revenue. The tariff was thus properly the business of the Ways and Means Committee, not the Committee on Manufactures to which Speaker Clay had sent it.[53]

This proposed compromise was not satisfactory to Clay or to the chair of the latter committee, John Tod of Pennsylvania, who in 1824 was, in effect, floor manager of the emerging tariff bill. A majority of the House favored the principle of protection, but it was impossible to establish the principle from the start. The traditions of the House prevented the bill's advocates from moving to strike out the enacting clause in order to force a vote on the general principle; they had first to proceed on an item-by-item basis, discussing and voting seriatim on each proposed rate. Only the bill's opponents could force a vote on the principle, but they avoided doing so, aware that they were more likely to defeat the tariff as a whole if it appeared to be a log-roll or pork-barrel effort to satisfy selfish special interests. However important the principle, the bill's advocates must balance particular interests and avoid excessive or disproportionate advantage if the bill were to become law.[54]

As with internal improvements, the tariff cause suffered from the tension between the general principle and the mass of detailed provisions. The House was besieged by petitions, proposals, and submissions from a myriad of producers and processors, and from special interests that were concerned in case some particular imports might achieve too much protection. As Clay remarked, "In the H. of R. there are 213 persons to satisfy & 1,000 interests to conciliate." A detailed package had been inherited from the unsuccessful bills of 1820 and 1823, and each item had to be defended as a necessary part of the whole. Key industries were given the protection they requested not by raising the rate on imports across the board but by adopting specific rates on particular items and using minimum valuations to covertly raise the duty on many cheap items to almost prohibitive levels. To avoid charges of bias, concessions were made to agricultural interests, most importantly to sugar producers in Louisiana and hemp growers in Kentucky and Missouri.[55]

The managers were aware that the 1820 bill had failed in the Senate, and they strove to make this bill acceptable there. Accordingly, on a number of items, industrial interests met defeat. As an exasperated Clay told one special pleader, "Congress is not legislating only for the Wolcott Woolen Manufacturing Company, but for a great nation & a great national interest." Chairman Tod pressed for mitigating amendments where a high rate on an item of consumption would alienate potential supporters or where a particular rate set one industry against another. These partial sacrifices ensured that some dissatisfied interests would turn against the bill, and so, "after much shuffling, grumbling and threatening," it passed a remarkably full House with a smaller majority (107–102) than that of 1820. Many proponents felt dissatisfied, and Niles regarded the outcome as "a sort of compromise between the two great parties," for and against protection.[56]

Once again, the pattern of voting in the House revealed the underlying tensions: it reflected the division over internal improvements, but with a more obvious North–South cleavage. The heart of the opposition remained the South Atlantic states, but they now found allies in the Southwestern states, while New England was evenly divided; "So you see," said one Ohio congressman, "codfish and Hickory men were against us." *Niles' Weekly Register* identified the opposition with the tobacco, cotton, and sugar states, alongside the three *"Navigating and fishing states"* of Massachusetts, New Hampshire, and Maine, which feared that a higher tariff might injure overseas commerce. In favor of protection were the "manufacturing" states of Rhode Island and Connecticut, and the "grain growing" states—the Northwestern and Middle Atlantic states, together with Vermont, Kentucky, and parts of Maryland and

Tennessee. The votes cast fully justified the view that the basic political conflict of 1824 set "the farming interests of the Middle and Western States" in contention with "the commercial monopoly of the East" and "the cotton growers of the South."[57]

Historians have focused on the great debate in the House and neglected what happened thereafter in the Senate, where, according to Rufus King, "the tariff absorbs all the interest and feeling." Here the bill faced determined opposition both from King and from Samuel Smith of Maryland, who happened to be chairman of the Senate Finance Committee. He viewed the word "Tariff" as having achieved a "cabalistic" power in the House "superior to all discretion of reason," and he saw his duty as restoring common sense. The Senate chipped away at the bill's provisions: it reduced the level of protection for many manufactures while retaining the House's enhanced iron duty, and returned the bill closer to the sort of revenue measure that Crawford and Buchanan had advocated. The changes brought over a few votes in some upper New England and Western states that had shown opposition in the House, and so passed the Senate by four votes, but Charles Hammond, for one, thought the modifications "not favourable to the principles of the bill." As Mangum said, it had been "gutted in the Senate." Even after a conference committee had settled the differences between the houses, the protectionist Niles saw that the revised bill was "far from meeting the views of the . . . 'American System,'" but he still advocated accepting it. When it finally passed both houses in late May, some opponents of protection regarded the new tariff act, "modified as it has been, . . . as a *revenue* bill," and a few even hailed it as a triumph for the South.[58]

Neither side had yet carried the day. The level of protection had been raised, but not as much as industry in general wanted, and the tariff was still fixed within the framework of revenue needs rather than the autarkic philosophy of the American System. The internal improvements cause had secured the General Survey Act, which was a great victory in principle and full of promise for the future, as well as appropriations worth $160,000 for various projects including harbor improvements, but no great measure of interest to the West had passed other than a $75,000 appropriation to improve the Ohio and Mississippi rivers. The continuing dependence of canal improvements upon a sympathetic federal executive was underlined by the considerable practical support Secretary of War Calhoun gave to the surveying of federal and state projects over the summer.[59] The policy struggle was still to be decided, but at least the legislative contest had made the battle lines clearer.

## DEFINING CANDIDACIES

The proceedings in Congress helped to define the election contest in two contradictory ways. First, the debates and votes on the American System brought into sharper relief the policy stances of the candidates. Representatives and newspapers reported the voting, conscious that it would help to underline the sectional identification of hostile candidates, and candidates were pressed to clarify where they stood on the issues. Second, as the exhausting session dragged on well into May, Washington became caught up in matters affecting the personal reputation of candidates, which some clearly thought might yet affect the outcome of the election. These scandals roused great excitement in the capital, though they arguably had little impact outside the Washington hothouse.

The debates and votes on the American System forced Adams to be more forthcoming about his views on tariffs and internal improvements. When approached for his views on the tariff in March, he had eschewed the idea that the tariff should be based on simple revenue needs and insisted on the need to balance industrial as well as agricultural and commercial interests. When later he was approached by George McDuffie and James Barbour, he said he was satisfied with the tariff as passed, which seemed to him a reasonable compromise between competing interests. He recognized that these views, if published, would operate against him in the South, where "a very strong feeling" existed. On internal improvements, by May he was willing to answer questions about his views, but asked that his responses be kept out of the newspapers. By June he was less insistent, and his response to questions put by a Maryland newspaper was widely reprinted. In it, he pointed out that in 1807 he had proposed the first-ever resolution for "a general system of internal improvements," and he still believed Congress had the power to make appropriations for roads and canals. This announcement caused some embarrassment on the Southern seaboard and especially in Virginia, where he was still regarded by many, including Crawford, as having an acceptable view on economic issues. However, he had never supported any specific proposal for congressional aid and was damned in the West, in any case, by New England's opposition to the General Survey Act, which Clay snidely suggested in debate reflected the secretary of state's own long-held private views.[60]

By contrast, Clay had clearly pitched his campaign on the American System, making him the first candidate ever to connect a presidential bid with a specific program. He may have mobilized visions of national integration and coherence, but he also appealed to specific regional grievances. He concluded his great House speech on internal improvements with a stirring recital of the West's sacrifices in return for little: the government's disbursements were all on the seaboard, but much of the revenue was raised from the West's lands; the National Road was accepted as a genuinely national measure, he said, but "not one stone has yet been broken, not one spade of earth has been yet removed in any Western State." While Clay won plaudits for championing the West, his commitment to a specific program of government activism undermined his continuing hopes for success in Virginia. Local meetings begin to denounce his abandonment of strict construction, and even some of those who approved of federal internal improvements, like Charles Fenton Mercer, were deterred by his enthusiasm for tariff protection. A growing reaction within the South against protectionism alienated some former supporters, including some in the Southwest who warned him to drop his support for the tariff or lose theirs. Even as the protective system ruined Clay yet further in the South in the summer of 1824, he gained no compensating reward in the seaboard states most interested in the policy, perhaps because Jackson had begun to steal his thunder as a nationalist candidate.[61]

Sectional divergence made the Senate tariff debates Jackson's toughest political test. His all-conquering appeal in Pennsylvania owed much to his reputation as a protectionist. In 1823 great publicity had surrounded the gift to Mrs. Jackson of a "Grass Bonnet or Hat" made by two little girls in New York. At the prompting of the donor—a Pennsylvania politician—the General was moved to reply that "Mrs. Jackson will wear with pride a hat made by American hands, and made of American materials: its workmanship . . . will be regarded as an evidence of the perfection which our domestic manufactures may hereafter acquire, if properly fostered and protected." Widely published, these "Grass Hat Letters" identified Jackson as an avowed economic nationalist. Some Southern supporters warned Jackson that those letters were too protariff to satisfy Southern sentiment. The day before the tariff debate began in the Senate, Jackson took the unprecedented step of sending a North Carolina supporter, Dr. Littleton H. Coleman, a letter clearly intended for general publication. In an attempt to straddle sectional differences, Jackson emphatically based his support for tariff protection on the needs of national defense. He had already voted consistently for the General Survey bill, and now, at decisive points, he voted for the tariff; his vote, and that of Eaton, saved the bill from defeat on its passage to its third reading in the Senate. To Charles Hammond in Cincinnati, the one mitigating feature of Jackson's presidential campaign was that it produced critical Southern votes for the tariff.[62]

The issue caused great strain on Jackson's Southern support, especially over the issue of cotton bagging, used to wrap raw cotton for export. The proposed duty was understood to benefit large manufacturing establishments in Kentucky, which the cotton-growing states of the Lower South found particularly obnoxious. Jackson's supporters in that region called on the General and Senator Eaton to oppose the duty on cotton bagging, but they cast the critical votes to pass it through the Senate, 24–23. According to Van Buren, who sat next to him in the Senate, the anxious Jackson tried to avoid blame for casting the critical vote by asking Van Buren to change his vote on this clause from opposition to support. However, when it was reconsidered a week later, Jackson and Eaton changed their votes and in effect removed the duty on cotton bagging from the bill. The clause was then saved on reconciliation by a conference committee of the two houses on which Jackson sat, but at a lower rate than protectionists wanted. Jackson also helped to ensure that lower-priced woolen goods, which slaves wore, were exempted from the higher duties that this tariff imposed more generally.[63]

Aware of rising criticism, notably in Tennessee and Alabama but also North Carolina, Jackson wrote several further letters—one drafted by Eaton and clearly intended for general publication—defending his support for "judicious" tariff protection. He emphasized three necessities: to enhance revenue so as to enable the rapid reduction of the national debt, to secure the materials of national defense, and to provide a future home market for cotton. He even argued that duties on sail duck, hemp, and iron should have been higher to boost revenue and avoid borrowing. The term *judicious*—which contemporaries and historians have enjoyed making fun of—deliberately echoed the wording of Crawford's report that pragmatically linked revenue needs with an element of selective protectionism.[64]

For Crawford, the American System was always fatal to his national appeal. His dilemma had been clear by February 1823: the suspicion that he opposed federal internal improvements and protective tariffs undercut him in the Middle and Border states, but if he came out in favor, he would lose at least Virginia and North Carolina because "every state south of the Potomac are more decided in their opposition to this manufacturing project, than even to Roads & Canals." Crawford might fudge the internal-improvement issue by favoring a constitutional amendment, but that would not satisfy those who insisted that the Constitution already gave the federal government sufficient authority. He was further damned when it was reported that forty-seven of the fifty-two representatives who attended the caucus voted against the General Survey bill. As a result, in many regions "a suspicion of attachment to or respect for Mr. Crawford" came to be "looked upon as a most heinous political sin."[65]

In the last weeks of the session, the excitement in Washington revolved round a scandal that affected Crawford's personal standing, suggesting how far he was still feared. In April Ninian Edwards, former Illinois senator and now newly appointed minister to Mexico, raised once more the charges that he had made the previous year against Crawford in fifteen anonymous newspaper articles signed "A.B." He had accused the secretary of the treasury of malfeasance, and he now asked Congress for a fuller investigation into the secretary's personal corruption. This new formal submission, Niles reported, "has acted in congress like a live coal thrown into a magazine of combustible matter" because it directly raised issues of financial mismanagement that had been somewhat submerged before. Edwards, whose ship had not yet left New Orleans for Mexico, was recalled to Washington by a high-powered ad hoc committee, and the investigation dragged on. Crawford's opponents enjoyed the embarrassing revelations and discussions. However, the committee decided that although the charges were factually justified, they did not provide hard evidence of a corrupt motive on Crawford's side. If anything, as Edwards himself had acknowledged earlier, Crawford's supposedly dubious actions had protected Western banks and land purchasers during the banking crisis. Curiosity may have been "on *tip-toe* to learn the cause of so great a bustle at Washington," and some thought the persecution created sympathy for Crawford, but the affair really resulted in nothing but Edwards's resignation in June and a general embittering of relations within Washington.[66]

Through the summer the Crawfordites were in full cry against both

Edwards and the administration. When the committee organizing the July Fourth celebration in Washington excluded Edwards before any charges were proved, the president and some of his Cabinet formally refused to attend, whereupon "about two-thirds of the subscribers withdrew their names." The *National Intelligencer,* since 1801 the official organ of the Republican Party, became so hostile to the administration that some Cabinet officers began to place government papers and notices in other newspapers. In this impassioned atmosphere, the grip on electoral reality among those confined to Washington became somewhat strained.[67]

Potentially of greater electoral impact was the "very unpleasant matter" of the Lowrie letter, which became public in April and made "much noise in the newspapers." In January former U.S. senator Walter Lowrie of Pennsylvania had claimed that in 1816 Jackson had written to Monroe urging the new president to appoint two Federalists and two Democrats to his Cabinet. Jackson and Monroe denied having written or received such a letter, but discovery of the original forced publication of the whole correspondence in May. Jackson had not used the precise words first reported, but he had advised Monroe that Federalists who had risked their lives to defend the republic should be "considered as Republicans." He believed the president should "consult no party or party feelings" in his choice of Cabinet officers.[68]

Some thought this amalgamationist proposal spelled death to his pretensions to be a Democratic Republican and so would "blow up Jackson in Pennsylvania." The General himself for a time feared its effect, but Adams predicted that the fuss "would not change five votes in Pennsylvania." Jackson refused to respond to the publication, and the state's Democratic press either ignored or, with extraordinary cheek, misrepresented the letter. In fact, according to Jackson's associate, William B. Lewis, the widespread publication of the letter in May "had the effect of rallying to the support of Genl. Jackson many of the Federalists, particularly that portion of them who supported the war and *hated John Quincy Adams* for having turned Traitor to his and their party."[69]

In the earlier stages of the campaign when Jackson's cause was thought bound to collapse, the General had scarcely ever been attacked personally, but after March 1824 his opponents took off their kid gloves. Nearly all the critical stories—mostly true—that would lard the 1828 campaign were first adumbrated in 1824: his dubious marriage, his execution of militia men, his refusal to obey legitimate civil power. A

"Caucus Curs in Full Yell, Or a War-Whoop, to Saddle on the People, a
Pappoose President." This cartoon, drawn by James Akin in 1824 and
probably published in Philadelphia, shows Jackson standing proud and
untouched in the face of the snarling dogs of the press. His sword bears
Caesar's words, "VENI, VIDI, VICI." Most of the newspapers supported
Crawford, notably (in the bottom left-hand corner) the Philadelphia editor
John Binns's Democratic Press; the many-headed dog next to it, though,
is labeled "Hartford Convention." Below the image are Shakespeare's lines
from Coriolanus: "What would you have, you Curs, that like not peace, nor
war? . . . Who deserves Greatness, deserves your hate; and your affections
are a sick man's appetite." This obvious reference to Crawford shows how the
Jacksonians continued to fear his appeal to traditional Democratic voters
in Pennsylvania. Courtesy: Library of Congress Prints and Photographs
Division.

cartoon published in Philadelphia portrayed Jackson as standing aloof and untroubled, with sword drawn but at rest, as the "curs" of the press snarled around him labelled with slanderous slurs. In fact, John Eaton had anxiously persuaded Jackson not to answer any newspaper attacks, and took on himself the task of defending the Hero.[70]

Crawford remained the prime target of press attacks in major states, but it was his health, both physical and mental, that remained the main matter of concern to his friends. Although it had improved early in the year, he suffered a relapse in May. He had begun to attend Cabinet meetings again in April, but he did not attend another till after the election in November. By June some of his friends feared for his life and talked about the possibility of finding a substitute candidate, preferably Clay. In July the Cabinet debated whether the Treasury was being properly and legally managed. Adams thought it was, and he found Crawford "so far restored" that there was no chance of his candidacy being withdrawn. Early in August three doctors confirmed to Monroe that Crawford was fit enough to conduct his office, and the Georgian took a convalescent holiday in Berkeley Springs in Virginia. By September most observers thought him remarkably recovered, except for persisting thick speech, and were confident that he would not withdraw from the race.[71]

In the struggle to find marginal advantages, attention turned to the vice presidential race. As Niles complained, though the office was important in its own right, politicians failed to consider that they might be choosing a replacement president and instead looked to conciliate key states. Crawford's managers had hoped that placing the reluctant Gallatin on the ticket—even though his foreign birth meant he was ineligible to become president—would attract old Democrats in Pennsylvania, but by September they had given up hopes of carrying the Keystone state. Because Gallatin brought little strength elsewhere, they somewhat clumsily persuaded him to withdraw from the ticket and allowed their state campaigns to choose as vice presidential candidate the man who seemed likely to bring most strength to the ticket locally.[72] Since his defeat in Pennsylvania and nomination for vice president by the Harrisburg convention, Calhoun had been generally regarded as Jackson's running mate, though the General did not acknowledge this situation until late in the campaign. Adams himself wanted Jackson as his running mate, partly because he thought Jackson would handle the Senate well and bring much-needed dignity to the office, but also because "no man has so solid a mass of popularity to secure in support of the administration."

When this proved impossible, Adams acknowledged Calhoun's claims, and by late October the two were usually bracketed together, though Calhoun insisted he remained neutral between Jackson and Adams. Thus Calhoun's success was made certain, and the second office would, after all, have little impact on the election to the first office.[73]

Since March, one watcher reported, "the most knowing" in Washington had been convinced that "the substantial controversy is now between Adams and Jackson." Yet despite all Crawford's travails, his many supporters among Washington officialdom remained optimistic. In June the usually well-informed Margaret Bayard Smith thought "his chance much better than that of either of the other candidates." Adams thought Crawford had recently lost little support and "his political prospects . . . remain much as they were from last Valentine's day." Many prominent men stood committed to his cause. They still hoped that old Democratic loyalties would carry a number of states, and they believed clever Senator Van Buren could yet control the great state of New York. However, the decision also depended on a handful of competitive popular-election states where Crawford had little chance.[74]

# 8 POPULAR BATTLEGROUNDS

By the spring of 1824 the combatants were geared for the critical conflict—but only in some states. Commentators generally agreed on giving New England to Adams, Pennsylvania and the Old Southwest to Jackson, and most of the Southeast to Crawford; Clay was regarded as the most prominent candidate in the Northwest, but with slim chances in any state south of Kentucky or on the seaboard. The greatest area of uncertainty lay in the heart of the nation, notably the Middle Atlantic and the Ohio Valley states. By March almost all commentators thought the chances slight for an outright decision in the Electoral College. Which three candidates would proceed into the House—and which would enjoy the political momentum—would be decided in only a handful of states.

As always, the outcome in the Electoral College depended mainly on the most populous states. By the spring of 1824, it was clear that the largest, New York, with 36 votes, was unpredictable and likely to be decided in the state legislature. The second and third—Pennsylvania (28 votes) and Virginia (24)—were regarded as one-sidedly safe for Jackson and Crawford, respectively. The four states ranked from sixth to ninth—Massachusetts (15), Kentucky (14), South Carolina (11), and Tennessee (11)—were all written off to their favorite-son candidate or, in Calhoun's case, his acknowledged replacement. In the remaining three top ten states—Ohio (16), North Carolina (15), and Maryland (11)—there were 42 electoral votes up for grabs, to be decided by popular election.

This handful of close contests in effect represented three distinctive battles, each to some extent reflecting and influencing the election in neighboring states. First, in the Old Northwest, dominated by Ohio, the struggle was three sided between Clay, Jackson, and Adams. Second, in the smaller middle states of New Jersey and Maryland, Jackson fought against Adams, with a Crawfordite distraction. Third, in North Carolina, Crawford struggled against a Jacksonian-led combination of his opponents who agreed only on whom they did not want. In all these states except Maryland, the voters decided on a statewide general ticket basis, which helped encourage statewide organizational efforts and gave a strong incentive to bring out every vote.

## THE CERTAINTIES

In the many one-sided states, few doubted the result, but some struggled against it. In Virginia, Crawford's supporters controlled the legislature after the state elections of August 1823, and they used it to nominate a slate of electors, a central committee of correspondence, and county committees. The opposition did not attack Crawford directly but rather stressed his lack of support elsewhere and the danger of handing the presidency to an unacceptable rival. The friends of the opposing candidates held state meetings that were not well attended, and some found difficulty in drawing up electoral tickets; they penetrated few of the counties dominated by Crawford's supporters. Local public meetings became the main local engine for the Jackson and especially the Adams campaigns, but "Crawford's friends have rested so confident of success," remarked the *Richmond Enquirer,* "that like Clay's friends in Kentucky, they have not held a single meeting of the people." The press predicted that the lack of a credible opposition would persuade thousands of Crawford's supporters not to vote: the Georgian duly carried the state with 56 percent of the vote in a turnout of about 24 percent of qualified voters.[1]

Likewise, in New England, Adams faced little effective challenge. In Maine, the opposition was "trifling," except in one county, which in any case he carried; in the end, he swept every district, defeating a rival unpledged ticket by three to one. In New Hampshire and Rhode Island, only his ticket ran, and he took over 90 percent of the vote. Such was Adams's predominance in New England that it is by no means clear whom the opposition votes were intended for. The lion's share undoubtedly were won by Crawford or by a ticket most likely to vote for him, but some were cast for Federalist tickets, as in Connecticut. Adams took almost 80 percent of the votes in that state, but the minority included 643 scattering votes that are usually credited to the opposition but were in fact votes for misspelled versions of the names of electoral candidates on the Adams ticket![2] In general, an opposition that drew together two contradictory traditions—old Democrats such as Isaac Hill who had been "too long engaged in the republican cause" and die-hard Federalists who could not forgive Adams for deserting their party in 1807—found great difficulty in cooperating politically.[3]

In Massachusetts, the opposition tried, unsuccessfully, to prevent Adams's supporters from converting the old district system into a general ticket system that would maximize his electoral vote. After the Republican caucus named an Adams electoral slate and a central committee of correspondence, his opponents within the party made a "combined and systematic effort . . . to secure the Federalists in support of Mr. Crawford." They got up a rival unpledged ticket, with individual electoral candidates named in separate county meetings, a ticket that represented the extremes, both partisan Democrats and die-hard Federalists. Ironically, they protested against state caucuses while voting for electors who would probably vote for the nominee of the congressional caucus. Personally, Adams welcomed Federalist opposition at home because it weakened the charge of Federalism leveled against him in some other states. Such was his hold in Massachusetts that his friends did little until the last weeks, when they held meetings and distributed tickets. They duly won with 82 percent of the state's popular vote in a low turnout.[4]

The situation was similar in Pennsylvania. After the Republican convention had nominated Jackson, even his firmest opponent thought "all opposition . . . worthless, at least at present," because "there is nothing to make an opposition of." Some of Jackson's Federalist supporters were soon alienated by "noisy democrats" who assumed "the exclusive right of supporting" him. Though the Lowrie letter confirmed some Federalists in their hope that the General would end their political proscription, overall "the imprudent and suspicious zeal" of the Democrats "materially reduced" Jackson's "strength" among them. Adams in particular found much support against Jackson from Philadelphia Federalists and Quakers.[5] In August the Crawfordites held their own state convention, but less than one quarter of the counties sent delegates, while Clay's lack of support ensured his friends could make only a feeble effort. Both campaigns relied on public meetings to name tickets, but they had too many areas of weakness, and both struggled to name representative statewide tickets. The Jacksonians, by contrast, showed "unceasing perseverance" locally and won 76 percent of the popular vote, compared to 11 percent for Adams, 9 percent for Crawford, and only 4 percent for Clay. Every county would give Jackson a majority.[6]

Paradoxically, Jackson's other main area of strength combined a similar assurance of victory with a greater sense of competition. The confidence was justified when Jackson carried both Alabama and Mississippi with at least two-thirds of the popular vote and failed to carry outright only three counties in each state. As in Tennessee—where he won 91.3 percent of the vote—most white people wished the federal government to remove the Indians and privatize their lands; in Mississippi, Choctaw and Chickasaw land still covered over half the state, whereas rapidly growing Alabama, "the wonder of the south," had already secured two-thirds of its territory, thanks to Jackson's treaty acquisitions of 1814 and 1816. Jackson's vote in favor of protective tariffs injured his support among the cotton interests, but adverse comment was quietened by his public letter advocating a revenue tariff, reduced government borrowing, and protection only for industries essential for national defense. His votes in favor of internal improvements, by contrast, were widely approved, thanks to the popular demand for improved transportation, especially in Alabama. However, despite Jackson's dominance, these two states saw the highest levels of popular participation in the presidential election in the whole country—51 percent in Alabama and 46 percent in Mississippi.[7]

This level of popular involvement in part reflected the extraordinarily high level of turnout aroused in recent state elections by the continuing disputes over debts, currency, and banks. Yet those contests had little relevance to the presidential election, as Jackson appealed across the board to the small farmers who made up most of the white population. The main opposition in both states came not from a Southern candidate but from Adams, who had won most newspaper endorsements before Jackson's national rise; his supporters had emphasized his high qualifications, his long record of service, and (ironically) his championing of Jackson's actions during the Seminole campaign. In Alabama the numerous planters from Georgia provided support for Crawford, but Adams pushed him into third place, with 17.62 percent of the popular vote compared to Crawford's 12.3 percent. In Mississippi, where Crawford had no constituency, Adams won one-third of the popular vote in an election that saw an extraordinarily high level of ticket voting. The Adams campaign enlivened the election in both states, agitating national issues through its strong representation in the local press and stimulating public attention in its areas of strength. Its attempt to persuade the Alabama legislature to adopt a district system was, however, a confession that Adams had no chance of carrying the state.[8]

Much of Adams's most enthusiastic support came from the New Englanders who numbered strongly among the mercantile community of the Old Southwest's commercial centers. However, despite his Yankee connections, he also attracted support from among cotton planters in the Alabama–Tombigbee basin in central Alabama, while in southwestern Mississippi he won over 40 percent of the vote cast in the five most southerly counties on the east bank of the Mississippi River near Natchez—the only plantation counties in the state—just as he did also in the upper east bank counties of neighboring Louisiana. Because of his home base, Adams was regarded as probably sounder on the tariff than Jackson, while reports that Adams privately favored internal improvements were no disadvantage in the Old Southwest. As in the areas of commercial agriculture around Baltimore, Adams offered a safe pair of hands for those well-situated Southerners who mistrusted Crawford and were wary of Jackson. Here lay the origins of the Southern Whig party of the next decade, but in 1824 the vigorous opposition of the Adams men had no chance of defeating the victor of New Orleans in the Old Southwest.[9]

## THE FOURTH STATE

By contrast, the states of the Old Northwest were unusual in 1824 in not having a favorite-son candidate. Their commitment to internal improvements and the tariff gave Clay great claims, but his connection with slave interests contradicted the antislavery views of many in the region. When Clinton proved unavailable, only a vote for Adams could express anti-Southern sentiment, but he never gave a satisfactory indication of immediate support for specific Western proposals. Forced to choose whether they were Northern or Western, the settlers finally gave the overwhelming majority of their votes to Southern candidates who seemed friendly to the American System.

The great prize in the region was Ohio, which possessed more than half the Old Northwest's electoral votes. Clay was consistently the front-runner here, and in the early months of 1824 his speeches in Congress confirmed him as the obvious Western preference. He had attracted a large number of Ohio's leading politicians, from both old parties and all state factions, and most of its established newspapers. In the legislative session of 1824, a meeting of his supporters drew up a list of electoral candidates from all parts of the state and created a state corresponding committee. Yet despite these advantages, Clay carried Ohio with less than 40 percent of the popular vote, thanks to the vigorous challenge from the supporters of Adams (25 percent) and Jackson (35 percent).[10]

The decline of Clinton had energized the Adams men, who called a legislative caucus of all those "opposed to the slave holding policy," which duly named a "FREE ELECTORAL TICKET." They developed a central organization fit to rival that already created by the Clay men and brought out more new newspapers than either of their rivals. They sent free copies to areas that lacked a friendly newspaper and established some energetic county, township, and (in Cincinnati) ward committees, which worked to ensure that their supporters "turn out, to a man." Partly as a result of their efforts, Adams's support would prove more generally diffused than that of Jackson or Clay, and he won a large proportion of his statewide vote in counties where he ran second.[11]

In achieving this result, the Adams campaign men used two striking lines of argument. On the one hand, they insisted that Adams was hostile to the "aristocratic" tendencies evident in the Crawford and Clay national and state campaigns: the Adams men claimed to rely on "the people," not caucuses, wishing to elect "a real democratic republican president" who would encourage "the growth and advancement of the middling and lower order of the people." To a greater extent than either of their rivals, they used local, popularly elected, delegate nominating conventions to endorse their man and give legitimacy to their local organizations. In many places, Adams men appealed to popular grievances against men in positions of influence and criticized Clay for being a lawyer and receiving the support of so many lawyers.[12]

On the other hand, the Adams press maintained the "cry of slavery" in a manner that was "loud, vehement, reiterated." One handbill entitled *Clay and Slavery!!* gave a long recital of Clay's role in the Missouri Compromise, which, it insisted, threatened the extension of slavery even into Ohio. If that happened, the state would be swamped by a rapidly growing "black population" and, within sixty years, forced "to participate in similar scenes of horror with those that have formerly been experienced in St. Domingo and Guadeloupe, which may gracious Heaven avert!" Adams was the only candidate "opposed to the extension of involuntary servitude," which, together with his experience, record of service, and "unblemished moral character," made him the ideal president for "a moral and religious people." Negrophobic overtones did not contradict the appeal of antislavery principle in the Ohio of the early 1820s.[13]

In southwestern Ohio, Adams carried those communities that were dominated by churches renowned for their uncompromising attitude to slavery, like the old Scottish denomination of Seceders, the Quakers, and some Presbyterian and Baptist congregations. In the main center of Quaker settlement in eastern Ohio, the Friends were said to "nauseate so greatly at slavery in Clay" and refused "to sacrifice principle at the shrine of WESTERN interest." Elsewhere, the "most active and persevering" support for Adams came from "emigrants from the New England states, who have not resided in the country long enough to divest themselves of sectional partialities," especially in communities that were islands in the midst of non–New Englanders. In Cincinnati, by 1822, cultural self-consciousness had distinctly sharpened among the New England community, which comprised about 30 percent of the town's population: measuring themselves against "the irish rabble" and "the antient inhabitants," they wanted "to mount the stalking horse slavery" in order to get a Northern president.[14]

But on the Western Reserve in northeastern Ohio, where New Englanders overwhelmingly predominated, a real dilemma was evident. According to the *Painesville Telegraph,* many local voters abandoned "their attachments to Mr. Adams, after more mature deliberation on the probable effects of his administration with regard to the interests of the western . . . states." Consequently, Clay ran much better on the Western Reserve than anticipated: whereas the Adams men had expected to win three-quarters of its vote, Clay won absolute majorities or a large plurality in four Yankee counties that might yet have the great Ohio canal built across them.[15]

In fact, in every county on the proposed routes of the Ohio canal or of the National Road, Clay usually won absolute majorities. He did well too in the backward and underpopulated hill counties of the southeast and in the newly opened northwestern counties. His supporters argued that his plurality (38.49 percent) gave a less valid indication of his popularity than the fact that he carried far more counties by an overwhelming margin than did his two rivals between them. Apparently many supporters in the interior counties were so convinced of his coming triumph that they did not bother to vote.[16]

Clay would have romped home had he been the only Western candidate. Jackson's advocates insisted that their man was as sound on the American System as Clay, while Clay's protagonists pointed to the support Jackson received from among the strongest antitariff men in the nation; they insisted that it was folly to divide the American System vote because the only beneficiary would be Adams. However, the Jacksonians knew that Clay was unelectable in some populous constituencies and believed that a large enough turnout in those areas could carry the state.

The center of Jackson's strength lay in Cincinnati, which had long served as the market and the source of news for an extensive area covering southwestern Ohio, southeastern Indiana, and adjoining parts of Kentucky. The whole metropolitan area had shared in Cincinnati's financial and economic collapse and had suffered again from the new recession that hit Cincinnati by May 1824. After the collapse of the Clinton and Calhoun campaigns, Jackson's popularity spread with a speed that amazed observers. As one Yankee visitor exclaimed in April, "Strange! Wild! Infatuated! All for Jackson! His victory at New Orleans was not more unaccountable than his political success is becoming. Two-thirds here are said to be for Jackson. But, surely, in February last, his name was not mentioned *in the Miami country*." By June Charles Hammond acknowledged that "Jackson here is all the rage—He is making innroads [sic] upon Clay almost entirely."[17]

As ambitious and disappointed politicians jumped on board the bandwagon, county and township meetings through the metropolitan area declared for Jackson and by late June had organized some influential county committees. Some newspapers shifted to Jackson and new ones started, but the Jackson press was always at a disadvantage compared to its rivals. Yet the demand for Jackson spread through these counties regardless of what local influential men and newspapers might say. Meetings called by the friends of Clay and Adams were often carried in favor of Jackson by overwhelming votes. In some counties "prominent men" found that "for once they have but little influence." According to one eve-of-election report, "*Tickets, handbills and pamphlets are in circulation here for Clay, direct from Cincinnati, but they are as uncurrent with our Farmers and Mechanics*" as the notes of discredited banks. Clearly the Jackson cause was almost irresistible among Western farmers who wanted internal improvements but resented Clay.[18]

# NATIONAL NOMINATION.

# THE PEOPLE'S TICKET.

### Gratitude, Glory, Pat___am!

## FOR PRESIDENT,
# ANDREW JACKSON.

Recommended to the People of the United States, by his Pure Democratic Principles, Stern Integrity, Long Experience, Eminent Talents, and Transcendent Services to his Country.

"Freemen, cheer the Hickory Tree,    O'er Freedom's Land its branches wave,
In storms its boughs have shelter'd thee;    'Twas planted on the Lion's Grave."

## FOR VICE PRESIDENT,
# JOHN C. CALHOUN.

The People's Ticket. Endorsement of Jackson in the Cincinnati Advertiser, June 23, 1824. As the election approached, such notices would also include the names of the electoral ticket committed to Jackson.

At the state level the Jacksonians faced a real organizational difficulty, which they solved by calling a state convention to meet in July in Columbus. Though thinly attended and denounced as a "farce," the convention named a ticket and a state committee of correspondence. However, they continued to depend for their organizing drive on politicians from their area of greatest concentrated strength, in southwestern Ohio, who through the late summer encouraged further organization in parts of central and eastern Ohio. Their efforts were, however, impeded by faulty information, as when they sent expensive packages of pamphlets and handbills to violent opponents.[19]

Despite organizational failings, Jacksonian activists knew that there was a great constituency for the General among the ethnic groups that had flooded into eastern Ohio from Pennsylvania during the previous twenty years. The Scotch-Irish, who were numerically predominant in the counties near Steubenville, gave "the immortal . . . hero" decisive absolute majorities. The Pennsylvania Dutch, whether on the belt of rich farming land that lay just south of the Western Reserve or in the more scattered German-speaking communities of central and southwestern Ohio, also gave substantial votes to Jackson. Attracted by his apparent republican simplicity, they were also deeply antagonistic to their New England neighbors in Ohio. Both Pennsylvania Dutch and Scotch-Irish could regard the victor of New Orleans as not only defending his country against English influences but also symbolizing the political virtue of Americans who were not of English stock.[20]

Clay was shocked by the narrow result in Ohio. He blamed his shortfall in votes on rumors that Clay electors would give their votes in the Electoral College to Crawford, the one absolutely unacceptable candidate.[21] In fact, Clay underestimated how extensively his unpopularity in Cincinnati had percolated into the city's hinterland, and he had ignored the Scotch-Irish and Pennsylvania Dutch in the state. Indeed, Jackson might well have carried Ohio in 1824 if the populous eastern counties had been better organized, their voters more aroused, and the level of turnout there not so disappointingly low—but the same might also be said of Clay's strongholds in the interior.

## VALLEY OF DEMOCRACY

Ohio's experience was replicated to some extent in every state in the Ohio Valley. In Indiana and Illinois a similar three-way fight played out in different electoral contexts. South of the river things were different partly because both Kentucky and Tennessee had favorite sons in the race, but also because Adams was not a serious contender there. Across the Mississippi, the new, lightly settled frontier state of Missouri proved in many ways a clone of Kentucky. However, everywhere, as a Yankee settler in Indiana remarked in December 1823, the presidential election became "the topic of the legislatures in each state, the hobby of every newspaper, and the chit chat of the counting room of the merchant, the bar room of the inn, the fireside of the farmer, and the workshop of the mechanic."[22]

In Indiana, early efforts were made to build up a Crawford party through land office and banking influence, but by 1823 the political class in general, including the Virginia group around the old territorial capital of Vincennes, recognized that local demand for internal improvements made Clay the obvious candidate. There is little evidence of organization before January 1824, when the legislature opted for the general ticket rather than a district system, in the state's first popular election for president. The first positive move came from the Adams men, who in April announced their electoral ticket, which had allegedly been named by his friends in the legislature in a secret caucus. By contrast, Clay's friends held various local meetings and formed some committees of correspondence, out of which emerged their electoral ticket, though not without overlap and confusion. The Jackson men faced similar difficulties deciding on their ticket because local meetings nominated conflicting lists, but they decided to follow the suggestion of the one Jackson newspaper, the Vincennes *Western Sun,* that they hold a state delegate convention in Salem in September. This thinly attended meeting agreed on a unified ticket, established a state central committee, and urged counties to establish their own correspondence committees and township vigilance committees. Three thousand copies of the ticket and 500 copies of an approved address were printed.[23]

The Adams men mounted an energetic campaign and gained the endorsement of half Indiana's newspapers. They defended Adams against the Clay men's claims that he was a Federalist at heart. They stressed that for voters to prefer Clay over Adams, "they must first learn to disregard all distinction between right and wrong—between freedom and slavery." Initially they emphasized that the debates over Missouri had "too forcibly illustrated" the dangers of slavery "to be obliterated from the public mind in so short a period"; in time, the issue broadened into the choice between a man of moral probity and "a plain old-fashioned slave holder" who "would use his influence to extend the blessings of slavery to every part of his government." They were helped by calls for a new state constitutional convention by those suspected of aiming to introduce slavery into Indiana, but Adams carried only those counties in eastern Indiana that were dominated by Quakers. Though in general he ran better in county seats, overall he came third, with less than 20 percent of the total vote. Compared to Ohio, the northern part of Indiana had scarcely been opened to settlement and the state had a relatively small Yankee population.[24]

Jackson was increasingly attacked along the same lines as Clay, with the added warning of the dangers posed by military chieftains. These essentially personal attacks were countered by the standard appeal to those cynical about the virtues of national politicians:

> Has he been to Europe? Has he ever bowed in the halls of royalty? Has he ever kissed a king's hand or a pope's toe? Has he ever played cards with royal dukes, dined with nobility, or intrigued with queens or princesses? Has he ever figured in a caucus, or rioted on the spoils of the public treasury?

Not surprisingly, straw polls taken at militia gatherings usually favored Jackson, with Clay ahead of Adams. However, the General's appeal proved most overwhelming in those older and more developed parts of Indiana that were dependent commercially and culturally on Cincinnati and Louisville, including their former banking services. These populous areas of south-central and southeastern areas of the state had been deeply affected by the economic collapse and hardship suffered by their metropolises, and they quickly caught their Jackson fever. Significantly, the counties closest to Louisville and Cincinnati saw not only Jackson win, but a low Adams vote push Clay into third place.[25]

Overall, Jackson won 7,447 votes (47 percent), Clay 5,318 (33 percent), and Adams 3,093 (20 percent). As in Ohio, Clay carried more counties than Jackson, running well in the western and less developed central part of the state. Clay did best on and near the Wabash and the West Fork of White River, possibly because of the internal improvement issue. The disappointing turnout—blamed by some on the "very bad" weather—may suggest that Clay's supporters in his strongholds underestimated the Jacksonian threat, but Clay himself once more blamed the rumors of a deal with Crawford for his disappointing showing in a state that had originally been counted for him. Indiana's five electoral votes would have made a critical difference later on.

Illinois also proved disappointing for Clay, where he came third in a most atypical popular election. From spring 1823 until summer 1824, this new state was obsessed with the struggle to decide whether a new constitutional convention should be called that would probably legalize slavery, which already existed de facto within the state. Since before statehood, Illinois had been dominated by Republican officeholders and land speculators who had guided Illinois along a proslavery route through the Missouri crisis. But then the notion that slavery could be officially extended into Illinois itself roused popular passions at home in what became "a long, angry, bitter, and indignant contest." As the later governor Thomas Ford recalled,

> The rank and file of the people were no less excited than their political leaders. Almost every stump in every county had its bellowing indignant orator on one side or the other; and the whole people for the space of eighteen months did scarcely anything but read newspapers, hand-bills and pamphlets, quarrel, argue, and wrangle with each other whenever they met together to hear the violent harangues of their orators. . . . The question of slavery was thoroughly discussed. The people took an undivided and absorbing interest in it; they were made to understand it completely . . . [producing] one of the most bitter, prolonged and memorable contests which ever convulsed the politics of this State.

On a steamy summer day in August, over 80 percent of Illinois voters— many having ridden long distances—went to the polls, and virtually 57 percent of them voted against the proposed convention and slavery. In comparison, the presidential election in November attracted a turnout of only 33 percent.[26]

To add confusion to distraction, the state assembly adopted a district system for the presidential election, but Governor Edward Coles did not announce the composition of the three districts until September. There is little evidence of a sustained campaign across the state for any candidate, and organization within each district was either perfunctory or nonexistent, though Jackson won endorsement from some county meetings. The older factions in the state were each divided within themselves by the presidential contest. In the August congressional elections, the Crawfordites made "extraordinary exertions" (but unsuccessfully) to block the reelection of the incumbent antislavery man, Daniel Cook, whose support for Adams could become critical in the event of a House election. In the presidential contest itself, each of the three districts suffered confusion over electoral candidates: too many were self-nominated, and it was not always clear which the followers of particular presidential candidates should concentrate their votes on. In the first district, James Turney stood as a "Jackson–Clay" candidate in opposition to Adams, even though there were already candidates for both Jackson and Clay; Turney was widely denounced as a closet Crawfordite because he had been nominated by a district convention of "Democratic Republican delegates." Although there are no signs of formal nominating machinery on the Adams side, his was the only campaign to put up a single candidate for elector in each district.[27]

Overall, Adams won the popular vote, with a plurality of 1,541 votes to 1,272 for Jackson and 1,047 for Clay, winning significant support from among the state's Southern majority. However, Adams piled up his lead in the first district, with 1,063 votes compared to 630 for the ambiguous James Turney, 343 for the Clayite, and 109 for Jackson's two candidates. In both the other districts, Jackson won the plurality, with Clay second in one and Adams in the other. Jackson thus won two of the three electoral votes even though he gained only 27 percent of the popular vote compared to Adams's 32 percent.

Did Adams do so well because of the preceding dispute over slavery in the state? Apparently no newspaper or presidential advocate, including supporters of Adams, made any connection publicly between the two contests. Yet all the identifiable Adams men who had taken a public stance on the convention question had opposed slavery, whereas very few of his opponents had. The first district covered most of the middle counties that in the previous two years had, it is thought, received an accelerated immigration of nonslaveholders from North and South and had certainly voted heavily against the convention. The district's Adams vote depended on considerably more than Yankee settlers, since it also included Madison County, across the Mississippi from St. Louis, a richly endowed, rapidly growing, highly populated, farming county in Illinois's American Bottom which contained relatively few slaves; though Southern settled, the county gave a large majority against the convention and almost half its votes to Adams. The popular vote for the Northern candi-

date in Illinois undoubtedly correlated with a raised antislavery awareness, and the extraordinary efforts of the anticonvention forces deserve
credit for the creation of an Adams constituency.[28]

The slavery dispute also had an adverse effect on the Clay campaign.
Initially the argument in Illinois had been between federal officeholders
who backed Crawford and Calhounites associated with Ninian Edwards,
Calhoun's brother-in-law. Then the slavery issue had divided the factions
in 1824, and differences on federal issues focused on the reelection of
the antislavery congressman Daniel Cook in August. By the time the
slavery issue had been decided and Clay could think of establishing a
campaign in Illinois, his thunder as the Western candidate was already
being stolen by Jackson. Instead, an effort was made in the press to eat
into Adams's support by presenting Clay as "the friend of universal freedom in all nations and all colors, and a strenuous friend for the gradual
. . . amelioration of the condition of the unfortunate blacks in our country." While Clay's vote was divided between the three districts, Jackson
did best in the most southerly counties of the state, which fortuitously
straddled two electoral districts.[29]

There was no possibility of Adams attracting as much popular support
in the adjacent slave states. In Missouri frontier politics were dominated
by conflicting land interests between French claimants under Spanish
law and new American claimants. Here too the presidential contest tran-
scended older divisions because of the strong Kentuckian influence, the
interest in internal improvements, and "the obligations" that Clay's "exertions [in the trials of statehood] have imposed on Missouri." Even the
state's senatorial pomposity, Thomas Hart Benton, gave up his initial
favorite, Crawford, to help engineer an early legislative nomination for
Clay and devoted the summers of 1823 and 1824 to stumping the state
for him. "This state," wrote an Adams editor on the eve of the election,
"is *betrothed* to Clay," though Adams did find some vocal support in populous and ethnically diverse St. Louis—especially in the city center and
among wealthy merchants from both older factions—and in affluent
Cape Girardeau. Clay won by a landslide two of the state's three electoral
districts, those up the Mississippi and Missouri valleys, and gained a
plurality in the third. Overall, Jackson attracted one-third of the popular
vote, doing well in some sparsely populated western counties and running Clay close (with 317 votes to Clay's 327) in the swampy country of
southeastern Missouri.[30]

Clay's favorite-son status was even more pronounced in Kentucky, but again Jackson found some sources of support. Clay carried the state— and each of its three multimember electoral districts—with about 70 percent of the vote or better. His success was almost universal, except on some fringes; he did just as well in the less well-endowed country south of the Green River as in the affluent Inner Bluegrass around Lexington. Jackson found his most numerous support in the Louisville area and in Campbell County across the Ohio from Cincinnati, but he won absolute majorities also in the Appalachian counties of eastern Kentucky and in the Jackson Purchase—secured from the Chickasaws only in 1818—on the banks of the Mississippi. These counties at opposite ends of the state had been created since 1820 and reflected the tendency for Jackson to do proportionately better in counties that had received more recent arrivals in the previous decade. Though unable to shake Clay's statewide command in 1824, four years later, these metropolitan and frontier footholds would provide—in Kentucky as elsewhere in the Ohio Valley—the basis for a spectacular overturn.[31]

The election in the Ohio Valley states, broadly defined, had demonstrated the power of the grass roots: political leaders found that they could not presume on the loyalty of their traditional supporters, and many shifted to follow their followers. In Illinois, for example, the triumph of antislavery persuaded the leaders of the convention cause to change policy because otherwise "every bob-tailed lad that could lisp his opposition to slavery might ride into office over the heads of men of talents and respectability."[32] The strength of each candidate was heavily regionalized within each state, according to settlement patterns and local interest in roads and canals. Organization tended to be strongest where backed by most popular support, but the Jackson and Adams campaigns were energetic enough to try to win support even in unpromising areas. Much the same would be true in the smaller states of the Middle Atlantic region, but in a very different political context.

### PARTIES OF THE MIDDLE STATES

As the giant Mid-Atlantic states moved beyond popular contention, so the presidential focus shifted to the minor players in the region. Unlike the Ohio Valley states, New Jersey, Delaware, and Maryland had all been deeply and evenly divided by the passions of the First Party System, the schisms of wartime, and the persistence of old rivalries. The appeal of the Democratic Republican Party remained strong, but so did the newer attractions of the American System. Right up to the eve of the election, some thought that Henry Clay would do well here, especially if he could make a local deal with one of his rivals, but he never developed an effective apparatus or elicited much response. Instead, the contest focused initially on the rivalry between Crawford and Calhoun and finally on that between Jackson and Adams, with Crawford's partisans running interference.

In New Jersey, a middle state of middling electoral weight (with eight votes), the presidential contest proved absolutely disruptive of existing patterns. Previously the home of one of the most highly organized Democratic Republican political machines, by the early 1820s the party focused essentially on the distribution of patronage by the state legislature. In several counties protests against excessive political management had seen the creation of independent bipartisan coalitions, but elsewhere old party lines held firm and politics remained competitive. The state was racked by sectional tensions between the south/west and north/east, which prevented the passage of constructive legislation. These differences were reinforced by the powerful external influences of Philadelphia and New York City, which some thought threatened the distinctive character of the state.[33]

Initially the state had been counted for Crawford as the likely regular Republican candidate, but Calhoun mounted an effective nationalist challenge under the careful guidance of his friend and Cabinet colleague, Samuel Southard. Clay too initially found support in the state's chief manufacturing center, Essex County, including a newspaper in Paterson, but his light soon flickered. The main opposition came from Adams, who had a strong appeal among both regular Republicans and the Quaker population of West Jersey; half the congressional delegation declared for him. The Jackson campaign began with an organizational initiative in Salem County by the New Yorker Samuel Swartwout, but it had little effect until Calhoun's cause collapsed in Pennsylvania early in 1824 and his partisans there urged their New Jersey colleagues to shift to Jackson. From nowhere, Jackson became a popular candidate, his military claims enhanced by Lafayette's visits to the Revolutionary battlefields in the state in the weeks preceding the election.

On September 1, Swartwout chaired a Jacksonian convention at Trenton that attracted men of both old parties from eight counties and drew up an electoral ticket consisting of five Republicans and three Federalists. The Adams and Crawford men, not unreasonably, branded the Jackson campaign as an amalgamationist device designed to help Federalists back into office. The issue of the Lowrie correspondence spilled over into New Jersey, but here too, rather than cast doubt on the General's Republican credentials, it gave Federalists reason to hope that he would end their political proscription.

The Republican label, however, remained as priceless in New Jersey as in Pennsylvania. That meant securing nomination by the Republican state delegate convention, which traditionally named the congressional and electoral candidates, all of whom were elected at large. Partisans of the three remaining presidential candidates all attempted to control the county meetings that nominated the delegates. Some meetings could not agree and split; in other counties, two or more Republican meetings named rival delegations. The convention met at Trenton in October and successfully agreed on a slate of congressional candidates, but none of the presidential campaigns enjoyed a majority. As one report said, "*Adams, individually,* was the most powerful; but the Crawford men came over to the Jackson party." This coalition settled disputes over membership to their own advantage and then named an electoral ticket consisting of five Jacksonians and three Crawfordites.[34]

The Adams group promptly walked out and held their own meeting. They confirmed the regular convention's congressional nominations but selected a rival electoral list committed to Adams. They accused their opponents of perverting the "the long established usage by which all other Republican conventions for the period of upwards of twenty years": they had allowed Federalists to sit and vote in a Republican meeting, they had ignored the privilege of each congressional district to propose its own candidate, and had excluded some Republicans who preferred Adams. No one could therefore be bound by the spurious regular convention's decisions. Accused by supporters of Jackson and Crawford of disrupting the Republican Party, the Adams men insisted that their opponents were destroying it by not allowing the people a free choice of Republican president.[35]

Many Jacksonians disapproved of the deal with the Crawfordites because the resulting ticket omitted the Federalist candidates from the earlier ticket. Within a week a new Jackson public meeting in Trenton had revised the ticket so as to exclude the Crawford men and reinstate at least one Federalist. The Jackson men energetically distributed the new tickets and discredited the compromise version, while the Crawfordites had little choice but to back the compromise in the hope of three electoral votes. They had bet on the old forms of the Democratic Republican Party, but they lacked the grassroots support to respond effectively when their opponents demonstrated that the old forms were now powerless.

By September Jackson was "all the cry" in the state. His campaign benefited from organization built up earlier by the Calhounites, especially in the southern part of the state, as well as the energetic involvement of Federalist leaders eager to break the Republican mold. Some reports claimed that those who preferred Clay also turned to Jackson, presumably because of his American System votes. Only one newspaper supported Jackson, compared to the overwhelming advantage that Adams had among the press.[36] However, the Adams men were even less well prepared for the contest than the Jacksonians; they did not finalize their electoral ticket until two weeks before polling day. In the end, the exclusive ticket of the Jacksonians carried the state with 9,283 votes, or 49 percent of the total vote, and majorities in half the counties, while the Adams men won 8,363 votes, or about 45 percent of the total. In addition, the top five Jacksonian candidates garnered an extra 1,216 votes each because their names were also on the Crawford ticket, which won less than 6.5 percent statewide but did rather better in counties still marked by ticket voting on old party lines in local elections.

The disappointing feature of the election was the low level of turnout—much lower than in the state and local elections one month earlier. In the old days, under the First Party System, New Jersey had played an innovative role in developing the use of committees, delegate conventions, and all the devices for stimulating voter turnout. In the November election of 1824 the old imperatives still worked in the at-large congressional election, and the Republican ticket was elected "without opposition."[37] However, in the presidential election held at the same moment, much confusion reigned: the campaigns were not certain where their strength lay, especially as the Jacksonians combined Federalist organizers with an appeal to traditional Republicanism. That sense of confusion may explain why many voters sat out the presidential election in New Jersey.

Delaware and Maryland maintained the same old party competitiveness as New Jersey but differed in their view of slavery and sectional issues. Both states retained Federalist strongholds, and regular Republicans traditionally followed the congressional nomination for president. As a result, according to the *New-York American* in March 1823, "Maryland and Delaware are counted on for Mr. Crawford, but we much suspect on the same grounds that have led his partizans [sic] into error with regard to other states, whose votes it has been supposed might be secured by gaining a few leading politicians, without consulting the inclinations of the people." In Delaware the contest would be decided in the state legislature, but Maryland now allowed a popular vote on a district system that gave seven districts one elector and two districts two.[38]

The Maryland Federalist Party had divided bitterly over the War of 1812 but had remained competitive. For all intents and purposes, it ceased formal operations in its own name after 1821, when it lost its postwar control of the state senate. The Republican Party survived as an office-holding machine but lost much of its authority at the county level as coalitions of independents and Federalists opposed all caucus nominations. The Crawford cause, led by General Samuel Smith, could not overcome popular antagonism to party dictation, and by July 1823 Smith was predicting that his own involvement would "probably sink my popularity, for *Maryland is against Crawford.*" The state was too interested in positive government programs to support a Radical program of retrenchment. The nationalist alternative was vigorously pressed by the Calhoun men, led by the former prowar Federalist Virgil Maxcy, who by late 1823 had built a network of supporters on the Eastern Shore as extensive as in Pennsylvania and the Carolinas.[39]

Baltimore—rapidly growing, commercial, and Democratic Republican—had long provoked a rural resistance that invigorated Federalist strength in outlying areas. Since 1815 the city had suffered an economic decline that was compounded by a severe banking collapse. The old merchant elite lost its prestige and influence amid undoubted evidence of corruption and speculation, which made the Panic even more destructive of social relationships. Rival elites began to emerge in the city as it rapidly industrialized, and at the grass roots, hardship and resentment among the working classes provided a fruitful seedbed for a popular Jackson movement. As early as October 1823 the future novelist (and Calhounite) John Pendleton Kennedy saw signs that the city's populace "would be in [Jackson's] favour two to one over every other candidate." With the collapse of Calhoun in Pennsylvania in March 1824, Jackson became ostensibly the most formidable candidate in the state.[40]

By 1824 Jackson's main opponent was Adams, who enjoyed the support of Republicans connected with the state administration. They took the lead in naming electoral candidates for Adams in the various districts. The Jacksonians followed suit and in Baltimore called a citywide convention. The statewide election proved very close, with Adams just narrowly beating Jackson by about 164 out of over 32,000 votes. However, thanks to the vagaries of the districting system—and the failure of the Adams men in the second district to unite on a single candidate—Jackson finished up with seven electoral votes to Adams's three and Crawford's one.[41]

In these states, the General's great appeal, especially to out-of-favor politicians, was his independence of party control. Roger B. Taney, who had led the prowar Maryland Federalists, thought Jackson honest, independent, and "not brought forward by any particular class of politicians, or any sectional interest. He is not one of the Secretaries. He is taken up spontaneously by the people, and if he is elected will owe obligations to no particular persons." In New Jersey, Federalists had long objected to a Republican machine politics that manipulated the electoral system so as to bar Federalists from public office. The consequence, they believed, was the creation of a self-serving political aristocracy, headed by the Cabinet members who were now trying to monopolize the presidency. Federalists who at one time believed office should be reserved for men of education, social position, and political experience now urged the voters to take their president "from your own body, untainted by the corruption of a court, and uninitiated in cabinet secrets." Electing "the last of the Revolutionary Patriots" would remove existing partisan detritus and offer a route back into national politics and officeholding for former Federalists and independent Republicans.[42]

Regardless of how politicians divided, in both New Jersey and Maryland Jackson tended to win votes in traditionally Republican and Adams in old Federalist counties. This correlation arose largely because some distinctive ethnocultural groups that historically preferred the Republicans favored Jackson, while the formerly Federalist Quakers wanted a nonslaveholding president. In New Jersey, Jackson did well in the northern counties, especially those adjacent to Pennsylvania and those settled by German, Dutch, or Scottish farmers. Adams carried nearly all the Quaker counties in West Jersey, from Trenton to Cape May, as well as the conspicuously New Englander counties in the northeast, including rapidly growing commercial and industrial Essex County. Overall, former Federalists divided between the two candidates, though they attained more prominent roles within the Jackson campaign.[43]

In Maryland, Jackson ran particularly well not only in Baltimore but also in the counties that were more diverse ethnically, religiously, and economically, and less involved in slaveholding. Adams could not rival

Jackson in Baltimore itself but beat him by 506 votes in the surrounding rural area, while Crawford won only nine votes in the whole district. Otherwise, Adams did best in the old English-settled, Anglican, and slave-holding strongholds in southern Maryland and on the Eastern Shore; as in Virginia and North Carolina, he ran well in the old coastal tobacco areas. In the southern part of the Delmarva Peninsula Adams competed against Crawford with Jackson quite out of the picture, whereas the Crawford ticket was withdrawn in most other counties and the Crawfordites there backed Jackson against Adams. Adams won in Maryland over half of the 22,000 votes he would win throughout the South.[44]

Crawfordite Republicans in Maryland accused their opponents of tacitly favoring the old enemy, but each electoral ticket contained former Federalists, with most on the Crawford and Jackson tickets. Indeed, while Adams did well in some Republican areas, much support for Crawford in the southern parts of both Maryland and Delaware conspicuously came from Federalists even though he was "par excellence *the* democratic candidate." Overall, traditional loyalties had little effect on the choice of sides throughout these states in 1824, amid what a long-established New Jersey newspaper described as the "general breaking up of the old parties of Federalists and Republicans."[45] The new voter formations of 1824 promised to become the bedrock of new national parties in both New Jersey and Maryland, whereas the more dramatic events in North Carolina in 1824 would turn out to have less effect on future alignments after 1825.

### A PEOPLE'S COALITION

Traditionally a satellite of Virginia, North Carolina had always taken its lead from Richmond. Its support for Crawford seemed certain in December 1823: the North Carolina delegation in Congress favored both him and a caucus nomination, and his friends quickly established their control of the state legislature in December. He had many local opponents, but they were divided between Calhoun, Adams, and Jackson; Clay's thunder had been entirely stolen by Calhoun. Because opposition was futile as long as it remained divided, the logic of the state's general ticket system encouraged the elements of opposition to combine behind a coalition ticket. Only in North Carolina did such a move work in 1824, in a way that might have been expected to be tried more widely, notably in Virginia itself.[46]

The first critical struggle in North Carolina was to determine the rules of the game. In 1812 the state party's leaders had replaced the district system used since 1796 by a legislative election in order to ensure that the state's electoral vote was not divided; then in 1815 they had adopted the general ticket system. In December 1823 the Calhounites, recognizing the regional nature of popular support on both sides, argued that the state should adopt a district system once more, but their effort was repelled in the House of Commons, 78–45. Simultaneously, the leading Calhounite, Charles Fisher of Salisbury, brought forward legislative resolutions to prevent central control of the nomination process; these condemned not only the congressional caucus but also state electoral nominations by a legislative caucus, at a time when overrepresentation of the eastern counties virtually ensured Crawfordite ascendancy. After long debate, the Fisher resolutions were indefinitely postponed, 82–46, but not before giving public exposure to the populist antiparty arguments of the anti-Crawford men. Finally, on Christmas Eve, a caucus of slightly under half of the legislature's members named an electoral ticket dedicated to Crawford, but without establishing Crawford's claim to represent the old party. The managers made the mistake of directing the invitation to attend the caucus not to all Democratic Republicans but to "Mr. Crawford's friends alone."[47]

The Calhoun men early recognized the need to combine with other opponents of Crawford in order to destroy "the yoke of proud Virginia." In July 1823 one observer noted that Adams had "a good many friends" in the state but was informed that "the friends of Calhoun & Adams will go Together Generally." By the year's end, Jackson's supporters, lacking confidence in their ability to carry the state and fearing above all the influence of the "caucus system," favored joint action with the Calhounites to overcome "a corrupt system of government." In January Fisher proposed a coalition ticket that would give Adams one vote, Jackson five, and Calhoun nine, on the understanding that if Calhoun withdrew, his friends would all vote for Jackson. To overcome Jacksonian reluctance, the Calhounites agreed to drop Calhoun's name and call it the People's Ticket. Every effort was then taken to have the ticket's candidates chosen incrementally by spontaneous popular meetings in the various counties, though the hand of a secret Calhoun committee in Raleigh was said to lie behind most meetings.[48]

The main threat to the cooperative effort came from the rapid expansion of Jacksonian support. Jackson's henchmen in Tennessee had found a North Carolina ally in the summer of 1823 in the old Federalist leader William Polk, who was attracted by the evidence that Jackson "would not proscribe and persecute the Federalists because they differ with him in opinion." Since then Polk had been working for Jackson in North Carolina, but there was little sign of an organized Jackson movement until after the legislative session closed on January 1. At that point some pamphlets advocating his cause were circulated and had a mighty effect on opinion, especially in the western counties. Though the air was "made to ring with the names of the other candidates," by February observers were confident that "General Jackson is decided[ly] the choice of the people." As a result, one key Calhounite in Raleigh found them so *"intoxicated with military glory"* that he feared the Jacksonians would nominate a ticket of their own and so hand the election to Crawford.[49]

The situation changed drastically with news of the Pennsylvania coup and Calhoun's acceptance of the vice presidential slot on the Jackson ticket. Most Calhounites reluctantly followed into the Jackson camp, with little choice now that "it seemed that the people of North Carolina are taking up Jackson, as Pennsylvania did, against their politicians and of their own mere will."[50] In the new situation, it was now agreed that the ticket's electors would vote for whichever candidate stood the best chance of defeating Crawford nationally, though mistrust persisted on both sides. The Jacksonians finally agreed to stick with the People's Ticket when they were allowed to choose the final remaining electoral candidates, and all but three of those already on the ticket gave open pledges to vote for Jackson. The three came from strong Adams districts and took the line that they would vote for the people's preference against the caucus candidate, though two privately agreed that meant Jackson.

The People's Ticket represented a formidable challenge to the old regime. Calhoun had already attracted considerable support in the western counties and around Albemarle Sound with his program of internal improvements, and his friends had built an effective organization, including the support of half the newspapers in the state. However, despite his cerebral appeal, Calhoun could not command raw popular opinion as Jackson could. Jackson's extraordinary appeal was ascribed by some to the high level of ignorance and illiteracy in many rural areas of North Carolina, where the names of national politicians were not well appreciated, whereas "the large majority whom opportunity have debarred from general information are more familiarly acquainted with those actions in the general history of Genl. Jackson which have been of general notoriety, and for which they are willing to promote him." In this vein, a Fay-etteville "retailer of whiskey and onions" named John Martin, who was running for the legislature in 1824 as a Jacksonian, asked his "friends who can read the newspapers" to recommend him "to their neighbor who can't read, particularly to the mechanic and laboring man, and to the friend of General Jackson." In North Carolina, at least, Jacksonism seemed to feed on the high level of illiteracy in the state.[51]

The Crawford men responded to the threat of a united opposition by mounting a vigorous campaign. They utilized all their candidate's strong points: a regular party nomination by Congress of the kind that had given the republic Jefferson, Madison, and Monroe; the support of thirteen out of fifteen North Carolina congressmen and a majority of the state legislature; and an experienced and capable candidate who had risen to eminence solely because of the "strength of his genius." They played down his ill health and circulated exaggerated reports of his re-covery in the fall of 1824. Above all, they emphasized that Crawford's views on public policy corresponded with the state's interests: opposition to the American System, a preference for economical government and low taxation, and a commitment to slavery and strict construction of the Constitution. By contrast, the hotheaded General Jackson was person-ally unreliable and could not be trusted to maintain peace and advance prosperity; he was a nationalist candidate, favoring Calhoun's policies and a protective tariff. In the circumstances, they argued, Adams men would be well advised to vote for the more statesmanlike Crawford, espe-cially as it would stand Adams in good stead in any House election, were Crawford no longer a candidate.[52]

Obviously the Crawford men recognized that the minority of voters who favored Adams could swing the statewide result. Never well orga-nized, the Adams men numbered several thousand and had the support of three newspapers by late 1823—five by the time of the election. They pitched their appeal on Adams's evident qualifications, long public ser-vice, republican manners, and the "stern moral principles" that made him oppose dueling. Some suggested that the selection of a Northern man would remove discontent and strengthen the Union, only to be told that North Carolina could never support "a President from a non-slave holding state." Jacksonian dominance of the People's Ticket made some Adams men fear that their dislike of Crawford was being exploited to trick them into voting, in effect, for Jackson, whom they disliked even more, but their suggestion of a separate Adams ticket fell on stony ground. It appeared that most Adams men, as long-term opponents of the regular Republicans, would opt for the ticket that stood the best chance of defeating the caucus candidate.[53]

The transformation of the presidential election into a two-horse race roused popular interest to almost unheard-of heights. Whereas around Raleigh before March "the great body of the people seemed to take no interest in the election," by April there was "not a farmer in our country but has formed his opinion. . . . We talk of nothing else and think of little besides." Two months later, a Salisbury newspaper reported that "all parties are beginning to feel something like a disgust at the mere mention of the Presidency." Yet, it continued, "It is nevertheless the all-absorbing topic of every circle: the political veteran of the legislative hall, and the novitiate of the school-room—the silver-headed matron and the blooming maiden—the wrinkled beldame, and the ruddy Miss—all, all must have much to say, and much to do in making a president." Little wonder that North Carolina produced the highest turnout in the nation after Alabama and Mississippi.[54]

In the end, the People's Ticket won 56 percent of the popular vote, with 20,148 votes to 15,629 and a majority in forty-two out of sixty-three counties. Crawford carried most of the counties in the eastern section of the state, excluding the coastal counties. This was the most developed part of the state, where plantations grew staple crops for export and possessed the densest slave population. The largest majorities were in the old tobacco country along the Virginia border and in the rice country of lower Cape Fear, where planters well appreciated the economic and political advantages of neo-Antifederalism, but also in three old Quaker counties; clearly many Friends disliked voting, even indirectly, for a dueling military chieftain. The People's Ticket carried the western counties and those bordering on Albemarle and Pamlico sounds—both areas largely underdeveloped and populated by nonslaveholding small farmers—as well as in a belt of counties isolated from Virginia markets in the north, plus more backward parts of the Cape Fear River region in the south. However, the sectional division, though pronounced, did not override older internal differences: old Federalists tended to vote for the People's Ticket as an expression of persisting opposition to partisan Republican predominance.[55]

Not all the People's votes came from supporters of Jackson and Calhoun. In a number of counties, their voters marked their ballot for the Electoral College with the name of their presidential preference, and in the thirteen counties for which returns survive, Adams men supplied about one-third of the People's vote. In Cumberland County, the "stronghold" of Adams sentiment, the New Englander outran General Jackson in the informal vote, thanks mainly to the support of lower-class Scottish settlers. Across the state as a whole, Adams's friends claimed that they supplied between 4,000 and 5,000 of the People's 20,000 statewide total. Some of his supporters therefore argued that five of North Carolina's fifteen electoral votes should be given to Adams, but that was never likely because the Adams men had played only a subsidiary part in developing the ticket, and almost all its nominees were committed to Jackson. Undoubtedly some Adams supporters voted for Crawford—"not that they love Crawford more, but that they love Jackson less"—which suggests the possibility that, had there been three tickets, Jackson might still have won a plurality even as Adams secured a significant minority vote.[56]

The success of the coalition ticket in North Carolina raises the issue of coalition making in other states. To some extent it was seen in New England between Crawfordites and Federalists, but could not remotely threaten Adams's advantage. In some other states, Calhoun's reluctant withdrawal created informal coalitions that redounded to Jackson's benefit. However, the state most akin to North Carolina was Virginia, where the opposition to Crawford was similarly divided into among three candidates: Clay was strong in the few National Road counties, Adams initially the favorite in the western counties, while Jackson found his stronghold in the southwestern corner known as "Little Tennessee." Like North Carolina, Virginia divided regionally over issues of internal improvement, providing a basis for joint resistance to eastern dominance and Junto control.[57]

There were critical differences between the two states. In Virginia the franchise was strictly limited, with about 60 percent of adult white men qualified to vote, compared to about 90 percent in North Carolina. The practice of Virginia politics remained strongly under oligarchical control, even though the state's regular use of oral voting did not apply in presidential elections. It was therefore harder to oppose dominant opinion than in North Carolina, and almost impossible to imagine a popular crusade arousing public opinion in Tidewater and Piedmont Virginia. Crawford's landslide with over 55 percent of the vote seemed inevitable from the start, except to the ever hopeful Clay.

Moreover, the character and circumstances of the various candidacies varied between the two states. In North Carolina the opposition came initially from Crawford's bitterest enemy and then from a reputedly nationalist candidate unacceptable to the neo-Antifederalists. In Virginia the loudest proponent of internal improvements was Clay, who was regarded as a sound Democratic Republican and a potential ally of Crawford's. In April Van Buren had virtually invited Clay to become vice presidential candidate on the Crawford ticket; Clay had hesitated before refusing. In September rumors abounded that Clay electors would vote for Crawford in the Electoral College, which his supporters denied so strongly that the rumors simply gained more currency. Many felt that Crawford's ill health guaranteed his withdrawal—if not soon, then at least before the House voted to settle a hung election. It was strongly in the interest of Clay men, in Virginia as in New York, to ensure that they did not create unnecessary bad blood that might prevent Crawford men from turning to Clay at some stage—and that meant not joining a coalition built solely on hostility to Crawford.

Such a juncture appeared unlikely in Virginia as the popular election approached because the Crawford men disapproved so strongly of broad construction and protective tariffs. Adams appealed partly because he was initially presumed to share the common economic outlook of seaboard interests and partly because he was considered most likely "to harmonize sectional sentiment," though his statements in favor of the 1824 legislation weakened both perceptions. In a situation where Jackson was regarded as entirely unacceptable to Crawfordites, Clay was as well placed as Adams to pick up Virginia's electoral vote. As it was, Virginia divided sectionally between the neo-Antifederalist East and the American System West, with three candidates dividing the West. Clay never managed to break out of his National Road heartland, while Adams, still reluctant to express unqualified support for the American System, found his support in the West and southern Piedmont ebbing away to Jackson. Even so, the West preferred "Adams with no statement" to "Crawford on a platform they disliked," and Adams won over 22 percent of the Virginia's popular vote, compared to less than 20 percent for Jackson and 3 percent for Clay. Whereas coalition had always threatened to win in North Carolina, in Virginia it could have succeeded only if it had persuaded potential but untapped anti-Crawford voters of its enhanced chances of defeating a Crawford landslide.[58]

## ORGANIZATION AND ENTHUSIASM

The politicians of 1824 in Northern and Border states knew perfectly well how to organize campaigns to win popular votes. Most of them had experienced the battles of the First Party System, and even those operating in new Western states had inherited knowledge of Eastern electoral practices. Many Southern states had been insulated from the heightened party passions of 1808–1815, but some, notably in the Southwest, had subsequently participated in boisterous state elections between 1819 and 1822. The historian Richard P. McCormick thought the political organization and campaigning in 1824 fell below the standard seen in state elections earlier, but the transference of those techniques to a presidential election, even in part, could be highly innovative. According to the historian James S. Chase, in 1824 "public meetings in the towns and counties, legislative caucuses, and statewide rallies and conferences, promoted by the friends of the presidential candidates, abounded in unprecedented numbers," giving great impetus for the development of political organization at state and local levels, especially in the contested states.[59]

In states where the result was not in doubt, the tendency was for the campaigns to organize using traditional methods, often relying on legislative caucuses to nominate electoral tickets and electioneering committees. In New England and Virginia, for example, the traditional dominance of arrangements made at the state capital continued, though scarcely needed in the one-sided contest. In contested states, well-established traditional methods could themselves be disrupted, as in New Jersey, or find their authority challenged. Overall, it was the challenging or less favored campaigns that took unusual measures to coordinate their efforts and attract favorable popular notice.

The unpopularity of caucus nominations at all levels encouraged the use of public meetings to demonstrate popular support and to initiate nominations. Though disdained by campaigns confident of their electoral majority, their rivals found the public meeting a vital way of distinguishing themselves from established political machines. In North Carolina Calhounites and Jacksonians alike emphasized that their organization grew out of public meetings, including militia musters and grand juries, which they insisted showed how much support they had from an aggrieved people. Jacksonians in Ohio were privately encouraged to hold local meetings, even "if not more than 10 or a dozen can be found in a county." [60] News of the meetings were widely reprinted in order to encourage action elsewhere. County nominations could be an embarrassment in that they produced a confusing number of candidates and tickets, unless the meeting accepted a nomination made elsewhere or privately agreed upon at the state level. The Clay men in Indiana found that nomination by county meetings could result in the nomination of men unwilling to stand, thus necessitating an embarrassing correction; as one spokesman explained, "The people had to bring about a selection unaided by a Legislative or Congressional caucus—and were of course liable to some misunderstandings previous to its adoption."[61] Elsewhere, meetings named too many (or too few) candidates; such confusions were particularly likely in states such as Illinois that used the district system.

The solution was to call a state delegate nominating convention on the pattern of the county and district conventions that had been regularly used earlier in the middle states and Ohio. The first state conventions ever called to give authority to a campaign for a particular presidential candidate—as opposed to a party convention—were called in 1824 by Jacksonians in Ohio and Indiana. In both states the campaign had little representation in the state assembly, and in any case did not emerge as a major competitor until the legislative session had ended. The Jacksonians summoned bona fide state delegate conventions to meet in July and September, respectively, to name a ticket, appoint a central committee of correspondence, and authorize the printing and circulation of an address to the people. Both were attended by fewer than twenty men and represented less than one-third of the counties in the state; they were far, far less numerous than public meetings held at the same time in the same place by their opponents. The conventions still faced the difficulty of finding candidates to represent parts of the state in which they were not strong, but each served the purpose of establishing an authoritative list of names for their supporters to concentrate their votes on. Both state parties, and their opponents, would follow the precedent in 1828, recognizing that the organization of delegate elections in the counties had the advantage of encouraging early local organization.

The Jacksonians in particular "invited mass participation in the campaign" through rallies and parades, usually in their areas of strength within the contested states. They also took straw votes at militia musters that were supposedly attended by all white men between the ages of 18 and 45. Opponents condemned these polls because they caught impressionable young men in a military context where they were susceptible to

the views of their officers. On such occasions in North Carolina, according to one observer,

> in almost every captain's company the drums were beating and fifes
> whistling for the hero of New Orleans. The officers would treat their
> men, make them drunk, and then raise the war whoop for General
> Jackson. Then the poor, staggering, drunken, and deluded creatures
> would sally forth for the place pointed out for them to vote. The
> result was always in favor of Jackson. I have conversed with some of
> them afterwards who told me they did not intend to vote that way at
> the proper election, they voted so just to please their officers.

The polarizing effect of having to indicate an opinion in public should
not be underestimated.[62]

Polls of all kinds attracted great interest because they gave a clue,
sometimes misleading, of how public opinion lay. Outside North Carolina, militia polls did not always favor the Jacksonians in areas where
other candidates were dominant. Far more balanced were sudden snap
straw polls, whether in grand jury proceedings, on steamboats, at market days, in barrooms, or at July Fourth celebrations, though often they
included people who did not qualify to vote. Of the groups that had no
formal say in the election, women often made their views known privately, and in Pennsylvania, Kentucky, and Indiana they assembled to
register their support for Jackson—in rare surviving examples of the
public involvement of women in the presidential election.[63]

Enthusiasm had to be harnessed, however. Township and ward committees were given the task of ensuring that likely supporters turned
out to the polls and were properly armed with voting tickets. Control
and vigilance at the voting place was, of course, also important. In some
states the election was conducted by officials elected for other purposes;
in others, the first group of people present at the poll were responsible
for electing clerks (or judges) of election. Either way, there seems little
evidence of the management of polling stations leading to disputes or to
complaints about legitimate votes being disallowed or illegitimate ones
permitted. In almost all the states voting was by ballot, which could be
specially printed, clipped from newspapers, or handwritten. Though less
secret than the later officially printed "Australian ballot," the careful voter
could usually conceal from the clerks how he had voted as he slipped his
paper into the locked ballot box. The only state that maintained public

viva voce voting in the 1824 presidential election was Kentucky, and here too there were almost no complaints of external influence on how individuals voted. The main disadvantage of oral voting was that the election dragged over three days, which, because the progress of the vote was known, could encourage voters to stay at home rather than travel to cast a useless vote.

Excitement could boil over and lead to excitable scenes, especially in metropolitan centers in contested states. One rare glimpse comes from Cincinnati, where on voting day a "contrivance" had to be used to control the thronging crowd at the polls: "A carpenter's bench was arranged in front of the window, leaving a narrow passage to admit about two or three at a time." Even so, according to a German resident, no one could get to the polls without being "squeezed almost to death, which means prevented several hundred votes getting in." The Jacksonians tried to crowd close to the entrance to make it easier for their own supporters to get to the polling window, but the Clayites and Adamsites responded by shouting, "Huzza for Jackson!" As a result, "they were soon helped thro' the crowd and some modest Jacksonites who did not huzza were push'd back. Thus they injured their own party."[64]

A similar combination of organization and enthusiasm was applied to fertile ground in North Carolina, where it resulted in Jackson winning his final margin of advantage in the Electoral College. Overall, in the three contested top ten states—Ohio, Maryland, and North Carolina—Jackson won twenty-two electoral votes, over half of those available, compared to Clay's sixteen, Adams's three, and Crawford's one. However, if all three states had been elected by general ticket and the same popular vote cast, Jackson would have slipped to second place with fifteen votes behind Clay's sixteen, while Adams went up to eleven. As it was, Jackson emerged from the general ticket and district elections the clear leader, with eighty-four electoral votes (44 percent), compared to Adams's forty-eight (25 percent), Clay's thirty-three (17 percent), and Crawford's twenty-five (13 percent). However, the popular elections did not decide the national contest in 1824. In the end, the result also depended on the outcome in those states where the legislature retained the power to choose the electors.

# 9 LEGISLATORS TAKE A HAND

In 1787–1788 the authors and ratifiers of the Constitution had assumed that members of the Electoral College would think for themselves in choosing the best man for president. By the time of the Twelfth Amendment in 1804, this assumption had been replaced by a presumption that the job of the electors was just to cast their ballots. That shift reflected a growing skepticism about politicians and representatives, who were thought likely to face irresistible temptations when choosing the chief magistrate; the only control came from the pressure of those who elected them. The growing belief that only the people were incorruptible was, in the long run, fatal to the practice of legislators choosing the electors and made it important to ensure that the popular will was accurately expressed in the election. Proposals for constitutional reform before the 1824 election tried to satisfy these assumptions, but without success. The effort, though, expressed the growing reaction against the signs that in 1824 legislatures were arrogating to themselves control over a decision that most thought should rest with the people. In the end the election marked the virtual end of legislative prerogative in presidential elections, but not until over one-quarter of the electoral votes at stake in 1824—71 out of 261—had been decided by state assemblies.

The attempt to change the election rules arose initially from efforts to introduce a uniform district system across the nation. In 1813 North Carolina congressmen had presented a memorial from their state legislature urging a constitutional amendment to divide the states into districts of equal population, with each district choosing one elector. This would end not only the choice of electors by legislators but also the trend toward the general ticket system: the proposers objected to a winner-take-all system because it exaggerated the power of the large states by disfranchising the dissenting minorities in their midst and gave too much power to the state party leaders who chose the electoral candidates. At the same time it exaggerated state unity and so encouraged sectionalism, because it obliterated the scattered minority interests that held union together. Moreover, the critics argued, the general ticket misrepresented the will of the people by counting minority votes as being in favor of the candidate they opposed, possibly resulting in the election of a president who was supported by fewer than half the voters. Only a district system would more accurately reflect the popular will.[1]

This proposal was renewed almost annually for the next decade, and received two-thirds approval in the Senate in 1813, 1819, and 1822. The House, however, reflected the voting strength of the large states, which were unwilling to reduce their own power; their representatives pointed out that in a hung election, power would shift to the small states, who, thanks to the unit rule in a House election, could equally elect an unpopular president. By December 1823 both chambers were considering the obvious compromise: a uniform district system combined with a replacement for the House election. Proposals that the Electoral College should be abolished ran into the objection that it left no room for settling a hung election. Senator Hayne of South Carolina and Senator Van Buren pointed out early in 1824 that it was better for the final decision to be taken not by legislators but by members of a body chosen for that specific purpose. Together with John Taylor of Caroline, they proposed that the Electoral College should be allowed a second ballot to choose between the two highest candidates. If a tie then resulted, it should be broken by a joint session of House and Senate, with each member voting individually. These constructive proposals not only met the demand that "the President should be elected by a majority, and not a minority, of the people" but also endeavored to preserve the separation of executive and legislative power.[2]

However, this reform effort came too late. Senator Rufus King—a voice from the Philadelphia convention of 1787—argued powerfully that the eve of a contentious election was the worst time to undertake fundamental revisions of the election rules. The Senate agreed and indefinitely postponed all the proposed amendments concerning the presidential election, by a vote of 30–13. In any case, the election was now too close to allow the passage and ratification of a constitutional amendment, the districting of states, and the mounting of focused campaigns in each district.[3]

These urgent efforts reflected a disillusionment with the power that legislatures in general had come to exercise in presidential elections. The Constitution instructed state assemblies to decide how the state's electors should be chosen, to determine how democratic the franchise should be in a popular election, and to organize the conduct of the election in time for the federally prescribed casting of electoral votes. Should they also influence or even decide which presidential candidate the state would vote for? In 1816 and 1820 it had scarcely mattered one way or the other; by 1824 it did matter, and public opinion had decided against the legislatures.

## REDUCING LEGISLATIVE INFLUENCE

In the long run the political influence of state legislatures suffered from the presidential campaign of 1824, but initially many feared that legislators in general were establishing an unprecedented and unjustified degree of control over the process. This was true not only of the congressional caucus but also of the various state legislatures. At the time of the Revolution the assemblies were regarded as the main defense of popular interests against governors who had generally been agents of an external imperialism, but the next generation came to view excessive legislative power as an evil to be counterbalanced by constitutional limitations and independently elected governors. By 1824 the federal government dictated the broad parameters of the timing of the election, but state legislatures determined the mode of the presidential election in their state. Even if they gave the choice to the people, they still usually exercised great influence over the nomination of electors. As regards the nomination of presidential candidates, the development of partisan devices designed to achieve a single national nomination—be it by congressional caucus or, in the case of the Federalists, some other form of national meeting—much reduced the scope of state assemblies to influence their selection. Only at moments of threatened party disintegration, notably in 1808 and 1812, had the occasional state legislature taken it upon itself to name a candidate for the nation.

In the likely free-for-all of the 1824 election, some legislatures were quick to pass caucus resolutions indicating their state's favorite candidate. The prime object was to influence opinion elsewhere but also to discourage dissent within the state. The first, unprecedented step had been taken by South Carolina in nominating Lowndes in December 1821, followed promptly in the West in 1822 when Kentucky and Missouri put down early markers for Clay and Tennessee for Jackson. Clay himself thought in November 1823 that, whatever the objections, legislative caucus nominations were still "the most influential expressions of public sentiment which have been yet employed." Objections to state legislatures speaking for the people were, however, becoming louder, and legislators hesitated to vote for resolutions that their constituents might find presumptuous and undemocratic. In December 1823 Clay's friends in Indiana decided to withdraw their call for a legislative resolution supporting him for exactly this reason. Legislators acknowledged that state assemblies had no constitutional right to express opinions on the choice of presidential candidates, but they insisted that they might properly hold informal caucuses in which legislators could express their preferences in a personal, nonofficial capacity. Given the need to take advantage of those few occasions when appropriate people were gathered together, there was little alternative but to use the meeting of the state assembly; in practice, every candidate in 1824 except Crawford secured at least one state legislative nomination.[4]

The state legislatures swiftly suffered from the backlash against "the caucus system that seems to be growing up in our land." At the national level, Crawford's leading supporters themselves provoked the reaction by giving exaggerated significance to the congressional caucuses of the past. In reality, the caucus had never chosen the Democratic Republican candidate, except perhaps in 1816; usually it had merely rubber-stamped the preeminent candidate who had emerged in informal discussion, whether in the press or between representatives in Washington and their friends and supporters back home. Often its real purpose was to find an acceptable vice presidential candidate. In 1824 great emphasis was placed on following correct procedure, when in fact previous meetings had been marked by informality and their importance had not been emphasized. Senator Samuel Smith of Maryland was regarded as the great authority on past caucuses when in fact he had not himself attended or approved of them all. After the event Smith faced much criticism at home for attending a caucus that was almost universally condemned in

Maryland; his response was to downplay its significance, insist on its informality, and declare that he had acted only in his personal capacity.[5]

In New York Rufus King expressed his anxiety that caucusing had infected the states as well as Congress. In April 1823 he objected when a state legislative caucus at Albany recommended their members of Congress attend the grand nominating caucus in Washington because it in effect extended the powers of state legislators to supervising the behavior of members of Congress. "This irregularity," he thought, impairs the distinct power of our divided Government, and . . . the expectation of a virtuous election of a President . . . must prove visionary." The solution was obvious to this prominent Federalist: "We must choose the electors by the people or the public liberties will be lost." He urged his son to propose that the New York assembly introduce—as it had in 1814— an amendment to the federal Constitution giving the choice of electors to the people. "They cannot be bribed," said the old Federalist, "they are safe agt. corruption: it may not be so if the Legislators choose the elect[or]s."[6]

The Wyoming pamphlets agreed that legislative encroachment at the state level derived from the perverse constitutional practice of allowing legislatures to choose a state's electors. However, widespread press criticism had a huge effect ahead of the election. In May 1823 Hezekiah Niles reported that ten states were due to use that method, but over the next year, four of them decided to allow the people to choose, two by general ticket and two in districts. All four lay in the West—Indiana, Illinois, Missouri, and Alabama—and their constitutions had been established for less than a decade. There had never been any intention of permanently denying the electorate its preeminence in the choice of chief magistrate, and consequently there was no serious argument over the change. Vermont was expected to follow suit, and its failure to do so was blamed on dilatoriness rather than principled resistance.

In many states it was felt that the change would not make much difference. In Missouri the legislature forgot to specify a time for the presidential election, but one newspaper argued that there was no point in calling it back into session just to remedy the omission. If there were no popular election, the choice would revert back to the assembly; then all the people needed to do was insist that their legislative candidates at the state election declare their presidential preference. That way, "the *people's* choice may be as fairly obtained as if they were directly to vote for Electors themselves." In the end, the governor, on dubious authority, announced the date himself, and the popular election was duly held as the new law required. In Vermont, the legislature chose the Adams ticket by a unanimous vote, with many members acting under instructions from their constituents. Certainly local opinion thought that "the result would be the same whether elected by the people or the legislature."[7]

Legislative choice could scarcely pervert the popular preferences of a state if opinion was as one-sided as in Vermont. If opinion was divided, the issue of apportionment became critical: was the assembly a micro-cosm of the electorate? As Niles complained in 1823, the four Upper South states from Delaware to North Carolina retained "the rotten bor-ough system of England," by which "a certain district of country, or space of land," had a representative in the legislature even when it was lightly populated. Thus counties with drastically different sizes of population could have equal numbers of representatives, which in practice meant that the Tidewater counties were overrepresented. Absolutely critical in internal state politics and the election of United States senators, this malapportionment affected the presidential election mainly by giving older areas undue influence in caucuses and the nomination of electoral candidates. The three largest of the four Upper South states had already conceded the election of presidential electors to the people, but in the Lower South the electors were still chosen by legislatures that were de-liberately apportioned to favor the Low Country and its special interests.[8]

## SOUTHERN SECTIONALISMS

The determination of the South Atlantic states to preserve tradi-tional structures arose essentially from their commitment to slavery. As spokesmen for the slave interest frankly stated, whereas statewide popular elections were unpredictable, control of the legislative power could be ensured by a suitable apportionment of seats, and the slave counties needed to be overrepresented in order to ensure political pro-tection. They needed to defend themselves, not so much against the threat of abolition from within the state, as to forestall the temptation for the popular majority to tax slave property inordinately and so prompt slave owners to release their slaves, which could be in no one's interests. Though this consideration was less pertinent in presidential elections, South Carolina and Georgia still retained legislative choice of electors, but in 1824 that did not prevent the accurate expression of the elector-ate's narrowing views on federal relations and national policy.[9]

In both those states the conflict between Crawford and Calhoun remained at the heart of the presidential contest, with each preferring its favorite son. Both conflicts reflected local faction fights, the more conspicuously in Georgia. In both states Jackson complicated the campaign by taking Calhoun's place in the spring of 1824 and introducing his own extraordinary appeal. Although the Lower South remained in deep economic depression, in the course of 1824 the public in both states became more concerned about the issues of sectional defense and white supremacy. Though their choice of presidential candidates differed, in both states the mediation of the legislature reflected local public opinion, producing outcomes in many ways similar to those in the more democratic states of the Southwest.

In South Carolina dramatic events at home rallied opinion around their favorite son at the same time as creating an intellectual problem for the state's nationalists. In June 1822 the Charleston authorities uncovered Denmark Vesey's slave revolt only two days before the planned uprising. Calhoun showed the benefits of federal protection—especially for the one state where slaves formed a majority of the population—when, as secretary of war, he sent a company of federal troops to Charleston "to remove the uneasiness in the public mind." In the racial panic that followed, white South Carolinians looked for outsiders to blame and lighted on visiting free black seamen. In December 1822 the assembly passed a law confining these subversives to jail for the duration of their ship's stay in a South Carolina port—although some of the sailors were citizens of other states and others were the subjects of foreign powers. This inevitably led to protests from Britain, whose black seamen were its main victims. In view of existing treaty protections, federal legal authorities inevitably upheld British protests. Thus by September 1823 South Carolina found itself in dispute with the federal government over an issue that local white folk believed involved their very survival.[10]

Interestingly, South Carolina responded to this challenge not by insisting on a careful reading of the Constitution—which must go against it—but by asserting state sovereignty. The Calhounites did not reverse their nationalist stance; they denied that it could affect the present issue. In the *South Carolina Protest* of December 1824, the assembly would declare that "the duty of the state to guard against insubordination or insurrection among our colored population . . . is paramount to all *laws*, all *treaties*, all *constitutions*." This determination would become more obvious after 1824, when Calhoun would contrive his doctrine of nullification as an ingenious means of giving state sovereignty a plausible appearance of constitutionality. Whereas neo-Antifederalists wished to limit federal power, Lower South nationalists chose to exercise power positively at whatever level. This contradiction of strict construction, as much as personal hostility to Calhoun, would ensure that states' rights men elsewhere refused to support South Carolina in the nullification crisis of 1832–1833.[11]

The conviction that Calhoun could be trusted to defend South Carolina transferred easily in 1824 to the slaveholding Jackson. The states' rights opposition led by former U.S. senator William Smith objected that Jackson had supported the protective tariff and federal internal improvements, which the South Carolina legislature was on the point of declaring unconstitutional; thus Jackson had conceded not only vital Southern economic interests but the only true ground of sectional defense, namely strict construction. This noisy little campaign in support of Crawford had relatively little impact: the presidency was not an issue in the elections to the assembly, and there was little opposition in the legislature to the Jackson–Calhoun ticket, which won 132–25. This margin was so wide that any bias in representation toward the Low Country made little difference.[12]

The white folks of Georgia were every bit as concerned to protect slavery as those of South Carolina, but a racial issue of a different hue overshadowed their politics in the 1820s. The political culture of Georgia also differed in that it accepted democratic presumptions that were still regarded with suspicion in South Carolina. In 1824 Georgia opened its governorship to popular vote and invited its voters to say whether they would like to elect the state's presidential electors; in November they voted overwhelmingly in favor, but that could not affect the current election. Alignments in that election were primarily dictated by the "mountain high" factional struggle between the Crawford–Troup men and the Clarke party. In 1823 the gubernatorial contest was "quiet, but steady and earnest" as Crawford's presidential standing was tested, and in a tense legislative election Troup at last emerged triumphant, by just four votes. The antagonism to Crawford of first Calhoun and then Jackson turned them to the side of William Clarke, who was in any case a warm personal friend of Jackson's. As favorite son, Crawford always had the edge, but Jackson had the advantage on the most urgent issue facing Georgia.[13]

Since the Yazoo settlement of 1802 the federal government had been committed to securing the removal of the Indians from Georgia. When Calhoun's civilization program persuaded Creek and Cherokee to dig in their heels in 1822, the state assembly in December 1823, at Governor Troup's suggestion, unanimously demanded action from the federal government. Ten million acres still remained in Indian hands, and Crawford men blamed the delay on Calhoun. A Cherokee delegation attended Washington to discuss the issue in March 1824 and was received with full diplomatic courtesy befitting a foreign embassy. In return the Cherokees (according to Adams) behaved "like well-bred country gentlemen," and Calhoun even addressed them as "Gentlemen." The Georgia delegation in Congress promptly remonstrated with the president, demanding more positive action to ensure their removal. Monroe publicly disagreed, insisting that the compact did not oblige the federal government to use force, and he refused to do so against the Creek and Cherokee. Crawford's position was not strong on this issue because of his proposal of 1816 that the Indians should not be compelled to move across the Mississippi but instead be allowed to remain as individuals and be absorbed by intermarriage. This amalgamationist suggestion rose to haunt him in 1824, while General Jackson's military and treaty-making record made his position on Indian removal quite clear.[14]

The contest between the two men was well canvassed in the elections to the Georgia assembly. All the candidates were identified as supporters of either Crawford or Jackson, and one ticket representing each side ran in most counties. The result was a clear victory for Crawford and the Troupites, whose votes for the various seats added up to a statewide vote of 19,007 votes, against 13,378 for Jackson and the Clarke men. In the assembly the margin was even greater: perhaps the Troup party's vote was better distributed than Clarke's or benefited from the overrepresentation of slaveholding areas under the 1798 constitution; perhaps sectional identity persuaded some Clarke men to vote for the favorite son. In the end, the Crawford slate won on joint ballot by 121 votes to 45 for the Jacksonians. This triumph for the seaboard statesman over the Western hero was just one in a series of victories that the Troup men were able to inflict on their local opponents between 1823 and 1825, before the state under Troup coalesced behind Jackson and Indian removal, with Crawfordite blessing.[15]

In spite of their reliance on legislative prerogative, the choice of presidential electors in these two states proved as reflective of political trends as in North Carolina or the Southwestern states that had adopted more directly democratic methods of selection. Overall Jackson was the great popular winner in the South, carrying more of the popular vote than all his opponents put together. His support came essentially from small farmers rather than the substantial slaveholders, except in South Carolina, where Calhoun's influence was powerful. On the whole the slaveholding interest preferred others—Crawford on the seaboard and Adams in the Southwest—who were regarded as more sympathetic to states' rights and less attracted to a positive national economic policy. Large slaveholders shared a suspicion of a federal government that might become an agent of Northern demands, and some saw the threat of a protective tariff as reinforcing the lessons of the Missouri crisis. However, views on economic issues differed: tariff protection did not yet rouse universal antagonism; those distant from the seaboard regarded internal improvements as necessary, while those primarily concerned about Indian removal and internal improvements viewed the prospect of a more active government with some enthusiasm. These tactical differences were exacerbated by the existence of favorite-son candidates, as Crawford's appeal in Georgia obstructed Jackson's sweep of the Lower South and revealed the barriers to Southern unity in the early 1820s.[16]

The expression of these differences in the Lower South was not obstructed by the survival of legislative voting in South Carolina and Georgia. Though the systems of apportionment adopted in Georgia in 1798 and South Carolina in 1808 gave a numerical advantage to the Low Country on joint ballot, the choice of electors was not seriously affected. The decision between popular and legislative election made little difference to the expression of public opinion—except in two small but deeply divided states set at opposite corners of the South.

## ROTTEN BOROUGHS

Tiny Delaware and frontier Louisiana differed drastically in character, yet together they helped decide who won the potentially critical third place in the Electoral College. Northern Delaware was penetrated by ideas and interests drawn from neighboring free states and dynamic metropolises, southern Delaware remained part of the old tobacco kingdom, and the state as a whole had become vigorously embroiled in the First Party System. Louisiana, by contrast, retained much of its French character and was a newcomer to the world of electoral politics. In both states legislative malapportionment and close divisions over the presidential contest combined to allow a choice of electors that did not necessarily reflect the wishes of most voters.

Federalism had long enjoyed power in Delaware, partly because it appealed to the conservative rural population in the two southern counties but also because the state constitution gave each of the three counties the same number of seats in each house of the assembly, regardless of population. The party therefore had an advantage in legislative elections that was less clear in the statewide popular elections for governor or Congress, which the Democrats occasionally won. The Federalists insisted on keeping the choice of presidential electors in the hands of the assembly despite Republican complaints. After 1815 party spirit persisted in state politics even as it subsided in national contests: in 1820 the parties competed to elect their own men as electors, but then the victorious Federalists voted for Monroe's reelection.

The northernmost county, New Castle, had a more diverse population, with many Scotch-Irish Presbyterians, and backed the Democratic Party. Their leaders favored economic development and protection for the industry established along the Brandywine. In 1820 this section, together with the Methodists further south, favored restrictions on slavery in Missouri, and the legislature duly passed resolutions instructing and advising their representatives in Congress to vote that way. Three of the state's four federal representatives protested that Congress did not have the power to impose restrictions and insisted that their oaths to support the Constitution must take priority over instructions. Voting in favor of Missouri's admission, they were roundly abused back home by men of both parties, especially in the Wilmington area. However, many Federalists in southern Delaware supported slavery—after two decades of decline, slave numbers had actually grown there since 1810—and their votes ensured the reelection in both 1820 and 1822 of the erring Federalist congressman, Louis McLane, despite the fact that he was associated with northern Delaware's economic interests. By 1824 McLane had turned to Crawford's support, partly out of personal admiration but also because he recognized the importance of states' rights for both the Union and the Chesapeake Bay planters in whose company he increasingly felt comfortable. The states' rights Federalists backing Crawford received strong support in Delaware's old tobacco-growing counties, just as in Maryland's neighboring Eastern Shore counties.[17]

Delaware politicians expressed confidence that public opinion "will be heard and respected" in the choice of electors because the election of representatives would take place so close to the voting for electors, yet in the event the October 1824 assembly elections did not offer clear choices. Adams attracted much support among the Democrats of New Castle County in the north, taking over a good deal of Calhoun's support through common hostility to Crawford, but their county ticket was pledged to support whomever was best placed to beat Crawford, no doubt hoping to appeal to the strong Jacksonian minority in the county. The Federalists were even less clear, with McLane and his friends backing Crawford and some Federalist leaders in Kent County opposing both McLane and Crawford. At this critical moment the county elections were once more fought along old party lines, and the Federalists once more secured control of the legislature. McLane narrowly won reelection to Congress, much assisted by his positive record on canals and protective tariffs.[18]

These results could not clearly reflect opinion on the presidential question. Whereas in a multicandidate general ticket election a candidate might win a popular majority without carrying a single county simply by running second everywhere, in an election for the legislature that same candidate would not elect a single representative or receive a single electoral vote. During the Delaware local elections Jackson was said to be vying with Adams on fairly equal terms, but his supporters elected only a handful of representatives. When the general assembly met, the press reported that fourteen members favored Adams, eleven Crawford, and five Jackson. Many of the thirty members did not feel bound by any prior commitment, and there was much "bargaining and intrigue" among the friends of the three presidential hopefuls. As a result, the election in the assembly showed no clear structure and little ticket voting, though ten members stuck with Adams throughout.[19]

Under Delaware's rules, the two houses voted together, with each legislator casting three votes, making ninety all together. To succeed, a candidate needed an absolute majority, or sixteen votes. On the only ballot held, ten candidates received between three and twenty-one votes each; the leading Adams candidate attracted the most and was immediately elected. The next two highest, both committed to Crawford, received fifteen votes, whereupon the speaker of the senate (who chaired the joint session and had already voted) gave a casting vote for each of them and declared them duly elected too. The members from New Castle County protested that the casting vote was illegal and that only those with a clear majority could be properly elected, but this "most miserable quibble," as the *Delaware Gazette* described it, was defeated with the support of the southern counties. Thus Crawford secured two critical electoral votes that he probably would not have won under a general ticket system.[20]

In Louisiana, by contrast, the commitment to legislative prerogative arose not from a concern to protect slave interest but from the determination of the *ancienne population* to preserve French dominance. The 1812 constitution imposed both a restrictive suffrage that enfranchised only 47.9 percent of adult white men in 1822, and an apportionment of the legislature that underrepresented New Orleans and gave the Creole parishes control. The long-lasting competition between the French-speaking population and newly arrived American settlers reached its all-time peak between 1823 and 1825, as Americans sued to move the state capital from New Orleans and the French proposed excluding the Florida parishes acquired after the West Florida rebellion of 1810. Yet amid talk of possible civil war, the French were internally divided between the ancient Creole population and the French foreigners who had settled in New Orleans over the last twenty years, as well as by long-standing family and factional rivalries. Internecine quarrels equally divided American settlers in both the Red River and Florida parishes. In July 1824 the gubernatorial election would be fought with "unprecedented virulence & ill-temper" in disregard of the national competition, though the presidential campaign had begun to carve its way through the state's complex cleavages.[21]

The one uniting factor in the early 1820s was the state's dire economic situation. The collapse in agricultural prices and the shortage of credit brought deep embarrassment to all producers for the market, while floods and rot destroyed two-thirds of the area's crops. Moreover, the state felt starved of federal care: its defenses had not been strengthened since the near disaster of 1814–1815; New Orleans was the nation's fifth most populous city but it still lacked road connections and a decent mail service; and the area west of the Mississippi needed to improve its navigable streams. The state required a fuller federal court system and sympathetic legal help with its land titles if it was ever to sell its vast public lands—amounting to half the state—to private owners.

As a consequence, Clay initially seemed the only candidate for Louisiana. He had many close contacts in the state, especially with French politicians, and was considered the only national politician concerned about Louisiana's problems. In April 1822 he was assured that he could rely on the support of "the agricultural part of our Community whether creole or American." His American System proved popular among business leaders in New Orleans, and the internal improvements program appealed to planters. The protective tariff was widely condemned in Louisiana as designed to satisfy Northern interests, but high import duties on sugar appealed powerfully in the sugar-growing southwestern parishes. In February 1823 the Clay forces confidently looked for a legislative nomination to establish his preeminence, only to find the assembly unwilling to commit itself so early in the campaign.[22]

The main challenge to Clay came inevitably from the man who had saved New Orleans from British invasion. Jackson had many connections in Louisiana dating back to those days, and his appeal as a "Patriot Redeemer" sang loudly in the New Orleans press. However, his record in dealing with Indians had less appeal in Louisiana than elsewhere in the Southwest, while many Louisianans remembered the insults and injuries that Jackson had inflicted upon French pride during his campaign, the imposition of martial law, and the arbitrary arrests. As a result a vigorous campaign pressed for a third candidate—not Crawford or Calhoun but Adams.

Opponents damned the Adams campaign as initiated by "dependants on the present administration and the expectants for office" and supported by the "few yankee pedlars and school masters stuck in every one of our villages, political priests, and federal lawyers." However, as in southwestern Mississippi and central Alabama, Adams appealed also to commercial centers and cotton planters looking for a safe pairs of hands. In American-settled St. Francisville—the small town on the east bank of the Mississippi that in 1810, for seventy-four days, had been the capital of the Republic of West Florida—an Adams newspaper made the presidential question the "only political subject that occupies much public attention," pressing local candidates to reveal their presidential preference and voters to write the name of their preference on their ballots for state legislators.[23]

Faced by such democratic pressures, Clay's local advocates relied on entrenched Creole strength in the legislature. In March 1823 the Clay men persuaded thirty-four of about sixty members to sign a set of resolutions that praised Jackson but declared Clay the only viable candidate, then tried to pass this off as a legislative nomination. The Jackson and Adams members protested loudly and moved to give the presidential decision to Louisiana's restricted electorate. The Clayites defended the traditional method, knowing that the French members would oppose any surrender of paternalist power. The overlap between signatories of the Clay resolutions and those voting against popular election proved damning: of those whom the press blamed for the outcome, all but three would be defeated in the July elections, thus weakening the Clay cause in the legislature that would make the critical choice.

Though the state election was fought primarily on local issues, in New Orleans the presidential question became central. The city Jacksonians pressed candidates to declare their preference and named a ticket committed to Jackson. Opponents objected that legislators must be allowed free choice and brought forward an Independent ticket made up of four Clay men and two Adamsonians. Working in each ward to bring out their vote, the Jacksonians won four out of six seats and the Independents two, one each for Adams and Clay. Outside of New Orleans and St. Francisville, the presidential contest was not agitated during the assembly elections, and many legislators turned up to its session without the restraint of prior pledges. This apathy was partly due to the comparative lack of newspapers outside of those two places, which between them had seven of the ten presses in the state. Though support cut across ethnic divisions, representatives of the sugar-growing, French-speaking slave parishes of southern Louisiana in general favored Clay, while Jackson had more supporters in the newly developing, American-settled parishes of cotton-growing northern Louisiana and of the Florida parishes. Some well-informed observers were puzzled to decide which of them had won in the state elections: early reports gave it to the Jacksonians, but most historians credit Clay with a narrow popular plurality (perhaps 41 percent to Jackson's 38 percent), though this may well be an optical illusion because the overrepresentation of the French parishes helped Clay win a majority in the assembly.[24]

After the gathering of the legislature, thirty-one (of fifty-eight) members attended a meeting of those who favored Clay, and there were two known supporters still to arrive in New Orleans. Those two never arrived—one apparently was diverted by a challenge to a horse race by an Adams man—and two of the thirty-one were prevented from attending the critical vote by injuries received when their gig overturned. Three more were apparently "seduced" away in the days of dark intrigue preceding the presidential vote.[25] As a result the Clay men were never able to concentrate more than twenty-eight or twenty-nine votes on their man, when thirty (or thirty-two if all sixty-three members attended) were needed to elect. This made the eleven Adams members critical. Clay men were unwilling to deal because they thought that Clay probably needed all Louisiana's five electoral votes to come in the top three nationally. Six Adams men agreed to vote with the Jacksonians in return for two of the five electors; some of the five other Adams men were probably among the thirty-one who had attended the initial Clay meeting. Five successive ballots proved necessary to clinch the Jackson–Adams victory. As an aggrieved Kentucky newspaper observed, the legislative system in Louisiana had given the strongest man in the state no electoral votes, while "the weakest got *two*."[26]

The electoral votes won in these two malapportioned legislatures proved critical for the nationwide election result. Crawford's two electoral votes in Delaware represented half his ultimate advantage over Clay nationally. That would have been more than overcome by the five electoral votes Clay would conceivably have won in Louisiana had the state adopted the general ticket system, in which case Clay rather than Crawford would have entered the House election. As it was, Clay's complete failure to win electors in states south of Kentucky meant that even more rested on the outcome of the New York election, which so many people had for so long seen as the key to the whole presidential election. As Eaton had said in March, the national contest rested "between the Genl & the man who may get N.Y."[27]

## THE PEOPLE'S PARTY

With one-seventh of the nation's population, the Empire State had thirty-five votes on offer, or 15 percent of the whole. After the failure of the electoral bill in March, the decision remained firmly in the hands of the state legislature elected in 1823. Governor Yates caused a brief flurry of excessive passion when he called a special session of the assembly in August to reconsider the electoral law, but Van Buren's Bucktails easily blocked proposals that in effect asked them to hand over their control of the election. The fall campaign would see a gargantuan struggle between the People's Men and the Regency-led Bucktails, but it could now have no direct influence on the outcome of the presidential election. However, the state election distinctly weakened Van Buren's ability to deliver the state to Crawford, as state legislators looked over their shoulders and pondered how the People's Party revolt might affect their future political careers.

Traditionally historians of New York explain the state election of 1824 in terms of Clinton's political martyrdom and an upsurge of popular sympathy that overwhelmed the Regency, but once more the old tale distracts from the real struggle. The People's Men were already a for-

"A Caucus Held at Albany on Sunday Evening, April 11th, 1824, by the N.Y. City Members." This anonymous cartoon satirizes the Democratic members from New York City, including leading People's Men, who decided to vote for the removal of De Witt Clinton as canal commissioner. The characters' comments all suggest guilt or self-interest, mixed with subservience to party dictation and apprehension of the likely popular response. The People's Party leader in the city, Henry Wheaton (directly in front of the dais, with arm raised), denounces Clinton for injuring the legal profession by laws he introduced. In a cloud above, Columbia says, "I renounce them and their ways." The cartoon demonstrates how Clinton's dismissal was blamed not just on the Bucktails but also on the People's Men, who are shown here resorting to the unpopular partisan devices normally associated with the Bucktails. Courtesy: Library of Congress Prints and Photographs Division.

midable challenge to the Bucktails, exploiting hostility to Crawford and the demand for the popular election of New York's electors. To meet the challenge, on the last day of the legislative session of 1823–1824, the Regency proposed firing Clinton as chairman of the state's canal commission, despite his devoted service and immensely successful enterprise. This maneuver was seen as "a *ruse de guerre*, to operate on the presidential election," by identifying the advocates of the electoral bill as Clintonians. If the anti-Clintonian People's Men voted against removal, they would be damned by loyal Democratic voters as closet Clintonians or worse; if they voted for it, cooperation between the two branches of the opposition would be difficult and the Bucktails' chances of winning the state election greatly enhanced. As it turned out, many of the People's Party leaders in the assembly did find a vote to defend Clinton too great a contradiction of all past political commitment, and so joined the Bucktails in firing him. The response was immediate: "Public feeling everywhere condemns the removal of Mr. Clinton," reported Rufus King in April, but this was an embarrassment to the People's Men as much as a weapon to help them win the state election.[28]

Throughout the months that followed, the Bucktails retained their confidence that they could control the state—or at least said that they did. Their newspapers repeatedly confirmed that New York would do its duty and support the official candidate of the Democratic Republican Party; to do so would be to fulfill the wishes of the people, whatever others said, because the party was, of course, by definition the expression of the popular will. The Bucktails had strengthened their hand by nominating the popular and eloquent Clay man Samuel Young as their gubernatorial candidate in place of Yates; as Thurlow Weed recognized, this "bold flank movement" reduced the chances of an effective Adams–Clay alliance in New York. Van Buren himself repeatedly reassured his correspondents that New York's votes could safely be counted for Mr. Crawford, and his confidence was all the more convincing because for two years he had always had his own way in New York. Even after the state election had gone wrong, Van Buren "to the last hour cheered his friends by the strongest assurances that all was safe."[29]

Whatever else happened, the Bucktails knew that Clinton would not be elected president. The assembly's decision in March had in effect destroyed his chances. Clinton duly gave up all hope for 1824 and instead asked his intimates to "prepare the minds of our friends in other states . . . in a *very confidential* manner to be for Jackson." Influenced no doubt by his Irish background, Clinton had long admired the victor of New Orleans and saw association with a real Republican hero as the best way of overcoming his own reputation as an opponent of the 1812 war. According to Jabez Hammond, Clinton was "the first eminent man at the north who announced a determination to support" Jackson.[30]

In March keen observers detected signs of a nascent Jackson movement in New York, though there was no outburst of public meetings as there had been in Pennsylvania and Ohio. One New York politician told Thurlow Weed that the "rapid march" of Jackson's popularity "far exceeded the expectations of his warm, decided friends"; he was become "the idol of the people." According to Henry Wheaton, "Jackson passes through the bowels of the common People, without any support from leading politicians of any party—where he will stop, heaven only knows." The signs were sufficiently worrying for Tallmadge to propose to Jackson—futilely—that he ally himself with Adams in a joint ticket headed by either of them, promising that it would carry New York. After the rejection of the electoral bill, Clintonian leaders in turn tried to get up a Jackson party in New York as a step toward creating a Jackson–Clinton party nationally, but observers dismissed this as a maneuver designed to strengthen Clinton's bid to become secretary of state in a Jackson or Adams administration. There was little evidence of persisting popular support; according to Parton, Jackson had "comparatively few adherents" there. Clinton's "zealous" supporters organized a meeting in New York City in April, but according to one local newspaper, those attending were "respectable, but . . . of little political weight," and it roused little popular enthusiasm; it was not followed by similar meetings around the state, as Jackson himself hoped.[31]

By May, as Plumer remarked, "The attempt to run General Jackson in New York seems to have failed—so that whatever strength there is in that state opposed to Mr. Crawford may be fairly set down to Mr. Adams." In July Jackson's campaign manager, John Eaton, visited New York City and agreed there was no point in organizing a campaign for Jackson there: "As Mr. Adams stands the only chance of successful opposition to Mr. Crawford in the Legislature, he will be taken up here on principle of policy if not of preference." In effect, the rejection of the electoral bill had "totally destroyed the hopes of the friends of Jackson in New York" as effectively as it had Clinton's.[32]

Henry Wheaton, leader of the People's Men in Manhattan and the southeastern counties, had advocated Calhoun into the early months of

1824, though never in opposition to Adams. Shortly after the electoral bill was postponed, Wheaton visited Adams in Washington to discuss the presidential election. Satisfied that he was committed against coalition with Crawford, Wheaton became one of Adams's most effective protagonists within New York.[33] Other dissidents preferred Clay, whose position in New York strengthened with the withdrawal of Calhoun and Clinton, the other internal improvements candidates. The Clay men had worked with the Regency in helping to defeat adoption of a general ticket system, but now they were freer to act independently.

The outcome of the presidential election, many realized, depended on the success of the People's Men in the state election, even though the selection of electors would be made by the incumbent lame duck legislature. According to Joseph Blunt, one of Adams's managers in New York, if the People's Men did not carry the statewide election, those Bucktails in the assembly who were marginally in favor of Adams would swing back to the regular side. However, if the People's ticket succeeded, the reverse would be true: the incumbent legislature would be overwhelmed by the campaign for governor. As Clinton had said after the 1823 elections, no ambitious man in the legislature would "turn his back on the people and commit political suicide."[34]

Whereas previously Clinton's supporters had been keeping quiet in order to encourage Democrats to rebel against the Regency, after his dismissal from the canal commission they insisted that their hero must head the opposition ticket. It had been expected that James Tallmadge would be the gubernatorial candidate, but he was damned by his vote to remove Clinton. The Democrats in the People's Party ranks now found that they must either swallow Clinton or face defeat. The decision had to be made at the state delegate nominating convention at Utica in September that the opposition leaders had agreed on in the dying days of the session. This was a complication that threatened to spoil their great symbolic moment.[35]

The People's Men insisted that their convention would avoid the entrenched evils of their opponents' political machine. The Bucktails' county and district nominating conventions, they claimed, were frauds, rubber-stamping decisions taken behind closed doors. "What are called 'Regular Nominations,'" said one handbill, "are a mere *hack*, a *machine*, which only serves to effect the purposes of the lordlings and office holders, to harness, hoodwink and break us in, to draw them coach like into office." These manipulated conventions scarcely differed from the caucuses they used to name governors and presidents, all amounting to "a dark and foul *aristocracy* in disguise." By contrast, the People's Party convention at Utica would be made up of "delegates freely chosen from almost all the counties in the state" and would therefore represent "the highest attainable evidence of public sentiment among that portion of our citizens who are determined to emancipate themselves from degrading thraldom to an unprincipled faction." Popular approval of the Utica nominating convention in September ensured that the Regency's gubernatorial nomination in April 1824 was the last ever made in New York by legislative caucus.[36]

In the campaign to elect delegates to Utica, Clinton's followers cashed in on his martyrdom and effectively commanded most of the resulting county meetings and conventions. The original People's Men of 1823 were strongly opposed to Clinton, but at Utica their choices were limited. They looked to John W. Taylor—like Tallmadge, a symbol of Northern antislavery—as a possible compromise candidate, but he chose to remain in Washington, where his vote would count in the event of a House election. When the convention decisively nominated Clinton for governor, the New York City delegation and other anti-Clintonians, including Tallmadge and Wheaton, walked out and refused to ratify his nomination. However, the young Thurlow Weed—already regarded as the Mr. Fix-it of the Adams campaign—worked hard to overcome the mutual prejudice of the old state parties, and with Tallmadge's reluctant permission, he persuaded both sides to nominate Tallmadge as lieutenant governor. Approved by an overwhelming vote in the convention, Tallmadge would attract 16,000 votes more than Clinton in the state election, showing that the People's victory was based on so much more than sympathy for the martyred father of the Erie Canal.[37]

The issues at stake in the state contest did not directly embrace the upcoming presidential election. The People's key demand for the popular election of presidential electors applied to future elections and was linked with promises to secure the popular election of justices of the peace, remove the last vestiges of property qualifications for voting, and assuage discontent with the taxation of personal property. The Bucktails did not oppose strenuously on these points, themselves coming out shortly before the November election in favor of the popular election of electors—next time! The original intention of the People's leaders had been to discuss presidential candidates at Utica, but no mention was made there. Wheaton in particular had hoped to emphasize Adams's claims, but like other "influential and active" Democratic supporters, he recognized that specific presidential candidacies had to be kept out of the state election in order to prevent internal disagreements from disrupting their chances. In the end, what proved "one of the most stirring" elections Weed would see in his long political career resulted in "the utmost excitement" triumphantly sweeping Clinton into the governor's mansion by 16,000 votes.[38]

The extra session of the state legislature called to choose the presidential electors met on November 2, which was also the first day of polling in the state election, in which both senate and house were up for reelection. The legislature agreed to postpone its vote for a week, allowing time to learn the full consequences of the "complete tornado" generated by the People's campaign. Whereas two years before the "Regency men" (or Bucktails) had held every senate seat, now their opponents carried six of the eight districts at stake. In the house more than three-quarters of the members elected were opposed to the Bucktails, either as Clintonians or People's Men. Only one of the seventeen senators who had voted to postpone the electoral law dared to run for reelection, and he was defeated "by a tremendous majority." Many of those regulars who did survive had been questioned about their presidential preferences, and all were aware of how their votes for electors might affect their future political careers. Some felt like Peter Smith of Montgomery County, who "had talked so strong and so much to his neighbors in favor of Mr. Adams . . . that he could not think of changing his ground."[39]

Clay and his American System had attracted much support among "the Yeomanry of the West," which provided him with his strongest bedrock support in any Atlantic state. He enjoyed the active support of the influential Peter B. Porter of Black Rock, on Lake Erie, and the Regency's gubernatorial candidate, Samuel Young. Yet Clay had not secured as many friends in the assembly as they had hoped because New York's western counties were divided in the same way as the Western Reserve in Ohio: Adams was unacceptable to some because of New England's opposition to internal improvements; Clay was unacceptable to others because of his identification with slavery. In places farther east on the canal—as in Weed's Rochester—Adams was by far the favorite candidate.

Formally, the People's Party did not have a preferred presidential candidate, but it was generally acknowledged that most of its members favored Adams. Plumer's informants spoke of a de facto alliance in New York that would enable both Clintonians and Adams men to achieve success, one in the state and the other in the presidential election. Certainly most of the anti-Clintonians among the People's Men were Adams's open advocates, and Clinton's personal preference for Jackson was not echoed by his gubernatorial campaign. Weed later claimed that "more than half, if not two-thirds, of the electors who made Mr. Clinton governor were friends of Mr. Adams," which would mean about 40 percent of those voting in the state election. His supporters did not make up an absolute majority of the newly elected house, but Adams was favorite: on all ballots he consistently won 40 percent of the representatives' votes. That compared with 34.4 percent for Crawford and 25.6 percent for Clay. It was, however, in joint session with the senate that the final decision would be made, and the senate still contained the Crawfordite majority that had killed the electoral law in March. The presidential outcome remained uncertain.[40]

## DECISION IN THE EMPIRE STATE

As in Delaware, the process of legislative election that had worked in the days of the First Party System proved a source of confusion in New York in the circumstances of 1824. The law required each chamber to choose its own list of electors; if the senate and house came up with the same list, the election was over. If they disagreed, the election was decided in a joint session of the two houses with electoral candidates restricted to those on the two lists. That system worked with two parties and two presidential candidates, but it proved cumbersome in 1824 with three viable candidates.

Van Buren evidently believed that the Regency could control the process through the party caucus. If the Bucktail caucus decided firmly in favor of Crawford, enough members who preferred other candidates would feel obliged to vote the party line, and that would be decisive. However, news of Clinton's triumphant election undermined confidence in the power and wisdom of the party and its leadership, and ensured that the governor's patronage would soon be under Clinton's control. The Regency still possessed means of persuasion: several banks were applying for charters, and, according to Jabez Hammond, "the interest of members in these applications for moneyed incorporations had an effect on the political action of some of them." One senator was overheard saying, "I am a Crawford man today, but unless the Chemical Bank passes I shall be a people's man tomorrow."[41]

The influence of the new governor was potentially decisive. According to Porter, had Clinton's opponent, Samuel Young, been elected, all New York's electoral votes would have been given to Clay. Clinton, by contrast, was personally committed to Jackson, but few of Clinton's followers in the legislature approved. When a Jackson ticket was proposed in the house, it attracted only 25 out of 125 votes. Instead, according to Porter, "a few Clintonian members" from western New York who were "warm advocates of Clay . . . were persuaded [by Clinton] as soon as the result of the election was known, to vote for the Adams ticket—Not that Clinton was in favour of Adams, but they would not vote for Jackson; & he was less afraid of Adams than of [Clay]."[42]

The Bucktail caucus at the opening of the extra session was attended by perhaps ten Clay supporters who were willing to take Crawford as their second choice but now thought his chances impossible and demanded that the caucus vote for Clay. This bid failed but the meeting agreed to adopt a ticket made up of twenty-nine Crawfordites and seven moderate Clay men. This was a necessary gesture of friendship designed to attract essential votes in the house in return for the understanding that the seven would vote for Crawford in the Electoral College if he had a chance of winning the state. The ticket passed the senate at the first attempt (seventeen for Crawford, seven each for Adams and Clay), passed by the same seventeen men who had obstructed the electoral law earlier in the year.[43]

The house proved more difficult. For three days it voted repeatedly, with the outcome changing by only a single vote from fifty Adams, forty-three Crawford, and thirty-two Clay; factional lines held and prevented a majority. Apparently the Adams men at an early point offered a deal whereby the ticket would be divided equally with the Clay men, but many of the latter were drawn to the Bucktail offer and made the "grand mistake" of not agreeing to close the deal while it was still practicable. The Bucktail leaders realized they could not carry the Crawford ticket in the lower house and, needing to bring the issue to a vote, decided to reduce the number of tickets to two by backing one of the opposition tickets. But which? They could at this point have killed off Adams's chances at a blow—but apparently because some were reluctant to back the Clay ticket that was headed by Governor Yates, whom they saw as a turncoat, the Bucktails decided to back Adams.[44]

This maneuver, according to one Bucktail, "threw the Clay men into convulsions" and forced an adjournment in "a high state of excitement."

That evening, in a meeting with Clay leaders, Van Buren promised that fifteen of the Crawford electors, if chosen, would vote for Clay, but the proposal was not accepted. Van Buren still believed that ultimately the Clayites would rally to the regular side, but they had lost trust in the Bucktail leadership. In any case, they had no interest in a deal that gave an advantage to Crawford because it was clear that the two men were now head-to-head in a struggle to decide which of them would gain third place in the Electoral College.[45]

The next day all three factions in the lower house voted for the Adams ticket and opened the way for the joint ballot. The Adams leaders now persuaded a significant portion of the Clay men to support a "Union ticket" made up of the seven Clay nominees on the Crawford ticket and twenty-nine names on the Adams ticket. Tallmadge and Wheaton undertook to ensure that the electors delivered the seven Clay votes in the College and even promised an eighth vote. During Sunday Weed, a printer by trade, secretly set the type in the offices of the anti-Regency Albany *Daily Advertiser* and printed off copies of the Union ticket, which were then discreetly distributed. Conscious that two crossovers would be enough to deprive the Adams–Clay union of its majority on joint ballot, Tallmadge, Wheaton, and Weed confronted three wavering Adams men whom they suspected—with some cause—of receiving promises of a financial nature from the Regency. Tallmadge and Wheaton initialed three Adams ballots and gave them to the suspects, threatening to expose them if the three marked ballots were not found in the ballot box after the count.[46]

The next day, the joint session met, with the gallery and lobbies "filled almost to suffocation." Adams and Clay supporters, needing every vote, turned up in strength to the joint session, many armed with the secret ticket. The first "printed split ticket" to be opened produced Crawfordite consternation: "Treason by God," Weed heard one shout, yet the Crawford men surely were the ones who had earlier given their Clay allies reason to mistrust their willingness to deliver the promised electoral votes. On the first ballot the Crawford–Clay ticket won seventy-six votes, the straight Adams ticket fifty-nine votes, and the Adams–Clay ticket nineteen. This gave the candidates who appeared on two tickets the advantage: seven Clay electoral candidates received ninety-five votes and twenty-five Adams men had seventy-eight, while the Crawfordites numbered seventy-six. Three individual ballots were invalidated, one because it scratched four names off a ticket, one because it voted for thirty-six Jacksonians and so was ineligible, and a third because it was blank. Some Bucktails argued that because a majority of those present was needed, only the seven Clay electors had been chosen. The joint session broke up "amid disgraceful scenes," and the houses met again separately. The senate finally accepted the house of assembly's opinion that, in view of the three technically blank ballots, only 154 members were present and voting, meaning that 78 constituted a majority, and so the twenty-five Adams candidates were also properly elected.[47]

The result was a great surprise to Van Buren, who blamed this substantial defeat on "the unyielding opposition of Mr. Clay's friends," who had practiced to "deceive." Four places remained unfilled; a second ballot, held the following day, gave them all to Crawford. Various theories were offered to explain this surprising twist. Porter claimed that "some half a dozen of Mr. Clinton's partizans" had voted for the Crawford electors on the understanding that, if in the Electoral College their votes could elect Jackson, they would transfer to him. Van Buren said some Clay men had voted for Crawford, but much later he offered a different explanation: though he had no suspicion at the time, Van Buren subsequently saw evidence to suggest the Adams men had thrown enough votes to Crawford to keep Clay out of the federal House election.[48]

The final detail of the electoral vote was yet to be determined because two weeks must pass before the Electoral College cast its vote. "Van B's intrigues will not cease," warned Wheaton, but he and Weed proved just as active in trying to subvert electoral candidates. Both Crawford and Adams men had a vested interest in keeping Clay out of the House of Representatives. When the New York Electoral College met on December 1, two Clayites were absent, and the other electors voted to replace them with men who then voted for Adams. The Regency persuaded one Adams elector to switch to Crawford. A fourth elector, a Crawfordite, was subjected to so many threats from different sides that he decided to satisfy no one and voted for Jackson. The main effect was to deprive Clay of three electoral votes and to give Crawford one extra.[49]

The Clay men accused their Adams allies of bad faith. Undoubtedly they were shortchanged in the Electoral College, as Tallmadge and Wheaton singularly failed to make sure that at least seven electoral votes were delivered to Clay. Weed later claimed that the deal had been conditional on Louisiana's voting for Clay and so its vote for Jackson had freed them from the promise, but in fact the Louisiana result was not known in New York until at least two weeks after the vote in the Electoral College. Only in retrospect was it fully clear that New York's shenanigans had ensured that Clay, instead of finishing with forty-one electoral votes to Crawford's forty, came fourth with thirty-seven to forty-one and so was excluded from the House election.[50]

A result that gave nearly 70 percent of New York's electoral votes to Adams, with nearly 20 percent to Clay and only 11 percent to Crawford, amounted to huge defeat for the Little Magician. "Van B.," wrote Wheaton, "looks like a wilted cabbage." In truth, Van Buren had entirely failed to appreciate how the forces generated by the presidential election were undermining the structures of the old party system, and in particular the New York Democratic Party upon which he relied. Jabez Hammond, always a shrewd observer, believed that the Crawfordites should have followed exactly the opposite course of action. They should have backed the electoral law as being "in accordance with our usage and practice ever since the organization of the government," and agreed that "a plurality of popular votes should decide the election" in New York. If then, after nominating Crawford, "they had denounced every man who should oppose such nomination as a traitor to the republican party, I sincerely believe that the discipline of party, the charm of names, and the high character and real merit of Mr. Crawford, together with the horror which at the time was felt whenever Clintonianism or federalism was mentioned, would have ensured a triumph to the Crawford party." Had Crawford carried New York, he would have stood second in the Electoral College with seventy-two votes compared to Adams's fifty-eight.[51]

Be that as it may, the converse strategy had stimulated a voter rebellion that put Adams's supporters in the driver's seat and rightly gave the New Englander the lion's share of New York's electoral kill. Adams had won most support in the newly elected house of assembly, and in the argument over the outcome of the first joint ballot, Crawford men knew that power lay with the lower house. Adams was favored even by men who were loyal supporters of the Regency; the young Bucktail representative Oran Follett, who "was at heart an Adams man," decades later told how, by an unauthorized initiative at the critical moment when Adams might have been excluded, he had pushed the Bucktails into backing the Adams ticket in the house. In truth, the New Englander's candidacy appealed to all New Yorkers who were reluctant to accept a slaveholder, be it Crawford, Clay, or Jackson; significantly, Weed later suggested that the bargain with the Clayites could not have been carried through in the Electoral College because no individual Adams elector was willing to vote for Clay, whatever collective undertakings had been given. Just as Jackson tapped broad reservoirs of support in the South and West and Pennsylvania, so Adams drew on a deep-rooted sentiment in the North that created a popular commitment rivaling that received by the Hero.[52]

Overall, the six legislatures gave Adams more than half their states' electoral votes—that is, thirty-six votes compared to sixteen for Crawford, fifteen for Jackson, and four for Clay. Excepting Delaware and Louisiana, these results more or less fairly reflected public opinion in those states: because all but one lay east of the Appalachians, the advantage went to the two seaboard candidates, who arguably took more than two-thirds of the underlying popular votes between them. Indeed, the figures (Table 3 in Appendix 1) suggest that Crawford enjoyed enough underlying voter support on the seaboard to easily beat Clay for third position in the national popularity stakes.[53] In terms of overall electoral votes, Jackson (99) and Adams (84) were by far the two leading candidates, with Crawford (42) a distant third. Clay (37) was excluded from the "contingent election" that now became necessary, but he was nicely placed to enjoy playing kingmaker in the House of Representatives.

# 10 THE CORRUPT BARGAIN

"The Election of a Chief magistrate, whether King, Doge or President," said Maryland's veteran U.S. senator, Samuel Smith, in November 1824, "is the rock on which all Republics are split." When it became certain the next month that the election would not be settled in the Electoral College, a Virginia newspaper writer warned that the current election now offered "the severest trial to which our invaluable constitution can be exposed." The example of 1801 showed how a House election could stagger on in prolonged stalemate and probably have to be settled by some backroom deal. In contrast to 1801, when the contest had been a relatively straightforward party fight, in 1825 all sorts of combinations might settle the result. The danger was, as Hezekiah Niles warned, that "such an election may shake the union, for it is possible one may be chosen, whom the people can regard only in the light of a usurper."[1]

These uncertainties were compounded, in many minds, by the perceived growth of "luxury and corruption" that was destroying the "republican virtue" upon which the liberty of the country depended. In this view, the very men who had the duty of resolving the election were themselves liable to be corrupted by their desire to win the favor of whoever succeeded. This not only meant that office seekers might well choose the next president for corrupt reasons but also that in the future an incumbent president could use the executive patronage to buy himself reelection almost in perpetuity. In 1823 Mahlon Dickerson had warned that "the broad road to monarchy is left open by those who formed our Constitution, by neglect or by design." A year later Thomas Hart Benton agreed when he presented his proposal to reform the election process.[2] Proposals to decide a hung election by allowing the Electoral College a second vote restricted to the top two candidates continued to be made in Congress only weeks before the House election was due, but in the end there was no alternative but to decide the election in the House of Representatives, as in 1801.[3]

As Congress reassembled in December 1824, excitement and intrigue quivered in Washington. The forthcoming House election became the sole topic of conversation as people tried to figure out what was likely to happen. All that was clear was that the contest was essentially between Jackson and Adams; it was not known in the federal city that Crawford, and not Clay, would be the third candidate until December 16. Very little was openly said, as candidates forbore public comment and most delegations kept their thoughts to themselves. Members of Congress apologized for not being able to give accurate news to their many pressing, curious correspondents; even "the most knowing ones seem to be but little better off." As different rumors made the rounds and suspicions of conspiracy mounted, some observers complained that those involved seemed to think only of their own selfish interests. To Congressman Mangum of North Carolina, any doubts there may have been in advance about the wisdom of having the House decide the outcome were justified daily.[4]

Yet when Niles went to Washington in early January, he was surprised by how "still and quiet" the members of Congress were about the election: "I have seen a much greater degree of excitement about some ordinary subject of legislation than appears to prevail as to the settlement of a question which has so long and so ardently agitated the people of the United States." Another observer suggested that the House election had been expected for so long that it had allowed time for reflection; in addition, "the fears of violence and intrigue generally entertained by the people have put every sober man upon his guard." Niles was confident that the election could be made without the "bitterness and agitation" of 1801, which "at one moment seemed almost sufficient to shake the union." He mused that "a difference of opinion as to persons does not appear to be a difference of principle as to things—nor is it"—though the outcome made him revise that judgment somewhat. Most members recognized that the House must not leave the country without a government after March 4. If that happened, according to the Twelfth Amendment the vice president would "act as president" (whatever that meant), but the thought of Calhoun in power did not please everyone.[5]

The crisis affected Washington's social life too. According to Margaret Bayard Smith, "Society is now divided into separate battalions as it were. Mrs. Adams collected a large party and went one night [to the theater], Mrs. Calhoun another, so it was thought by our friends that Mrs. Crawford should go too, to show our strength." Van Buren and Louis McLane obligingly roused senators and congressmen to make up "a strong Crawford escort." For her part, Mrs. Adams's fortnightly soirees were better attended than ever, especially as the day of election approached. Louisa Catherine's dinners were "unusually good" and the guests carefully chosen, but one targeted visitor thought "the graces and fascinations of a man of ease & urbanity" sat on her husband "like the lowering feathers of a city milliner on a raw country girl." Despite his awkwardness, Quincy found time during his busy day to visit and receive congressmen.[6]

New to Washington, Mrs. Jackson thought "the extravagance" of the "great city" was "in dressing and running to parties." She and the General attended few, "staying at home smoking our pipe," and were seen in public mainly at church. Many were eager to catch a glimpse of "her majesty of two husbands," as she was dubbed in the wake of reports of her dubious marital status, but Mrs. Jackson disappointed those who had expected to find an uncivilized, immoral frontierswoman. When they visited the Senate, she seemed but "an ordinary looking old woman dressed in the height & *flame* of fashion." Jackson himself was daily mobbed by well-wishers, sometimes between 50 and 100 persons a day. Late in the session, however, he would be incapacitated when an old wound flared after a fall. Certainly he spent less time visiting congressmen on the Hill or in their messes than Adams did.[7]

As in the previous session, the candidates dined together frequently, at each other's and at other people's houses, and maintained cordial relations. On one occasion after dinner, Adams and Jackson took their seats on chairs placed before the fire, each diplomatically leaving a chair between them. Clay insouciantly nipped in and sat on that central chair, saying, "Well, gentlemen, since you are both so near the chair, but neither can occupy it, I will slip in between you and take it myself!" Apparently the two candidates were not amused, but everyone else within earshot could laugh. Mrs. Smith found that the friends of each candidate, though "divided and known," were, "when they meet, perfectly good-natured and polite. . . . I cannot perceive any animosity, any bitterness, or suspicion. . . . It is all done, (as far as respects society) in a fair and pleasant manner and I really hope the crisis will pass without turbulence or difficulty of any kind."[8]

Amid the bonhomie, the politicians were hard at work. The congressmen had, of course, been elected in 1822–1823, not in 1824, and the balance in each state delegation did not necessarily reflect that in the recent popular or legislative election. Jacksonians could be confident of only five state votes: Pennsylvania, Tennessee, Alabama, Mississippi, and South Carolina. Adams could count on the six New England states, and Crawford on three Southeastern states (Virginia, Georgia, and Delaware). That left ten states initially uncertain. The maneuvers to capture the critical number of thirteen were potentially labyrinthine and opened the way to deep suspicion. The historian Robert Remini described the outcome as the "Theft of the Presidency," but that does less than justice to the real significance of all the politicking.[9]

## THE LIMITS OF CHOICE

Initially observers—in and out of Washington—assumed that Jackson was in a prime position. News of his extraordinary popular triumphs in states as diverse as New Jersey, Indiana, and North Carolina created a momentum that few thought could be resisted by any politician looking forward to future usefulness. Willie P. Mangum thought that "the opinion of the house, take the men as individuals, is much against him, but many are afraid of the vote" that the people have given him. On top of that, the presence of Lafayette in Washington for most of the session introduced to the capital the "military enthusiasm" that his visit occasioned elsewhere in the country. Aware of this possibility, Lafayette avoided wearing military uniform even in parades, and with deliberate discretion, he endeavored to emphasize civilian attainments.[10]

Second thoughts soon set in. Daniel Webster, who was willing to play all sides, reported "a re-action agt. Genl. Jackson—a *feeling* somewhat adverse to giving the Presidency to *mere* military character." John Sloane of Ohio was not the only congressman to see evidence in Jackson's disposition, common among military men, "to contemn [sic] the salutary agency of the law, and rely on the application of force, for effecting all objects." Who else, other than Cromwell and Bonaparte, had "dissolved the legislature of a sovereign State, and suspended the operation of all its laws"? Mangum thought the shift against Jackson also owed something to a recalculation of his chances. Particularly decisive seemed reports that Illinois's sole congressman, Daniel P. Cook, "it is pretty certain will vote for Adams." Cook had "pledged himself to vote with his State," but "the parties [are] so balanced that he feels at liberty to pursue the dictates of his own Judgt. . . ., & without him Jackson cannot succeed."[11]

Moreover, the argument that congressmen were obliged to vote for the man who won most votes in the Electoral College began to seem silly: otherwise, why did the Constitution insist on an absolute majority and refer a hung election to the House? It was not as though a lead in the Electoral College necessarily reflected majority popular opinion. The three-fifths clause biased the Electoral College toward Southern candidates; without it, Adams would have led Jackson by eighty-three votes to seventy-seven. True, on the face of things, Jackson had a plurality of the popular vote in those states that allowed their voters to choose the electors. However, in North Carolina Jackson owed victory to the open support of many Adams men; had they held aloof and Crawford won the state, Adams and Jackson would have tied in the Electoral College with eighty-four votes each. Moreover, in Maryland and Illinois the accidents of districting had given Jackson the lion's share of the electoral votes even though Adams had won a popular majority. "These facts," according to Congressman Sloane, "were known to congress at the time of making the choice," and he was convinced that Jackson "was not the choice of a majority of the American people."[12]

For Jackson may have won a popular plurality in those states where the electorate choose its Electoral College, but what of the six states where the state legislature had chosen the electors and popular presidential preferences had not been directly measured? In Georgia, the preceding state election provided a clear and measurable indication of Crawford's advantage; Vermont and South Carolina were emphatically one-sided, and the size of the popular vote there could be calculated from contemporaneous elections. In Delaware and Louisiana the popular preference could only be guessed, though these lightly populated states could not change any nationwide calculation. Jackson certainly had at least plurality support across all four Southern states taken together, while Vermont belonged to Adams. The sixth state was New York where, in the state elections in November, 193,000 votes had been cast—enough to swamp the entire national popular vote of the leading presidential candidates. Had the proposed electoral bill passed back in March, New York's presidential election would have been held at the same time as the state election, and the indications were that Adams would have won 40 percent of the 193,000, Crawford 34 percent, Henry Clay 26 percent, and Jackson none. If that is correct, then across the nation, Adams in effect had 34,000 more popular votes than Jackson. Such precise calculations may not have been made in early 1825, but politicians knew that in the most populous part of the country, Adams had tapped a broad current of popular feeling as powerful as that which buoyed Jackson.[13]

However, both popular currents were less than nationwide. As one U.S. senator observed, "I cannot learn that the delegations from the States south of the Chesapeake will support Mr. Adams, nor those from east of the Hudson, the General. In this aspect of affairs the friends of Mr. Crawford do not abandon the field." On the face of things, however, Crawford's chances were slim. His health was still an issue: he had begun attending Cabinet meetings again in November, but those who saw him thought him still handicapped. According to one supporter in December, "His articulation will even now operate against him, for . . . he is not the commanding man that he once was in conversation. . . . His tongue is so much affected that he lisps and with some difficulty expresses himself." Moreover, he had been fortunate to be returned third in the Electoral College, narrowly ahead of Clay. Whereas both Jackson and Adams soon thought they had six or seven states already lined up, Crawford could boast only three or four.[14]

In spite of his disadvantages, Crawford's supporters showed great loyalty to their man. According to Congressman Mangum, "The members from No. Ca. have not looked to any other result than a vote for Crawford . . . his claims are not to be surrendered." For himself, he added, "I cannot bring myself for purposes of popularity, to abandon what in my heart I believe to be those principles that make for the welfare of our common country." Louis McLane, who held Delaware's vote in his sole hand, maintained his personal commitment to Crawford, who after all had won two of his state's three electoral votes: "I cannot *think* of a *second* choice, until it becomes necessary for *me* to elect one, or prevent an election." The Crawfordites were "not inactive, delegates have been appointed from our five States to meet & confer."[15] They thought admiration for Crawford to be widespread among the members. Senator Ruggles believed that Crawford would win a ballot in the House if it were decided by individual votes rather than by states. Van Buren and John Holmes looked to work on individuals among the New England delegations in the hope that when the election approached paralysis, covert Crawfordites would come together behind the candidate of the good old party. If that didn't happen, they would be well served in the long run by holding aloof and bearing no responsibility for whatever inadequate administration emerged from the House. "At all events," said Van Buren, "we will come out of the contest with clean hands."[16]

The congressmen of 1825 were in any case unlikely to opt for Crawford because they well knew the situation in their own states and had a firm sense of how public opinion lay. They well understood just how unpopular Crawford was outside the Southeast. This may have been a lame duck session, but many of them had faced reelection in the fall of 1824 and had promised their electorates that, regardless of their own personal predilections, they would follow the popular preferences expressed at the ballot boxes in their state and district.

Thus, as the various state delegations canvassed the varied personal opinions of their members, the overwhelming imperative that emerged was to obey local public opinion. As one newly reelected congressman predicted, "The members will generally consider themselves bound by the sentiments expressed by their constituents." Adams was not personally favored by the New Hampshire members, but Plumer predicted they "will vote for him because their constituents have done." Similarly, most congressmen from Pennsylvania and New Jersey were thought to prefer Adams but would vote for Jackson. In the end, nearly every delegation from a state that had demonstrated a clear statewide popular preference in the election of electors would cast its vote that way in the House election.[17] Even the eighty-one lame ducks, who were not returning to Congress after March, by and large followed the demands of the "electoral connection."[18]

The testing exceptions to this democratic rule were those congressmen who had given presidential pledges at the time of their election in 1822–1823, as had some Adams men in parts of the North and some Crawfordites in New York. However, the most conspicuous example was North Carolina, where many in the congressional delegation had been elected in 1822 after giving public commitments to vote for Crawford. The Georgian may have lost North Carolina to a coalition of his opponents in 1824, but the delegation preferred to stick by the pledges already given, even though they came under strong pressure from Jacksonians back home who threatened to oppose their reelection. Overall, eighteen of the twenty-four delegations decided, in the face of dissent-

*The Fourth Runner. David Claypoole Johnston's cartoon of "A Foot-Race" includes a study of the disappointed Clay, whose fourth place gives him no choice but to "draw up." His supporters are told not to be so "CLA-morous," as "your old Kentuck's come to a stand-still." An adviser, dressed as a jockey, comforts him that "there'll be some scrubbing by & by & then you'll have a chance." Meanwhile, an armed ruffian swears, "D——n my leather breeches if I won't always stand up for the GINeral." The House of Representatives, within the Capitol, dominates the horizon. Courtesy: American Antiquarian Society.*

ing minorities, to honor the preferences stated at some point by their electorates.

That commitment ensured that Henry Clay could not have won, even had he qualified for the House election in place of Crawford. For two years men had been saying that Clay was bound to win any House election he entered; they assumed that his energetic advocacy of the American System and his personal standing in the House would guarantee a winning coalition. His election as Speaker on his return to the House in December 1823 was interpreted by some as demonstrating his personal command, though the more acute pointed out that Clay owed his election to the North's determination to defeat the Virginia candidate for Speaker. The disappearance of Clay's popular support in the Southwest, the many-sided opposition he faced in the Northwest, and his failure to embody support in Middle Atlantic states deprived him of democratic credibility. In late November he himself had anticipated that, even if he came in the top three, he would "enter the H. so crippled that my election can scarcely be anticipated." Either way, whether in or out of the House election, most congressmen believed that Clay could still make Western policies and the American System the deciding factor in the election.[19]

## MR. CLAY'S BARGAIN

Still, twenty years later, during his third run for the presidency in 1844, Henry Clay had to defend his behavior in the House election. Jacksonian Democrats insisted as an article of faith that in 1825 Clay had delivered his states to Adams in return for the state department and the presumed succession to the presidency. This bargain was corrupt because he had not preferred Adams as the best choice but had hawked his support around the other contenders to see who would pay his price. These charges always lacked substantiation. When Congressman George Kremer of Pennsylvania first made the accusation on the eve of the House election, he initially supported Clay's demand for a committee of inquiry, then refused to give evidence. When Jackson himself later claimed that he had been approached by Clay's representatives, his witness turned out to be the shifty Jacksonian James Buchanan, whose evidence suggested it was the Jacksonians who had approached Clay and been rebuffed, not vice versa.[20]

Clay himself found the approaches of "the friends of the three returned candidates . . . very amusing," as each group pressed for his support in its own distinctive way. Jacksonians emphasized the need for a Western president; Crawfordites stressed that he and Crawford were the "only genuine Republican Candidates," the only ones who could preserve the Republican Party; and Adamsonians begged him "to consider seriously whether the public good & your own future interests do not point most distinctly to the choice which you ought to make." They all believed that Clay could control his friends and that Clay himself was biddable.[21]

In fact, Clay had already made his personal decision before the meeting of Congress. He had expressed it in private letters to confidants who could release the letters subsequently if needed. They included not only Lafayette but also Benton, who as a prominent Jacksonian would later stoutly defend Clay against Jacksonian attacks on this point.[22] Clay made it clear he could support neither Crawford nor Jackson. Though Clay and Crawford had long been thought the most obvious bedfellows, Clay had two objections. Crawford was too ill, and Clay's opinion was not changed by what he saw during the session. More to the point, there was "reason to fear . . . from his position and Southern support . . . the principles of administration" that Crawford would adopt, especially as public meetings in Virginia increasingly expressed deep disapproval of Clay's adoption of "the new-fangled will-o'-the-wisp doctrines of 1824" that betrayed the old states' rights doctrines of 1798. As Clay had told the Crawford men "again and again," there was no likelihood of his being able to persuade his allies in the West to support a political cause tainted with hostility to the American System.[23]

Clay's objection to Jackson was that most widely expressed in Washington. Jackson stood essentially as a military chieftain, a potential threat to the republican system, and lacking the qualities of a statesman. Jackson himself may or may not be a threat, but the example of promoting this military chieftain could be dangerous to the young republic. He and his friends were also well aware that Clay was unlikely to be adopted as successor to a Western candidate, whereas he would stand well as heir presumptive to a Yankee president. The same sort of logic persuaded Clinton to use his influence for Jackson, who would prefer a Northern secretary of state and presumed successor.

Though his early determination is well attested, Clay resolved to keep quiet to avoid alienating his Western friends by an early declaration against Jackson. The initial response of many of them was to support the latter as a Western president who had voted for their favorite measures. Adams had been identified in the West during the campaign as opposing, or at least not enthusiastically supporting, the American System, and he was regarded by many, including Clay, as not possessing the personal qualities desirable in a head of state. It would take some effort to persuade them that Adams should be preferred to the charismatic Jackson. Even after his famous private meeting with Adams on the evening of January 9, Clay asked Adams to keep their understanding confidential in order to allow time for his friends to come round to Adams's support.[24]

The run-up to that meeting was carefully managed by Clay. The go-between was Robert P. Letcher, a Kentucky congressman and personal friend of Clay, who visited Adams several times. Adams had privately long mistrusted Clay's gambling disposition, but he also recognized that Clay possessed a core of political principle and now welcomed his approach. Seated next to each other at a dinner in honor of Lafayette, they agreed to meet for a private conversation. At that meeting on January 9, Clay and Adams had "a long conversation explanatory of the past and prospective of the future." Adams's diary is famously silent on the details of the conversation—he left a page blank for further elaboration but never completed it—but enough is said to leave no doubt about the thrust. They had disagreed so frequently, and sometimes publicly, in the past that some explanation was needed and an agreement that no ill will survived.[25]

As regards the future, Clay wished Adams, as far as he may think proper, "to satisfy him with regard to some principles of great public importance, but without any personal considerations for himself." Those principles must, in the circumstances, have included Clay's American System. Nine months earlier, at dinner at Jackson's lodgings, Adams had thought Clay too "warm, vehement, and absurd upon the tariff," and he had later told whoever asked that he himself approved the more limited degree of protection finally embraced in the 1824 measure. On internal improvements, Adams could give fuller approval, especially as he had gone on record agreeing that the Constitution gave Congress full power to build and support roads and canals of national importance. Clay was satisfied. He assured Adams of his support, and though there was no specific assurance, he soon told confidants he could have *"any"* office he wished under an Adams presidency. The question was, would the states that had voted for Clay agree with his judgment?[26]

Congressmen like Willie P. Mangum who thought Clay held "in his hands the vote of 5 states" overrated his control in a way Clay himself did not. Many in those states thought that Jackson's surprisingly strong showing made it difficult to avoid voting for the alternative Western candidate. Sometime before January 15 five Western delegations—Ohio, Kentucky, Missouri, Illinois, and Louisiana—met in secret and decided that they would act together but keep their preferences secret. They were inclined to Adams but wished to see how things developed. Almost everyone recognized that the decision really lay in the hands of Ohio, the largest and most influential of the Western states, and to a lesser extent Kentucky.[27]

From within Ohio came much advice. Jacksonians argued that the Hero stood second only to Clay in the state's affections, and many neutrals reluctantly agreed that Jackson would win a straight race against Adams. Others disagreed, saying that opinion among Clay voters was overwhelmingly in favor of Adams. Some suggested that the general assembly pass resolutions; this was thought unwise, though "two-thirds of . . . the present legislature" had voted for Clay and now preferred Adams. It was argued that what mattered was not who came second to Clay in Ohio but rather who the second choice was of those who had voted for Clay. Whichever way those people leaned, their favorite was bound to have a majority of the votes cast in October, and if Adams were chosen, it would be a fitting reward for the hard work of the Adams campaign in winning a quarter of Ohio's popular vote.[28]

When the Ohio delegation met in caucus in December, it was "about equally divided between Adams and Jackson," balanced between "the wish to have a Western president now, in the person of Jackson, whom they do not much like; and the certainty of having Clay, by the aid of the northern states [i.e., New England], at some future period." Though this could mean they were at Clay's command, a New Hampshire member noted that Clay's friends "profess to attach less importance to men than to measures—Give us, they say, a man who is for internal improvement; & we do not care whether he is from the east or the west." By early January—before Clay's meeting with Adams—"a large majority" of Ohio's representatives had come to favor Adams, the first of the Clay states to do so, "and *that too* without having ascertained Mr. Clay's views on the subject." However, they decided for the present to maintain close silence, preserve their neutrality, and seek out full information before committing themselves. After all, they had "several western measures on hand that would in no way be injured through the favorable expectations of the friends of the different presidential candidates."[29]

The decision was critical for Congressman John C. Wright, a Clay man whose district in eastern Ohio had voted overwhelmingly for Jackson. Wright insisted that in this instance he must follow not the sentiments of his immediate constituents but rather the opinion of the state and the best interests of the Union. This meant that he must "find out [the candidates'] sentiments on internal improvements before I can cheerfully vote." By January 22 he had learned enough to decide that Jackson, despite his American System votes in Congress, had "a natural affinity" with "the cotton-growing policy, which is in direct war with our own. . . . He is a western man to be sure in residence but not in feelings and policy; he would be *charged* to the *account* of the west while in fact he belonged to the south." New England was less hostile to the West: "While the east are commercial they are also manufacturing and are free." Did it not make more sense to unite upon Adams, "a man who agrees with us on the questions of internal improvement and domestic industry, elect him, make him feel he owes his elevation to us & throw our state into an influential attitude in relation to the new administration?"[30]

Behind this judgment lay some significant developments in the House. The previous session had passed the strategic General Survey Act but had largely failed to support specific improvement measures of national import. The president had proposed in his annual message that Congress give financial aid to the company planning to build the long-planned Chesapeake and Delaware Canal, which would connect two major Atlantic inlets. The 1824 session expired without the House pressing the bill to a third reading. On January 14, 1825, the same proposal passed to its third reading, 86–83, and finally passed the House, 113–74, on January 21. The swelling support owed much to Adams men from New England and New York, whose switch some thought had established the principle of federal internal improvements.[31]

More pertinent for Ohioans, the National Road had long been promised to connect Washington with the state capitals of the Northwestern states and the Mississippi. Construction from central Maryland had reached the Ohio River in 1818, then stopped; successive bills to extend the road across Ohio failed to make progress, even in 1824. The renewed proposal—to appropriate $150,000 to start construction across eastern Ohio—roused a heated debate in January 1825 that, according to Plumer, "exhibited so many of Adams's friends in favor of this western measure, and most of the Atlantic friends of Jackson against it." Webster's remarks in favor of the bill, Plumer later recalled, "were particularly gratifying to the Western members; & were not without their influence in bringing them to vote for Adams." The bill passed to its third reading, 93–82, on January 18 and finally 97–72 on January 21, with New Englanders prominent among those shifting to its support, both now in the House and after the election in the Senate. As Congressman Duncan McArthur later wrote, the course of Jackson's friends in Congress "put it out of our power to support the pretensions of the General without at the same time abandoning" the interests of Ohio, while "it was evident that for the support of those measures, our only reliance was upon the friends of Mr. Adams, the identity of interest between the Northern and Western States, and the liberality of the Eastern members of Congress."[32]

In Ohio's House vote for president, two congressmen from southwestern Ohio voted for Jackson, two for Crawford from personal and partisan considerations, and the remaining ten for Adams. Eight of the ten could claim to have not contradicted the wishes of their constituents because Clay had run ahead of Jackson in their districts. After Clay had been appointed secretary of state, he asked Ohio's congressmen, who included some men of considerable reputation, to comment publicly on their decision. They all insisted that the delegation had made up its own mind, there had been no input from Clay, and they had never considered Clay's immediate future or ambitions. In effect, their decision meant that Ohio had finally voted for what its electorate had been looking for through the campaign: a Northern president who favored Western policy.[33]

The decision was less straightforward for the Kentucky delegation. In January news arrived that the newly elected state legislature had formally requested them to vote for Jackson. Local elections in August had given a majority to the Relief Party, which decided to exploit the ancient practice of legislative instruction but recognized that, by convention, congressmen could only be requested, not instructed; despite the current reaction against legislative interference, they insisted that this was an unusual situation because the delegation had to vote as a bloc to express the state's opinion. Outsiders believed that Kentucky's congressmen could not stand against such a public statement in favor of Jackson, but their devotion to Clay and his Western policy encouraged two-thirds of them to resist the request, which they thought based on ignorance of

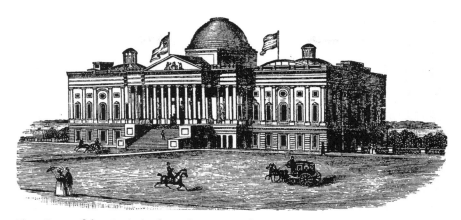

*East Front of the Capitol, 1825. The House of Representatives, where the election was decided, occupied the south wing of the rebuilt Capitol, to the left of the dome in this view. This engraving was published in Ben: Perley Poore,* Perley's Reminiscences of Sixty Years in the National Metropolis, *2 vols. (Philadelphia: Hubbard Bros., 1886), 1:45.*

the real choices. In any case, the delegation despised their local opponents, who not only favored relief measures even though the pressing need had now passed but were also commencing a war against the state judiciary that could only bring the state into disrepute. Though by 1828 the Jackson party would benefit hugely from the resentments of the Relief or New Court party, in 1825 Clay's supporters believed that a vote for Adams would accurately reflect the outlook of the overwhelming majority in Kentucky that had backed Clay and Western policies. Even Amos Kendall, who by now preferred Jackson, said that he would be content "if our interest in the west can be promised by any other arrangement."[34]

On January 24, two weeks before the day of election, the Ohio and Kentucky delegations called the friends of Jackson and Crawford into a committee room and informed them of their decision to vote for Adams. This "sudden & unexpected" announcement immediately caused a "buzzing in the hive" because it created the likelihood that Adams would win. That depended on the other Clay states following suit, and on Adams attracting two more seaboard states from south of New England.[35]

### WINNING THE MARGINALS

Everything was still up for grabs. The joint Ohio and Kentucky announcement at first depressed the friends of other candidates, but they soon recovered. Adams himself feared that his coalition with Clay would prompt a Jackson–Crawford combination that could equally count on the support of eleven states and would prove more unscrupulous in persuading the fickle members of wavering states. For their part, the Jacksonians believed that they could attract some of Adams's Western support away from him, especially where the state's vote was in the hands of a single congressman. Conversely, some Crawfordites thought that they could find ways of frustrating the influence that the American System forces threatened to acquire over the next administration.[36]

Clay himself felt great anxiety about Jacksonian pressure on the single members from Illinois and Missouri. Daniel P. Cook of Illinois had been elected as a prominent antislavery protagonist in 1820 and 1822 and had committed himself to Adams at an early stage in the presidential election. He had been willing to vote for Jackson if the rest of the West did so, but he determined to vote for Adams "the moment he learned the course of Mr. Clay and his friends." Yet Cook was also a son-in-law of Ninian Edwards, himself Calhoun's brother-in-law, which opened Cook to Calhoun's ambition to be Jackson's kingmaker. The combined forces of George McDuffie, John Eaton, and Samuel Ingham of Pennsylvania laid an "electioneering siege" on Cook, but none of their blandishments or threats had any effect.[37]

Missouri's vote, by contrast, lay in the hands of the aristocratic, Virginia-born lawyer John Scott. On arriving in Washington in December 1824, he avowed himself in some circles to be a Crawford man and kept open his links with that side till the end. In the previous July, however, he had publicly committed himself to Clay but promised in the event of a House election to be "the organ of the people." When reality struck, he found there was no clear indication of the popular will in Missouri. The state legislature refused to make a recommendation when he asked for guidance, taking the line that it was improper to instruct in this instance. The state's two senators disagreed with each other. David Barton insisted that in this one instance a congressman must act on behalf of the whole country rather than his own state, which meant acknowledging Adams's superior qualifications. Senator Benton decreed that the people demanded Jackson and converted to his cause; he then maintained "a screw upon Scott" that the proud Virginian deeply resented.[38]

Scott equally refused, according to one Pennsylvania Jacksonian, to be "sold like sheep" by Clay, and he was personally hostile to Adams because of past appointments in Missouri and the Arkansas territory. In an interview with Scott on January 22, Adams explained past misunderstandings and gave assurances about future appointments in the frontier West. When Scott said he hoped Clay would be part of any Adams administration, Adams refused to comment, other than to say that "if . . . elected by the suffrages of the West I should naturally look to the West for much of the support that I should need." Scott appeared satisfied, but he made it clear that he was not trying to make a bargain and had not promised to vote for Adams because he intended to "act with his friends." Scott later insisted that he had throughout been "very well disposed to go with the other Western delegations" in seeking to influence the incoming administration. In fact his vote remained in doubt to the end because, as Adams judged, he wished above all to go with the winner, and the Crawfordites later claimed they had lost the "irresolute" Scott's vote mainly because Clay spent hours with him the night before the vote.[39]

Likewise, Louisiana's vote long remained uncertain. In February 1824 the state's congressmen had said that they would not consider themselves bound to follow the assembly's choice if "contrary to the known will of the people." The uncertainties of the election gave the three congressmen a free choice, though each had a sense of opinion in his own district. By the end of January Rufus King understood William Brent to be firm for Adams while Edward Livingston, from the New Orleans area, was equally committed to Jackson. The balance was held by Henry Gurley, a Clay man who had been born in New England. The Clay forces thought, though not with absolute certainty, that this meant Louisiana would go with them to Adams.[40]

If Jacksonian efforts to break down the unity of the Western Clay states proved of doubtful effect, their hope to attract the support of Crawford's friends was always a nonstarter. The bad blood between the two men did not help: Crawford was the one prominent former enemy in Washington with whom Jackson had not already reconciled himself. In January Mrs. Jackson visited Mrs. Crawford, presumably with the General's knowledge, but Jackson never followed it up before the election, even when an easy opportunity presented itself on Capitol Hill.[41] The Virginia delegation was absolutely unwilling, in 1825, to support a military man, as their correspondence and conversation consistently emphasized. Rather than do so, they were willing to either leave the country without a president after March 4, despite the inevitability of Calhoun taking the reins of power, or shift decisively to Adams as part of a broad-based coalition.[42]

Such an outcome the Western forces were determined to avoid if at all possible. Clay's "confidential friends" told Adams that Clay wished to throw "Virginia and the South[east] into a minority," but there was more than one way of doing that. By January 15, according to Congressman Philemon Beecher of Ohio, the five Western Clay states had "come to an understanding":

> If . . . Maryland and New Jersey will not vote for Adams [which would mean he could not win thirteen states], we of the west will make Jackson the President at once. . . . If the Atlantic states will not . . . put it into our power to make Adams president, we are not going to jeopardize ourselves by giving an ineffectual vote. . . . [This] understanding between us of the west is a matter kept to ourselves at present.

As Scott of Missouri said, future influence on the incoming administration depended on giving the decisive vote: "I had rather my state should be the party courted than the party courting."[43]

The combination of New England and the American System strengthened Adams's chances of winning some seaboard states south of New England. In mid-January both the New Jersey and Maryland delegations were "yet quite unsettled, a majority of both are inclined to vote for Adams, but are afraid of the people." Ten days later the New Jersey delegation decided for Jackson, but Adams's position in Maryland decisively improved, especially as it became clear that Adams had won a fraction more of Maryland's popular vote than Jackson. The nine-man delegation was equally divided between Jackson and Adams, 3–3, with one Crawfordite; the other two were thought likely to "go with Clay's friends in the west." Though that seemed to imply it would go for Adams, Maryland's vote was still considered doubtful at the end of January. However, even with it, Adams would be one short of the magic number.[44]

## SECURING NARROW CONTROL

Even as Adams neared the target, Jacksonians still had hopes. Two days before the House voted, Senator Eaton believed that Jackson would probably command the votes of Missouri and Louisiana, giving the General six of the nine Western states, though it seemed less likely that public pressure from home could yet operate on congressmen from Illinois, Ohio, or even Kentucky. He remained confident of Maryland and New Jersey, as well as Pennsylvania and South Carolina. New York he expected to be evenly divided and possibly "give no vote to the end," but he thought it more likely that after several ballots Adams would win New York and also Delaware. At that stage, with Adams and Jackson holding nine and ten states respectively, he thought the remaining Crawford states—Virginia, North Carolina, and Georgia—would shift to the only other Southern candidate and give Jackson the victory. However, he recognized that it was all uncertain.[45]

On their side, the Crawford men persisted in believing they could play the decisive role. Adams predicted that they would ultimately ally with the Jackson men; though prescient, he was premature. In the circumstances of February 1825, the Crawfordites maintained their determination not to allow the election of a military chieftain. On December 22 James Barbour, U.S. senator for Virginia and a leading Crawfordite, had a long, confidential conversation with Adams and assured him that Virginia would stick with Crawford as long as there was any hope of success, but a majority of the delegation would then shift to Adams. A wartime Republican governor of Virginia, Barbour had supported nationalist policies after the war but shifted his ground as views at home changed. Unwilling to enter into constitutional arguments, he opposed the protective system but was willing to support some internal improvements on practical grounds where appropriate. During his visit he enquired closely into Adams's views on the American System. His host assured him his purpose was "*conciliation, not collision.*" Adams said he found the new tariff satisfactory, but if it "should be found to bear hard upon the agricultural and commercial interests, I should incline toward an alleviation of it in their favor." As for internal improvements, he had no doubt about Congress's constitutional power, but he agreed that there needed to be caution that the power was not misused. Barbour left Adams "with the impression that the interview had been entirely satisfactory to him." Despite his Northern political character, Adams provided an acceptable alternative for Virginia.[46]

At the end of January, as relations between Jackson and Adams men deteriorated, some Crawfordites continued to hope that a stalemate between the leading candidates would persuade one of the rival groupings to compromise on Crawford in order to defeat the other. Others thought rather of stopping Adams from winning on the first few ballots. Van Buren himself believed that old party loyalties could persuade Samuel Eddy of Rhode Island to vote for Crawford and so tie that two-man delegation, while he understood that one of the Adams supporters in the Maryland delegation would shift to Jackson after the first ballot, thus depriving Adams of two states. Such politicking would enable them to sustain a stalemate and then offer to break it by swinging their votes en bloc to Adams. Apparently Van Buren told Eddy that the reason he desired him to "hold out" was not to prevent Adams's ultimate election but to help the Crawfordites secure "terms." As the reluctant McLane acknowledged, as kingmakers they could then "have control" of the new administration.[47]

On the other hand, the Adams men could still enhance their chances of early success by cultivating the Federalists scattered through most delegations. Jackson's appeal, especially in the Middle Atlantic states, had partly been as a nonpartisan, as the national hero who in 1817 had urged President Monroe not to discriminate against patriotic Federalists in his appointments to office. Adams was thought prejudiced against them because of the recriminations leveled at him ever since he abandoned the Federalist Party in 1807. Adams now gave private assurances that he would appoint suitable Federalists to office, though in fairness he added that both the other candidates would undoubtedly do the same. Such assurances had already confirmed the support of Webster, who now looked to Adams for promotion, ideally to the coveted London mission; critically, they clinched the uncertain Henry Warfield of Maryland, who spread the news to other Middle State Federalists. Thus Adams confirmed the support not only of Maryland but also of critically placed individuals in the New York delegation.[48]

As throughout the long campaign, the Empire State held the key. Inscrutable as ever, many observers simply omitted the state from their calculations of the likely result because, according to a North Carolina member, every New York congressman "now seems to desire rather to find out the course of others than to disclose his own." The most organized element in the delegation consisted of loyal Bucktail men, a majority originally elected in 1822 and committed to the Democratic candidate. Their numbers had been sapped by the dramatic events in New York in 1824 and the experience of struggling for reelection, which ensured that the largest bloc within the delegation consisted of Adams men, now strengthened by Clay's personal supporters. Clinton tried to direct his acolytes toward Jackson, even though most Clintonians preferred Adams; in the decisive ballot, two did vote for the General. In this situation the Crawfordites had little chance of carrying the delegation, but they could hope to prevent it from casting a vote. Well-placed observers thought that New York was most likely to go for Adams, "possibly in the first instance, certainly in the end," but the Adams ranks suffered a blow when one of their presumed members, John J. Morgan, a congressman for Manhattan, announced he would vote for Jackson. Plumer thought that "even the New York members did not know, with certainty, which way it would be, till their votes were counted"—a situation that encouraged the Crawfordites to hope that the seduction of just one man could prevent a majority.[49]

Of the eighteen Adams congressmen, they focused their hopes on Stephen Van Rensselaer. Far from the weak and foolish old man sometimes portrayed, the dignified but affable Patroon was the greatest landholder in New York, a figure of independent standing and political influence. Though a Federalist, he had taken charge as major general of the invasion of Canada's Niagara frontier in 1813, had served as lieutenant governor, twice run as a gubernatorial candidate, and would serve on the state's canal commission for twenty-three years, fourteen of them as president following Clinton. In 1824 he knew all the presidential candidates and had their confidence. Tending to "glide with the stream," he had at one point favored Clay, though in August 1823 his cousin, Solomon, had forecast he would in the end prove a "firm friend" to Adams.[50]

Contrary to Van Buren's distant memory, there is no contemporary evidence that the Patroon ever promised to vote for Crawford. Initially in December 1824 Van Rensselaer agreed with Clinton that Jackson was most likely to win and decided to back him; as he reassured one former party colleague, "You and I are too old to fear any molestation from him—we were not Hartford Convention men but good federalists." As he came to realize Adams could win, Van Rensselaer appreciated his own vote might become critical. Assuring Clay that New York would in the end vote for Adams, he directly asked the latter to confirm that he would appoint "the most able & worthy men, without reference to parties." By these conversations Van Rensselaer considered himself pledged, and he later insisted that he had told Van Buren of his decision. His intention "could not have been unknown to the opponents of Adams." Certainly Adams himself claimed later that he had known before the vote that he was going to win, probably on the first ballot.[51]

However, the highly sociable Van Rensselaer was vulnerable to pressure because he shared a mess with Van Buren and McLane, who certainly believed that the day before the ballot they had persuaded him not to vote for Adams on the first ballot. The man himself repeated that assurance on the day itself to others, including Charles Fenton Mercer of Virginia, who was also thought to be "in favor of Jackson." Recognizing that several critical members were intending to vote for Adams partly because they wanted to go with the winner, Crawford leaders communicated Van Rensselaer's statement to Scott of Missouri and the "timid & indecisive" Gurley of Louisiana in an effort to swing those states.[52]

Clay and Webster fiercely resisted this attempt to counter the expectation of victory that held the Clay–Adams forces together. Neither wished to see a stalemate that would eventually be broken by the Crawford men, giving the Radicals a strong voice in the new administration. Clay and his Western allies were determined to keep out men who would negate the influence of Western policy in an Adams presidency. Nor did Webster and the Federalists wish to see the most partisan of Democratic Republicans retain a position to influence future appointments. Together, Clay and Webster nobbled Van Rensselaer in his way to the House and emphasized the need for a prompt resolution of the election to avoid "disorganization of the government." If he intended to support Adams

Engraved by G.Parker from a Miniature by C.Fraser

STEPHEN VAN RENSSELAER.

*Stephen Van Rensselaer. This engraving by George Parker (d. 1868) is based on a miniature by Charles Fraser, painted about 1835, when Van Rensselaer was about seventy, ten years after the election of Adams in the House of Representatives. The Patroon has been calculated to have been the tenth richest man in American history, worth the equivalent of $88 billion at 2007 prices at the time of his death in 1839. Courtesy: Library of Congress Prints and Photographs Division.*

at some point, he must do so immediately. Clay also had Scott of Missouri speak to him a few minutes before the vote, presumably to confirm that Scott was voting for Adams. There can be no doubt that Van Buren and McLane felt betrayed by Van Rensselaer's vote and made life miserable for him in their mess, but equally they had been grasping at straws and trying to exploit fallibilities that did not exist. Their tactics failed not only with the Patroon but also with Samuel Eddy of Rhode Island, John Scott of Missouri, and Henry Gurley of Louisiana.[53]

So it was that on February 9, in the midst of a snowstorm, Congress met in joint session to hear the announcement of the indecisive electoral vote. The Senate then withdrew to allow the House to make its choice. Each congressman dropped his ballot in the box provided for each delegation. Duplicate certificates of the state results were placed in two boxes and examined by separate committees. The two chairmen, Randolph and Webster, announced the result of their counts, which agreed: thirteen states out of twenty-four had voted for John Quincy Adams. According to Niles, "Everything in this election was conducted with perfect propriety and decorum on the part of the House"—though when the result was announced, "some clapping and exultation took place in the galleries, and some hissing followed," whereupon Speaker Clay had the galleries cleared. The conclusive vote brought general surprise—not that Adams had won, but that he had done so on the first ballot.[54]

That was the point: if he hadn't, the course of future ballots was unpredictable. As Van Buren foresaw, "the push on the part of the Mr. Adams' supporters" had "to succeed on the first ballot." They had hopes that New Jersey and Indiana would swing their way on subsequent votes, but they also knew that in three or four states, their advantage rested on a single vote. Once their state count began to reduce, the coalition would wobble as some elements came to fear that Adams would now gain victory through the support of Crawfordite states. In that case, as Congressman Beecher had earlier suggested, some Western Clay men might well look to secure the triumph of Western interests by preemptively shifting their votes to Jackson.[55]

An immediate vote for Adams was therefore a way of avoiding uncertainty, but it was also for many the straightforward path. To accept Van Buren's policy of tactically shifting votes meant playing a subtle game that had begun to look dishonorable. McLane had earlier been willing to consider a Crawfordite shift en bloc to Adams in order to "have control of the administration," but in the last days, even he was upset by hints that "the *New Yorker*" was thinking of leading his men into the Adams camp. Equally, Eddy was "shocked" by Van Buren's suggestions and "resolved not to be used by others." He chose to show constancy of purpose and cast his vote as the people of Rhode Island and of New England clearly wanted. The sense of democratic obligation in the end was fulfilled rather than betrayed by the election of John Quincy Adams.[56]

## BARGAIN AND CORRUPTION

The manner of election in the House, John C. Wright thought, was "well calculated to make a favourable impression on the nation and on strangers of the great moral force of our Republican institutions." One witness from Salem, Massachusetts, thought it "astonishing, after so much excitement, to see how quietly and with how much dignity and propriety the crisis was met even by those who had the most intense feelings on the subject. . . . I could not but feel gratified that Adams had been chosen, altho' I wish it had been a better man." In the evening after the election, the visitor attended President Monroe's last evening reception at the White House:

> Such a crowd! . . . General [Winfield] Scott had his pocket picked there, with $800 in it. It occurred to me that it was a fine place for the business. . . . The excitement that has so long existed and from which so much was feared seemed to have passed away in a moment. Genl. J. had many more smiles than his successful rival—whose muscles by the way are not often relaxed by smiles.

Many in the crowd witnessed the critical moment when Jackson approached Adams and shook hands, with the latter looking much the more embarrassed. In the days that followed, the city filled with "strangers and people of distinction from every part of the country," many of them office seekers, and the atmosphere of celebration continued through the inauguration.[57]

The Senate accepted the legitimacy of the new administration, confirming Adams's senior appointments without opposition, except for Clay's nomination as secretary of state. Even that controversial appointment passed by a vote of 25–13, with opposition coming from the Jacksonians and half the Crawfordites. Van Buren voted for Clay, and Nathaniel Macon made it plain that he voted against him "not on account of his conduct on the election of President, but for his construction of the constitution."[58] Those congressmen who voted for Adams were later held to account back home for their vote, especially if they represented a district where Jackson had won more votes than Adams. Yet in the congressional elections of 1826–1827 those who had voted for Adams retained a higher proportion of their seats (90 percent) than did the Jackson men (85 percent).[59]

Among the public at large, the bitterest complaints came from the Jacksonians. Their newspapers sent up a howl of disappointment and disapproval and insisted the Hero had been cheated. The Cincinnati *National Republican,* which had warned that "the Clay party in Ohio" was about to betray "domestic measures," announced the virtual end of the republic with the headline, *"The Bourbons are restored."* In Philadelphia the *Columbian Observer* wanted to see Clay *"tarred and feathered";* indeed, according to one count, Clay was "burned in effigy 153 times in the different states of the Union, and buried formally 7 times." The abuse was so extreme—and so unsubstantiated—that one Ohio lawyer thought it proved conclusively that "not monkies [sic] alone throw their own excrement for want of better weapons."[60]

Yet for all that, it appears that majority opinion favored the outcome, and no Jacksonian actually offered insult to Clay. Even in Cincinnati the Jackson men put on "more good natured faces than might have been expected," while the inaugural did much to conciliate local opinion because it "demonstrated that Mr. Adams is with us—He is sold to Mr. Clay, not Mr. Clay to him." The new secretary of state's correspondents assured him that most of the West was not just satisfied but "enthusiastic" about the result, except "in the huckster and the barber shops." In the summer, with the president's encouragement, Clay took a leisurely journey home and made many public appearances. He was delighted by the warmth of his reception in nearly every village "from the Alleghany [sic] to Lexington going and returning through Ohio. . . . The demonstrations which were made of public esteem and consideration, in the case of Genl. La Fayette, hardly exceeded those of which I was the object."[61]

This approval seemed to answer those who thought Clay unwise to accept the offer of the state department. Many voices advised him against. Some, like Crawford, thought Adams would make a poor president and drag down anyone associated with him. More said Clay ought not to accept because it would gave substance to the charge of a corrupt bargain; some added that he would do more good to the Western cause by staying in the House and smoothing the course of favorable legislation. However, others thought that if he refused, his opponents would in any case seize on it as proof of a guilty conscience, while the appointment of Clay to a Cabinet post was necessary to confirm that the new administration would remain committed to Western policies. As one minor Western politician wrote, "If Mr. A. performs ⅔ of what he hints at in his inaugural speech, I am satisfied—and if Clay is his right hand man the Republic is safe, and the West will be tolerably satisfied." After all, under Monroe, executive decisions were usually discussed by the five-man Cabinet, even if the president sometimes made his own decision, and all five senior members were considered important in the formulation of policy.[62]

In any case, what were the alternatives? After Adams, Clay was best qualified for the office and agreed with Adams on the main issues of foreign policy, at least since the recognition of the independent Latin American republics. If Clay did not take the office, the alternative secretary of state would become a rival for the succession—and if the office went to someone as self-focused as Clinton (as Monroe wanted), the administration would suffer, in Calhoun's words, "much trouble and . . . much distraction."[63]

If the appointment was entirely reasonable and honorable, why did the charge of corruption gain such force and become the widely accepted narrative of the 1825 negotiations? Clay would never manage to throw off the accusation of bargain and corruption, and late in life he thought his acceptance of the office a great mistake. Van Buren later claimed to have warned Kentucky congressman Frank Johnson in advance that if the Clay men made Adams president, "they would sign Mr. Clay's political death warrant. He will never become President, be your motives as pure as you claim them to be." To the suspicious mind, the coming together of two men who had frequently disagreed in the past and who had been supported on different grounds during the election campaign could be explained only by an unprincipled bargain to further each other's political interests.

Jackson immediately leapt to that conclusion: "the *Judas* of the West has closed the contract and will receive the thirty pieces of silver—his end will be the same. Was there ever witnessed such a bare faced corruption in any country before?"[64] This refrain echoed through Jackson's correspondence, and some of his comments later reached the press. No matter that Adams appointed not one lame duck congressman to federal office, even though they were the most open to corruption; no matter that the evidence of a crude hawking of Clay's support was nonexistent.[65] The mere fact that candidates had not sat back, like Jackson himself, and held themselves aloof from all negotiation was proof of corruption. The thought that a hung election could only be settled by discussion and compromise did not enter his thinking. All Jackson could do was assume his suspicions were true, bemoan the corruption of modern men and the threat to the republic, and accept that civic duty now required him to heed the people's call to save "the liberty of my country." The role of Patriot King, suitably republicanized, was one that Jackson could not now refuse.[66]

If the belief in corruption provided Jackson with his motivation for opposing the Adams administration from its very threshold, it gave his protagonists and supporters the ideological cover they needed to justify organizing an opposition party. When Richard M. Johnson said that the Jacksonians would oppose the Adams administration even "if they act as pure as the angels that stand at the right hand of the throne of God," his statement met with public indignation because opposition for its own sake was still frowned on.[67] Many observers expected those excluded from the Adams–Clay combination to oppose the new administration's policies, but the presumption remained that only differences based on high principle could justify partisan behavior. Adams himself hoped to maintain the nominally consensual basis of Monroe's presidency, and to that end, he had offered to keep Crawford at the treasury. Crawford had politely declined and urged his followers to give the administration time to reveal its policies; as Van Buren later wrote, they did not enter into opposition until the president's statements in his inaugural address, and then developed in his first annual message, gave them decent cause. By contrast, the Jacksonians argued that an administration created by a corrupt bargain could not have the best wishes of the republic and the people at heart.[68]

Furthermore, the cry of corruption had the electoral merit of appealing to all the suspicions of men in power that had built up over the years of panic and depression. If there was an "Era of Corruption" (as the historian Robert Remini argued), it was not in the 1820s but had peaked in the heady days of speculation immediately after the war, when bankers, land speculators, and their legal associates had exploited control of government at all levels to line their own pockets. The voter rebellions of 1819–1822 in local and congressional elections had already reduced both their influence and the financial means of government, and the agents of the Adams administration would keep their hands remarkably clean. Attempts by congressional committees in 1828 to find waste and corruption found little to complain about and had no proposals for further retrenchment. In Cincinnati a Jackson editor set up a campaign newspaper in 1828 entitled *The Friend of Reform and Corruption's Adversary* to expose the current "system of corruption and prodigality," but he could find enough material to fill only twelve pages out of the 400 published. Yet regardless of the facts, the memory of hard times created a popular presumption of corruption that the Jacksonians would exploit in 1827 and 1828, as they harked on the need for a patriotic hero "to sweep the Augean stables."[69]

Such rhetoric could draw on the long tradition of Country Party ideology that predated the American Revolution. It also gained strength from the peculiar character of the 1824 election. Since 1796 the choice of president had increasingly fallen into the hands of a popular electorate, as the conflict between Federalist and Democratic Republican simplified the choice of president to two names, clarified the political character of each candidate, and gave the electorate the opportunity to vote, directly or indirectly, for the man of their choice. Mechanisms such as the caucus and the legislative choice of electors may appear now to have obstructed the free expression of the popular voice, but few at the time doubted that the choice of presidents elected since 1801 met with popular approval. Then in 1824 the established democratic system ceased to work, the choice became more complex, the old guidelines no longer held, and the choice of electors inevitably failed to produce a clear result. The election had to be settled in conclave—even if the doors were open to the public—and it was all too easy to presume that politicians would take advantage of such a situation to feather their own nests. The House election became the manifest warning, as the masthead of the leading Jacksonian newspaper would have it in 1828: "POWER IS ALWAYS STEALING FROM THE MANY TO THE FEW."[70] Circumstances encouraged a popular suspicion that the choice of Adams had been corrupt, even as many other considerations prompted the revival of a two-party conflict that ensured that the election of president would in future return into the hands of the electorate.

In May 1829 Chile went to the polls under the democratic constitution devised and approved the previous year. Modeled on the original U.S. Constitution, it provided for the indirect election of the chief executive through an electoral college. The incumbent president, General Francisco Antonio Pinto, won an absolute majority in the college, but because he was expected to resign soon after taking office (as he did), the critical election was for vice president. Political opinion had become strongly polarized over the previous decade between liberals and conservatives, but the majority liberal grouping could not agree on its candidate. As a result there was no majority in the electoral college and the final choice had to be made by the congress. The liberal majority decided, quite plausibly, that it had a free choice among those returned to the college and chose the third-placed candidate. Unhappy with the outcome, conservatives and dissident liberals insisted that the congress was obliged to choose between the top two candidates and refused to accept the result. They carried out a coup in Santiago and created an alternative government. The country then suffered a two-battle civil war that confirmed the overthrow of the liberals who had apparently won the 1829 election.[1]

Five years earlier it had, for a moment, appeared that the United States election might similarly be decided by force. Two weeks before the joint announcement by Ohio and Kentucky delegations, the mere rumor of an Adams–Clay coalition roused threats of physical violence from within Pennsylvania. Lafayette's secretary, Auguste Levasseur, attended a dinner in York at which he met some Pennsylvania militiamen who "talked of laying siege to Washington if Jackson were not chosen." Adams himself received anonymous letters from Philadelphia threatening civil war if he were elected, and Senator Richard Johnson of Kentucky told him it had been seriously proposed to set up the General's standard in opposition to a new Adams government. Similar noises came from other centers, notably Cincinnati and New York, where they "are quite as hot as . . . in Philadelphia." Clay's confidant, Josiah S. Johnston, claimed there were "a set of violent men writing letters to inflame . . . the people" of Philadelphia and "aggravate their minds to produce effect" in

Washington. "Suppose they succeed in making an impression that the election is carried by corruption—would it not end in civil war"?[2]

Yet all was sound and fury. As Adams said, the threat of violence had "an air of desperation" as Jacksonians recognized their Hero could not win the House election. A few days after the event, the Pennsylvanian Edward Ingersoll remarked that "one might infer from reading the *Columbian Observer* that preparations were making for an actual march on Washington—but it is a fact except among the grog-shops . . . there is very little excitement—and the 'eleventh-hour men' as they have been called, or friends of Calhoun, are positively glad, as are the Crawfordites." In the evening after the House chose Adams, Levasseur too attended Monroe's last White House reception and witnessed the two rivals cordially shaking hands. He then bumped into two of the Pennsylvania militia officers he had dined with in York and asked what they intended to do. Laughing, one replied:

> You remember our threats, then; we were then in a good condition for making a noise; but our opponents paid no attention to it, and they have done well. They have judged us more justly than we desired. Now, since the law has spoken, we have only to obey. We shall second Mr. Adams with the same zeal as if we had chosen him; but at the same time, we shall watch his administration a little more closely, and according as it proves good or bad, we shall defend or attack it. Four years are soon gone; and the consequences of a bad election are easy to be repaired.

However much noise Jacksonian partisans might make, the defeated candidates made no attempt to resist the peaceful transfer of power, embarrass Adams's inauguration, or prevent the smooth establishment of his administration.[3]

The United States in 1825 differed from Chile in 1829 simply because of its long-established tradition of accepting the results of elections, even when the process did not work as opponents wished. Unlike former Spanish and French possessions, the British colonies had for two centuries chosen their provincial and local legislatures through voting and in the late eighteenth century had learned to trust representative institutions to defend the interests of local communities against imperial power. Since 1789 the electorate had even controlled central authority and chosen its chief executives, and the opposition had enjoyed freedom to organize within the established political order. However disturbing the disappearance of established political landmarks, however divisive the events of recent years, there still existed a broad consensus on constitutional and electoral procedures. In 1825 the disappointed may have doubted the moral rectitude of the victors, but they did not doubt the constitutional legitimacy of Adams's election.[4]

## THE NOVELTY OF 1824

The comparison with Chile in 1829, if a little stretched, indicates how far the election of 1824 departed from the almost comfortable routine of presidential elections since 1800. For twenty years the imbalance of voters' party loyalties had made a single party dominant nationally, the reelection of the incumbent in 1804 and 1820 had become almost automatic, and the main contest in 1808 and 1816 had been for the Republican nomination. Only in 1812, when Clinton's insistence on running against Madison seemed to give the Federalists a chance, had there been any doubt about the outcome. However, once the parties had lost their ability to command voter loyalty across a large number of states, the election became an unpredictable crisis in which candidates and politicians had to rely on personal contacts and vestigial party institutions to try to shape the outcome. In the process they were obliged to innovate, often on the basis of earlier experience but as never before required in a presidential election.

The first new demand imposed by the election was for active leadership of each campaign. In most previous presidential elections candidates had been able to stand back because the party did the necessary organizational work, and candidates were identified by party label rather than as individuals. Thus the candidates were relieved of the need to push their candidacy and could fulfill the expectations of a "mute tribune." In 1824 virtually every candidate directed his own campaign through personal correspondence or relied on close associates. Crawford was notably active before his illness, and afterward good friends, notably Van Buren, came to the rescue. Jackson insisted he would do nothing to advance his own cause, but Eaton and Lewis acted effectively as his managers while Jackson himself maintained a considerable correspondence, subscribed to eighteen newspapers, and had to be cautioned by Eaton against being drawn into newspaper controversies. Only as the day of voting approached did he fall into a dignified silence in the summer and fall of 1824.

Adams too may have sincerely believed he should maintain a passive role, but as the election got closer he became more active. When his friends set up a Washington paper, the *National Journal,* to promote his cause in November 1823, he made a point of ensuring that the state department placed its advertising there. In the weeks before the House election, he conspicuously began to discuss future possibilities with potential allies, privately walking on fiery coals as he doubted his own probity.[5] Clay proved the least effective organizer, partly because he was so distracted by family and personal illness and, until late 1823, the demands of his bank job. He found few willing to act for him in distant states, and his attempt to found a devoted newspaper in Washington in 1823 got little further than the prospectus. In the summer of 1824 the Louisiana senator Josiah S. Johnston tried to boost Clay's cause in the Middle States, bemoaning how it had sunk everywhere "under the want of direction & management," when "a little activity & money" would have "engaged . . . a sufficient number of presses." Clay would never neglect party organization again.[6]

The press was recognized as the key means of communication by every campaign. Crawford and Calhoun both understood from an early date that an effective press in the capital was an absolute necessity, and by the summer of 1823 newspapers had also appeared there for Adams and, for a brief moment, Clay. The Washington press, together with prominent newspapers in New York, Philadelphia, Boston, and Baltimore, exchanged with local newspapers free of postal charges, thus creating an interchange of information and a means of disseminating favorable news and argument in a system that had developed over the previous thirty years. Newspaper support sometimes arose spontaneously, notably when an established paper volunteered its support, but sometimes means—financial, technical, and editorial—had to be found, as Calhoun demonstrated so successfully in the early part of the campaign. One of Adams's advantages was the number of literate young men, like Thurlow Weed, who volunteered their literary efforts up and down the land.[7] Once acquired, the press was used in innovative ways: for example, campaign biographies were published for the first time (for every candidate except Clay), and candidates now began to issue policy statements through letters to private individuals, which—like the supposedly nonpolitical Jackson's letter to Dr. Coleman—newspapers were then permitted to reprint because it would be wrong to deprive the public of information they deserved to have.

The nomination of candidates in a way that established the serious-ness and identity of their campaign also required fresh thought. The congressional caucus could carry weight only for so long as it could demonstrate that it did so; the moment the Democratic Republican Party lost its ability to command its voters, the caucus became pointless, though it took the experience of 1824 to demonstrate this simple truth to all. Crawford's opponents faced the difficulty of finding some alter-native authority to recognize their candidacies, and their regional focus made state legislatures seem the obvious solution. Contrary to received historical opinion, there was no accepted tradition of formal nomination by state legislatures, and very quickly opponents objected so strongly to legislative interference in the choice of president that assemblies began to refuse the opportunity. The resort to separate nominations by county meetings proved popular, but it led to confusion and contradictory nomi-nations on the same side; if it didn't, opponents complained (as in North Carolina) that the county meetings were following a prearranged script prepared in private caucus.

Undoubtedly this election marked the passage from caucuses to con-ventions. That transition was less significant than might be thought because of the extensive prior experience of delegate nominating con-ventions at grassroots levels in the Middle Atlantic states and Ohio and even at state level in Pennsylvania and New York. In 1816 William Duane and his followers in Pennsylvania and Ohio had proposed a national nominating convention, but it was regarded as an unnecessary incon-venience when representatives from around the nation were already gathered at Washington. By 1827 Van Buren, attracted by the association of delegate conventions with Democratic Republican tradition, was dis-cussing the possibility of a national convention with Thomas Ritchie, though agreement on the opposition candidates for 1828 made a meet-ing of any sort unnecessary. The main obstacle to a specially convened national convention was long-distance transportation. By 1824 the in-crease in steamboats in the coastal trade and on the Ohio and Missis-sippi, as well as the convenience of an (unrepaired) National Road from the Ohio through Maryland, were already easing travel from the West, but considerable difficulties still existed in many parts of the nation. Those problems would reduce in the late 1820s, thanks to an acceler-ation in canal and road building; indeed, the ability of three parties to hold national conventions in 1831–1832 owed a good deal to the stimulus given to internal improvements during the Adams presidency.

In many states, legislatures preserved their traditional role of naming, in caucus, both electoral tickets and committees of correspondence. This was convenient for any candidate with a reasonable number of supporters within a legislature but could not serve a candidacy that lacked such support or that took off after the assembly had closed its session. In such circumstances the Jacksonians in Ohio and Indiana organized state delegate conventions—the first in the nation called in a presidential election—which, however badly attended, did the job; the public relations advantage of relying on popularly elected delegates also induced the Crawford men in Pennsylvania and the Jacksonians in Virginia to hold their own state conventions.[8] Delegate conventions had the additional advantage of requiring early organization at the grass roots, which could then be used by local committees to bring out the voters on Election Day.

The part that legislatures still played in the process made protagonists eager to make the presidential question an issue in state elections held long before October 1824. Ironically, the more indirect the democracy, the more it stimulated partisan organization to control and scrutinize the action of legislators. Crawfordites and Calhoun men in North Carolina raised the issue in 1823, as did Adams men in the Old Northwest, in attempts to control state legislatures. Such efforts became more serious as 1824 approached in those states where the assembly still chose the electors: the presidential question was introduced into state elections, and in some states, notably Vermont and Georgia, the people in effect controlled the choice. Delaware and Louisiana remained inscrutable, but in New York the power of voters out of doors effectively swayed the assembly's decision, though they could not control or determine it. The same awareness was expressed in some congressional elections of 1822–1823, but on the whole the contest was too ill-defined at that moment for many congressmen to have given pledges. The elections held in 1824–1825 could have no direct effect on the personnel involved in the House election, but congressional candidates seeking reelection in 1824 had to explain, if necessary, their involvement in the congressional caucus the previous February and state their intentions in the coming House election; usually they promised to respect the wishes expressed by the voters.

In effect, the presidential election had the effect of democratizing state politics. Voters who made their wishes known to legislators were likely to be informed if any representative betrayed his trust. Similarly, the respective campaigns kept an eye on those chosen as presidential electors. Whereas in the past party ties and party command of patronage could keep electors faithful to the ticket they were elected on, in 1824 independent politicians feared that the old party men might use their advantages to seduce some into casting rogue votes in the Electoral College. Eaton warned fellow Jacksonians that "craft & management may slip improper men in who may deceive," but only in New York did this fear prove justified. In most states such vigilance was the job of the state committee of correspondence, which became the essential enforcers and energizers.[9]

The committees of correspondence also had to energize the campaign across the state including areas where they lacked visible support. Thus they were largely responsible for the county meetings that in 1824 were called in numbers unprecedented in a presidential election. Campaigns confident of carrying a particular state—be it Vermont, Virginia, or Kentucky—did not usually call such meetings, but challenging campaigns often did. The meetings sometimes nominated electors, but more often they were designed for their effect elsewhere, even when not well attended. The committees were also responsible for organizing parades, administering straw polls, and exploiting occasions when crowds mustered, which could enthuse voters and make good news copy. The Jacksonians were at the forefront of such initiatives, especially parades and militia musters, but they were closely matched by the Adams men in many constituencies. Indeed, any notion that anti-Jacksonians had a built-in cultural resistance to partisan activity cannot survive close attention to the 1824 campaign.[10]

Overall, state politics had little effect on the presidential contest, at least outside New York. Elections for other offices often ignored the fight for the White House and looked to more local issues, such as the plans for the proposed state canal program in Ohio, the contest over slavery in Illinois, and the relief struggle in Kentucky. These campaigns had their effect on the presidential contest in terms of introducing new election techniques and heightening issue awareness, as in Illinois; from the reverse view, the presidential election could impact on state elections whenever a local candidate—like Mr. Martin in Fayetteville, North Carolina—tried to defeat an established local rival by appealing to popular presidential preferences. That same logic would lead to the growing consonance between local and national politics over the next fourteen years.

As was true federally, local communication with the voters depended on the printing press. Long a key part of the political arena, existing local newspapers in 1823–1824 took up particular candidates and acted as a means of coordination and spread their favorite's message. The number of candidates on this occasion encouraged the foundation of new newspapers to support those who were otherwise ignored locally. Adams attracted the support of many local editors; Jackson ran well behind, except in North Carolina, where he inherited the fruits of Calhoun's work. These papers took much of their campaign material from other newspapers, and frequently their articles reflected materials elsewhere; in the case of Jackson, that commonly meant the *Letters of Wyoming*. Campaign spoofs were popular, defining the contest in everyday terms, as horse races or family arguments; the few cartoons that survive were too difficult (and too expensive) to print in newspapers and were usually restricted to handbills sold on city street corners. Local presses also printed tickets that could be used at the polls, and handbills, sometimes scurrilous, that were designed for the local electorate. These circulated freely, reaching a large audience, often too late for effective contradiction; in New York historian Alvin Kass found them "thrown on doorsteps, tacked on fence rails, and on the backs of wagons." They were commonly handed out by the campaigners who in the final days visited voters to persuade them to the polls.[11]

There can be no doubt of Andrew Jackson's popular appeal in some particular places. He found enthusiastic support in many backcountry areas, most notably in North Carolina and the Southwest, though in some states the backcountry preferred Clay or even Adams. The Hero thrived most in those metropolises that had been heftily hit by the Panic and depression, and these places were the source of most Jacksonian organizational energy; strikingly though, the largest cities—the great seaports—were either immune to Jackson, like Boston, or too socially complex, like Philadelphia, for one candidate to have an easy ride there. Votes were more likely to pile up in surrounding areas close to the metropolis, as in the case of Cincinnati, though around Baltimore the main beneficiary was Adams. In addition, Jackson's candidacy had huge, often underspoken, appeal to particular ethnic groups, notably the Scotch-Irish and Pennsylvania Dutch, wherever they lived. The support of Irish Catholics for Jackson in New York City helps explain De Witt Clinton's attraction to his cause, even while most of his supporters in state politics preferred a Northern man.

Adams enjoyed a similarly broad appeal, but to a different section of the population, usually better educated and more cultivated religiously. However uninspiring personally, he attracted the votes of New Englanders spread throughout the country, including the more secularly minded as well as those who considered themselves (in Josiah Quincy's phrase) members of "a religious and moral people." Their moral sense had been reinvigorated by the Missouri crisis, and moderate antislavery sentiment, often marred by racist overtones, undoubtedly created votes for Adams; the correlation between hostility to Southern slavery and an Adams vote in New York, Ohio, and Illinois is too strong to deny, however sublimated in New England itself. Significantly, though, that association did not prevent Adams from becoming the leading opposition candidate in Maryland or the lower Southwestern states, as the two-party logic of the electoral system made him increasingly the obvious repository for the votes for those who could not accept either Jackson or Crawford.

The complexities of the 1824 election guaranteed that a straight two-horse race would not develop. The line of policy that was initiated by the Monroe administration and embodied in Clay's American System provoked strong regional disagreements that overrode simple North–South differences. The division between Atlantic interests and those who looked to the development of the interior prevented unity within the South and limited the appeal of the Northern candidate west of the Appalachians. "After all," as Wheaton said of the settlers of western New York, "though a portion of the 'universal Yankee nation,' they are *western* in their feelings & interests."[12] At the same time the salience of ethnocultural differences prevented the appearance of political divisions based simply on economic interest and outlook, with the result that many in New York and Pennsylvania failed to see that agreement on government policy meant that they should support the proposed Adams–Clay deal. During the preceding months Clinton may have defined the outlook of the future Whig Party, but he could see no contradiction in throwing his personal support to General Jackson.

The majority voting system created a pressure for voters to focus their votes on the two candidates with the best chance of success, as it had done in 1796 and 1800, but the campaigns of Clay and especially Crawford won enough states to prevent either Jackson or Adams from winning an Electoral College majority. That created the need for a contingent election, which duly revealed the unsatisfactory nature of the processes laid down by the Founding Fathers for settling any election in which more than two candidates were capable of carrying a significant number of electoral votes. That experience prompted what has proved to be the last serious attempt to correct a defect that may yet, at some time, prevent a satisfactory conclusion to a presidential election.

## CONSTITUTIONAL REFORM, AGAIN

When Andrew Jackson was nominated for 1828 by the Tennessee legislature in October 1825, his acceptance message pointed immediately to what he thought were the two necessary reforms: the restriction of presidents to a single term and a ban on appointing members of Congress to federal office. There was no great demand for either reform—the latter was clearly just a sideswipe at Clay—and neither proposal got anywhere. Nor was there any great demand for the suffrage to be extended even further among adult white men, because they already had it, at least outside Rhode Island, Virginia, and Louisiana. However, there was a widespread feeling that the election process could be made to reflect the popular will more effectively.

The election had clearly shown the disadvantages of allowing state legislatures to choose the presidential electors. There was an inherent difficulty in deciding the best way to hold the vote in a bicameral legislature; as Delaware and New York had demonstrated, the method adopted could have a real effect on the outcome. A legislative election was certainly open to corruption (or the suspicion of corruption) in a way that a popular election could not be. There were few guarantees that those elected to the Electoral College by a legislature would vote as intended, whereas popularly elected electors absolutely felt obliged to do so. The awareness of these drawbacks resulted in four of the six legislative-vote states adopting the general ticket by 1828 and Delaware following suit in 1829; only South Carolina stuck to legislative privilege, right down to the Civil War.

A major effort was made in Congress in February 1826 to correct more general inadequacies of the current presidential system. The Jacksonian leader in the House, George McDuffie, pointed out that "different rules prevail in the same State at different times, and in the different states at the same time, all liable to be changed according to the varying views and fluctuating fortunes of political parties." He wanted a standardized but democratic system and advocated a resolution calling for a simplified version of the Dickerson proposal of two years before: introduce a uniform district system and prevent the reversion of a hung election to the House. This proposal, however, faced strong opposition from Crawford men, who argued that a district system would violate the "federative principle" upon which the United States was based, whereas the general ticket system recognized the key role of "the states in their political character."[13]

The House concurred overwhelmingly on the need to avoid future House elections, but the committee it appointed could not agree on any alternative plan. Inevitably the Jacksonians used the occasion to beat the administration for lacking democratic legitimacy, thus alienating potential supporters among their opponents. Some Adams men responded that the presidential election should be made genuinely democratic: abolish the Electoral College and let the president be chosen in a single nationwide ballot. The House approved reference to a committee, but as its proponents had foreseen, the South would never accept this sacrifice of the three-fifths advantage. As for the district system, the large states refused to surrender the advantage they gained from the general ticket, which rapidly became accepted as the norm. Proposals for reform did not emerge from committee and have never been successfully revived since, mainly because the reemergence of the two-party system after 1825 greatly reduced the chances of a hung election recurring again.[14]

## ON WITH THE NEW

The election of presidential electors in 1824 did not mark the beginning of the Second Party System but rather the end of the old system. The various candidates had chosen to slug it out in 1824, ignoring those who argued that they needed to join forces; the campaign was therefore destructive for both the old parties, as the issues and passions of the election cut across preexisting groupings. The House election faced a different imperative—the need to find a government by creating a coalition—and the establishment of the ruling formation in itself provoked a counterunion among those excluded. Charles Hammond in Cincinnati later mused that regardless of who won the House election, those left out would have created an opposition party—but that judgment exaggerates the chance nature of the winning combination that had been created.

The House election in effect created a coalition that would, in the next decade or so, develop into what came to be called the Whig Party. That combination was made up of two strands: on the one hand, the blend of Yankee pride, moral reform and antislavery sentiment that had produced a great bloc of support for Adams across most Northern states; on the other, the broad demand for American System policies so evident in the support Clay won in the Ohio Valley states. This coalition first provided most of the congressional support for the new administration's legislative program, then fought as a coherent party to reelect Adams in 1828, broke apart under the strain of political Antimasonry during Jackson's first term, substantially reunited in 1832, and then provided the backbone of the Northern and Border state branch of the Whig Party in the later 1830s. Through all the changes of name, it represented much the same impulses, constituencies, and political identities as came together in 1825.[15]

Though routinely condemned as a failure, the Adams administration was in fact a landmark. As Adams emphasized in his inaugural address (Appendix 2), he wished to continue Monroe's work in assuaging old party feelings, but he also planned to advance "improvement"—and in fact his tenure was important for providing a more positive example of effective federal encouragement of economic development than Alexander Hamilton had managed. Though these measures were essentially the work of Congress and passed by bipartisan log roll, the existence of a sympathetic and encouraging executive released the pent-up demand in Congress for roads, canals, and improvements to rivers and harbors. Under the Adams presidency the federal government spent as much on internal improvements in four years as it had in the previous twenty-four years. Moreover, the projects begun under Adams covered a wider variety of proposals than the previous concentration on the National Road, and they would continue to draw on the treasury long after President Jackson had cast his 1830 Maysville veto against future grand schemes. Thus it is quite inappropriate to describe the Adams administration, as did the political scientist Stephen Skowroneck, as identified with a set of commitments that had failed or were deemed irrelevant. In fact it marked the beginnings of a program that the Whig Party would strive to expand for the next quarter century.[16]

Adams failed to win reelection in 1828 partly because of the nature of his victory in the House election. To win in 1825, the Adams men had needed thirteen states, regardless of the size of their populations, but small states, by definition, cannot carry a similar degree of power in either the Electoral College or the regular proceedings of the House. More importantly, they had of necessity relied on a number of divided, competitive states, notably New York and Ohio. In the 1826–1827 congressional elections, the administration held most of their seats, including some where Adams men represented districts that had voted overwhelmingly for Jackson in 1824, but they suffered from their lack of support in the South and from the pockets of support enjoyed by Jacksonians and Crawfordites in the North. As a result, the loss of just ten seats was enough for them to lose control of the House, as the speakership election of December 1827 revealed. In the presidential election of 1828 the thirteen Adams states of 1825 possessed 139 electoral votes out of 261, but only the six New England states, with 51 electoral votes, could be regarded as safe; in comparison, the opposition commanded 101 votes in seven safe states in the South and Pennsylvania. An Adams victory depended on winning most of the marginal states in the face of the most charismatic presidential candidate of the nineteenth century armed with a message of democratic restoration.

The Jacksonian opposition took significantly longer to blend into a unified electoral force. The personal supporters of Jackson were from the start committed to opposition, and they nominated their Hero for the 1828 election as early as October 1825. The problem was that the Crawfordites had absolutely rejected Jackson in 1824, as both a military chieftain who could not be trusted with civil power and as a nationalist hostile to strict construction of the Constitution. Through 1825 their resistance weakened as they saw with alarm the growing conjoined threats of a new de facto Federalism and open menaces to their systems of racial control.[17] In the congressional session of 1825–1826 they joined the Jacksonians in opposing the Panama Congress, but the action of the two groups was not coordinated. Van Buren's great achievement was to persuade the former Crawfordites that, as Crawford himself was now hors de combat, their only hope was to rally on Jackson. That process, however, took time.

One complicating factor was, as ever, De Witt Clinton. Though most of his followers preferred Adams, Governor Clinton used his personal influence to carve out a separate position for himself in future presidential politics. Some of those close to him spoke of his running against Adams in 1828. Failing that, Clinton advocated Jackson, partly in the belief that he would be Jackson's natural successor. Such a stance was a major obstacle to persuading old Democrats in New York to back Jackson. Van Buren concentrated on restoring the old party's dominance in New York state politics and allowed the party's nomination for governor in 1826 to go to an old Democrat, George Rochester, who supported Clay in 1824 and now the new administration; Van Buren was not displeased when Governor Clinton won reelection. Thereafter Van Buren strove to bring his supporters in state politics to recognize that the real threat to their old principles was not Clinton but rather a federal administration that could be branded as neo-Federalist. By September 1827 he had substantially achieved that task, even healing the personal rift with Clinton; any possibility of future difficulties with that unreliable man disappeared with Clinton's death in February 1828. Even then, it was regarded as necessary to reinforce the party loyalty of Dutch farmers by having Van Buren himself run for governor in 1828 on the same ticket as Jackson.

Southern Crawfordites were drawn into a united opposition party by the argument that Jackson may have been a nationalist in 1824, but his future course as president would be different if he owed his election to Southern states' rights men. Van Buren pointed out that "the General was at an earlier period well grounded in the principles of our party"; and John Tyler, now senator for Virginia, told his party friends at home that, if surrounded in cabinet by reliable men, Jackson would adopt Virginia principles and even come right on the American System. This argument proved well justified when, as president, Jackson adopted a modified strict construction formula as his own and destroyed federal policies and institutions that threatened the South. As one historically minded Democrat of the 1870s would remark, the policy of the party as it emerged from Jackson's presidency owed less to the Jacksonians of 1824 than to the Crawfordites.[18]

The attraction of the neo-Antifederalists into the Jacksonian coalition obviously owed much to events under President Adams. The South came together in the late 1820s under the combined pressure both of perceived threats to its control of black slaves and native tribes and of the hostile economic policy demanded by the Northern majority in Congress. So powerful was this double pressure south of the Border states that all sorts of antagonistic groups came together in support of Jackson. Crawfordite joined with Calhounite, leaving their differences to be settled after Jackson's victory. Calhoun himself had tried in 1824 to keep his vice presidential campaign independent of both Jackson and Adams, but the political sensitivities of the South made it clear he had no political future backing the Adams administration.[19]

The contest of 1828 would see presidential campaigning carried to a new intensity. None of the campaigning techniques used was new, but they had never been used so extensively in a presidential election. Many of the means used to promote particular candidates, notably political biographies and campaign newspapers, had been pioneered in 1824 but had not reached the whole nation because of the internal agreement within many states. The main impact in 1824 had been limited to the battleground states; 1828 simply widened the battleground. The result was to arouse new levels of interest and draw crowds of new voters to the polls, to an extent far beyond the expectation of anyone involved in the election—and such a "surge" of voters has always redounded to the advantage of the party out of power.[20]

How voters responded to the blitz of propaganda and agitation that hit them in 1828 depended on their political background and their location. Some saw the current contest through their experiences in the 1824 election, which had given them a political view and a loyalty that affected how they now responded. Evidence from New Jersey, Maryland, Ohio, and Cumberland County, North Carolina, suggests that those who had become caught up in a close contest in 1824 stuck with their choice, and a pamphlet published in New York assumed that the votes cast in 1824 and in the 1826–1827 congressional elections provided a fair benchmark against which to measure developments in 1828. For many, like the young lawyer Robert J. Walker of Pittsburgh, loyalties were created then that could persist a lifetime.[21]

However, that experience was limited and overtaken by events. The fusion of the Crawford and Jackson forces by 1828 meant that the battle lines had changed in all the South Atlantic states and created virtual one-party situations; only for the Adams and Clay minority was there any continuity of political alignment. In the broadening number of states now open to a two-party contest, the excitements of a close struggle brought floods of new voters to the polls who would, in many states, make their choices on different grounds from those that had operated in 1824. In particular, they would now have to consider the charges of bargain and corruption that linked the Adams administration with their deepest suspicions of politicians.

As important as the corrupt bargain, however, was the argument that the General, who in 1824 had transcendentally exemplified heroic independence, was now the man who could restore the old Democratic Republican Party. Faced by an amalgamationist president who had appointed six Federalists to significant office, Van Buren by 1827 was arguing that the best way of restoring "a better state of things" was to combine

"Genl. Jackson's personal popularity with the portion of old party feeling yet remaining." It was an identification that obviously worked well in the South, but he insisted that traditional loyalties remained powerful in the "North" too for large numbers of voters. In 1828 he was proved right, not only in New York but also in unlikely places like southeastern Ohio, and thereafter the Jacksonians began to build their support in New England largely on an appeal to old-time party men. Of course, the shift of the Jacksonians toward reviving the sensitivities of the First Party System—which Van Buren thought Jackson took too far after 1832—caused complications for the Democratic Party because of the support he had attracted from some Federalists, and it provoked a major shift of old Federalists back into the ranks of the opposition.[22]

In time the voter choices made in 1824 and 1828 would develop into partisan loyalties that generated a particular mind-set, and in time the internal dynamic of the party and the binding experience of fighting a common enemy could develop that persuasion into an ideological commitment. They would, however, come under strain as the events of 1830–1838 defined the Democratic Party in ways not apparent in the late 1820s. The Maysville veto shocked some who thought Jackson a firm internal improvements man; the issues surrounding banking alienated some, especially in commercial cities, who had not expected the Democratic Party to launch attacks on the principal means of financing economic enterprise. Repeatedly Democratic administrations challenged the interest of Pennsylvania in national banking and protective tariffs, and it is testimony to the power of party loyalty that the state remained loyal for so long. In the end the Democrats appeared to challenge the interests of the cotton South too, and the consequence was a political revolution in the South after 1834 that would destroy the Democrats' easy national predominance and reinvigorate the Second Party System.

On the anti-Jacksonian side, tensions within the national party arose because loyal supporters who were attracted to its side in 1824 were disillusioned by the party's reaction to later developments. After 1829 the former Adams, now National Republican, party always had within it a tension between the moral and antislavery wing and the economic wing. That distinction underlay the Antimasonic secession that resulted in the disruption of the opposition to the Jacksonians in several Northern states between 1829 and 1833, which was overcome sufficiently in 1832 to provide a united opposition in the three largest states and after 1833 to reunite as the embryonic Northern Whig Party. Similar tensions would embarrass the Whigs on questions relating to slavery in subsequent years, resulting in the free soil secessions of 1848 and 1854.

In many Northern and Middle states, the Democrats and Whigs of the 1830s and 1840s appear in many ways to be reincarnations of the Democratic Republicans and Federalists of former times. Some historians have pointed to the cleavage within the Democratic Republican Party after 1801 as providing a better parallel, at least in those states where the Jeffersonians had established an overwhelming predominance. Yet there was little direct continuity between political cleavages before 1818 and those of the later 1830s and 1840s. In effect, the multiple crises that hit the country after 1818–1819 disrupted existing political formations, and the events of 1824–1825 recast them on somewhat different lines from what had gone before and what came immediately afterward. Much of the political history of the Second Party System derives from the simple fact that what appear to be recurring tensions within the body political were at odds with the structures deriving from the crisis of 1818–1822 that took form in the unusual but defining presidential election of 1824.

## THE PARTICULARITY OF 1824

Knowledge of what happened after 1825 stands in the way of understanding the presidential election of 1824; the future does not reveal much about past situations. The men who fought the presidential campaign of 1824 simply cannot be understood by examining the ideological positions of the later Whig and Democratic parties. Jackson publicly favored nationalist policies in 1824, not those with which his name is usually identified. Crawfordites could not accept a military chieftain in 1824–1825, even if they found their route back to power and influence when they changed their mind. Clay's American System was restricted to tariff and internal improvements and would not come to incorporate policies toward national banking and the public lands until after 1830. Adams ran in 1824 as a firm Democratic Republican, even if he attracted much Federalist support and in 1825 agreed to adopt an amalgamationist course. Though he shared in the widespread acceptance of the need for positive national economic policies, Adams did not entirely agree in all respects.

In particular, Adams had reservations about Clay's American System. He agreed substantially on internal improvements, especially on the key constitutional issue, but he was wary of the possible corrupting power of grand schemes. He never approved of Clay's autarkic ideas for a protective tariff and remained conscious of the existing needs and interests of agriculture and commerce across the nation. As president, Adams never officially recommended raising tariff levels, and in Congress in 1832 he would take the lead in watering down the Tariff of Abominations of 1828 in a bill that deserves to be considered the real compromise of the tariff issue before the nullification crisis complicated the situation.[23] However, as president, Adams did advance the policies of the coalition that had elected him, allowing his Cabinet officers to advance specific proposals, including a higher tariff, and signing all measures passed by Congress.

The response of politicians and voters to the policy proposals of 1824 was conditioned by their recent experiences of domestic crisis rather than by any awareness of where events would lead them. Memory of the Missouri crisis slowly forced a unity on New Englanders that contradicted previous and continuing internal divisions and proved powerful enough to make even Adams seem a supportable candidate. In return, the South rejected all Northern candidates—except for the minority that thought the most popular Southern candidate less reliable than the safe hands of the civilized and honest Adams. The Panic of 1819 and the subsequent depression affected the whole country, producing a sense of the republic's moral failure and the need for repair and restoration. Once the immediate needs for relief had been addressed and the worst moments of need and desperation overcome, then people reacted in different ways: some looked for a savior, others for an appropriate response from the federal government.

Inevitably their political expectations were strongly influenced by their experience of party politics over the previous generation. Many believed that the old Democratic Republican Party of Jefferson and Madison held the secret of continued political rectitude and disapproved of candidates who were considered great men superior to party values. Pragmatically, they also believed the party's hold on voter loyalties was an iron fact of life that would determine the election. When that hope crumbled, they were left not only without safe moorings but also without familiar signposts to indicate their political course. These Old Republicans were opposed by the many others, both Federalist and Republican, who over the last decade had come to believe that the party machine was the great stifling influence in political life and the source of corruption; for them a popular independent candidate—a Calhoun, a Clinton, a Jackson—was essential to break the stranglehold that was epitomized by the congressional caucus. The two most successful candidates were both independent in nature and appeal, yet each was conscious of the need to maintain a Democratic Republican identification.

Undoubtedly Jackson was a force of nature, a charismatic figure who had extraordinary appeal for many ordinary Americans of his own day. Initially a military hero, he became a new Washington, a Patriot King who could rescue a failing republic by his own moral force. His appeal to small farmers living in rural isolation, especially in the South, was almost absolute in 1824, and that was reinforced by the growing spirit of Southern sectionalism that would sweep many planters into his ranks within very few years. In the large commercial cities outside New England, he found further enthusiastic support, often among ethnic minorities but also based on a working-class conservatism that wished to reverse the new economic pressures on their status and independence. Yet for many others he was a deeply divisive figure. The revulsion of the "universal Yankee nation" against slaveholder rule saw Jackson as the prime example of the Southerner who knew no civil discipline or respect for law because he came from a slave society that ultimately rested on violence. Old Republicans feared that the election of such a military chieftain would undermine true republican values and destroy the work of the Founding Fathers. In such circumstances Jackson could not win majority support in the America of 1824, and the voting figures show that he did not.

To become president, Jackson needed the support of some of his opponents of 1824, and that required coalitions and concessions of the sort he scorned the Adams administration for making on its way to power. He had already learned to attract the support of Federalists to an extent that was possible only for a Republican hero whose patriotism was beyond rebuke. He was successfully managing to satisfy both sides of the tariff question by judicious qualifications. He still had to learn to conciliate the Old Republicans who had opposed his election in 1824–1825 but now had nowhere else to go. He had to allow himself to move from the nationalism of 1824 to the states' rights views of the Crawfordites, with the result that his first administration would be notable for its assault on the nationalist programs of the last fifteen years. Except during the nullification crisis, President Jackson would not be the patriot of 1824.

For the others too, the whole experience of the 1824 election was one of political education. Crawford learned not to trust the power of party loyalty in all situations nor to rely on continuing good health. Calhoun moved from being the architect and executive of national programs along his first steps toward becoming a sectionalist spokesman, as his allies in the House of Representatives revealed in the debates over the National Road in January 1825. Clay discovered that charisma must be reinforced by thorough organization, and he saw his grand vision of the American System diminished by the need for log rolling to build congressional majorities. Adams's views on domestic issues shifted from a suspected Atlantic perspective to an open continental one, in keeping with the Monroe Doctrine and the views of those who finally elected him. What had begun as a contest of personalities, suitably described in terms of a horse or foot race, finished in the House election as a struggle to determine the character and policy stance of the next presidency, regardless of which runner finished up in the chair directly in front of the warming White House fire.

# ELECTORAL AND POPULAR VOTES

## Table 1. Electoral Vote

| State | For President | | | | For Vice President | |
|---|---|---|---|---|---|---|
| | Jackson | Adams | Crawford | Clay | Calhoun | Other |
| Maine | — | 9 | — | — | 9 | — |
| New Hampshire | — | 8 | — | — | 7 | 1 Jackson |
| Vermont | — | 7 | — | — | 7 | — |
| Massachusetts | — | 15 | — | — | 15 | — |
| Rhode Island | — | 4 | — | — | 3 | — |
| Connecticut | — | 8 | — | — | — | 8 Jackson |
| New York | 1 | 26 | 5 | 4 | 29 | 7 Sanford |
| New Jersey | 8 | — | — | — | 8 | — |
| Pennsylvania | 28 | — | — | — | 28 | — |
| Delaware | — | 1 | 2 | — | 1 | 2 Clay |
| Maryland | 7 | 3 | 1 | — | 10 | 1 Jackson |
| Virginia | — | — | 24 | — | — | 24 Macon |
| North Carolina | 15 | — | — | — | 15 | — |
| South Carolina | 11 | — | — | — | 11 | — |
| Georgia | — | — | 9 | — | — | 9 Van Buren |
| Alabama | 5 | — | — | — | 5 | — |
| Mississippi | 3 | — | — | — | 3 | — |
| Louisiana | 3 | 2 | — | — | 5 | — |
| Kentucky | — | — | — | 14 | 7 | 7 Sanford |
| Tennessee | 11 | — | — | — | 11 | — |
| Missouri | — | — | — | 3 | — | 3 Jackson |
| Ohio | — | — | — | 16 | — | 16 Sanford |
| Indiana | 5 | — | — | — | 5 | — |
| Illinois | 2 | 1 | — | — | 3 | — |
| Total | 99 | 84 | 41 | 37 | 182 | 78 |

*Note:* The vice presidential race was won easily in the Electoral College by Calhoun. Of the others, Nathan Sanford of New York won thirty electoral votes as Clay's running mate; Crawford's supporters voted for Clay in Delaware (2), Nathaniel Macon in Virginia (24), and Van Buren in Georgia (9); and Jackson won thirteen votes in Missouri (3) and from Adams men elsewhere.

## Table 2. Unofficial Figures for the Popular Vote

| State | Jackson | Adams | Crawford | Clay | Other |
|---|---|---|---|---|---|
| Maine | — | 10,432 | 3,117 | — | 35 |
| New Hampshire | — | 10,209 | — | — | 643 |
| Massachusetts | — | 31,851 | 6,246 | — | 614 |
| | | | [+614][a] | — | [−614][a] |
| Rhode Island | — | 2,145 | 200 | — | |
| Connecticut | — | 7,741 | 1,992 | — | |
| New Jersey | 9,283 | 8,363 | 1,216 | — | |
| Pennsylvania | 35,893 | 5,405 | 4,186 | 1,701 | |
| Maryland | 14,535 | 14,698 | 3,371 | 694 | |
| Virginia | 2,975 | 3,514 | 8,558 | 426 | |
| North Carolina | 20,148 | — | 15,629 | — | |
| | [−4,500][b] | [+4,500][b] | | | |
| Ohio | 18,411 | 12,308 | — | 19,165 | |
| Indiana | 7,447 | 3,093 | — | 5,318 | |
| Illinois | 1,272 | 1,541 | 847 | 1,047 | |
| Missouri | 1,166 | 191 | 35 | 2,042 | |
| Kentucky | 6,668 | 120 | 3 | 17,383 | |
| Tennessee | 11,285 | 224 | 530 | 36 | |
| | [+6,215][c] | | | | |
| Alabama | 9,461 | 2,406 | 1,679 | 106 | |
| Mississippi | 3,314 | 1,718 | 121 | 21 | |
| Totals | 141,858 | 115,959 | 47,730 | 47,939 | |
| Amended totals[d] | 143,573 | 120,459 | 48,334 | 47,939 | |

*Source:* This table was originally published in Donald Ratcliffe, "Popular Preferences in the Presidential Election of 1824," *Journal of the Early Republic* 34 (2014): 55, unfortunately with a basic error that is corrected here. In the original, I put Maryland's votes for Jackson and Adams the wrong way round; the correction made here has the effect of taking 163 votes from Jackson and giving them to Adams. The totals are corrected here and elsewhere.

*Note:* Drawn from the election returns collected by Philip Lampi of the American Antiquarian Society, which are now largely available on the *A New Nation Votes: American Election Returns, 1787–1825* website, at http://elections.lib.tufts.edu/. The results given here benefit from Lampi's more recent minor revisions of the figures, as reported in Donald Ratcliffe, "Popular Preferences in the Presidential Election of 1824," *Journal of the Early Republic* 34 (2014): 45–77. These returns include all votes cast where the voter's intentions are clear, even when the votes were disallowed officially because of some (often trivial) technicality. They therefore differ marginally from the official returns, which may be found in Michael J. Dubin, *United States Presidential Elections, 1788–1860: The Official Results by County and State* (Jefferson, NC: McFarland, 2002), 31–42.
[a] Votes in Massachusetts cast for a Federalist ticket that included candidates who also appeared on a Crawford ticket.
[b] Votes in North Carolina cast for the People's Party ticket but by voters who specifically preferred Adams.
[c] Lampi's estimate of Jackson's vote in the Tennessee counties for which the results are missing, in many of which he was unopposed.
[d] Total vote including the extra items in the notes above.

**Table 3. Estimated Popular Vote in States Where the Legislature Chose**

| State | Jackson | Adams | Crawford | Clay |
|---|---|---|---|---|
| Vermont | — | 11,000 | — | — |
| Delaware | 1,090 | 3,058 | 2,043 | — |
| South Carolina | 18,000 | — | 3,400 | — |
| Georgia | 13,378 | — | 19,007 | — |
| Louisiana | 1,843 | 842 | — | 1,983 |
| New York | — | 77,338 | 66,511 | 47,497 |
| Totals | 34,311 | 92,238 | 91,321 | 51,480 |
| Vote in popular vote states (from Table 2) | 143,573 | 120,459 | 48,334 | 47,939 |
| Estimated grand total | 177,884 | 212,697 | 139,655 | 99,419 |

*Source:* Reprinted with permission from Donald Ratcliffe, "Popular Preferences in the Presidential Election of 1824," *Journal of the Early Republic* 34 (2014): 71, corrected as explained in Table 2. The methods used to assess the underlying popular vote are explained in ibid., 68–73.

# JOHN QUINCY ADAMS'S INAUGURAL ADDRESS, MARCH 4, 1825

The inauguration of John Quincy Adams as sixth president of the United States marked more than the peaceful triumph of constitutional processes amid unstructured competition and confusion. Adams represented a new generation coming to maturity after the Revolution. He was the first to take the oath of office wearing trousers rather than breeches, the first to describe the American republic officially as a "democracy." The opening third of the address was a hymn of praise to the Constitution and to the great gains that the republic had made during the previous half-century. But though promising to maintain the policies and practices of his predecessors, his understanding of both past and present was seen as threatening by some of his hearers.

Martin Van Buren insisted long after that Adams could have effected "a hearty and effective union" with those who had supported other candidates in the election, but he alienated them by his inaugural address in two ways. First, Adams declared that no difference of political principle now divided the two old parties, and so there was no justification for their continuance. This description, Van Buren claimed, was bound to offend "the scattered members of one of those great parties"—the Democratic Republicans—who "could not be expected to listen with complacency to this description, by their successful rival, of a state of things which they had discovered to be 'a delusion and a snare.'" Second, Adams declared his support for federal internal improvements and argued that surviving constitutional scruples on the matter would soon be satisfied by the practical advantages brought by such public works; he would flesh out his program in his first annual message in December. Van Buren insisted that "not one of the followers of the old Republican faith . . . could fail to see in [this policy] the most ultra latitudinarian doctrines" (*MVBA*, 194–195).

These objections arose in spite of Adams's admiration for the provisions of the Constitution that he expressed in the first third of his Inaugural Address. He praised the balancing of liberty and law, the releasing of individual enterprise, the economy of its government. He promised to abide by its restrictions, yet also pointed to its clear purpose to "form a more perfect union . . . provide for the common defense, [and] promote the general welfare." It had made possible the growth of the nation and the improvement of the condition of its people. "All the purposes of human association have been accomplished as effectively as under any other government on the globe, and at a cost little exceeding in a whole generation the expenditure of other nations in a single year." Moreover, the republic had triumphed over foreign threats, the extremities of war, and "dissensions among ourselves . . . which have more than once appeared to threaten the dissolution of the Union." The remainder of the address moved on to more contentious terrain:

It is a source of gratification and of encouragement to me to observe that the great result of this experiment upon the theory of human rights has at the close of that generation by which it was formed been crowned with success equal to the most sanguine expectations of its founders. Union, justice, tranquillity, the common defense, the general welfare, and the blessings of liberty—all have been promoted by the Government under which we have lived. Standing at this point of time, looking back to that generation which has gone by and forward to that which is advancing, we may at once indulge in grateful exultation and in cheering hope. From the experience of the past we derive instructive lessons for the future. Of the two great political parties which have divided the opinions and feelings of our country, the candid and the just will now admit that both have contributed splendid talents, spotless integrity, ardent patriotism, and disinterested sacrifices to the formation and administration of this Government, and that both have required a liberal indulgence for a portion of human infirmity and error. The revolutionary wars of Europe, commencing precisely at the moment when the Government of the United States first went into operation under this Constitution, excited a collision of sentiments and of sympathies which kindled all the passions and embittered the conflict of parties till the nation was involved in war and the Union was shaken to its center. This time of trial embraced a period of five and twenty years, during which the policy of the Union in its relations with Europe constituted the principal basis of our political divisions and the most arduous part of the action of our Federal Government. With the catastrophe in which the wars of the French Revolution terminated, and our own subsequent peace with Great Britain, this baneful weed of party strife was uprooted. From that time no difference of principle, connected either with the theory of government or with our intercourse with foreign nations, has existed or been called forth in force sufficient to sustain a continued combination of parties or to give more than wholesome animation to public sentiment or legislative debate. Our political creed is, without a dissenting voice that can be heard, that the will of the people is the source and the happiness of the people the end of all legitimate government upon earth; that the best security for the beneficence and the best guaranty against the abuse of power consists in the freedom, the purity, and the frequency of popular elections; that the General Government of the Union and the separate governments of the States are all sovereignties of limited powers, fellow-servants of the same masters, uncontrolled within their respective spheres, uncontrollable by encroachments upon each other; that the firmest security of peace is the preparation during peace of the defenses of war; that a rigorous economy and accountability of public expenditures should guard against the aggravation and alleviate when possible the burden of taxation; that the military should be kept in strict subordination to the civil power; that the freedom of the press and of religious opinion should be inviolate; that the policy of our country is peace and the ark of our salvation union are articles of faith upon which we are all now agreed. If there have been those who doubted whether a confederated representative democracy were a government competent to the wise and orderly management of the common concerns of a mighty nation, those doubts have been dispelled; if there have been projects of partial confederacies to be erected upon the ruins of the Union, they have been scattered to the winds; if there have best dangerous attachments to one foreign nation and antipathies against another, they have been extinguished. Ten years of peace, at home and abroad, have assuaged the animosities of political contention and blended into harmony the most discordant elements of public opinion. There still remains one effort of magnanimity, one sacrifice of prejudice and passion, to be made by the individuals throughout the nation who have heretofore followed the standards of political party. It is that of discarding every remnant of rancor against each other, of embracing as countrymen and friends, and of yielding to talents and virtue alone that confidence which in times of contention for principle was bestowed only upon those who bore the badge of party communion.

The collisions of party spirit which originate in speculative opinions or in different views of administrative policy are in their nature transitory. Those which are founded on geographical divisions, adverse interests of soil, climate, and modes of domestic life are more permanent, and therefore, perhaps, more dangerous. It is this which gives inestimable value to the character of our Government, at once federal and national. It holds out to us a perpetual admonition to preserve alike and with equal anxiety the rights of each individual State in its own government and the rights of the whole nation in that of the Union. Whatsoever is of domestic concernment, unconnected with the other members of the Union or with foreign lands, belongs exclusively to the administration of the State governments. Whatsoever directly involves the rights and interests of the federative fraternity or of foreign powers is of the resort of this General Government. The duties of both are obvious in the general principle, though sometimes perplexed with difficulties in the detail. To respect the rights of the State governments is the inviolable duty of that of the Union; the government of every State will feel its own obligation to respect and preserve the rights of the whole. The prejudices everywhere too commonly entertained against distant strangers are worn away, and the jealousies of jarring interests are allayed by the composition and functions of the great national councils annually assembled from all quarters of the Union at this place. Here the distinguished men from every section of our country, while meeting to deliberate upon the great interests of those by whom they are deputed, learn to estimate the talents and do justice to the virtues of each other. The harmony of the nation is promoted and the whole Union is knit together by the sentiments of mutual respect, the habits of social intercourse, and the ties of personal friendship formed between the representatives of its several parts in the performance of their service at this metropolis.

Passing from this general review of the purposes and injunctions of the Federal Constitution and their results as indicating the first traces of the path of duty in the discharge of my public trust, I turn to the Administration of my immediate predecessor as the second. It has passed away in a period of profound peace, how much to the satisfaction of our country and to the honor of our country's name is known to you all. The great features of its policy, in general concurrence with the will of the Legislature, have been to cherish peace while preparing for defensive war; to yield exact justice to other nations and maintain the rights of our own; to cherish the principles of freedom and of equal rights wherever they were proclaimed; to discharge with all possible promptitude the national debt; to reduce within the narrowest limits of efficiency the military force; to improve the organization and discipline of the Army; to provide and sustain a school of military science; to extend equal protection to all the great interests of the nation; to promote the civilization of the Indian tribes, and to proceed in the great system of internal improvements within the limits of the constitutional power of the Union. Under the pledge of these promises, made by that eminent citizen at the time of his first induction to this office, in his career of eight years the internal taxes have been repealed; sixty millions of the public debt have been discharged; provision has been made for the comfort and relief of the aged and indigent among the surviving warriors of the Revolution; the regular armed force has been reduced and its constitution revised and perfected; the accountability for the expenditure of public moneys has been made more effective; the Floridas have been peaceably acquired, and our boundary has been extended to the Pacific Ocean; the independence of the southern nations of this hemisphere has been recognized, and recommended by example and by counsel to the potentates of Europe; progress has been made in the defense of the country by fortifications and the increase of the Navy, toward the effectual suppression of the African traffic in slaves, in alluring the aboriginal hunters of our land to the cultivation of the soil and of the mind, in exploring the interior regions of the Union, and in preparing by scientific researches and surveys for the further application of our national resources to the internal improvement of our country.

In this brief outline of the promise and performance of my immediate predecessor the line of duty for his successor is clearly delineated. To pursue to their consummation those purposes of improvement in our common condition instituted or recommended by him will embrace the whole sphere of my obligations. To the topic of internal improvement, emphatically urged by him at his inauguration, I recur with peculiar satisfaction. It is that from which I am convinced that the unborn millions of our posterity who are in future ages to people this continent will derive their most fervent gratitude to the founders of the Union; that in which the beneficent action of its Government will be most deeply felt and acknowledged. The magnificence and splendor of their public works are among the imperishable glories of the ancient republics. The roads and aqueducts of Rome have been the admiration of all after ages, and have survived thousands of years after all her conquests have been swallowed up in despotism or become the spoil of barbarians. Some diversity of opinion has prevailed with regard to the powers of Congress for legislation upon objects of this nature. The most respectful deference is due to doubts originating in pure patriotism and sustained by venerated authority. But nearly twenty years have passed since the construction of the first national road was commenced. The authority for its construction was then unquestioned. To how many thousands of our countrymen has it proved a benefit? To what single individual has it ever proved an injury? Repeated, liberal, and candid discussions in the Legislature have conciliated the sentiments and approximated the opinions of enlightened minds upon the question of constitutional power. I can not but hope that by the same process of friendly, patient, and persevering deliberation all constitutional objections will ultimately be removed. The extent and limitation of the powers of the General Government in relation to this transcendently important interest will be settled and acknowledged to the common satisfaction of all, and every speculative scruple will be solved by a practical public blessing.

Fellow-citizens, you are acquainted with the peculiar circumstances of the recent election, which have resulted in affording me the opportunity of addressing you at this time. You have heard the exposition of the principles which will direct me in the fulfillment of the high and solemn trust imposed upon me in this station. Less possessed of your confidence in advance than any of my predecessors, I am deeply conscious of the prospect that I shall stand more and oftener in need of your indulgence. Intentions upright and pure, a heart devoted to the welfare of our country, and the unceasing application of all the faculties allotted to me to her service are all the pledges that I can give for the faithful performance of the arduous duties I am to undertake. To the guidance of the legislative councils, to the assistance of the executive and subordinate departments, to the friendly cooperation of the respective State governments, to the candid and liberal support of the people so far as it may be deserved by honest industry and zeal, I shall look for whatever success may attend my public service; and knowing that "except the Lord keep the city the watchman waketh but in vain," with fervent supplications for His favor, to His overruling providence I commit with humble but fearless confidence my own fate and the future destinies of my country.

*Source:* James D. Richardson, *A Compilation of the Messages and Papers of the Presidents, 1789–1907,* 11 vols. (Washington, D.C., 1897–1907), 2:294–297.

# NOTES

### ABBREVIATIONS

AJP    *The Papers of Andrew Jackson,* ed. Sam B. Smith et al., 9 vols. to date (Knoxville: University of Tennessee Press, 1980–)

CHP    Charles Hammond Papers, OHS

DWP    *The Papers of Daniel Webster,* series 1, *Correspondence,* ed. Charles M. Wiltse, 7 vols. (Hanover: University Press of New England, 1974–1986)

HCP    *The Papers of Henry Clay,* ed. James F. Hopkins et al., 11 vols. (Lexington: University of Kentucky Press, 1959–1992)

HSP    Historical Society of Pennsylvania, Philadelphia

JCCP    *The Papers of John C. Calhoun,* ed. W. Edwin Hemphill et al., 28 vols. (Columbia: University of South Carolina Press, 1959–2003)

JHNY    Jabez D. Hammond, *The History of Political Parties in the State of New York, From the Ratification of the Constitution to December, 1840,* 2 vols. (Albany: printed by C. Van Benthuysen, 1842)

JQAM    *Memoirs of John Quincy Adam, Comprising Portions of His Diary from 1795 to 1848,* ed. Charles Francis Adams, 13 vols. (1874–1877)

LC    Library of Congress, Washington, D.C.

MHS    Massachusetts Historical Society, Boston

MVBA    *The Autobiography of Martin Van Buren,* in *Annual Report of the American Historical Association for the Year 1918* (Washington: Government Printing Office, 1920; reprint, New York: Da Capo Press, 1973)

MVBP    Martin Van Buren Papers, mainly from the Presidential Papers microfilm, LC

NWR    *Niles' Weekly Register,* 47 vols. (Baltimore: Hezekiah Niles, 1811–1837)

OHS    Ohio Historical Society, Columbus

RKC    *The Life and Correspondence of Rufus King,* ed. Charles R. King, 6 vols. (New York: G. P. Putnam's Sons, 1900)

WPL    *The Missouri Compromises and Presidential Politics, 1820–1825: From the Letters of William Plumer Jr.,* ed. Everett Somerville Brown (St. Louis: Missouri Historical Society, 1926)

WRHS    Western Reserve Historical Society, Cleveland

### CHAPTER 1 MYTH AND REALITY

1    *MVBA,* 149–152.

2    Richard P. McCormick, *The Presidential Game: The Origins of American Presidential Politics* (New York: Oxford University Press, 1982), 21–26.

3    The Twentieth Amendment of 1933 makes the current position clear. Previously (and in 1824–1825) the Twelfth Amendment of 1804 provided only

that, in the event of a nonelection before the end of the previous president's term on March 4, the newly elected vice president would "act as president" as though the president had died. Nothing was said about what would happen if no vice president had been elected by March 4.

4 *MVBA*, 152–153; the story was not published until 1920. For "theft," see Robert V. Remini, *Andrew Jackson and the Course of American Freedom, 1822–1832* (New York: Harper & Row, 1981), chap. 5.

5 Donald Ratcliffe, "Popular Preferences in the Presidential Election of 1824," *Journal of the Early Republic* 34 (2014): 66–74.

6 Roy F. Nichols, *Invention of American Political Parties* (New York: Macmillan, 1965), 271; Morton Keller, *America's Three Regimes: A New Political History* (New York: Oxford University Press, 2007), 79; John A. Munroe, *Louis McLane: Federalist and Jacksonian* (New Brunswick, N.J.: Rutgers University Press, 1973), 172–173.

7 Jeffery J. Jenkins and Brian R. Sala, "The Spatial Theory of Voting and the Presidential Election of 1824," *American Journal of Political Science* 42 (1998): 1158; H. W. Brands, *Andrew Jackson: His Life and Times* (New York: Random House, 2005), chap. 29; George Dangerfield, *The Era of Good Feelings* (New York: Harcourt, Brace, and World, 1952), 313–314.

8 Charles Sellers, *The Market Revolution: Jacksonian America, 1815–1846* (New York: Oxford University Press, 1991), 172–201; Sean Wilentz, *The Rise of American Democracy: Jefferson to Lincoln* (New York: Norton, 2005), 240–257; Daniel Walker Howe, *What Hath God Wrought: The Transformation of America, 1815–1848* (New York: Oxford University Press, 2007), 203–211, 237–241.

9 A common error is to assume that in most states the legislature chose the state's presidential electors, which had not been true since the election of 1800.

10 Tom W. Smith, "The First Straw? A Study of the Origins of Election Polls," *Public Opinion Quarterly* 54 (1991): 23. For the "electoral connection," see William T. Bianco, David B. Spence, and John D. Wilkerson, "The Electoral Connection in the Early Congress: The Case of the Compensation Act of 1816," *American Journal of Political Science* 40 (1996): 145–171; Jenkins and Sala, "Spatial Theory of Voting," 1176–1177; Jamie L. Carson and Erik J. Engstrom, "Assessing the Electoral Connection: Evidence from the Early United States," *American Journal of Political Science* 49 (2005): 746–757.

11 Thomas M. Coens, "The Formation of the Jackson Party, 1822–1825" (Ph.D. diss., Harvard University, 2004), 110–157; Daniel Peart, *Era of Experimentation: American Political Practices in the Early Republic* (Charlottesville: University of Virginia Press, 2014), 120–124.

12 Joel H. Silbey, *Martin Van Buren and the Emergence of American Popular Politics* (Lanham, Md.: Rowman & Littlefield, 2002), 45.

13 James S. Chase, *The Emergence of the Presidential Nominating Convention, 1789–1832* (Urbana: University of Illinois Press, 1973); M. J. Heale, *The Presidential Quest: Candidates and Images in American Political Culture, 1787–1852* (New York: Longman, 1982). Roger Fischer, *Tippecanoe and Trinkets Too: The*

*Material Culture of American Presidential Elections* (Urbana: University of Illinois Press, 1988), 8–16, 24, decided that although material objects celebrating Jackson's victories had been on sale since 1815, there is no evidence that such "trinkets" were sold to promote any candidacies in 1824; but see Melba Porter Hay, "1824," in *Running for President: The Candidates and Their Images*, ed. A. M. Schlesinger, Fred L. Israel, and David J. Frent (New York: Simon & Schuster, 1994), 85–99.

14 Rufus King, Memoranda, February 9, 1825, *RKC*, 6:585–586.

15 "Political Horse Racing and Presidential Contest," *Nashville Gazette*, widely reprinted, for example in the Chillicothe, Ohio, *Supporter and Scioto Gazette*, July 5, 1823.

16 Ratcliffe, "Popular Preferences," 66–74.

17 *JQAM*, 4:388 (June 4, 1819).

18 Chase C. Mooney, *William H. Crawford, 1772–1834* (Lexington: University Press of Kentucky, 1974), 238–239, 240–241.

19 *Supporter and Scioto Gazette*, July 5, 1823.

20 Heale, *Presidential Quest*, 1–22.

21 John B. [H.] Eaton to R. King, March 5, 1821, *RKC*, 6:389.

22 Donald Ratcliffe, "The Right to Vote and the Rise of Democracy, 1787–1828," *Journal of the Early Republic* 33 (2013): 219–254.

23 C. Edward Skeen, "*Vox Populi, Vox Dei:* The Compensation Act of 1816 and the Rise of Popular Politics," *Journal of the Early Republic* 6 (1986): 253–274, esp. 266.

24 The traditional power of legislatures to choose the presidential electors continues to be grossly exaggerated, e.g., in Andrew Burstein, *America's Jubilee* (New York: Knopf, 2001), 146; cf. Ratcliffe, "Right to Vote," 249–251.

25 St. Clairsville *Ohio Federalist*, September 4, 1817; Jabez D. Hammond, in *JHNY*, 1:475; *NWR*, 23 (March 1, 1823), 401.

26 *Albany Argus*, September 12, 1823, quoted in Dixon Ryan Fox, *The Decline of Aristocracy in the Politics of New York, 1801–1840* (1919; reprint, New York: Harper & Row, 1965), 275–276; William Duane to Jefferson, October 19, 1824, in Kim Tousley Phillips, *William Duane, Radical Journalist in the Age of Jackson* (New York: Garland, 1989), 589–590.

27 Coens, "Formation of the Jackson Party," 161–164; *JHNY*, 1:437–439; Philip S. Klein, *Pennsylvania Politics, 1817–1832: A Game without Rules* (Philadelphia: Historical Society of Pennsylvania, 1940), 92; *MVBA*, 98.

28 John King to Van Buren, February 23, 1823, MVBP. The age profile is based on *Historical Statistics of the United States* (Washington, D.C.: Bureau of the Census, 1975), 1:16. For the impact of Independent politics, see James A. Kehl, *Ill Feeling in the Era of Good Feeling: Western Pennsylvania Political Battles, 1815–1825* (Pittsburgh: University of Pittsburgh Press, 1956), and Donald J. Ratcliffe, *Party Spirit in a Frontier Republic: Democratic Politics in Ohio, 1793–1821* (Columbus: Ohio State University Press, 1998), 148–248.

29 Gorham A. Worth to Thomas Sloo Jr., August 2, 1820, in "Selections from the Torrence Papers," ed. Isaac Joslin Cox, pt. 6, *Quarterly Publications of*

the *Historical and Philosophical Society of Ohio* 6 (1911): 32; Samuel Rezneck, "The Depression of 1819–22: A Social History," *American Historical Review* 39 (1933): 30–32.

30  *NWR*, 23 (January 11, 1823), 290; Thomas H. Greer, "Economic and Social Effects of the Depression of 1819 in the Old Northwest," *Indiana Magazine of History* 44 (1948): 230.

31  Murray N. Rothbard, *The Panic of 1819: Reactions and Policies* (New York: Columbia University Press, 1962), 16.

32  Ibid., 95.

33  Emil Pocock, "Popular Roots of Jacksonian Democracy: The Case of Dayton, Ohio, 1815–1830," *Journal of the Early Republic* 9 (1989): 489–515, sees the divisions of 1820–1822 as preparing the way for the later national party division but fails to notice that almost all his "democrats" supported Adams in 1828. Donald J. Ratcliffe, *The Politics of Long Division: The Birth of the Second Party System in Ohio, 1818–1828* (Columbus: Ohio State University Press, 2000), 265, 396–397.

34  *JQAM*, 5:128.

35  Daniel Feller, *The Public Lands in Jacksonian Politics* (Madison: University of Wisconsin Press, 1984), 22–38.

36  Rufus King to Charles Gore, February 9, 1823, *RKC*, 6:500; *Liberty Hall and Cincinnati Gazette*, January 6, February 10, 1824; John Lauritz Larson, *Internal Improvement: National Public Works and the Promise of Popular Government in the Early United States* (Chapel Hill: University of North Carolina Press, 2001).

37  Norris W. Preyer, "Southern Support for the Tariff of 1816: A Reappraisal," *Journal of Southern History* 25 (1959): 306–322.

38  Thomas Cobb of Georgia, in Robert Pierce Forbes, *The Missouri Compromise and Its Aftermath: Slavery and the Meaning of America* (Chapel Hill: University of North Carolina Press, 2007), 144; Rufus King, quoted in *MVBA*, 139; Jefferson to John Holmes, April 22, 1820, Thomas Jefferson, *The Writings of Thomas Jefferson*, ed. Paul Leicester Ford, 10 vols. (New York: G. P. Putnam's Sons, 1892–1899), 10:157.

39  Margaret Bayard Smith to Mrs. Kirkpatrick, October 12, 1822, in Margaret Bayard Smith, *The First Forty Years of Washington Society: Portrayed by the Family Letters of Mrs. Samuel Harrison Smith*, ed. Gaillard Hunt (New York: Scribner, 1906), 158–160; Calhoun [to Monroe], September 24, 1823, *JCCP*, 8:284; Robert P. Hay, "The American Revolution Twice Recalled: Lafayette's Visit and the Election of 1824," *Illinois Magazine of History* 69 (1973): 43–72; Heale, *Presidential Quest*, 23–25.

40  Mrs. Catharina V. R. Bonney, comp., *A Legacy of Historical Gleanings*, 2 vols. (Albany, N.Y.: J. Munsell, 1875), 1:415; Peart, *Era of Experimentation*, 5, 151. In ten of the eighteen popular-vote states with the lowest turnout, the winner beat his nearest rival by over 25 percent of the total vote; in six of the eight other popular elections, the lead was down to 13 percent.

1    Mooney, *William H. Crawford*, 7; J. E. D. Shipp, *Giant Days: The Life and Times of William H. Crawford* (Americus, Ga.: Southern Printers, 1909), 152.

2    Gallatin to John Badollet, July 29, 1824, in Mooney, *William H. Crawford*, 26.

3    Lowndes, quoted in Langdon Cheves to Clay, November 9, 1822, *HCP*, 3:314; William Plumer to his father, November 24, 1820, in *WPL*, 56–58; Malcolm J. Rohrbough, *The Land Office Business: The Settlement and Administration of American Public Lands, 1789–1837* (New York: Oxford University Press, 1968), 191–194. In Indiana, Crawford's choice of banks to act as public depositories was seen as a means of building a party for him.

4    *National Intelligencer*, September 27, 1834, in Mooney, *William H. Crawford*, 341–342; see also 119–126. Leonard White, *The Jeffersonians: A Study in Administrative History, 1801–1829* (New York: Macmillan, 1951), 387–388.

5    Jackson to James Gadsden, December 6, 1821, *AJP*, 5:121.

6    Greer, "Economic and Social Effects," 36.

7    Ninian Edwards of Illinois, reported in *JQAM*, 5:327 (March 10, 1821).

8    This and following paragraphs draw heavily on Norman K. Risjord, *The Old Republicans: Southern Conservatism in the Age of Jefferson* (New York: Columbia University Press, 1965), and Harry Ammon, "The Richmond Junto, 1800–1824," *Virginia Magazine of History and Biography* 61 (1953): 395–418. I borrow the term "neo-Antifederalist" from Larson, *Internal Improvement*, 111.

9    In Virginia, the Lynchburg *Virginian* introduced the term *junto* in April 1823 when it accused a named group of Richmond politicians of controlling the state through party mechanisms. *Richmond Enquirer*, May 6, 1823. Historians have argued whether the Junto ever existed, but it seems reasonable to say that an informal grouping of Republican leaders exercised significant political influence. Trenton E. Hizer, "Virginia Is Now Divided: Politics in the Old Dominion, 1820–1833" (Ph.D. diss., University of South Carolina, 1997).

10   Kenneth C. Martis and Gregory A. Elmes, *The Historical Atlas of State Power in Congress, 1790–1990* (Washington, D.C.: Congressional Quarterly, 1993), 46–49. Virginia's relative power had slipped by 2.4 percent, while New York's and Ohio's had increased by over 1 percent each.

11   Macon to Bartlett Yancey, March 8, April 15, 1818, in Risjord, *Old Republicans*, 198.

12   William W. Freehling, ed., *The Nullification Era: A Documentary Record* (New York: Harper & Row, 1967), 8–9; Risjord, *Old Republicans*, 244.

13   Plumer to his father, February 21, 1821, in *WPL*, 41.

14   Ibid., 35–42, quotations at 41, 37.

15   Thomas G. Watkins to Jackson, March 13, 1822, *AJP*, 5:155–156.

16   *RKC*, 6:494, 496–497, 500.

17   Risjord, *Old Republicans*, 149–150 (first quotation), 224–225; John Taylor to James Monroe, April 29, 1823, [W. E. Dodd, ed.], "Letters of John Taylor of Caroline County, Virginia," *John P. Branch Historical Papers of Randolph-*

*Macon College* 2 (1908): 350–353. Taylor had doubts about both Adams and Calhoun, but thought either preferable to Crawford.

18  *MVBA*, 129; Jefferson to Gallatin, October 29, 1822, in Albert Gallatin, *The Writings of Albert Gallatin*, ed. Henry Adams, 3 vols. (Philadelphia: J. B. Lippincott, 1879), 2:259; John S. Pancake, *Samuel Smith and the Politics of Business, 1752–1839* (Tuscaloosa: University of Alabama Press, 1972), 160.

19  Jackson to Allan Campbell, March 31, 1821, in Andrew Jackson, *Correspondence of Andrew Jackson*, ed. John Spencer Bassett (Washington, D.C.: Carnegie Institution, 1928), 3:46; *RKC*, 6:373, 378; R. H. Walworth to Azariah C. Flagg, December 28, 1821, in Thomas Robson Hay, "John C. Calhoun and the Presidential Campaign of 1824," *North Carolina Historical Review* 12 (1935): 24.

20  *Richmond Enquirer*, December 11, 1823; *HCP*, 3:890–891; Clinton to Van Rensselaer, January 31, 1821, in Bonney, *Legacy of Historical Gleanings*, 1:362; *JQAM*, 5:361.

21  Charleston *Patriot*, in *Bangor Register* (Maine), July 4, 1822; *JQAM*, 6:56; Plumer to his father, December 11, 1821, in *WPL*, 68.

22  Plumer to his father, January 13, 1821, *WPL*, 27; Rufus King to J. A. King, January 19, 1821, *RKC*, 6:378; Noble E. Cunningham Jr., *The Presidency of James Monroe* (Lawrence: University Press of Kansas, 1996), 111.

23  Calhoun, August 1822, quoted in *JQAM*, 6:57.

24  Plumer to his father, January 27, 1821, in *WPL*, 63–64; *JQAM*, 5:327.

25  *JQAM*, 5:466; Hay, "John C. Calhoun," 23–24, 36.

26  Mrs. St. Julien Ravenel, *Life and Times of William Lowndes of South Carolina, 1782–1822* (Boston: Houghton Mifflin, 1901), 211, 223–229; Calhoun to Virgil Maxcy, December 31, 1821, *JCCP*, 6:595–597. See also Carl J. Vipperman, *William Lowndes and the Transition of Southern Politics, 1782–1822* (Chapel Hill: University of North Carolina Press, 1989); Charles M. Wiltse, *John C. Calhoun: Nationalist, 1782–1828* (New York: Bobbs-Merrill, 1944), 237. The cynical interpretation of Calhoun's hasty nomination in Washington follows Gerald M. Capers, *John C. Calhoun: Opportunist* (Gainesville: University of Florida Press, 1960), 83–85.

27  *Supporter and Scioto Gazette*, July 5, 1823; Van Buren, reported later in Clay to Peter B. Porter, June 15, 1823, *HCP*, 3:432; Rufus King to Charles King, January 8, 1822, King to Jeremiah Mason, May 17, 1822, in *RKC*, 6:437, 471; Hay, "John C. Calhoun," 24, 38.

28  Calhoun to Maxcy, March 18, 1822, in Hay, "John C. Calhoun," 37; Heale, *Presidential Quest*, 51–53. The memoir was probably written by George M. Dallas: Wiltse, *John C. Calhoun*, 254.

29  Calhoun to Ninian Edwards, June 12, 1822, *JCCP*, 7:160–161; Thomas L. McKenney, *Prospectus of the Washington Republican and Congressional Examiner* [Washington, D.C., 1822], broadside, American Antiquarian Society. See also *HCP*, 3:316; Herman J. Viola, *Thomas L. McKenney: Architect of America's Early Indian Policy, 1816–1830* (Chicago: Swallow Press, 1974), 84–91.

30  James A. Hamilton, *Reminiscences of James A. Hamilton, or Men and Events, At Home and Abroad* (New York: Charles Scribner, 1869), 62; *JCCP*, 7:542,

547, 8:264–266, 287; Wayne Cutler, "The A.B. Controversy," *Mid-America* 51 (1969): 24–38.

31  *JQAM*, 6:8; John Allen Trimble, "Memoirs of an Old Politician in the National Capital at Washington," ed. Alice M. Trimble, *Journal of American History* 3 (1909): 617.

32  *Richmond Enquirer*, December 11, 1823, in Hay, "John C. Calhoun," 31.

33  *RKC*, 6:469, 499–500, 508 (quotation).

34  *JQAM*, 6:56, 62.

35  Jefferson to Gallatin, October 29, 1822, and to Van Buren, June 29, 1824, in Jefferson, *Writings of Thomas Jefferson*, 10:235, 316.

36  *MVBA*, 182–183; Dickerson in U.S. Senate, 1823, quoted by Herbert Ershkowitz, *The Origin of the Whig and Democratic Parties: New Jersey Politics, 1820–1837* (Washington, D.C.: University Press of America, 1982), 2.

37  Jonathan Roberts, Memoirs, photocopy of MS, Roberts Papers, HSP; quotations from 1:96, 2:9–10.

38  *Evening Post*'s correspondent in Washington, January 7, 1822, in Bonney, *Legacy of Historical Gleanings*, 1:380.

39  Wirt quoted by the *Evening Post*'s correspondent in Washington, January 7, 1822, Van Buren to Charles E. Dudley, January 10, 1822, in Bonney, *Legacy of Historical Gleanings*, 1:380, 382, 388.

40  Tompkins and Van Buren to Republicans at Albany, in *MVBA*, 126, 127; Bonney, *Legacy of Historical Gleanings*, 1:378, 382–384; Van Buren to Rufus King, May 31, 1822, *RKC*, 6:473, and February 18, 1822, in Robert V. Remini, *Martin Van Buren and the Making of the Democratic Party* (New York: Columbia University Press, 1959), 26; *JQAM*, 6:127–128.

41  Rush to Roberts, October 25, 1823, Jonathan Roberts Papers, HSP; Risjord, *Old Republicans*, 250. Please note that I am using the term "Old Republicans" in a different sense to Risjord, who specifically applied it to Southern conservatives, while I use the term to describe Democratic Republican Party loyalists wherever they lived.

42  Quoted in Heale, *Presidential Quest*, 40.

43  Gallatin to Walter Lowrie, May 22, 1824, in Gallatin, *Writings of Albert Gallatin*, 2:290.

44  Rufus King to Van Buren, January 22, 1822, MVBP.

45  Peart, *Era of Experimentation*, 102.

46  Crawford to Van Buren, August 1, 1823, in "Ten Letters from William Harris Crawford to Martin Van Buren," ed. William Henry Williams, *Georgia Historical Quarterly* 49 (1965): 69.

47  Klein, *Pennsylvania Politics*, 124, 131.

48  Steubenville, Ohio, *Western Herald*, April 12, 1823. This and the following paragraph draw heavily on Ratcliffe, "Popular Preferences," which in turn draws on the *New Nation Votes* website. For the persistence of old-party prescriptions in Boston during the revolt of the "Middling Interest," see Peart, *Era of Experimentation*, 15–46.

49  New York *National Advocate, for the Country*, October 23, November 18, 1823.

50 William G. Shade, *Democratizing the Old Dominion: Virginia and the Second Party System, 1824–1861* (Charlottesville: University of Virginia Press, 1996); Douglas R. Egerton, *Charles Fenton Mercer and the Trial of National Conservatism* (Jackson: University Press of Mississippi, 1989).

51 *Richmond Enquirer*, February 12, 1824; Calhoun to Swift, August 24, 1823, in Hay, "John C. Calhoun," 33; Egerton, *Charles Fenton Mercer*, 188.

52 This and the following paragraphs draw heavily on Albert Ray Newsome, *The Presidential Election in 1824 in North Carolina* (Chapel Hill: University of North Carolina Press, 1939).

53 Calhoun to Virgil Maxcy, March 25, 1823, *JCCP*, 7:542; Thomas E. Jeffrey, *State Parties and National Politics: North Carolina, 1815–1861* (Athens: University of Georgia Press, 1989), 17–19, 24–25.

54 Calhoun to unknown, March 18, 1823, *JCCP*, 7:530; Salisbury *Western Carolinian*, September 9, 1823, in Newsome, *Presidential Election*, 54. Contemporaries estimated that between 90 and 100 out of the 196 members now elected were committed to Crawford. Newsome, *Presidential Election*, 57, 72, 76–78.

55 *JCCP*, 8:281; Newsome, *Presidential Election*, 73, 77–78.

56 New York *National Advocate, for the Country*, November 25, 1823; Ulrich B. Phillips, *Georgia and States Rights* (1902; reprint, Antioch Press, 1968), 93–108.

57 Wiltse, *John C. Calhoun*, 237; William W. Freehling, *Prelude to Civil War: The Nullification Controversy in South Carolina, 1816–1836* (New York: Harper & Row, 1966), 91–106.

58 Philemon Beecher to Thomas Ewing, January 2, 1823[4], Thomas Ewing Family Papers, LC.

**CHAPTER 3  A NORTHERN MAN**

1 Charles Hammond to John C. Wright, February 2, 1820, CHP.

2 Plumer to his father, April 10, 1820, November 24, 1820, in *WPL*, 49, 55.

3 James Riley to Ethan Allen Brown, December 24, 1819, Ethan Allen Brown Papers, OHS; Plumer to his father, March 4, 1820, in *WPL*, 13–14. The original amendment proposed by James Tallmadge in 1819 included a requirement for the gradual emancipation of *post-nati* slaves, but this was not included in the later provisos proposed by Jonathan Roberts in the Senate and John W. Taylor in the House and at issue in the 1820 session. Donald J. Ratcliffe, "Captain James Riley and Antislavery Sentiment in Ohio, 1819–1824," *Ohio History* 81 (1972): 85n28.

4 Matthew Mason, *Slavery and Politics in the Early American Republic* (Chapel Hill: University of North Carolina Press, 2006); Donald J. Ratcliffe, "The Decline of Antislavery Politics, 1815–1840," in *Contesting Slavery: The Politics of Bondage and Slavery in the New American Nation*, ed. John Craig Hammond and Matthew Mason (Charlottesville: University of Virginia Press, 2011), 269–273.

5   *NWR*, 23, supplement to vol. 22 (March 27, 1822), 65–66.

6   Herman V. Ames, ed., *State Documents on Federal Relations* (1900–1906; New York: Da Capo Press, 1970), 203–205.

7   Auguste Levasseur, *Lafayette in America, in 1824 and 1825; or, Journal of Travels in the United States*, 2 vols. (New York, 1829), 1:91, 222; Stephanie Kermes, *Creating an American Identity: New England, 1789–1825* (New York: Palgrave Macmillan, 2008), 134–135.

8   John Wood Sweet, *Bodies Politic: Negotiating Race in the American North, 1730–1830* (Baltimore: Johns Hopkins University Press, 2003), 353–397.

9   *Strictures Addressed to James Madison on the Celebrated Report of William H. Crawford, Recommending the Intermarriage of Americans with the Indian Tribes. Ascribed to Judge Cooper and Originally Published by John Binns in the Democratic Press* (Philadelphia, 1824); *Caucus Curs in Full Yell, or A War Whoop, to Saddle on the People, a Papoose President*, a cartoon by James Akin, published in Philadelphia, 1824. I am grateful to Nicholas Guyatt and Daniel Peart for help on this point.

10  Zanesville, Ohio, *Muskingum Messenger,* June 10, 1820, March 25, 1823.

11  Van Buren to Thomas Ritchie, January 13, 1827, MVBP; Charles Gore to Rufus King, June 14, 1820, *RKC*, 6:346–347; *MVBA*, 131–132, 137–140.

12  John Sloane to Benjamin Tappan, March 29, May 4, 1820, Benjamin Tappan Papers, LC; King to Gore, April 9, 1820, and Gore to King, June 14, 1820, *RKC*, 6:329, 346–347.

13  Gore to King, June 14, 1820, *RKC*, 6:346–347.

14  Donald B. Cole, *Jacksonian Democracy in New Hampshire, 1800–1851* (Cambridge, Mass.: Harvard University Press, 1970), 41.

15  William Plumer to his father, December 3, 1821, *WPL*, 65.

16  Charles Gore to King, June 2, 1822, *RKC*, 6:473–474. For proslavery Federalists, see Larry E. Tise, *Pro-Slavery: A History of the Defense of Slavery in America, 1701–1840* (Athens: University of Georgia Press, 1987).

17  Zanesville *Muskingum Messenger,* February 25, May 13, June 10, November 25, 1823.

18  Plumer to his father, April 7, 1820, in *WPL*, 16; *JQAM*, 4:529–530 (February 23, 1820), 6:35–37, 39, 45.

19  Ratcliffe, "Popular Preferences," 55; *JQAM*, 6:135.

20  King to Gore, February 9, 1820, King to J. A. King, March 2, 1823, *RKC*, 6:500, 505.

21  William Plumer to his father, November 13, 1820, *WPL*, 51–52; Ravenel, *Life and Times of William Lowndes*, 231.

22  William Henry Harrison to James Findlay, January 24, 1817, transcript, Josiah Morrow Papers, Cincinnati Historical Society; *JQAM*, 6:54–55 (August 19, 1822); Henry R. Warfield to Clay, May 30, 1822, and Henry Shaw to Clay, April 4, 1822, *HCP*, 3:212, 185.

23  William Plumer to his father, January 27, 1820, *WPL*, 64; Joseph Storey, quoted in Lynn Hudson Parsons, *John Quincy Adams* (Madison, Wis.: Mad-

ison House, 1998), 165; King to Gore, February 9, 1823, *RKC*, 6:500; James Buchanan to Hugh Hamilton, March 22, 1822, James Buchanan Papers, HSP.

24  *JQAM*, 6:94–96 (August 19, 1822).

25  Adams, quoted in Parsons, *John Quincy Adams*, 167; *JQAM*, 6:170 (August 9, 1823).

26  Joseph Hopkinson to Mrs. Adams, in *JQAM*, 6:130–131; Charles Francis Adams, *JQAM*, 6:129.

27  *JQAM*, 5:38, March 25, 1820; Plumer to his father, November 24, 1820, *WPL*, 55; *RKC*, 6:337, 367; *JCCP*, 7:249. In April 1822 one of Clay's correspondents thought antislavery would give Clinton New York, Pennsylvania, and the Old Northwest. *HCP*, 3:200.

28  Benjamin Gorham, quoted in Henry R. Warfield to Clay, May 30, 1822, and Frank Johnson to Clay, December 10, 1822, *HCP* 3:212, 334; R. Goldsborough to King, April 17, 1822, *RKC*, 6:469.

29  King to Charles King, January 9, 1823, *RKC*, 6:494.

30  King to Gore, February 9, 1823, *RKC*, 6:501; New York *National Advertiser, for the Country*, December 15, 1823.

31  "The Macbeth Policy," January 1823, *JQAM*, 6:135–136; Henry Shaw to Clay, February 11, 1823, *HCP*, 3:373.

32  Charles Gore to King, May 15, 1822, June 2, 1823, King, Memorandum, February 24, 1823, King to Gore, February 9, 1823, *RKC*, 6:470–471, 473–474, 510, 501, and 508n; *NWR*, 23 (January 18, February 1, 1823), 322, 342–343.

33  Van Buren to King, May 31, 1822, Charles Gore to King, June 2, 1822, King to Gore, February 9, 1823, *RKC*, 6:472–473, 473–474, 501. See also Andrew R. L. Cayton, "The Fragmentation of 'A Great Family': The Panic of 1819 and the Rise of the Middling Interest in Boston, 1818–1822," *Journal of the Early Republic* 2 (1982): 143–168, and Peart, *Era of Experimentation*, 15–46.

34  Concord *New-Hampshire Statesman*, March 8, 1823 (quotation), August 4, 1823, October 25, 1824; Ezekiel Webster to Daniel Webster, April 3, 1823, *DWP*, 1:324.

35  Ezekiel Webster to Daniel Webster, January 28, 1822, April 3, 1823, *DWP*, 1:304, 323.

36  Isaac Parker to Webster, February *c*.13, 1823, *DWP*, 1:322; Independent Federalists of Lincoln, "To the Federal Electors of Lincoln District" [Wiscasset, Maine, September 1823], broadside, American Antiquarian Society; *NWR*, 25 (November 22, 1823), 177.

37  *New-Hampshire Statesman*, March 29, April 12, May 31, 1824; Cheves to Clay, November 9, 1822, *HCP*, 3:315; *RKC*, 6:500, 507–508, 510–511.

38  See the discussion of the 1824 tariff in chap. 7 below.

39  David W. Kling, *A Field of Divine Wonders: The New Divinity and Village Revivals in Northwestern Connecticut, 1792–1822* (University Park: Pennsylvania State University Press, 1993); William G. McLoughlin, *New England Dissent, 1630–1883: The Baptists and Separation of Church and State*, 2 vols. (Cambridge, Mass.: Harvard University Press, 1971), 2:1199–1200; Randolph A.

Roth, *The Democratic Dilemma: Religion, Reform, and the Social Order in the Connecticut River Valley of Vermont, 1791–1850* (New York: Cambridge University Press, 1987), 80–116.

40  McLoughlin, *New England Dissent*, 2:1189–1206.

41  Kermes, *Creating an American Identity*, esp, 15–56, 182–183 (quotation); Joseph A. Conforti, *Imagining New England: Explorations of Regional Identity from the Pilgrims to the Mid-Twentieth Century* (Chapel Hill: University of North Carolina Press, 2001), esp. 79–202; Harlow W. Scheidley, *Sectional Nationalism: Massachusetts Conservative Leaders and the Transformation of America, 1815–1836* (Boston: Northeastern University Press, 1998).

42  Conforti, *Imagining New England*, 79–202.

43  P. P. F. De Grand to Adams, January 17, 22, 1824, Adams Papers, MHS; Scheidley, *Sectional Nationalism*, 67.

44  P. P. F. De Grand to Adams, April 22, 1823, Adams Papers, MHS; Scheidley, *Sectional Nationalism*, 66–67, 74–75; William Lloyd Garrison, *The Letters of William Lloyd Garrison*, ed. Walter H. Merrill (Cambridge, Mass.: Harvard University Press, 1971), 1:4 n.; Arthur B. Darling, *Political Changes in Massachusetts, 1824–1848* (New Haven, Conn.: Yale University Press, 1925), 45; Troy *New York Sentinel*, August 1824, in Concord *New-Hampshire Statesman*, September 13, 1824.

45  Troy *New York Sentinel*, August 1824, and Norfolk, Va., *Herald*, in *New-Hampshire Statesman*, September 13, 1824, May 5, 1823.

46  *Boston Centinel*, September 1822; Henry R. Warfield to Clay, December 18, 1821, *HCP*, 3:148–149; William Plumer to his father, November 24, 1820, *WPL*, 58.

47  Philadelphia *National Gazette*, November 6, 1822, in Shaw Livermore Jr., *The Twilight of Federalism: The Disintegration of the Federalist Party, 1815–1830* (Princeton, N.J.: Princeton University Press, 1962), 96–97.

**CHAPTER 4  THE DREAD OF APOLLO**

1  Evan Cornog, *The Birth of Empire: De Witt Clinton and the American Experience, 1769–1828* (New York: Oxford University Press, 1998), 147.

2  Ambrose Spencer to Armstrong, May 4, 1813, in Jerome Mushkat, *Tammany: The Evolution of a Political Machine, 1789–1865* (Syracuse, N.Y.: Syracuse University Press, 1971), 53.

3  *New-York Statesman*, May 6, 1820.

4  *JHNY*, 1:537–538.

5  Robert Greenhalgh Albion, *The Rise of New York Port, 1815–1860* (1939; reprint, Newton Abbot, U.K.: David & Charles, 1970), 417; Matthew L. Davis to William P. Van Ness, August 1808, in Mushkat, *Tammany*, 36.

6  *JHNY*, 1:489; Nathan Williams to Van Buren, December 19, 1819, MVBP; *Albany Argus*, October 22, 1824, in Michael Wallace, "Changing Concepts of Party in the United States: New York, 1815–1828," *American Historical Review* 74 (1968): 457.

7  *JHNY*, 1:502–503, 455–456, 486, 487.

8   *JHNY*, 1:437, 454, 500, 450.

9   Clinton to Henry Post, October 21, 1822, in John Bigelow, ed., "De Witt Clinton as a Politician," *Harper's New Monthly Magazine* 50 (1875): 567; *MVBA*, 123.

10   *JHNY*, 1:573–578, 479 (quotation), 477–482, 479–480 (quotation), 531; *MVBA*, 90.

11   *JHNY*, 1:527–531, 118, 537–538, 2:3; Bonney, *Legacy of Historical Gleanings,* 1:344.

12   Bonney, *Legacy of Historical Gleanings,* 1:353; *JHNY,* 1:565–570; Mushkat, *Tammany,* 70–73.

13   *JHNY,* 2:102, 104, 115; *RKC,* 6:382–383; William Plumer Jr. to his father, January 3, 1822, in *WPL,* 74.

14   *MVBA,* 513; Van Buren to Thomas Ritchie, January 13, 1827, MVBP.

15   Van Buren to Mr. Dudley, January 10, 1822, in Bonney, *Legacy of Historical Gleanings,* 1:382.

16   Bonney, *Legacy of Historical Gleanings,* 1:388.

17   Plumer to his father, January 3, 1822, in *WPL,* 74, also 65–66, 68; *MVBA,* 131–140; Bonney, *Legacy of Historical Gleanings,* 362.

18   *JQAM,* 6:113 (November 1822); King, Memorandum, March 4, 1823, in *RKC,* 6:511.

19   Bonney, *Legacy of Historical Gleanings,* 382; Risjord, *Old Republicans,* 231; *MVBA,* 126; *JQAM,* 6:160; *HCP,* 3:300.

20   Rufus King to Charles King, February 26, 1823, Memoranda by Rufus King, April 7, 1823, *RKC,* 6:504, 521, also 519, 527; *MVBA,* 131.

21   *RKC,* 6:511, 504.

22   *JHNY,* 2:128.

23   Rufus King to Charles Gore, February 9, 1823, *RKC,* 6:500; Chilton Williamson, *American Suffrage: From Property to Democracy, 1760–1860* (Princeton, N.J.: Princeton University Press, 1960), 196–197; *JHNY,* 1:544.

24   Timothy Flint, *Arthur Clenning* (n.p.: Towar & Hogan, 1828), 22–23.

25   *JHNY,* 2:127, 129; James O. Morse to Adams, quoted in Mushkat, *Tammany,* 80.

26   *JQAM,* 6:62; Memoranda by R. King, April 28, 1823, Van Buren to R. King, May 2, 1823, and King, Memorandum, February 3, 1823, *RKC,* 6:527–529, 510.

27   *New-York American,* April 28, 1823, in Craig Hanyan with Mary L. Hanyan, *De Witt Clinton and the Rise of the People's Men* (Montreal: McGill–Queen's University Press, 1996), 85; King to John A. King, December 22, 1823, *RKC,* 6:489; *MVBA,* 131–132, 139–140.

28   King to Charles King, February 26, 1823, King to J. A. King, January 1823, *RKC,* 6:504, 495.

29   Calhoun to Samuel Southard, April 9, to Micah Sterling, April 28, and to J. G. Swift, April 29, 1823, *JCCP,* 8:11, 36–39; Henry Wheaton to Virgil Maxcy, quoted in Maxcy to Lemuel Williams Jr., September 10, 1823, *JCCP,* 8:266; Hanyan, *De Witt Clinton,* 76–79.

30  Nathaniel Rochester, quoted in Adam Beatty to Clay, June 30, 1823, *HCP* 3:446; *National Advertiser, for the Country,* October 10, 1823.

31  David Woods to Clay, August 27, 1823, William B. Rochester to Clay, November 1, 1823 *HCP,* 3:475, 510, 500–501.

32  William B. Rochester to Clay, November 1, 1823, *HCP* 3:510; *New-York Patriot,* April 1823; Jacob Barker to Butler, October 23, 1823, in Remini, *Martin Van Buren,* 42.

33  *JHNY,* 2:129; Mushkat, *Tammany,* 83–84; Hanyan, *De Witt Clinton,* 126.

34  Henry Wheaton to Levi Wheaton, October 19, 1823, in Elizabeth Feaster Baker, *Henry Wheaton, 1785–1848* (Philadelphia: University of Pennsylvania Press, 1937), 46; *NWR,* 25 (November 1, 1823), 131; Calhoun to Maxcy, October 31, 1823, *JCCP,* 8:338.

35  *National Advertiser, for the Country,* October 31, 1823; Robert V. Remini, "The Albany Regency," *New York History* 39 (1958): 342; De Witt Clinton Diary, October 28, 30, 1823, in Hanyan, *De Witt Clinton,* 128.

36  *Philadelphia Sentinel,* in *National Advertiser, for the Country,* November 11, 1823; Calhoun to S. L. Gouvernour, November 9, 1823, *JCCP,* 8:354; Hanyan, *De Witt Clinton,* 132.

37  *JHNY,* 2:131–132.

38  Hanyan, *De Witt Clinton,* 141–142.

39  *National Advertiser, for the Country,* September 16, 23, 1823.

40  *Portland Argus,* in *National Advocate, for the Country,* December 5, 1823; ibid., November 21, 28, 14, 1823; *MVBA,* 142.

41  *National Advertiser, for the Country,* November 11, 25, 1823; *JHNY,* 2:140; Saunders to Yancy, December 4, 1823, in "Letters of Romulus M. Saunders to Bartlett Yancy [sic], 1821–1828," ed. A. R. Newsome, *North Carolina Historical Review* 8 (1931): 435–436. This last letter contains a fuller account of the election, but apparently the manuscript is torn, obliterating the name of the author of the report, who was "a source entitled to the fullest credit." Could it have been Van Buren, who would perhaps tend to emphasize to a Southerner that the Bucktails were the South's main defense against Northern antislavery sentiment?

42  Rufus King to Edward King, July 8, 1823, *RKC,* 6:531.

43  *New-York American,* July–October 1823, 122, and *National Advocate,* August, November, 1823, in Hanyan, *De Witt Clinton,* 122–123, also 113.

44  *MVBA,* 142; Peter B. Porter to Clay, November 17, 1823, *HCP,* 3:522.

45  Benjamin F. Butler to Jesse Hoyt, January 29, 1824, in *The Lives and Opinions of Benjamin Franklin Butler and Jesse Hoyt,* comp. William Lyon McKenzie (Boston: Cook & Co., 1845), 38; Virgil Maxcy to [Charles Fisher?], November 16, 1823, in *North Carolina Historical Review* 7 (1930): 601; Henry Wheaton to Levi Wheaton, January 15, 1824, in Baker, *Henry Wheaton,* 52–53; Peter B. Porter to Robert Fleming, March 12, 1824, Peter B. Porter papers, Buffalo Historical Society.

46  Bigelow, "Clinton as Politician," 567; Clinton to Henry Post, March 4, 1824, ibid., 568; Webster to Jeremiah Mason, November 20, 1823, *DWP,* 1:333. See also Hanyan, *De Witt Clinton,* 88–116.

47 Hanyan, *De Witt Clinton,* 58–59; William B. Rochester to Clay, December 20, 1823, *HCP,* 3:547.

48 *JHNY,* 2:139; Daniel Webster to Ezekiel Webster, November 20, 1823, *DWP,* 1:334–335.

49 *JHNY,* 2:144–147.

50 *JHNY,* 2:154.

### CHAPTER 5 THE WESTERN INTEREST

1 Plumer to his father, November 13, 1820, *WPL,* 51–53; Frances Wright, *Views of Society and Manners in America* (New York, 1821), 374–375; Jabez D. Hammond, *The History of Political Parties in the State of New York, From the Ratification of the Constitution to December, 1840,* 2 vols. (Albany, N.Y.: printed by C. Van Benthuysen, 1842), 2:126.

2 Plumer to his father, February 15, 1821, November 24, 1820, *WPL,* 38, 56; Benton to James P. Preston, December 22, 1822, in William Nisbet Chambers, *Old Bullion Benton: Senator from the New West* (Boston: Little, Brown, 1956), 117.

3 Peter B. Porter to Clay, July 8, 1822, *HCP,* 3:252; Robert V. Remini, *Henry Clay, Statesman for the Union* (New York: Norton, 1991), 194; Webster to Jeremiah Mason, November 30, 1823, *DWP,* 1:336; Erastus Root to Clay, February 9, 1824, *HCP,* 3:634.

4 Clay, Speech on the Tariff, April 26, 1820, *HCP,* 2:826–847; quotation, 828.

5 Chambers, *Old Bullion Benton,* 84; Plumer to his father, November 24, 1820, *WPL,* 55–56.

6 Bonney, *Legacy of Historical Gleanings,* 1:409–410; Coens, "Formation of the Jackson Party."

7 *St. Louis Enquirer,* in Chambers, *Old Bullion Benton,* 88; Ratcliffe, *Politics of Long Division,* 58–60.

8 Charles Hammond to John C. Wright, December 15, 1822, CHP.

9 Feller, *Public Lands,* 31–58. An increase in circuits meant an increase in judges because each Supreme Court judge was responsible for conducting a particular circuit court.

10 Feller, *Public Lands,* 40–48.

11 Richard L. McCormick, *The Party Period and Public Policy: American Politics from the Age of Jackson to the Progressive Era* (New York: Oxford University Press, 1986), 14.

12 Ethan Allen Brown to William Trimble, May 12, 1820, Brown Papers; John Sloane to Benjamin Tappan, April 15, 1820, Benjamin Tappan Papers, LC.

13 Chillicothe *Scioto Gazette,* October 21, 1824.

14 [Elgius Fromentin?] to Clay, April 26, 1822, *HCP,* 3:200–201.

15 Arndt M. Stickles, *The Critical Court Struggle in Kentucky, 1819–1821* (Bloomington: Indiana University, 1929).

16 Amos Kendall to Clay, June 20, 1822, *HCP,* 3:237.

17 Clay to Benjamin W. Leigh, December 22, 1823, *HCP,* 3:550; ibid., 478–479, 551n3, 4; Francis Johnson to Clay, December 10, 1822, *HCP,* 3:333–334.

18  Francis Johnson to Clay, December 10, 1822, *HCP*, 3:334.

19  [Elgius Fromentin?] to Clay, April 26, 1822, *HCP*, 3:200–201.

20  Clay to Brooke, September 1, 1823, *HCP*, 3:480; King to Charles Gore, February 9, 1823, *RKC*, 6: 500.

21  Ralph D. Gray, *The National Waterway: A History of the Chesapeake and Delaware Canal, 1769–1965* (Urbana: University of Illinois Press, 1967), 25–66.

22  Clay to Porter, April 14, 1822, Porter to Clay, January 29, [1823], *HCP*, 3:191, 356.

23  Porter to Clay, September 6, 1823, *HCP*, 3:486–487.

24  William B. Rochester to Clay, December 20, 1823, *HCP*, 3:547.

25  Cheves to Clay, November 9, 1822, *HCP*, 3:314; also 575, 593n, 743; Thomas I. Wharton to Clay, August 13, 1823, Clay to Josephus B. Stuart, December 19, 1823, *HCP*, 3:467, 545.

26  Thomas I. Wharton to Clay, August 13, 1823, *HCP*, 3:466–467.

27  *JCCP*, 8: xxiii–xxiv; Adams's MS diary, MHS, in ibid., xxiv (final quotation).

28  Cheves to Clay, November 9, 1822, *HCP*, 3:316 (also 213, 317); Calhoun to Virgil Maxcy, January 20, 1823, *JCCP*, 7:432.

29  Whittlesey to Charles Hammond, February 14, 1824, CHP; Q. F. Atkins to Whittlesey, February 6, 1824, Elisha Whittlesey Papers, WRHS; Whittlesey to Joshua R. Giddings, May 13, 1824, September 18, 1824, Joshua R. Giddings Papers, OHS.

30  Joseph Richardson to John H. Larwill, September 23, 1824, Larwill Family Papers, OHS; Steubenville *Western Herald*, April 12, 1823; Edward King to Rufus King, November 24, 1822, January 23, 1823, *RKC*, 6:487, 497.

31  John Sloane to Charles Hammond, January 1, 1824, CHP.

32  Thomas, quoted in Edward King to Rufus King, July 22, 1823, *RKC*, 6:532.

33  Hammond to Wright, February 18, 1824, CHP.

34  James A. Paxton to Duncan McArthur, January 10, 1824, Duncan McArthur Papers, LC; Clay to Francis Brooke, March 16, 1824, *HCP*, 3:673.

35  Clay to Francis Brooke, February 23, 1824, *HCP*, 3:656.

36  Ephraim Cutler, Nahum Ward, Samuel Hildreth, "Address to the Free and Independent Electors of the 7th Congressional District" [June 1824], Samuel P. Hildreth Papers, Marietta College.

37  Clay, quoted in Georgetown, D.C., *Metropolitan*, 1821, *HCP*, 3:19–20 n.

38  William S. Merrill, 1820, in Ophia D. Smith, *The Life and Times of Giles Richards, 1820–1860* (Columbus: Ohio State Archaeological and Historical Society, 1936), 14–15; *Liberty Hall and Cincinnati Gazette*, [June] 1821, in *HCP*, 3:103 n.

39  Charles Hammond to Elisha Whittlesey, February 2, 1824, Whittlesey Papers.

**CHAPTER 6  ENTER THE GENERAL**

1  Steubenville, Ohio, *Western Herald*, September 1, 1815; Toasts Given, July 4, 1815, Mantua, Ohio, John Harmon Papers, WRHS; Gabriel L. Lewis Jr., "John H. Eaton, Jackson's Campaign Manager," *Tennessee Historical Quarterly* 11 (1952): 100.

2   Jonathan Roberts, "Memoirs," 2:125–126. In the 1680s the *dragonnades* had billeted troops on Protestant families to persuade them to convert to Catholicism.

3   *JQAM*, 4:197–198, 4:221–222, 5:327; Louisa Catherine Adams, Diary, February 3, March 4, 1819, Miscellany, *Microfilms of the Adams Papers*, 608 reels (Boston: Adams Manuscript Trust, MHS, 1954–1959), MHS; Jessup N. Couch to Peter Hitchcock, February 9, 1819, Charles E. Rice Papers, OHS.

4   Jackson, in James Parton, *Life of Andrew Jackson*, 3 vols. (New York: Mason Bros., 1861), 2:354; Monroe and Wirt, quoted in *AJP*, 5:96.

5   *AJP*, 5:89–90, 141, 159.

6   William Carroll to Clay, February 1, 1823, John W. Overton to Clay, January 16, 1822, *HCP*, 3:361, 156–157. The following paragraphs follow Charles Grier Sellers Jr.'s classic article, "Jackson Men with Feet of Clay," *American Historical Review* 62 (1957): 537–551.

7   White to Overton, January 30, 1823, in Sellers, "Jackson Men," 546.

8   Benton to Clay, July 23, 1823, *HCP*, 3:460; White, in Nashville *Union*, September 25, 1835, in Sellers, "Jackson Men," 542.

9   *AJP*, 5:294–295; "Major Lewis's Narrative," in Parton, *Andrew Jackson*, 3:21–23. Only three of the twenty-five survived the next state election.

10  Thomas B. Reed to Clay, September 5, 1822, John McKinley to Clay, June 3, September 29, 1823, in *HCP*, 3:284, 427, 490–491.

11  *NWR*, 23 (January 11, 1823), 291; Clay to Porter, January 31, 1824, *HCP*, 3:630.

12  Jonathan Roberts, "Memoirs," 2:142, and Roberts to Mathew Roberts, February 29, March 5, 7, 9, 1824, Jonathan Roberts Papers, HSP.

13  Plumer to his father, February 29, 1824, in *WPL*, 102.

14  Crawford to Gallatin, July 24, 1819, in Gallatin, *Writings of Albert Gallatin*, 2:117.

15  Philadelphia *Franklin Gazette*, October 8, 1822, in Phillips, *William Duane*, 528.

16  Klein, *Pennsylvania Politics*, 117.

17  Cameron, in Lee F. Crippen, *Simon Cameron, Ante-bellum Years* (Oxford, Ohio: Mississippi Valley Press, 1942), 5; *NWR*, 24 (November 8, 1823), 156.

18  Simpson to Jackson, July 5, 1823, in Phillips, *William Duane*, 564; Kim T. Phillips, "The Pennsylvania Origins of the Jackson Movement," *Political Science Quarterly* 91 (1976): 497.

19  Henry Baldwin to Jackson, January 1, 1823, in Jackson, *Correspondence of Andrew Jackson*, 3:184n; Jackson to H. W. Peterson, February 23, 1823, *AJP*, 5:252–254; Phillips, "Pennsylvania Origins," 498.

20  *JCCP*, 7:515–518, 530; Louisville *Public Advertiser*, May 3, 1823.

21  Virgil Maxcy to R. S. Garnett, November 16, 1823, in *American Historical Review* 12 (1907): 601; William Darlington to Lewis Coryell, February 18, 1824, Lewis Coryell Papers, HSP; Jonathan Roberts to Mathew Roberts, December 21, 1823, Roberts Papers, HSP.

22  Jonathan Roberts to Mathew Roberts, December 20, 1823, Roberts Papers, HSP.

23 Jonathan Roberts to Mathew Roberts, January 14, 1824, Roberts Papers, HSP; Dallas to William Darlington, January 27, in Klein, *Pennsylvania Politics*, 158; Calhoun to Maxcy, February 27, 1824, *JCCP*, 5:554; Peart, *Era of Experimentation*, 130.

24 Clay to Peter B. Porter, February 19, 1824, *HCP* 3:653; Klein, *Pennsylvania Politics*, 163.

25 Coens, "Formation of the Jackson Party," 39–46. See also chap. 7 below.

26 George McDuffie to ———, January 13, 1823 [probably 1824], in "Correspondence of John C. Calhoun, George McDuffie and Charles Fisher, Relating to the Presidential Campaign of 1824," ed. A. R. Newsome, *North Carolina Historical Review* 7 (1930): 486.

27 William Cooper Howells, *Recollections of the Life in Ohio, 1813–1840* (Cincinnati: Robert Clarke, 1895), 99, 119–121, 157–158; Steubenville, Ohio, *Western Herald*, September 1, 1815; William Foulks to Peter Hitchcock, February 16, 1819, Peter Hitchcock Family Papers, WRHS; Edward Patchell to Jackson, August 16, 1824, Jackson, *Correspondence of Andrew Jackson*, 3:262–265.

28 Philip S. Klein, *President James Buchanan: A Biography* (University Park: Pennsylvania State University Press, 1962), 45–48.

29 *NWR*, 27 (November 3, 1824), 149; Henry Simpson, *The Lives of Eminent Philadelphians, Now Deceased, Collected from Original and Authentic Sources* (Philadelphia: William Brotherhead, 1859), 893–895; Adams to Louisa Catherine Adams, August 28, 1822, in John Quincy Adams, *Writings of John Quincy Adams*, ed. Worthington Chauncey Ford, 7 vols. (New York: Macmillan, 1913–1917), 7:297.

30 Philadelphia *Columbian Observer*, n.d., in Phillips, *William Duane*, 567–568, and August 3, 1822, in Hanyan, *De Witt Clinton*, 58; Philadelphia *Franklin Gazette*, August 17, 1824, in Phillips, *William Duane*, 583–584.

31 *Strictures Addressed to James Madison on the Celebrated Report of William H. Crawford, Recommending the Intermarriage of Americans with the Indian Tribes. Ascribed to Judge Cooper and Originally Published by John Binns in the Democratic Press* (Philadelphia, 1824), iii–iv. See also David A. Wilson, *United Irishmen, United States: Immigrant Radicals in the Early Republic* (Ithaca, N.Y.: Cornell University Press, 1998), 39–40, 55, 62–64; Phillips, *William Duane*, 204–209; Klein, *Pennsylvania Politics*, 146–147.

32 *Cincinnati Advertiser*, November 3, 1824.

33 Hon. Edward Stanley, *Journal of a Tour in America, 1824–1825* (n.p.: privately printed for Lord Derby, 1931), 178; Adam Hodgson, *Letters from North America: Written during a Tour of the United States and Canada*, 2 vols. (London: Hurst, Robinson & Co., 1824), 1:102.

34 J. P. Kennedy to Virgil Maxcy, October 11, 1823, in Heale, *Presidential Quest*, 60; *NWR*, 27 (January 10, 1824), 291; Charles Hammond to John C. Wright, October 1, 1824, CHP.

35 *Liberty Hall and Cincinnati Gazette*, May 18, 1824.

36 R. Goldsborough to Rufus King, April 17, 1822, *RKC*, 6:468.

37 *Political Thoughts, No. 1: Idea of a Patriot President* (Washington City: Davis

& Force, 1823). Written in December 1822, the pamphlet was reviewed in January 1823 in *The United States Gazette and Literary and Political Repository* 1:1 (New York: Charles Wiley, January 1823). For the continuing appeal of the idea of a republican Patriot King, see Ralph Ketcham, *Presidents Above Party: The First American Presidency, 1789–1829* (Chapel Hill: University of North Carolina Press, 1984), which underestimates its power in Jackson's campaigns.

38  For Jacksonism as a "revolt against politics," see Coens, "Formation of the Jackson Party," 18–65.

39  *The Letters of Wyoming, to the People of the United States, on the Presidential Election, and in Favour of Andrew Jackson* (Philadelphia: S. Simpson & J. Conrad, 1824). Jackson learned of Eaton's authorship in April 1824 (*AJP*, 5:388, 389n6). Apparently there were at least eighteen letters, with some of the later ones being reprinted separately in the press. Gabriel L. Lowe Jr., "John H. Eaton, Jackson's Campaign Manager," *Tennessee Historical Quarterly* 11 (1952): 106n28. The following paragraphs draw heavily on Robert P. Hay, "The Case for Andrew Jackson in 1824: Eaton's 'Wyoming Letters,'" *Tennessee Historical Quarterly* 29 (1970): 139–151.

40  *Columbian Observer*, August 3, 1822, in Hanyan, *De Witt Clinton*, 58, and n.d., in Vincennes *Western Sun and General Advertiser*, August 23, 1823, in Adam A. Leonard, "Personal Politics in Indiana, 1816 to 1840," part 1, *Indiana Magazine of History* 19 (March 1923): 19. The latter source is cited by Leonard as the Columbus *Ohio Observer* (which did not exist) for 1825 (which the content contradicts); I guess that he means the *Columbian Observer*.

41  Calhoun to Jackson, March 30, 1823, *AJP*, 5:266.

42  A Nashville pastor to a New York clergyman, August 13, 1824, in Hagerstown, Md., *Torch Light and Public Advertiser*, December 14, 1824, *AJP*, 5:290.

43  Plumer to his father, February 29, 1824, in *WPL*, 102–103; *AJP*, 5:370–371.

**CHAPTER 7  A SEASON IN WASHINGTON**

1  *JQAM*, 6:276.

2  James Sterling Young, *The Washington Community, 1800–1828* (New York: Columbia University Press, 1966); [Alexander Hamilton], *Federalist Papers*, no. 27.

3  Constance McLaughlin Green, *Washington: Village and Capital, 1800–1878* (Princeton, N.J.: Princeton University Press, 1962–1963), 1:106. *NWR*, 23 (February 22, 1823), 387, gives the population as 13,247 in 1820 and probably 14,856 in January 1823.

4  Young, *Washington Community*, 98; Van Rensselaer's letters, in Bonney, *Legacy of Historical Gleanings*, 1:338, 379, 397, 402; Allan G. Bogue and Mark Paul Marlaire, "Of Mess and Men: The Boardinghouse and Congressional Voting, 1821–1842," *American Journal of Political Science* 19 (May 1975): 207–230, esp. 226–228.

5  Van Rensselaer, in Bonney, *Legacy of Historical Gleanings*, 1:340, 343, 353;

Jonathan Roberts, Diary, Jonathan Roberts Papers, HSP, 2:9; C[yrus] W. Trimble to John Allen Trimble, January 29, 1821, Papers of John Allen Trimble and the Trimble Family, 1787–1908, OHS; St. Clairsville *Ohio Federalist,* in Cincinnati *Western Spy,* August 2, 1816.

6   *Letters of Wyoming,* 47, 51; Thomas G. Watkins to Jackson, March 13, 1822, *AJP,* 5:156; Catherine Allgor, *Parlor Politics: In Which the Ladies of Washington Help Build a City and a Government* (Charlottesville: University of Virginia Press, 2000), 147–149.

7   Washington *National Intelligencer,* July 13, 1822, in Green, *Washington,* 108; Philadelphia *Columbian Observer,* August 3, 1822, in Hanyan, *De Witt Clinton,* 58.

8   *Letters of Wyoming;* Noble E. Cunningham Jr., ed., *Circular Letters of Congressmen to Their Constituents, 1789–1829,* 3 vols. (Chapel Hill: University of North Carolina, 1978), 3:1151–1309.

9   Charles Francis Adams, quoted in Allgor, *Parlor Politics,* 180, 176–182. The verse was written by John Agg and appeared in the Washington *National Intelligencer,* January 8, 1824; reprinted in *New-Hampshire Statesman,* February 2, 1824, and Nathan Sargent, *Public Men and Events, 1817–1853,* 2 vols. (Philadelphia: J. B. Lippincott, 1875), 1:40–42.

10  Parton, *Life of Andrew Jackson,* 3:14. Parton pointed out that Jackson was already a serious candidate within several states.

11  John Sloane to Charles Hammond, January 1, 1824, CHP.

12  Jackson to George Washington Martin, July [January] 2, 1824, *AJP,* 5:334; Daniel to Ezekiel Webster, February 22, 1824, in Daniel Webster, *The Private Correspondence of Daniel Webster,* ed. Fletcher Webster, 2 vols. (Boston: Little, Brown, 1857), 1:346.

13  *JCCP,* 7:298; John Henry Eaton to Jackson, February 23, 1823, *AJP,* 5:255; Leverett Saltonstall to his wife, Mary, February 26, 1824, Leverett Saltonstall, *The Papers of Leverett Saltonstall, 1816–1843,* ed. Robert E. Moody, 5 vols. (Boston: Massachusetts Historical Society, 1978), 1:124.

14  Eaton to Jackson, February 23, 1823, *AJP,* 5:255; Green, *Washington,* 108–109.

15  Smith, *First Forty Years,* 162, 165; *JCCP,* 8:xxvi–xxviii.

16  *NWR,* 25 (November 15, 22, 1823), 161, 185.

17  *Letters of Wyoming,* 89; Newsome, *Presidential Election,* 105–106.

18  Ernest R. May, *The Making of the Monroe Doctrine* (Cambridge, Mass.: Harvard University Press, 1975).

19  Samuel Flagg Bemis, *John Quincy Adams and the Foundations of American Foreign Policy* (New York: Knopf, 1949), 369–376, quotation at 375; *JQAM,* 6:177–180; Bemis, *John Quincy Adams and the Foundations of American Foreign Policy,* 363–381.

20  *JQAM,* 6:173 (August 14, 1823), and also 6:477. So much for May's claim that Adams opposed recognizing Greece because he did not wish to appoint a well-known Federalist, such as Edward Everett. May, *Making of the Monroe Doctrine,* 229–233.

21  *JQAM,* 6:185–186, November 15, 1823.

22  William Duane, *The Two Americas, Great Britain, and the Holy Alliance* (Washington, D.C., 1824); Phillips, *William Duane,* 493–527.

23  *JQAM,* 6:194–195, November 21, 1823; Wright to Hammond, December 9, 1823, CHP.

24  Clay, Remarks on Resolution on European Intervention in America, [May 26, 1824], *HCP,* 3:764–765.

25  *JQAM,* 6:198–199, November 24, 1823.

26  Clay, Speech on Mission to Greece, [January 23, 1824], and controversy with Ichabod Bartlett, *HCP,* 3:603–618.

27  Rufus King to Charles King, May 22, 23, 1824, *RKC,* 6:571; Bemis, *John Quincy Adams and the Foundations of American Foreign Policy,* 408–435.

28  Plumer, *WPL,* 48–49.

29  Ruggles to Hammond, January 1, 1824, CHP, and Ruggles to Ephraim Cutler, February 8, 1824, in *Life and Times of Ephraim Cutler, Prepared from His Journals and Correspondence,* ed. Julia Perkins Cutler (Cincinnati: R. Clarke, 1890), 184–185.

30  Ruggles to Hammond, January 1, 1824, CHP; Mrs. Smith to Mrs. Boyd, December 19, 1823, in Smith, *First Forty Years,* 162–163; Plumer to his father, April 1, 20, 1824, *WPL,* 108.

31  Romulus M. Saunders to Bartlett Yancy, December 4, 7, 1823, in "Letters of Romulus M. Saunders to Bartlett Yancy," 435–438.

32  Jonathan Roberts to brother Mathew, December 6, 20, 1823, Roberts Papers, HSP; David Scott to Lewis Coryell, February 18, 1824, Coryell Papers, HSP; Ruggles to Charles Hammond, January 1, 1824, CHP; Elian Kent Kane to Jesse B. Thomas, January 8, 1824, in Peart, *Era of Experimentation,* 114–115.

33  James Geddes to John W. Taylor, February 22, 1823, in Chase, *Emergence of the Presidential Nominating Convention,* 290–291; *NWR,* 23 (March 1, 1823), 401; Mooney, *William H. Crawford,* 237, 249–250, 256–257.

34  Jackson to Andrew Donelson, January 21, 1824, Jackson, *Correspondence of Andrew Jackson,* 3:225.

35  Address by Senator Benjamin Ruggles to the Republicans of the United States, Washington, February 21, 1824, in *History of American Presidential Elections, 1789–1968,* ed. Arthur M. Schlesinger and Fred L. Israel, 4 vols. (New York: Chelsea House, 1971), 1:401–404. Surprisingly, perhaps, the Virginia House decided by a vote of 76–77 not to act on the Tennessee resolutions, but a party caucus passed unanimously resolutions supporting the principle of a congressional caucus. Lyon G. Tyler, *The Letters and Times of the Tylers* (1884; reprint, New York: Da Capo, 1970), 1:341–342.

36  Chase, *Emergence of the Presidential Nominating Convention,* 56–57; Klein, *Pennsylvania Politics,* 150–157.

37  May, *Making of the Monroe Doctrine,* 238–239.

38  Henry Wheaton to Levi Wheaton, December 24, 1823, in Baker, *Henry Wheaton,* 49; Clay to Josephus B. Stuart, December 19, 1823, Clay to Peter B.

Porter, December 24, 1823, *HCP*, 3:544–545, 553–554; Wright to Hammond, January 8, 1824, CHP.

39 Elisha Whittlesey to Robert Harper, December 18, 1824, Robert Harper Papers, WRHS; William Plumer Jr. to his father, December 31, 1823, February 29, 1824, *WPL*, 92–93, 103.

40 Rufus King to Charles King, December 19, 1823, *RKC*, 6:539–540; Risjord, *Old Republicans*, 308n47; Remini, *Martin Van Buren*, 44–45.

41 *JQAM*, 6:226 (January 4, 1824); Ruggles to Ephraim Cutler, February 8, 1824, in Cutler, *Life and Times of Ephraim Cutler*, 184–185.

42 Ruggles to Cutler, February 8, 1824, in Cutler, *Life and Times of Ephraim Cutler*, 184–185, and to Thomas Worthington, February 5, 1824, Thomas Worthington Papers, OHS; Clay to Peter B. Porter, October 4, 1823, *HCP*, 3:494; *National Intelligencer*, February 3, 1824, in Charles Seymour Thompson, *An Essay on the Rise and Fall of Congressional Caucus As a Machine for Nominating Candidates for the Presidency* (New Haven, Conn.: [Yale, 1902]), 43.

43 John Patterson to Hammond, February 3, 1824, Whittlesey to Hammond, February 14, 1824, Wright to Hammond, January 26, 1824, CHP; Ruggles to Worthington, February 5, 1824, Worthington Papers, OHS.

44 Walter Lowrie to Gallatin, February 21, 1824, in Dangerfield, *Era of Good Feelings*, 311; Risjord, *Old Republicans*, 252–253.

45 "Address by Senator Benjamin Ruggles to the Republicans of the United States, Washington, February 21, 1824," in Schlesinger and Israel, *History of American Presidential Elections*, 1:401–404; Ruggles to Abraham Tappan, March 17, 1824, VFM 430, OHS.

46 Gallatin to Walter Lowrie, May 22, 1824, in Chase, *Emergence of the Presidential Nominating Convention*, 62; *Pennsylvania Intelligencer*, March 12, 1824, in Crippen, *Simon Cameron*, 16; Plumer to his father, May 3, 1824, *WPL*, 117. The ditty was reported as "Fifty-two / Won't do," a clear error.

47 Sloane to Hammond, January 1, 1824, Ruggles to Hammond, October 9, 1824, CHP; *Liberty Hall and Cincinnati Gazette*, March 5, 1824. The verse comes from Stephen Colwell to Thomas Ewing, March 4, 1824, Ewing Family Papers, LC.

48 Philemon Beecher to Thomas Ewing, February 25, 1824, Ewing Family Papers, LC; *Cincinnati Advertiser*, March 3, 1824; Zanesville *Ohio Republican*, January 11, 1823, and as quoted in Chillicothe *Scioto Gazette*, May 31, 1823.

49 Edward Stanwood, *American Tariff Controversies in the Nineteenth Century*, 2 vols. (Westminster: Archibald Constable, 1904), 1:220–223, 226.

50 These paragraphs draw heavily on Larson, *Internal Improvement*, chap. 4.

51 *NWR*, 25 (February 29, 1824), 387; Feller, *Public Lands*, 58–59.

52 Clay, Speech on Tariff, [March 30–31, 1824], *HCP*, 3:683–730.

53 James Buchanan, *The Works of James Buchanan*, ed. John Bassett Moore, 12 vols. (1908–1911; reprint, New York: Antiquarian Press, 1960), 1:56–70.

54 These paragraphs draw heavily on Jonathan J. Pincus, *Pressure Groups and Politics in Antebellum Tariffs* (New York: Columbia University Press, 1977), and Stanwood, *American Tariff Controversies*, 2:200–242.

55 Clay to ———, February 15, 1824, *HCP*, 3:639; Pincus, *Pressure Groups and Politics*, 45. Louisiana still voted against.

56 Clay to ———, February 15, 1824, *HCP*, 3:639–640; Wright to Tappan, April 18, 1824, Benjamin Tappan Papers, LC; *NWR*, 26 (April 17, 1824), 97. See also Pincus, *Pressure Groups and Politics*, 68, 69, 71.

57 Wright to Tappan, April 18, 1824, Benjamin Tappan Papers; *NWR*, 26 (April 17, 24, May 1, 15, 1824), 112, 113–114, 127, 137, 173; *Cleaveland [sic] Herald*, October 22, 1824.

58 King, reported in *JQAM*, 6:317 (May 2, 1824); Pancake, *Samuel Smith*, 167–168; Hammond to Ruggles, [May 9, 1824], CHP; Willie P. Mangum to Seth Jones, May 24, 1824, in Willie Person Mangum, *The Papers of Willie Person Mangum*, ed. Henry Thomas Shanks, 5 vols. (Raleigh, N.C.: State Department of Archives and History, 1950), 1:146; *NWR*, 26 (May 15, 22, 29, 1824), 161, 171, 202.

59 *JCCP*, 9:xliv–xlvi.

60 Plumer to his father, March 8, 1824, *WPL*, 105–106; *JQAM*, 6:323, 353, 451; Clay, Speech on Internal Improvements, [January 14, 1824], *HCP*, 3:572–593.

61 Clay, Speech on Internal Improvements, [January 14, 1824], *HCP* 3:590–592. See also Heale, *Presidential Quest*, 45–47.

62 Marquis James, *Life of Andrew Jackson* (Indianapolis, Ind.: Bobbs-Merrill, 1938), 373; Jackson to Littleton H. Coleman, April 26, 1824, *AJP*, 5:398–400 and 400n; Heale, *Presidential Quest*, 49–50; Hammond to Wright, May 3, 1824, CHP. In May 1821 Clay himself had advocated "a judicious tariff, carefully devised"; *HCP*, 3:81.

63 *MVBM*, 239–243; *AJP*, 5:411, 412 n.; Stanwood, *American Tariff Controversies*, 232.

64 *AJP*, 5:400–401, 404, 409–413, 417–420, 425–429.

65 King to Gore, February 9, 1823, in *RKC*, 6:500, also 496; *Cincinnati Advertiser*, March 3, 1824; *Proceedings and Address of the Convention of Delegates, that Met in Columbus, Ohio, December 28, 1827, to Nominate a Ticket of Electors Favorable to the Reelection of John Quincy Adams, President of the United States, To Be Supported at the Electoral Election of 1828* (Columbus: P. H. Olmsted, 1827). The *Advertiser*'s report of the voting was inaccurate: sixty-six attended the caucus and sixty-two voted for Crawford.

66 *NWR*, 26 (April 24, 1824), 116, 129; Smith to Mrs. Kirkpatrick, June 28, 1824, in Smith, *First Forty Years*, 165–166; Remini, *Martin Van Buren*, 58–59. See also Thomas Hart Benton, *Thirty Years' View, or A History of the Workings of the American Government for Thirty Years, from 1820 to 1850*, 2 vols. (New York: D. Appleton & Co., 1859), 1:34–36; Mooney, *William H. Crawford*, 242–248.

67 *JQAM*, 6:374–376, 384–398.

68 Monroe to Jackson, February 22, 1824, *AJP*, 5:365–366; Klein, *Pennsylvania Politics*, 166–169.

69 John H. Eaton, G. Sullivan of Massachusetts, and Adams, April 24, 1824, in

JQAM, 6:307–308; J. S. Bassett, "Major Lewis on the Nomination of Andrew Jackson," *Proceedings of the American Antiquarian Society* 33 (1923): 20. See also Coens, "Formation of the Jackson Party," 40–46.

70  *Caucus Curs in Full Yell;* Lowe, "John H. Eaton," 104n27, 110–114.

71  Adams to Plumer, July 26, 1824, in *WPL*, 117; Mooney, *William H. Crawford,* 263–268; Risjord, *Old Republicans,* 253–254.

72  Mooney, *William H. Crawford,* 275–279; Robert P. Hay, "The Pillorying of Albert Gallatin: The Public Response to his 1824 Vice-Presidential Nomination," *Western Pennsylvania Historical Magazine* 65 (1982): 181–202.

73  *NWR,* 27 (November 6, 1824), 147–148; *JQAM,* 6:332–333 (May 1824); John Adams Dix, *Memoirs of John Adams Dix,* comp. Morgan Dix, 2 vols. (New York: Harper, 1883), 2:309–314.

74  George M. Bibb to J. J. Crittenden, March 8, 1824, in Mrs. Chapman Coleman, ed., *The Life of John J. Crittenden: With Selections from His Correspondence and Speeches,* 2 vols. (Philadelphia: Lippincott, 1871): 1:60–62; Smith to Mrs. Kirkpatrick, in Smith, *First Forty Years,* 166; Adams to Plumer, July 26, 1824, *WPL,* 117.

**CHAPTER 8 POPULAR BATTLEGROUNDS**

1  *Richmond Enquirer,* August 6, 1824, in Peart, *Era of Experimentation,* 129; Shade, *Democratizing the Old Dominion,* 84–85; Joseph Clinton Clifft, "The Politics of Transition: Virginia and North Carolina and the Presidential Election of 1824" (Ph.D. diss., University of Tennessee, 1999), 94–111, 113–116.

2  *NWR,* 27 (November 13, 1824), 161; Ratcliffe, "Popular Preferences," 55, 64.

3  Isaac Hill to Plumer, April 22, 1824, *WPL,* 111–112.

4  *JQAM,* 6:291 (April 15, 1824); Peart, *Era of Experimentation,* 124–127.

5  Jonathan Roberts to Mathew Roberts, March 5, 1824, Jonathan Roberts Papers, HSP; Phillips, *William Duane,* 505; Philadelphia *United States Gazette,* October 1824.

6  Klein, *Pennsylvania Politics,* 170–175; Peart, *Era of Experimentation,* 130.

7  *NWR,* 27 (December 25, 1824), 259–260; *AJP,* 5:413 n.; Thomas P. Abernethy, *The Formative Period in Alabama, 1815–1828* (Montgomery, Ala.: Brown Printing, 1922), 124–134, 128; Edwin A. Miles, *Jacksonian Democracy in Mississippi* (Chapel Hill: University of North Carolina Press, 1960), 5, 15, 21–22, 23; Peart, *Era of Experimentation,* 151.

8  Charles S. Sydnor, *The Development of Southern Sectionalism, 1819–1848* (Baton Rouge: Louisiana State University Press, 1948), 108–120; Abernethy, *Formative Period,* 103–119, 124, 129–130; Miles, *Jacksonian Democracy,* 6–8, 23.

9  Sydnor, *Development of Southern Sectionalism,* 172; Abernethy, *Formative Period,* 42, 91, 132–134; Miles, *Jacksonian Democracy,* 18.

10  The following paragraphs draw heavily on Ratcliffe, *Politics of Long Division,* 80–92, 98–104, 111–122.

11  *Delaware Patron,* April 29, 1824; Charles Hammond to [John C. Wright], January 7, 1824, CHP; *Chillicothe Times,* October 20, 1824.

12  E. Cutler, N. Ward, and S. Hildreth, "Address to the Free And Independent Electors of the 7th Congressional District," [June 1824], SPHP; *Cleaveland* [*sic*] *Herald*, March 6, 1823; *Painesville Telegraph*, September 4, October 30, 1824.

13  Hammond to Whittlesey, February 2, 1824, Whittlesey Papers; A Citizen of Ohio, *Clay and Slavery!!*, n.p., October 22, 1824, political broadside, OHS, and reprinted in *Cincinnati Emporium*, October 28, 1824.

14  Hammond to Wright, December 11, 1823, February 18, March 19, and April 16, 1824, CHP; Cincinnati *National Republican*, October 5, 1824; *Western Post*, in Ripley *Castigator*, August 24, 1824; Chillicothe *Scioto Gazette*, October 21, 1824.

15  *Painesville Telegraph*, March 5, April 30, 1823.

16  Chillicothe *Scioto Gazette*, November 18, 1824; *Painesville Telegraph*, October 30, 1824; *Cincinnati Gazette*, November 16, 1824. In seventeen of the twenty-four counties in which Clay won an absolute majority, the level of turnout was below the average for the state.

17  Henry Dana Ward to Cutler, April 14, 1824, Ephraim Cutler Papers, Marietta College (emphasis in original); Hammond to Wright, June 7, 1824, CHP.

18  Cincinnati *National Republican*, October 15, 29, 1824.

19  Sloane to Whittlesey, August 9, 1824, Whittlesey Papers.

20  Steubenville *Western Herald*, September 1, 1815; Cincinnati *Advertiser*, November 3, 13, 1824.

21  Clay to Francis Brooke, November 26, 1824, *HCP*, 3:887.

22  Calvin Fletcher, *The Diary of Calvin Fletcher*, ed. Gayle Thornbrough (Indianapolis: Indiana Historical Society, 1972), 1:99 (entry for December 2, 1823).

23  And the only ones in 1824, except for an equally weak Crawford convention in Pennsylvania and a Jackson one in Virginia. The Pennsylvania and New York conventions of 1824 were equally novel but were called by parties seeking to decide on an agreed candidate. Leonard, "Personal Politics," 23–26; Peart, *Era of Experimentation*, 128, 130.

24  Richmond (Ind.) *Public Leger*, May 15, 1824, June 12, 1824, and Corydon *Indiana Gazette*, April 9, 1823, in Thomas W. Howard, "Indiana Newspapers and the Presidential Election of 1824, *Indiana Magazine of History* 63 (1967): 193–197.

25  Vincennes *Western Sun*, quoted in Donald F. Carmony, *Indiana, 1816–1850: The Pioneer Era* (Indianapolis: Indiana Historical Society, 1998), 481, and 482–483.

26  Thomas Ford, *A History of Illinois: From Its Commencement as a State in 1818 to 1847*, ed. Rodney O. Davis (1854; reprint, Urbana: University of Illinois Press, 1995), 33; *Edwardsville Spectator*, July 6, October 19, 1824. See also David Ress, *Governor Edward Coles and the Vote to Forbid Slavery in Illinois, 1823–1824* (Jefferson, N.C.: McFarland, 2006), 141–142; Peart, *Era of Experimentation*, 47–72.

27  Gerard Leonard, *The Invention of Party Politics: Federalism, Popular Sovereignty, and Constitutional Development in Jacksonian Illinois* (Chapel Hill:

University of North Carolina Press, 2002), 65–70; Peart, *Era of Experimentation*, 132–134.

28 Eleven of the seventeen counties that had voted against a convention gave Adams more votes than his statewide average, while nine of the eleven counties that had voted in favor of a convention gave less than 15 percent of their votes to Adams. Charles M. Thompson, *The Illinois Whigs before 1846* (Urbana: University of Illinois, 1915), 16–31, emphasized the significance of Northern immigration into Illinois in the early 1820s, which he considered larger than generally assumed (see esp. 17n26 and 26–27); see also James Simeone, *Democracy and Slavery in Frontier Illinois: The Bottomland Republic* (DeKalb: Northern Illinois University Press, 2000), 6, and Kurt E. Leichtle and Bruce G. Carveth, *Crusade against Slavery: Edward Coles, Pioneer of Freedom* (Carbondale: Southern Illinois University Press, 2011), 90. For the extraordinary efforts, see Peart, *Era of Experimentation*, 47–72.

29 Vandalia *Illinois Intelligencer*, October 29, 1824.

30 Franklin *Missouri Intelligencer*, February 21, 1824; St. Louis *Missouri Republican*, May 10, 1824; Alan S. Weiner, "John Scott, Thomas Hart Benton, David Barton, and the Presidential Election of 1824: A Case Study in Pressure Politics," *Missouri Historical Review* 60 (1965–1966): 475–476.

31 Lynn Marshall, "The Genesis of Grass-Roots Democracy in Kentucky," *Mid-America* 47 (October 1965), 269–287, reveals a significant county-level correlation between Jackson's vote in 1824 and population growth, 1810–1820. In addition, we can add that of the eight new counties created since 1820, two on the Ohio River gave Clay massive majorities but the other six— at the eastern and western extremes of the state—were the only counties to give absolute majorities to Jackson in 1824 besides those either containing Louisville or across the Ohio from Cincinnati. For the contrast between the Inner Bluegrass and the Green River country, see Stephen Aron, *How the West Was Lost: The Transformation of Kentucky from Daniel Boone to Henry Clay* (Baltimore: Johns Hopkins University Press, 1996), 124–169.

32 *Edwardsville Spectator*, April 27, 1824.

33 This and subsequent paragraphs draw heavily on Ershkowitz, *Origin of the Whig and Democratic Parties*, 1–21.

34 Philadelphia *Franklin Gazette*, in Zanesville *Ohio Republican*, October 30, 1824; NWR, 27 (October 23, 1824), 113–114, which gives the balance as 7:1.

35 Trenton *True American*, October 23, 1824; *New-York Spectator*, October 26, 1824.

36 Isaac Southard to Samuel Southard, September 17, 1824, quoted in Ershkowitz, *Origin of the Whig and Democratic Parties*, 43. See also NWR, 27 (October 23, 1824), 113; Trenton *True American*, November 6, 1824; Plumer to father, December 9, 1824, in WPL, 121.

37 NWR, 27 (November 13, 1824), 162.

38 *New York American*, in *Painesville* [Ohio] *Telegraph*, March 5, 1823.

39 Samuel Smith to Mrs. Mansfield, July 25, 1823, in Pancake, *Samuel Smith*, 166. See also ibid., 159–166; JCCP, 6:620–621, 7:181–183.

40 Kennedy to Maxcy, October 11, 1823, in Mark H. Haller, "The Rise of the Jackson Party in Maryland, 1820–1829," *Journal of Southern History* 28 (1962): 311. For the metropolis, see Gary Lawson Browne, *Baltimore in the Nation, 1789–1861* (Chapel Hill: University of North Carolina Press, 1980), 90–113.

41 The Maryland votes are discussed in Ratcliffe, "Popular Preferences," 66–67.

42 Taney to William Beal, March 19, 1824, in Carl Brent Swisher, *Roger B. Taney* (New York: Macmillan, 1935), 121–122; Trenton *Emporium*, September 25, October 30, 1824, in Walter R. Fee, *The Transition from Aristocracy to Democracy in New Jersey, 1789–1829* (Somerville: Somerset Press, 1933), 255–257.

43 Michael J. Birkner and Herbert Ershkowitz, "'Men and Measures': The Creation of the Second Party System in New Jersey," *New Jersey History* 107 (1989): 44–47; Rudolph J. Pasler and Margaret C. Pasler, *The New Jersey Federalists* (Cranbury, N.J.: Associated University Presses, 1975), 153–155, 170–171. Breaking the pattern, the Dutch in New Jersey had formerly been Federalist.

44 *NWR*, 27 (November 13, 1824), 162; Sydnor, *Development of Southern Sectionalism*, 172.

45 In northern Delaware Jacksonians threw their votes to Adams to keep Crawford out. The quotations are from J. G. Brinklé to John M. Clayton, September 24, 1824, in Richard Arden Wire, "John M. Clayton and the Rise of the Anti-Jackson Party in Delaware, 1824–1828," *Delaware History* 14 (1973): 259–260, and *Trenton Federalist*, November 8, 1824, in Fee, *Transition from Aristocracy*, 259. See also Livermore, *Twilight of Federalism*, 170.

46 This section draws most heavily on Newsome, *Presidential Election*, supplemented by Jeffrey, *State Parties*, 21–33, and Clifft, "Politics of Transition."

47 Romulus M. Saunders to Bartlett Yancy, December 31, 1823, in "Letters of Romulus M. Saunders to Bartlett Yancy," 441; "Debate on the Fisher Resolutions," ed. A. R. Newsome, *North Carolina Historical Review* 4 (1927): 428–470, 5:65–96, 204–223, 310–328; Newsome, *Presidential Election*, 74–75.

48 Charles Fisher to William Polk, February 3, 1824, in Newsome, *Presidential Election*, 87; William Davidson to Fisher, July 10, 1823, "Correspondence of John C. Calhoun," 494.

49 William B. Lewis to William Polk, March 15, 1824, in Jeffrey, *State Parties*, 26–27; John D. Hawkins to William Polk, February 14, 1824, in Newsome, *Presidential Election*, 93; B. B. Smith to Charles Fisher, January 24, 1824, "Correspondence of John C. Calhoun, George McDuffie, and Charles Fisher, Relating to the Presidential Campaign of 1824," ed. A. R. Newsome, *North Carolina Historical Review* 7 (1930): 499, 502.

50 George M. Bibb to John J. Crittenden, March 8, 1824, in Coleman, *Life of John J. Crittenden*, 1:61.

51 Thomas Jefferson Green to William Polk, February 2, 1824, in Newsome, *Presidential Election*, 93; Mr. Martin, quoted in Harry L. Watson, *Jacksonian*

Politics and Community Conflict: The Emergence of the Second American Party System in Cumberland County, North Carolina (Baton Rouge: Louisiana State University Press, 1981), 101–102.

52 Newsome, Presidential Election, 102–104.

53 Quotations from Newsome, Presidential Election, 144–145.

54 William H. Haywood Jr. to Willie P. Mangum, April 17, 1824, in Mangum, Papers of Willie Person Mangum, 1:137; Salisbury Western Carolinian, June 8, 1824, in Newsome, Presidential Election, 140.

55 William Gaston to Daniel Webster, October 10, 1824, DWP, 1:365; Jeffrey, State Parties, 30. For an emphasis on economic distinctions, see Jeffrey Normand Bourdon, "'All Must Have a Say': Internal Improvements and Andrew Jackson's Political Rise in North Carolina in 1824," North Carolina Historical Review 91 (2014): 89–92.

56 Robert Williamson to Bartlett Yancey, July 26, 1824, "Letters to Bartlett Yancey," ed. J. G. De Roulhac Hamilton, James Sprunt Historical Publications 10 (1911): 46–47; Ratcliffe, "Popular Preferences," 67–68. For the "stronghold," see Watson, Jacksonian Politics, 99–102, 147–149.

57 The following paragraphs draw heavily on Charles H. Ambler, Sectionalism in Virginia from 1776 to 1861 (Chicago: Chicago University Press, 1910), 116–132; Clifft, "Politics of Transition," 94–118; Peart, Era of Experimentation, 127–129.

58 Richmond Enquirer, December 4, 1823, in Clifft, "Politics of Transition," 34–35; Ambler, Sectionalism in Virginia, 129–130.

59 Chase, Emergence of the Presidential Nominating Convention, 290–291, 63–66.

60 Elijah Hayward to John Larwill, August 30, 1824, Larwill Family Papers, OHS.

61 Quoted in Carmony, Indiana, 1816–1850, 478.

62 Wilentz, Rise of American Democracy, 248; Robert Williamson to Bartlett Yancey, July 26, 1824, "Letters to Yancey," 46; Smith, "First Straw?" 25–30.

63 Philadelphia Columbian Observer, August 21, 1824, in Coens, "Formation of the Jackson Party," 196.

64 Jacob Deterly, "Remarks," Diary from 1819 to 1848 (MS, Genealogical Society, Salt Lake City, Utah), 2 vols., typescript, OHS, 2:1.

## CHAPTER 9 LEGISLATORS TAKE A HAND

1 David P. Currie, "Choosing the Pilot: Proposed Amendments to the Presidential Selection Process, 1809–1829," Green Bag 2d 4 (Winter 2001): 142–143; Heale, Presidential Quest, 23–32; McCormick, Presidential Game, 110–114, 155–157. In 1823 James Madison claimed that the 1787 constitutional convention had had a district system in mind; Madison to George Hay, August 23, 1823, in H. Clay Reed, "Presidential Electors in Delaware, 1789–1829," Delaware History 14 (1970–1971): 19n.

2 NWR, 25 (December 13, 20, 27, 1823, January 3, 17, 1824), 240–242, 260, 270–271, 273, 317; Mooney, William H. Crawford, 261–262; Currie, "Choosing the Pilot," 143–144.

3    Currie, "Choosing the Pilot," 145.

4    Vipperman, *William Lowndes*, 259; Clay to William Hendricks, November 10, 1823, *HCP*, 3:517; Chase, *Emergence of the Presidential Nominating Convention*, 43, 51.

5    Pleasant M. Miller to Charles Fisher, January 3, 1824, in "Correspondence of John C. Calhoun," 498; Pancake, *Samuel Smith*, 170. See also Chase, *Emergence of the Presidential Nominating Convention*, 18–28.

6    Rufus King to J. A. King, April 20, 1823, *RKC*, 6:519–520. Clinton published some essays treating legislatures as the source of corruption; Hanyan, *De Witt Clinton*, 104–106.

7    Franklin *Missouri Intelligencer*, February 14, September 13, 1824; *Political Tables, Shewing the Population of the Different States, and Exhibiting the Return of Votes at the Elections in 1824 and 1826* (New York, 1828), 9 (quotation); *Woodstock Observer*, in *NWR*, 27 (November 6, 1824), 148.

8    *NWR*, 25 (November 29, 1823), 192.

9    Fletcher M. Green, *Constitutional Development in the South Atlantic States, 1776–1860* (1930; reprint, New York: Norton, 1966), passim.

10   *JCCP*, 7:210, 220–221 (quotation), 227; Freehling, *Prelude to Civil War*, 53–61, 108–116 (quotation, 59).

11   Ames, *State Documents on Federal Relations*, 207; Donald Ratcliffe, "The Nullification Crisis, Southern Discontents, and the American Political Process," *American Nineteenth Century History* 1, no. 2 (2000): 1–30.

12   Freehling, *Prelude to Civil War*, 91–106. Since 1808 apportionment for the legislature had been based on a combination of population and taxable wealth that automatically gave the backcountry a greater voice as slavery expanded there. Rachel N. Klein, *Unification of a Slave State: The Rise of the Planter Class in the South Carolina Backcountry, 1760–1808* (Chapel Hill: University of North Carolina Press, 1990), 262–268. In the October congressional elections, four of the state's nine districts had competitive elections, but in only one district were the presidential preferences of the candidates stated. This was the Cheraw district, which, untypically, heavily backed the states' rights opposition. The Crawford man gained 3,692 votes, the Adams man got 1,869, and Jackson's supporter only 933. One local newspaper, the *Cheraw Intelligencer and Southern Register*, had strongly backed Adams. The district lay on the border with North Carolina: the neighboring counties there voted for the People's Ticket, with a strong endorsement for Adams. I owe this information to the kindness of Philip Lampi.

13   *NWR*, 27 (November 6, 1824), 148; *Western Carolinian*, quoted in Green, *Constitutional Development*, 206; Phillips, *Georgia and States Rights*, 102; Anthony Gene Carey, *Parties, Slavery and the Union in Antebellum Georgia* (Athens: University of Georgia Press, 1997), 21–22. Georgia backed South Carolina's stand over black seamen.

14   *JQAM*, 6:255–256; Wiltse, *John C. Calhoun*, 295; Phillips, *Georgia and States Rights*, 54–55, 69–71; Mary Young, "Racism in Red and Black: Indians and

Other Free People of Color in Georgia Law, Politics, and Removal Policy," *Georgia Historical Quarterly* 73 (1989): 493–495.

15 *Georgia Journal,* October 12, 1824; Phillips, *Georgia and States Rights,* 100–103; Carey, *Parties, Slavery and the Union,* 20–23.

16 Sydnor, *Development of Southern Sectionalism,* 170, 172.

17 Munroe, *Louis McLane,* 99–111, 141–143.

18 Ibid., 143–148, 163–165; Wire, "John M. Clayton," 259–260.

19 *NWR,* 26 (May 29, 1824), 203, 27 (November 13, 1824): 687; Wilmington *Delaware Gazette,* November 16, 1824.

20 *Delaware Gazette,* November 16, 1824; *NWR,* 27 (November 13, 20), 687, 688. Calhoun interpreted the initial news of the voting to mean that Delaware "has lost her vote . . . except for one elector for Mr. Adams." Calhoun to unknown, November 14, [1824], *JCCP,* 9:382. At its next session the assembly passed a law establishing that in future there must be "a distinct balloting for each elector" and "a majority of all votes given shall be necessary for an appointment." Reed, "Presidential Electors in Delaware," 14–18.

21 *NWR,* 23 (March 1, 1823), 402. This and the following paragraphs draw heavily on Joseph G. Tregle Jr., *Louisiana in the Age of Jackson: A Clash of Cultures and Personalities* (Baton Rouge: Louisiana State University Press, 1999), 54–167. The 1822 figure comes from Samuel Hyde, *Pistols and Politics: The Dilemma of Democracy in Louisiana's Florida Parishes, 1810–1899* (Baton Rouge: Louisiana State University Press, 1996), 47.

22 [Eligius Fromentin?] to Clay, April 26, 1822, Clay to Brooke, March 9, 1823, *HCP,* 3:201, 392.

23 [Eligius Fromentin?] to Clay, April 26, 1822, *HCP,* 3:200–201; *Louisiana Gazette,* November 17, 1824, in Tregle, *Louisiana,* 155; John M. Sacher, *A Perfect War of Politics: Parties, Politicians, and Democracy in Louisiana, 1824–1861* (Baton Rouge: Louisiana State University Press, 2003), 19.

24 Sacher, *Perfect War,* 19–20; *AJP,* 5:436 n.4.

25 Clay to Brooke, December 22, 1824, Clay to Porter, December 26, 1824, *HCP,* 3:249, 904–905.

26 New Orleans *Mercantile Advertiser,* November 22, in *Louisville Public Advertiser,* December 15, 1824; Frankfort *Argus of Western America,* in Remini, *Henry Clay,* 249.

27 Eaton to John Coffee, March 2, 1824, in Lowe, "John H. Eaton," 110.

28 *NWR,* 26 (April 24, 1824), 116–117; Rufus King to Charles King, April 21, 1824, *RFK,* 6:567.

29 Thurlow Weed, *The Life of Thurlow Weed Including His Autobiography and a Memoir,* ed. Harriet A. Weed and Thurlow Weed Barnes, 2 vols. (Boston, 1883–1884), 1:108–109, 118, 127; Van Buren to Samuel Smith, August 7, 1824, in Pancake, *Samuel Smith,* 225.

30 Clinton to Henry Post Jr., March 13, 1824, in Hanyan, *De Witt Clinton,* 179; *JHNY,* 2:127.

31 J. B. Mower to Weed, March 5, 1824, in Remini, *Andrew Jackson,* 78; Whea-

ton, quoted in Hanyan, *De Witt Clinton*, 179–180; Tallmadge to Jackson, March 6, 1824, *AJP*, 5:373–375; Parton, *Life of Andrew Jackson*, 3:30, and a New York paper, April 24, 1824, quoted ibid., 3:30n; *AJP*, 5:388. See also Coens, "Formation of the Jackson Party," esp. 187; *WPL*, 110, 114–116.

32  Plumer to Levi Woodbury, May 1, 1824, Levi Woodbury Family Papers, LC (I owe this reference to the kindness of Daniel Peart); Eaton, in Hanyan, *De Witt Clinton*, 201–202; *Philadelphia Gazette*, October 21, 1824, in *New York Spectator*, October 26, 1824.

33  *JQAM*, 6:256–257 (March 13, 1824); Baker, *Henry Wheaton*, 44–55, 62; Hanyan, *De Witt Clinton*, 244.

34  Clinton to Henry Post Jr., December 24, [1823], in Hanyan, *De Witt Clinton*, 161; also 197.

35  *JHNY*, 158–166; Weed, *Life of Thurlow Weed*, 1:109–111.

36  "The People's Nomination," April 15, [1824], handbill, and "Proceedings of a Meeting of the Citizens of Albany," 3, quoted in Chase, *Emergence of the Presidential Nominating Convention*, 64. See also *NWR*, 26 (April 10, 24, 1824), 85–86, 114.

37  Weed, *Life of Thurlow Weed*, 1:119–121; *NWR*, 27 (October 2, 1824), 68.

38  Weed, *Life of Thurlow Weed*, 1:117, 120–121; Alvin Kass, *Politics in New York State, 1800–1830* (Syracuse, N.Y.: Syracuse University Press, 1965), 120. Tallmadge won the lieutenant governor's election by 32,000 votes.

39  *JHNY*, 2:175; Weed, *Life of Thurlow Weed*, 1:125.

40  *WPL*, 115, 143; *JQAM*, 6:292–294, 302, 441–442; Weed, *Life of Thurlow Weed*, 1:166–167.

41  *JHNY*, 2:175, 178.

42  *NWR*, 27 (November 20, 1824), 186; Porter to Clay, January 14, 1825, *HCP*, 4:17.

43  Remini, *Martin Van Buren*, 73–75.

44  Porter to Clay, January 14, 1825, *HCP*, 4:17; Oran Follett to the editor, February 10, 1881, *New York Tribune*, 1881, in Weed, *Life of Thurlow Weed*, 1:130–136. Had the Bucktails nominated the Clay ticket, the Adams men might well have backed it in joint session, thus keeping Crawford out of the House, or else, as Van Buren feared they contemplated, simply paralyzed the legislature and so deprived New York of its electoral vote. Van Buren to Crawford, November 17, 1824, MVBP.

45  Benjamin F. Butler to Jesse Hoyt, November 13, 1824, in Remini, *Martin Van Buren*, 76, 76–77; *NWR*, 27 (November 20, 1824), 185.

46  Weed, *Life of Thurlow Weed*, 1:122–126. Van Buren's proposal of sixteen electoral votes for Clay was less generous than it seemed because Crawford would receive twenty votes, putting Clay four down in comparison. The Weed plan offered only seven electors, but they would all be a net gain for Clay over Crawford.

47  *NWR*, 27 (November 20, 1824), 185, 193–194, 225; Weed, *Life of Thurlow Weed*, 1:126–128.

48  Van Buren to Samuel Smith, November 17, 1824, in Pancake, *Samuel Smith*,

174; Van Buren to Crawford, November 17, 1824, MVBP; Porter to Clay, January 17, 1825, *HCP*, 4:17; *MVBA*, 2:147.

49  Wheaton to Samuel L. Gouverneur, November 21, 1824, in Remini, *Martin Van Buren*, 81, 82; Weed, *Life of Thurlow Weed*, 1:129–130.

50  Weed, *Life of Thurlow Weed*, 1:128. Without the last-minute shenanigans in New York, Clay and Crawford might have tied at forty electoral votes each, in which case both would have been excluded from the House election because the number of candidates was limited to "not exceeding three." *NWR*, 27 (December 4, 1824), 215.

51  Wheaton to Gouverneur, November 21, 1824, in Remini, *Martin Van Buren*, 81; *JHNY*, 2:179; *NWR*, 27 (November 20, 1824), 185.

52  Oran Follett to the editor, February 10, 1881, *New York Tribune*, 1881, in Weed, *Life of Thurlow Weed*, 1:130–136. Note that Weed's own account of the incident, 130, mistakes the timing of Follett's motion; cf. Weed, *Life of Thurlow Weed*, 1:128–129.

53  Ratcliffe, "Presidential Preferences," 68–74.

**CHAPTER 10  THE CORRUPT BARGAIN**

1  Samuel Smith to his grandson, November 16, 1824, in Pancake, *Samuel Smith*, 174; *Richmond Enquirer*, December 23, 1823, in Heale, *Presidential Quest*, 23; *NWR*, 23 (December 20, 1823), 242.

2  Dickerson, January 13, 1819, February 11, 1823, and Benton, February 3, 1824, in Heale, *Presidential Quest*, 27, 30–31. Federalists like Webster were more likely to fear a diminution in the power of the president as he became more dependent on Congress for his election. *DWP*, 1:363.

3  *NWR*, 25 (December 13, 20, 27, 1823, January 3, 17, 1824), 240–242, 260, 270–271, 273, 317; Mooney, *William H. Crawford*, 261–262; Currie, "Choosing the Pilot," 143–144.

4  Willie P. Mangum to Duncan Cameron, January 10, 1825, in Mangum, *Papers of Willie Person Mangum*, 1:173–174, 185.

5  *NWR*, 27 (January 15, 1825), 305; letter from Washington, January 12, 1825, Marietta, Ohio, *American Friend*, January 28, 1825.

6  Smith, *First Forty Years*, 170–171; *JQAM*, 6:443, 501; McLane to his wife, December 29, 1824, in Munroe, *Louis McLane*, 173.

7  Parton, *Life of Andrew Jackson*, 3:52–53; Jackson to Coffee, December 27, 1824, in *AJP*, 5:457–459; Charles Hammond to John C. Wright, January 10, 1825, CHP; McLane to his wife, December 9, 1824, in Munroe, *Louis McLane*, 174.

8  Smith, *First Forty Years*, 170–171; Louis McLane to his wife, January 13, 1825, in Remini, *Henry Clay*, 257.

9  Remini, *Andrew Jackson*, chap. 5.

10  John Johnston to Ethan Allen Brown, December 15, 1824, E. A. Brown Papers, OHS; Philemon Beecher to Thomas Ewing, December 15, 1824, Thomas Ewing Family Papers, LC; Shipp, *Giant Days*, 189–190.

11  Webster to Jeremiah Mason, December 29, 1824, *DWP* 1:379–380; John

Sloane, "Address to the People of the Counties of Columbiana, Stark, and Wayne, in the State of Ohio," Wooster, August 1, 1826, handbill, Richard P. Morgan Ohio Imprint Library, Willoughby, Ohio (which I owe to the great generosity of Rich Morgan); Mangum to Yancey, December 25, 1824, in Mangum, *Papers of Willie Person Mangum*, 1:161.

12  Sloane, "Address to the People," 7, 11; Ratcliffe, "Popular Preferences," 66–67.

13  Ratcliffe, "Popular Preferences," 67–74.

14  Ethan Allen Brown to John Johnston, January 2, 1825, John Johnston Papers, OHS; Romulus M. Saunders to Bartlett Yancey, December 10, 1824, in "Letters of Romulus M. Saunders to Bartlett Yancy," 447.

15  Mangum to Yancey, December 25, 1824, Mangum to John Robertson, January 3, 1825, in Mangum, *Papers of Willie Person Mangum*, 1:161, 170; McLane to his wife, January 13, 1825, in Munroe, *Louis McLane*, 174; Romulus M. Saunders to Bartlett Yancey, January 11, 1825, in "Letters of Romulus M. Saunders to Bartlett Yancy," 449. The five states included New York as well as four South Atlantic states.

16  Ruggles to Worthington, December 18, 1824, Thomas Worthington Papers, OHS; Mangum, *Papers of Willie Person Mangum*, 1:169; Van Buren to Mrs McLane, February 6, 1825, in Remini, *Andrew Jackson*, 91.

17  Elisha Whittlesey to George Tod, December 12, 1824, in "Letters from the Samuel Huntington Correspondence, 1800–1812," ed. Elbert J. Benton, *Tracts of the Western Reserve Historical Society* 95 (1915): 161–163; Plumer to his father, December 15, 1824, January 4, 1825, *WPL*, 122, 128. For Indiana's three congressmen, who came by different routes to vote for Jackson, thus respecting the statewide plurality, see Carmony, *Indiana, 1816–1850*, 483–486.

18  Jenkins and Sala, "Spatial Theory of Voting," 1176–1177; Carson and Engstrom, "Assessing the Electoral Connection."

19  Plumer to his father, December 23, 1823, *WPL*, 83–84; Clay to Francis Brooke, November 26, 1824, *HCP*, 3:888.

20  These maneuvers stemming from Pennsylvanians, with Eaton's presumed involvement, are well discussed in Klein, *Pennsylvania Politics*, 175–185; Lowe, "John H. Eaton," 117–124.

21  Clay to Francis Preston Blair, January 8, 1825, *HCP*, 4:9.

22  Benton's letter, in *Cleveland Herald*, February 15, 1828; Benton, *Thirty Years' View*, 1:48–49.

23  Clay to Hammond, October 25, 1824, and to Benjamin W. Leigh, December 22, 1824, *HCP*, 3:871, 901; *NWR*, 27 (January 1, 1825), 276.

24  Plumer to his father, January 20, 1825, *WPL*, 133.

25  *JQAM*, 6:446–447, 452–453, 456–458, 464–465.

26  *JQAM*, 6:464–465 (January 9, 1825), 258 (March 15, 1824); Clay to James Brown, January 23, 1825, *HCP*, 4:39. For Adams's views, see *JQAM*, 6:343 (May 20, 1824), 353 (May 22, 1824), 418 (September 22, 1824), 451–452 (December 17, 1824).

27  Mangum to Duncan Cameron, January 10, 1825, Mangum, *Papers of Willie*

*Person Mangum*, 1:174; Philemon Beecher to [Governor Allen Trimble?], January 15, 1825, Beecher–Trimble Collection, Cincinnati Historical Society.

28  Edwin Currier to Ephraim Cutler, December 30, 1824, Ephraim Cutler Papers, Marietta College, Ohio; Hammond to Wright, January 10, 1825, CHP; Timothy Fuller to Cutler, January 8, 1825, Cutler Papers. This and the subsequent paragraphs draw heavily on Ratcliffe, *Politics of Long Division*, 92–95.

29  Plumer to his father, December 16, 1824, January 4, 1825, *WPL*, 123, 129; Duncan McArthur to Tobias Watkins, May 18, 1827, Duncan McArthur Papers, LC; Wright to Hammond, January 22, 1825, CHP.

30  Wright to Hammond, December 18, 1824, January 22, 1825, CHP; Wright to Tappan, February 12, 1825, Benjamin Tappan Papers, LC.

31  Gray, *National Waterway*, 53–55; Larson, *Internal Improvement*, 161–165. The votes may be found in *Register of Debates in Congress* (Washington, D.C.: Gales and Seaton, 1824–1837), 18 Cong., 2 sess., 223–224, 333–334.

32  Plumer's journal and Ohio correspondence, quoted in Peter J. Parish, "Daniel Webster, New England, and the West," *Journal of American History* 54 (1967): 535–537; McArthur to Tobias Watkins, May 18, 1827, McArthur Papers; Feller, *Public Lands*, 65–67.

33  *An Address of Henry Clay to the Public, Containing Certain Testimony in Refutation of the Charges Against Him, Made by Gen. Andrew Jackson, Touching the Last Presidential Election* (Washington, 1827), reprinted in *NWR*, 33 (January 5, 12, 1828), 296–315.

34  Kendall to Clay, January 21, 1825, *HCP* 4:35. For the practice of instruction, see Clement Eaton, "Southern Senators and the Right of Instruction, 1789–1860," *Journal of Southern History* 18 (1952): 303–319; C. Edward Skeen, "An Uncertain 'Right': State Legislatures and the Doctrine of Instruction," *Mid-America* 73 (1991): 29–47.

35  Plumer to his father, January 24, 1825, *WPL*, 135–136.

36  *JQAM*, 6:478, 501.

37  Plumer's Journal, March 1825, quoted in William Plumer to Clay, January 8, 1828, *HCP*, 7:20–21; *JQAM*, 6:443, 444, 472, 476–477, 495, 501, 507 (quotation), 512.

38  St. Louis *Missouri Republican*, July 19, 1824; *JQAM*, 6:507. See also "Letters of Romulus M. Saunders to Bartlett Yancy," 448; Weiner, "John Scott," 476–493; and, for the uncertainties in the General Assembly, Perry McCandless, *A History of Missouri, 1820–1860* (Columbia: Missouri University Press, 1972), 75n.

39  George Kremer, in James, *Life of Andrew Jackson*, 428; *JQAM*, 6:443, 456, 473–475, 507; John Scott, "To the People of the State of Missouri," St. Genevieve, Mo., June 26, 1826, Broadsides, American Antiquarian Society; Smith, *First Forty Years*, 185.

40  Plumer to his father, February 29, 1824, *WPL*, 103; Rufus King, Notes, January 29, 1825, in *RKC*, 6:584.

41  Plumer to his father, January 24, 1825, *WPL*, 133–135; *JQAM*, 6:478; R. King, Notes, January 29, 1825, *RKC*, 6:583.

42  Smith, *First Forty Years*, 182, 195.

43  Plumer to his father, December 24, 1825, *WPL*, 124; Philemon Beecher to [Governor Allen Trimble?], January 15, 1825, Beecher–Trimble Collection, Cincinnati Historical Society; Scott, "To the People of the State of Missouri," June 26, 1826, American Antiquarian Society.

44  Beecher to [Trimble?], January 15, 1825, Beecher–Trimble Collection, Cincinnati Historical Society; Plumer to his father, January 4, 1825, *WPL*, 126–127; *JQAM*, 6:479–480; Rufus King, Notes, January 29, 1825, *RKC*, 6:584.

45  Eaton to Overton, February 7, 1825, in Lowe, "John H. Eaton," 116–117.

46  *JQAM*, 6:450–452 (December 22, 1824); Charles D. Lowery, *James Barbour: A Jeffersonian Republican* (University: University of Alabama Press, 1984), 84–150. Crawford himself said later that he would have voted for Adams rather than Jackson: Crawford to Ingersoll, April 4, 1828, Charles Jared Ingersoll Papers, HSP (I owe this last reference to the kindness of Daniel Peart).

47  McLane to his wife, February 20, 1825, and to J. A. Bayard, January 9, 1825, in Munroe, *Louis McLane*, 172, 170; *MVBA*, 152. The claim that in the last days Van Buren schemed to shift Crawfordite votes to Adams was later made by Jabez Hammond "from the best authority" (*JHNY*, 2:190), but he withdrew the claim in a later edition after Van Buren protested in a personal letter (August 21, 1842, MVBP). Sargent repeated the claim in *Public Men and Events*, 1:75–77, citing the testimony of two congressmen of 1825. Remini, *Martin Van Buren*, 85–90, 221–223, argues against the claim, but his evidence comes from Van Buren's letters written before the end of January, supplemented by a touching trust in Van Buren's later claims and a surprising misunderstanding of the references to "Eddy." I find the contemporary evidence of others who were aware of the February conversations more persuasive.

48  *JQAM*, 6:469, 474, 492–494, 497–498; *RKC*, 6:586–587; Remini, *Martin Van Buren*, 223–224; Livermore, *Twilight of Federalism*, 172–196.

49  Romulus Saunders to Bartlett Yancey, December 10, 1824, in "Letters of Romulus M. Saunders to Bartlett Yancy," 446; Rufus King, Notes, January 29, 1825, in *RKC*, 6:584, 587; *JQAM*, 6:497–498 (February 6, 1825); Plumer to his father, February 13, 1825, *WPL*, 137–138.

50  Bonney, *Legacy of Historical Gleanings*, 1:409, 415; John W. Taylor to Adams, August 2, 1823, in Cornog, *Birth of Empire*, 206n28, 153–154.

51  Correspondence with Clinton, December 7, 11, 18, 1825, and Van Rensselaer to Ebenezer Foote, January 25, 1825, in William B. Fink, "Stephen Van Rensselaer and the House Election of 1825," *New York History* 32 (1951): 326–329; *JQAM*, 6:493–494; King, Memoranda, February 9, 10, 1825, *RKC*, 6:585–587; Samuel Flagg Bemis, *John Quincy Adams and the Union* (New York: Knopf, 1956), 47 n.

52  King, Memoranda, February 9, 1825, *RKC*, 6:585–586; Plumer to his father, February 13, 1825, *WPL*, 138. See also *JQAM*, 6:493–494; *MVBA*, 149–152; Smith, *First Forty Years*, 175–176, 181–182.

53   *MVBA*, 151, 152; Smith, *First Forty Years*, 175–176, 184–186, 190–193. See also Livermore, *Twilight of Federalism*, 179–182.

54   *NWR*, 27 (February 12, 1825), 383–384. Niles thought the offenders numbered fifteen or twenty out of the thousand present.

55   Van Buren to James A. Hamilton, January 26, 1825, in Hamilton, *Reminiscences of James A. Hamilton;* Plumer to his father, February 13, 1825, *WPL*, 138; Beecher to [Trimble?], January 15, 1825, Beecher–Trimble Collection, Cincinnati Historical Society. Clay's emissary, Letcher, had told Adams in late January that victory on the first ballot was essential: *JQAM*, 6:452–453.

56   McLane to J. A. Bayard, January 9, 1825, and to his wife, February 9, February 20, 1825, in Munroe, *Louis McLane*, 170–172. In "Spatial Theory of Voting," 1157–1179, Jenkins and Sala argue that the congressmen who voted for Adams were voting in accord with their ideological affinity to him and not because their votes were bought. Though revealing, their methodology is not totally convincing because they define Adams's ideological stance as being what it proved to be after reaching his understanding with Clay—and it also does not enable them to explain why congressmen from New York and Pennsylvania who also agreed with Adams voted for Crawford and Jackson.

57   Wright to Hammond, February 13, 1825, CHP; Leverett Saltonstall to William Minor, February 22, 1825, and to his wife, Mary, February 9, 11, 1825, in Saltonstall, *Letters of Leverett Saltonstall*, 1:155, 1:143, 1:144–145, and 1:142–159.

58   William Henry Harrison to Hammond, March 9, 1825, quoted in Hammond to [Clay], October 18, 1827, *HCP*, 6:1160.

59   Jenkins and Sala, "Spatial Theory of Voting," 1175; Carson and Engstrom, "Assessing the Electoral Connection," 746–757.

60   Cincinnati *National Republican*, December 28, 1824, February 18, 1825; Philadelphia *Columbian Observer*, March 10, 1825, in Klein, *Pennsylvania Politics*, 186; *Washington City Gazette*, April 19, 1825, in Coens, "Formation of the Jackson Party," 205 (and for the Jacksonian response in general, 203–240); Thomas H. Genin to Hammond, May 4, 1825, CHP.

61   Diary of John H. James, 1825, in *A Buckeye Titan*, ed. William E. Smith and Ophia D. Smith (Cincinnati: Historical and Philosophical Society of Ohio, 1953), 386; Hammond to Wright, March 16, 1825, CHP; Clay to Francis Brooke, March 4, 1825, CHP, 4:87–88; Sloane to Whittlesey, June 13, 1825, Elisha Whittlesey Papers, WRHS; Clay to James Brown, September 4, 1825, *HCP*, 4:617.

62   James Heaton to John McLean, March 19, 1825, James Heaton Papers, LC. The role of the Cabinet is best described in *JQAM* for 1817–1825, passim, and Cunningham, *Presidency of James Monroe*, esp. 124–126.

63   Calhoun to Smith Thompson, November 10, 1824, *JCCP*, 9:379. See also "Monroe on the Adams–Clay 'Bargain,'" ed. Barnes F. Lathrop, *American Historical Review* 42 (1937): 273–276.

64   *MVBA*, 150; Jackson to William B. Lewis, February 14, 1825, *AJP*, 6:29–30.

65 Jenkins and Sala, "Spatial Theory of Voting," 1176.

66 Jackson to Lewis, February 20, 1825, *AJP*, 6:36–38. Richard R. Stenberg, in his "Jackson, Buchanan, and the 'Corrupt Bargain' Calumny," *Pennsylvania Magazine of History and Biography* 58 (1934): 61–85, argues that the obsession in Jackson's correspondence with the corrupt bargain charge amounted to a cynical and deceitful manipulation of the truth; this view underestimates Jackson's ability to deceive himself.

67 Richard M. Johnson to William Seaton (of the *National Intelligencer*), early in the 1825–1826 session, reported in *NWR*, 32 (April 28, 1827), 152–154.

68 *MVBA*, 194–196.

69 Remini, *Andrew Jackson*, 12–38; Ratcliffe, *Politics of Long Division*, 235–236. For Jacksonian use of the corrupt bargain charge in 1828, see Donald B. Cole, *Vindicating Andrew Jackson: The 1828 Election and the Rise of the Two-Party System* (Lawrence: University Press of Kansas, 2009).

70 Washington *United States Telegraph*, 1828 passim.

**EPILOGUE**

1 J. Samuel Valenzuela, "Political Polarization, Institutional Failure, and Regime Breakdown: The Contentious 1829 Elections in Chile," in *The Oxford Handbook of Revolutionary Elections in the Americas, 1800–1911*, ed. Eduardo Posada-Carbó and Andrew Robertson (New York: Oxford University Press), forthcoming.

2 Levasseur, *Lafayette in America*, 2:24; *JQAM*, 6:483; Josiah S. Johnston to Chandler Price, February 1, 1825, in Klein, *Pennsylvania Politics*, 183.

3 *JQAM*, 6:483; Edward Ingersoll to J. S. Johnston, February 18, 1825, in Klein, *Pennsylvania Politics*, 186; Levasseur, *Lafayette in America*, 2:23–30. The story could well be apocryphal because the liberal Levasseur was particularly keen to emphasize that democracy would be safe for France. I am grateful to Daniel Peart for drawing this moment to my attention.

4 Donald Ratcliffe, "Political Disintegration and Losers' Consent: The U.S. Presidential Election of 1824," in Posada-Carbó and Robertson, *Oxford Handbook of Revolutionary Elections* (forthcoming).

5 Culver H. Smith, *The Press, Politics, and Patronage: The American Government's Use of Newspapers, 1789–1875* (Athens: University of Georgia Press, 1975), 56–59; Dangerfield, *Era of Good Feelings*, 331–343; Bemis, *John Quincy Adams and the Union*, 32–55.

6 Josiah S. Johnston to Clay, September 22, 1824, *HCP*, 3:844–845.

7 Calhoun to Ninian Edwards, June 12, 1822, *JCCP*, 7:160; Jeffrey L. Pasley, *"The Tyranny of Printers": Newspaper Politics in the Early Republic* (Charlottesville: University of Virginia Press, 2001).

8 Peart, *Era of Experimentation*, 128, 130.

9 Eaton to Overton, March 7, 1824, in Lowe, "John H. Eaton," 110. For the role of committees of correspondence, see Kass, *Politics in New York State*, 35–39.

10 Cf. Ronald P. Formisano, "Political Character, Antipartyism, and the Second Party System," *American Quarterly* 21 (1969): 683–709.

11  Kass, *Politics in New York State*, 39.

12  Wheaton to Maxcy, June 19, 1823, in Livermore, *Twilight of Federalism*, 97.

13  McDuffie, 1826, quoted in Lucius Wilmerding, *The Electoral College* (New Brunswick, N.J.: Rutgers University Press, 1958), 47; McCormick, *Presidential Game*, 157–158.

14  Currie, "Choosing the Pilot," 145–146; Ratcliffe, *Politics of Long Division*, 202–203; McCormick, *Presidential Game*, 159–163.

15  Donald J. Ratcliffe, "The Forgotten Origins of the Northern Whigs, 1827–1833," *Proceedings of the Ohio Academy of History* (2002): 69–78, and "Antimasonry and Partisanship in Greater New England, 1826–1836," *Journal of the Early Republic* 15 (1995): 197–237.

16  Sydnor, *Development of Southern Sectionalism*, 180; Stephen Skowroneck, *The Politics Presidents Make: Political Leadership from John Adams to George Bush* (Cambridge: Harvard University Press, 1993), 39.

17  Coens, "Formation of the Jackson Party," 247–282.

18  *MVBA*, 198; John Tyler to John Rutherfoord, December 8, 1827, in Tyler, *Letters and Times of the Tylers*, 376–378; Charles Reemelin, "Reminiscences of Moses Dawson," *Cincinnati Commercial*, December 11, 1869.

19  Van Buren to Thomas Ritchie, January 13, 1827, MVBP; Duff Green to Jackson, June 9, 1827, *AJP*, 6:339. See also Richard H. Brown, "The Missouri Crisis, Slavery, and the Politics of Jacksonianism," *South Atlantic Review* 65 (1966): 55–72; Ratcliffe, "Nullification Crisis."

20  Angus Campbell, "Surge and Decline," *Public Opinion Quarterly* 24 (1960): 397–418. For the 1828 election, see Cole, *Vindicating Andrew Jackson;* Ratcliffe, *Politics of Long Division*, 131–310.

21  Richard P. McCormick, *The Second American Party System: Party Formation in the Jacksonian Era* (Chapel Hill: University of North Carolina Press, 1966), 128–130, 159–160; Ratcliffe, *Politics of Long Division*, xi–xv, 161–163; Watson, *Jacksonian Politics*, 110, 114–115, 208–209, 288; *Political Tables, Shewing the Population of the Different States, and Exhibiting the Return of Votes at the Elections in 1824 and 1826, and in Several of the States in 1828, With Remarks* (New York: Elliott & Palmer, 1828), iii–iv.

22  Van Buren to Ritchie, January 13, 1827, MVBP; Ratcliffe, *Politics of Long Division*, 277–310; Cole, *Jacksonian Democracy.*

23  Ratcliffe, "Nullification Crisis," 12–15.

# BIBLIOGRAPHIC ESSAY

This is the first book-length study of this unusual and testing election as a whole. Only two books have been devoted to the election in particular states, one by Albert Newsome on North Carolina published in 1939 and the other by Harry Stevens on Ohio in 1955. While the elections of 1800 and 1828 never cease to attract authors, the elections in between remain neglected except in anthologies and encyclopedias that endeavor to provide a systematic survey. Indeed, relatively little has been published in recent decades on the politics of the early 1820s except in biographies and studies of the politics of slavery. George Dangerfield's graphic *The Era of Good Feelings* (New York: Harcourt, Brace, and World, 1952) remains essential reading; the same author's *The Awakening of American Nationalism, 1815–1828* (New York: Harper & Row, 1965) is briefer but blander. Daniel Peart's recent *Era of Experimentation: American Political Practices in the Early Republic* (Charlottesville: University of Virginia Press, 2014) stands out as a welcome, fresh-thinking analysis of these very years, but its emphasis on political activity that fell outside the party paradigm and its focus on a handful of states led the author to underestimate this key presidential election.

Short treatments of the election are overall of low standard. The best short essay remains James F. Hopkins, "Election of 1824," in *History of American Presidential Elections, 1789–1968*, ed. Arthur M. Schlesinger Jr. and Fred L. Israel, 4 vols. (New York: Chelsea House, 1971), 1:349–381. Melba Porter Hay, "1824," in *Running for President: The Candidates and Their Images*, ed. A. M. Schlesinger, Fred L. Israel, and David J. Frent (New York: Simon & Schuster, 1994), 85–99, presents a reasonable summary and provides some striking images. Donald R. Deskins Jr., Hanes Walton, and Sherman C. Puckett, eds., *Presidential Elections, 1789–2008: County, State and National Mapping of Election Data* (Ann Arbor: University of Michigan Press, 2010), 80–84, combines fascinating maps with an inaccurate text.

Useful introductions may also be found in three colossal works of the last quarter century that reasserted the significance of 1824 in American political development: Charles Sellers's stimulating if idiosyncratic *The Market Revolution: Jacksonian America, 1815–1846* (New York: Oxford University Press, 1991), Sean Wilentz's neo-Progressive *The Rise of American Democracy: Jefferson to Lincoln* (New York: Norton, 2005), and Daniel Walker Howe's monumental and insightful *What Hath God Wrought: The Transformation of America, 1815–1848* (New York: Oxford University Press, 2007), 203–211, 237–241. Though Howe's approach is Whiggish compared with the Jacksonian bias of the others, all three stress democratic transition as the chief issue of the election. These views tended to overlook the lessons of Chilton Williamson, *American Suffrage: From Property* to *Democracy, 1760–1860* (Princeton, N.J.: Princeton University Press, 1960), which showed that, with a few state exceptions, the United States operated a political system based on near-universal manhood suffrage long before 1815. In part historians have been misled by the confused coverage of suffrage reforms between the Revolution and the Civil War in Alexander Keyssar's influential *The Right to Vote: The Contested History of Democracy in the United States* (New York: Basic Books, 2000). A recent attempt to restore clarity may be found in Donald Ratcliffe, "The Right to Vote and the Rise of Democracy, 1787–1828," *Journal of the Early Republic* 33 (2013): 219–254.

Newspapers were the essential means of communicating news and views by the 1820s. Their expansion and influence in the Jeffersonian era are authoritatively revealed in Jeffrey L. Pasley, *"The Tyranny of Printers": Newspaper Politics in the Early Republic* (Charlottesville: University of Virginia Press, 2001), as are the means of exchange in Richard R. John, *Spreading the News: The American Postal System from Franklin to Morse* (Cambridge, Mass.: Harvard University Press, 1995). My own understanding of the period is derived from a wide reading of Ohio newspapers, as listed in my *The Politics of Long Division: The Birth of the Second Party System in Ohio, 1818–1828* (Columbus: Ohio State University Press, 2000). Insights into the reactions and behavior of different publics can be gained best by a systematic reading of newspaper files rather than by using the search facilities of modern online collections. However, these collections provide access to otherwise unobtainable newspapers and cannot be ignored: I have used both *Proquest Historical Newspapers* and the *19th Century U.S. Newspapers* database from Gale Cengage Learning. *Niles' Weekly Register* provides an extraordinary compendium of news from across the nation and is available online from Proquest American Periodical Series New Platform.

All students of this election owe a great debt to the magnificent documentary letterpress collections relating to leading politicians that have been produced over recent decades. There are disadvantages, indicated below, with one or two of the collections, and there is nothing comparable for such key figures as Adams, Crawford, Van Buren, and Clinton. Equally, some older collections are valuable for 1824, notably Charles R. King's highly revealing collection of *The Life and Correspondence of Rufus King*, 6 vols. (New York: G. P. Putnam's Sons, 1900), vol. 6. *The Papers of Daniel Webster*, series 1, *Correspondence*, ed. Charles M. Wiltse, 7 vols. (Hanover: University Press of New England, 1974–1986), vols. 1 and 2, also include valuable summaries.

For Jackson, see *The Papers of Andrew Jackson*, ed. Sam B. Smith et al., 9 vols. to date (Knoxville: University of Tennessee Press, 1980–). Unfortunately the volumes for these years (volumes 5 and 6) deliberately omit some well-known Jackson letters that were already available; it is therefore still necessary to consult the older collection edited by John Spencer Bassett, *Correspondence of Andrew Jackson* (Washington, D.C.: Carnegie Institution, 1928). James Parton, *Life of Andrew Jackson*, 3 vols. (New York: Mason Bros., 1861), vol. 3, reprints some important memoirs and contradicts some early myths. Robert V. Remini's three-volume biography is the fullest and most graphic modern account; the relevant volume is entitled *Andrew Jackson and the Course of American Freedom, 1822–1832* (New York: Harper & Row, 1981). Gabriel L. Lowe Jr., "John H. Eaton, Jackson's Campaign Manager," *Tennessee Historical Quarterly* 11 (1952): 99–147, reveals the management of the Jackson campaigns.

Calhoun's political letters are submerged beneath the monumental record of his work at the War Office in *The Papers of John C. Calhoun*, ed. W. Edwin Hemphill et al., 28 vols. (Columbia: University of South Carolina Press, 1959–2003), vols. 6–9, and so some older collections remain useful, especially A. R. Newsome, ed., "Correspondence of John C. Calhoun, George McDuffie and Charles Fisher, Relating to the Presidential Campaign of 1824," *North Carolina Historical Review* 7 (1930): 477–504. One of the most informative sources on Calhoun's campaign is Thomas Robson Hay, "John C. Calhoun and the Presidential Campaign of 1824," *North Carolina Historical Review* 12 (1935): 20–45. Charles M. Wiltse's admiring three volumes provide the fullest biography; for this period, see his *John C. Calhoun: Nationalist, 1782–1828* (New York: Bobbs-Merrill, 1944), to which Gerald M. Capers, *John C. Calhoun: Opportunist* (Gainesville: University of Florida Press, 1960) offers a useful counterirritant. Of more recent biographies, Irving H. Bartlett, *John C. Calhoun: A Biography* (New York: Norton, 1993) provides the best introduction, and John Niven, *John C. Calhoun and the Price of Union* (Baton Rouge: Louisiana State University Press, 1988) has the more penetrating political insights.

Henry Clay is well served by James F. Hopkins et al., editors of *The Papers of Henry Clay*, 7 vols. (University of Kentucky Press, 1959–1992), vols. 2–4. The fullest biography is Robert V. Remini's *Henry Clay, Statesman for the Union* (New York: Norton, 1991), though the author's treatment of 1824 forgets some of the insights in his earlier biography of Jackson. Maurice G. Baxter, *Henry Clay and the American System* (Lexington: University Press of Kentucky, 1995), is a brief biography rather than a study of Clay's economic program.

Our knowledge of William Crawford is limited by the destruction of his papers. He has received thorough and sympathetic treatment in Chase C. Mooney, *William H. Crawford, 1772–1834* (Lexington: University Press of Kentucky, 1974). Some revealing materials may be found in J. E. D. Shipp, *Giant Days: The Life and Times of William H. Crawford* (Americus, Ga.: Southern Printers, 1909); in "Ten Letters from William Harris Crawford to Martin Van Buren," ed. William Henry Williams, *Georgia Historical Quarterly* 49 (1965): 605–632; and in Albert Gallatin, *The Writings of Albert Gallatin*, ed. Henry Adams, 3 vols. (Philadelphia: J. B. Lippincott, 1879), vol. 2.

John Quincy Adams's correspondence is available in the microfilms of the Adams Family Papers deposited in the Massachusetts Historical Society. His diary is highly revealing, sometimes not intentionally so, even in its published version, which produces only half of the original text: *Memoirs of John Quincy Adams, Comprising Portions of His Diary from 1795 to 1848*, ed. Charles Francis Adams, 12 vols. (1874–1877; reprint, Freeport, N.Y.: Books for Libraries Press,

1969). Recent biographies of Adams tend to be too narrowly focused to advance our understanding of this election or politics in general.

The Library of Congress's collection of the Martin Van Buren Papers is available on microfilm in the Presidential Papers series (36 reels, Library of Congress, 1948–1980) and is used here; the more comprehensive microfilm, based on a broad trawl of American repositories (55 reels, Alexandria, Va.: Chadwyck-Healey, 1989), is less easily obtainable. "The Autobiography of Martin Van Buren," edited by John C. Fitzpatrick, *Annual Report of the American Historical Association for 1918* (Washington, D.C., 1920), contains some invaluable and revealing passages but is at times misleading on 1824. Van Buren is taken too much at his own estimate in Robert V. Remini's lively *Martin Van Buren and the Making of the Democratic Party* (New York: Columbia University Press, 1959), but useful correctives may be found in John Niven, *Martin Van Buren: The Romantic Age of American Politics* (New York: Oxford University Press, 1983), and especially Donald B. Cole's thoroughly researched *Martin Van Buren and the American Political System* (Princeton, N.J.: Princeton University Press, 1984).

Those unable to use the De Witt Clinton's Papers at Columbia University can find scattered correspondence in John Bigelow, ed., "De Witt Clinton as a Politician," *Harper's New Monthly Magazine* 50 (1875): 409–417, 563–571, and in Mrs. Catharina V. R. Bonney, comp., *A Legacy of Historical Gleanings*, 2 vols. (Albany, N.Y.: J. Munsell, 1875), which reprints some valuable Van Rensselaer family papers. Evan Cornog's brief *The Birth of Empire: De Witt Clinton and the American Experience, 1769–1828* (New York: Oxford University Press, 1998) introduces the career, while Craig Hanyan with Mary L. Hanyan, *De Witt Clinton and the Rise of the People's Men* (Montreal: McGill–Queen's University Press, 1996), provides fascinating data and interesting perceptions, especially from Clinton's perspective, of events at this critical moment in New York.

Some minor politicians wrote deeply observant letters that have been published. William Plumer's revealing letters to his father from within the Adams camp appear in *The Missouri Compromises and Presidential Politics, 1820–1825: From the Letters of William Plumer Jr.*, ed. Everett Somerville Brown (St. Louis: Missouri Historical Society, 1926). For a Southern (and North Carolina) perspective, see "Letters to Bartlett Yancey," ed. J. G. De Roulhac Hamilton, *James Sprunt Historical Publications* 10 (1911): 25–76, and "Letters of Romulus M. Saunders to Bartlett Yancy [sic], 1821–1828," ed. A. R. Newsome, *North Carolina Historical Review* 8 (1931): 427–462. This book reveals my own debt to a reading of the Charles Hammond Papers at the Ohio Historical Society, which are available on microfilm in the Ohio Political Leaders microfilm series. Margaret Bayard Smith's keen observation of Washington society and her involvement in the Crawford campaign are revealed in *The First Forty Years of Washington Society: Portrayed by the Family Letters of Mrs. Samuel Harrison Smith*, ed. Gaillard Hunt (New York: Scribner, 1906).

The official voting figures are available by county in Michael J. Dubin, *United States Presidential Elections, 1788–1860: The Official Results by County and State* (Jefferson, N.C.: McFarland, 2002), 31–42. The best source for this and preceding elections is the American Antiquarian Society's A New Nation Votes website (http://elections.lib.tufts.edu/), which holds the state- and county-level voting data for 1787–1825 collected by Philip Lampi. The nature of the collection as it applies to this election is explained, with Lampi's help, in Donald Ratcliffe, "Popular Preferences in the Presidential Election of 1824," *Journal of the Early Republic* 34 (2014): 45–77.

Modern secondary works on this election are few, and the student of this election has to browse among ancient texts. The ignoring of this election owes much to uncertainty about the nature of political development in this period; it lacks the clarity of the regular two-party situation, which brings the comfort of simple definition to voters and historians alike. Charles S. Sydnor brought some clarity by defining it as "The One-Party Period of American History," *American Historical Review* 51 (1946): 439–451. Richard P. McCormick's *The Second American Party System: Party Formation in the Jacksonian Era* (Chapel Hill: University of North Carolina Press, 1966) introduced the concept that a series of "party systems" (better described as "electoral systems") has marked U.S. political development, summarizing the work on partisanship before 1815 that had been published in recent years and discussing the uneven route by which a "second party system" came into existence by the late 1830s. This heightened the problem of describing politics in the 1820s, which did not fit the dominant model.

Subsequently some political historians argued that the party system approach was mistaken in that it imposed on politics before 1815 a framework of interpretation derived from later periods. This view was an article of faith for proponents of the New Political History, as expressed in the essays of Ronald P. Formisano and William G. Shade in *The Evolution of American Electoral Systems*, ed. Paul Kleppner et al. (Westport, Conn.: Greenwood Press, 1981). The same assumption also underlies the work of those historians who preferred to think in terms of a party period from the 1830s to the 1890s when partisan considerations reigned supreme compared to the weaker partisan structures before and after. Ronald P. Formisano recognized the need to explain politics before the 1830s in a much-cited essay, "Deferential-Participant Politics: The Early Republic's Political Culture, 1789–1840," *American Political Science Review* 68 (1974): 473–487, and in a monumental state study, *The Transformation of Political Culture: Massachusetts Politics, 1790s–1840s* (New York: Oxford University Press, 1983). Richard P. McCormick underlined the prevailing view in his *The Presidential Game: The Origins of American Presidential Politics* (New York: Oxford University Press, 1982), by describing the politics of the period from 1824 to 1832 as marked by factions rather than parties.

The main qualification to this trend was an important essay by Joel H. Silbey, "The Incomplete World of American Politics, 1815–1829: Presidents, Parties and Politics in 'The Era of Good Feelings,'" *Congress and the Presidency* 11 (1984): 3–17, which pointed out that memories of earlier partisan conflict persisted and created a situation that helped to explain subsequent political developments. This argument drew on three books, all important for understanding the 1824 election, which demonstrated the persistence of the concerns of the First Party

System. Robert V. Remini's lively *Martin Van Buren and the Making of the Demo-cratic Party* revealed the determination to revive the old Jeffersonian party. Shaw Livermore, *The Twilight of Federalism: The Disintegration of the Federalist Party, 1815–1830* (Princeton, N.J.: Princeton University Press, 1962), demonstrated the persistence of Federalism and the reluctance of Democratic Republicans to admit its adherents to the political mainstream. Norman K. Risjord, *The Old Republicans: Southern Conservatism in the Age of Jefferson* (New York: Columbia University Press, 1965), examined the extreme Jeffersonian ideologues in the Old South and showed how they extended their influence in the 1820s.

The role of serious issues in the 1824 campaign, often reflecting cultural concerns about the health of the republic, was emphasized by Paul C. Nagel, "The Election of 1824: A Reconsideration Based on Newspaper Opinion," *Journal of Southern History* 26 (1960): 315–329. The theme was developed in the early 1970s by Robert P. Hay in a series of essays: "The Case for Andrew Jackson in 1824: Eaton's 'Wyoming Letters,'" *Tennessee Historical Quarterly* 29 (1970): 139–151; "'The Presidential Question': Letters to Southern Editors," *Tennessee Historical Quarterly* 31 (1972): 170–186; and "The American Revolution Twice Recalled: Lafayette's Visit and the Election of 1824," *Illinois Magazine of History* 69 (1973): 43–72. This line of thought culminated with M. J. Heale's perceptive, and now classic, *The Presidential Quest: Candidates and Images in American Polit-ical Culture, 1787–1852* (New York: Longman, 1982), which inter alia emphasized the significance of the 1824 election.

Other historians were more concerned to demonstrate the inadequacy of Mc-Cormick's mechanistic approach to party formation by showing how societal forces, voter perceptions, and ideological considerations helped mold the 1824 election. Both Donald J. Ratcliffe, "The Role of Voters and Issues in Party For-mation: Ohio, 1824," *Journal of American History* 59 (1973): 847–870, and Kim T. Phillips, "The Pennsylvania Origins of the Jackson Movement," *Political Science Quarterly* 91 (1976): 489–508, sought to create a more satisfactory interpretation that brought voters, their concerns, and the articulation of issues into the elec-toral picture. Robert E. Shalhope, "Jacksonian Politics on Missouri: A Comment on the McCormick Thesis," *Civil War History* 15 (1969): 210–225, showed the role the 1824 election played in Missouri's political development through the creation of lasting party persuasions. These approaches were dismissed as inter-esting but of no significance for the later party system, which the New Political History believed arose essentially out of the social and cultural tensions of the 1830s; this view was sustained by the work of the ethnocultural historians, who brilliantly demonstrated the importance of noneconomic influences on voting behavior but tended to divorce the concerns of voters from both political issues and the behavior of politicians. Ethnocultural research rarely reached back to the 1820s; two helpful exceptions were William G. Shade, "Pennsylvania Poli-tics in the Jacksonian Period: A Case Study, Northampton County, 1824–1844," *Pennsylvania History* 39 (1972): 313–333, and Donald J. Ratcliffe, "Politics in Jack-sonian Ohio: Reflections on the Ethnocultural Interpretation," *Ohio History* 88 (1979): 5–36. My *Politics of Long Division* (2000) was an attempt to show in detail how in the 1820s political pressures; social, economic, and cultural realities; the work of politicians; and the facts of voter behavior created the dynamic out of which the classic party system of the late 1830s arose.

That process began in the extraordinary crisis that hit the United States in 1818–1819 and led to the 1824 election. To understand that context, see the key writings on the Monroe presidency: Dangerfield's *Era of Good Feelings*, Harry Ammon's *James Monroe: The Quest for National Identity* (Charlottesville: University Press of Virginia, 1990), and Noble E. Cunningham Jr., *The Presidency of James Monroe* (Lawrence: University Press of Kansas, 1996). The international context is best explained in Samuel Flagg Bemis, *John Quincy Adams and the Foundations of American Foreign Policy* (New York: Knopf, 1949), and James E. Lewis Jr., *The American Union and the Problem of Neighborhood: The United States and the Collapse of the Spanish Empire, 1783–1829* (Chapel Hill: University of North Carolina Press, 1998). Ernest R. May, *The Making of the Monroe Doctrine* (Cambridge, Mass.: Harvard University Press, 1975), combined the overseas crisis with a fascinating analysis of the election campaign as it stood by December 1823, but he was misled by the gossip and sycophancy of politicians. An informed critique that emphasizes Monroe's control is provided by Harry Ammon, "The Monroe Doctrine: Domestic Politics or National Decision?," *Diplomatic History* 5 (1981): 53–70.

The significance of political life within the republic's isolated capital is discussed by James Sterling Young's influential *The Washington Community, 1800–1828* (New York: Columbia University Press, 1966), which suffers from a tendency to generalize across totally different political situations. For a correction of its distinctive argument about congressmen's messes, see Allan G. Bogue and Mark Paul Marlaire, "Of Mess and Men: The Boardinghouse and Congressional Voting, 1821–1842," *American Journal of Political Science* 19 (May 1975): 224–226. Catherine Allgor's interesting *Parlor Politics: In Which the Ladies of Washington Help Build a City and a Government* (Charlottesville: University of Virginia Press, 2000), exaggerates female participation in politics, accepts Young's picture of Washington's isolation, and so interprets the 1824 election in too narrow a compass. "Washington's Political Press and the Election of 1824" are briefly surveyed by William E. Ames and S. Dean Olsen in *Journalism Quarterly* 40 (1963): 343–350, while another means of communication with voters is illustrated in Noble E. Cunningham Jr., *Circular Letters of Congressmen to Their Constituents, 1789–1829*, 3 vols. (Chapel Hill: University of North Carolina Press, 1978).

On the great sectional crisis of 1819–1821, Glover Moore's *The Missouri Controversy, 1819–1821* (Lexington: University of Kentucky Press, 1953) fails to take antislavery sentiment seriously, while Robert Pierce Forbes, *The Missouri Compromise and Its Aftermath: Slavery and the Meaning of America* (Chapel Hill: University of North Carolina Press, 2007), underplays both the antislavery buildup to the crisis and popular pressures during it. Their accounts should be supplemented by two recent demonstrations of the vigor of antislavery before and through 1820: Mathew Mason, *Slavery and Politics in the Early American Republic*

(Chapel Hill: University of North Carolina Press, 2006), and John Craig Hammond, *Slavery, Freedom, and Expansion in the Early American West* (Charlottesville: University of Virginia Press, 2007). See also Major L. Wilson, *Space, Time, and Freedom: The Quest for Nationality and the Irrepressible Conflict, 1815–1861* (Westport, Conn.: Greenwood Press, 1974), 22–48; Leonard L. Richards, *The Slave Power: The Free North and Southern Domination, 1780–1860* (Baton Rouge: Louisiana State University Press, 2000), 52–54; and Sean Wilentz, "Jeffersonian Democracy and the Origins of Political Antislavery in the United States: The Missouri Crisis Revisited," *Journal of the Historical Society* 4 (2004): 375–401. For changing racial attitudes, see John Wood Sweet, *Bodies Politic: Negotiating Race in the American North, 1730–1830* (Baltimore: Johns Hopkins University Press, 2003). My own understanding is expressed in "The Decline of Antislavery Politics, 1815–1840," in *Contesting Slavery: The Politics of Bondage and Slavery in the New American Nation*, ed. John Craig Hammond and Matthew Mason (Charlottesville: University of Virginia Press, 2011).

The Panic of 1819 and the subsequent depression deserve a modern in-depth and extensive treatment. We still rely on Murray N. Rothbard's *The Panic of 1819: Reactions and Policies* (New York: Columbia University Press, 1962), which was concerned more with policy arguments than events, and had a distinctly anti–hard money bias, as had Bray Hammond, *Banking and Politics in America: From the Revolution to the Civil War* (Princeton, N.J.: Princeton University Press, 1957). The broader social effects were best dealt with in even older short treatments: Thomas H. Greer, "Economic and Social Effects of the Depression of 1819 in the Old Northwest," *Indiana Magazine of History* 64 (1948): 227–243, and Samuel Rezneck, "The Depression of 1819–22: A Social History," *American Historical Review* 39 (1933): 28–47, which is reprinted in his *Business Depressions and Financial Panics: Essays in American Business and Economic History* (Westport, Conn.: Greenwood, 1968), 53–72.

On the national economic issues that followed the Panic, see in particular John Lauritz Larson, *Internal Improvement: National Public Works and the Promise of Popular Government in the Early United States* (Chapel Hill: University of North Carolina Press, 2001). Daniel Feller's well-researched *The Public Lands in Jacksonian Politics* (Madison: University of Wisconsin Press, 1984), is illuminating on far more than its narrow title suggests. On the protective tariff, Edward Stanwood, *American Tariff Controversies in the Nineteenth Century*, 2 vols. (Westminster: Archibald Constable, 1904), 1:200–242, remains useful, though largely displaced by Jonathan J. Pincus's treatment of the 1824 tariff in his *Pressure Groups and Politics in Antebellum Tariffs* (New York: Columbia University Press, 1977), which provides invaluable economic and legislative information before embarking on econometric and theoretical speculations.

Valuable perspectives on the election at both national and state level can be gained through some highly readable biographies of minor characters. The most revealing include Charles Sellers, *James K. Polk, Jacksonian, 1795–1843* (Princeton, N.J.: Princeton University Press, 1957), for Tennessee; John A. Munroe, *Louis McLane: Federalist and Jacksonian* (New Brunswick, N.J.: Rutgers University Press, 1973), for Delaware; and Charles D. Lowery, *James Barbour: A Jeffersonian Republican* (University: University of Alabama Press, 1984), for Virginia. For Missouri, see William Nisbet Chambers, *Old Bullion Benton: Senator from the New West* (Boston: Little, Brown, 1956).

On the revolution in nominating methods, the classic statement remains M. Ostrogorski, "The Rise and Fall of the Nominating Caucus, Legislative and Congressional," *American Historical Review* 5 (1899): 255–283. The best modern treatment is James S. Chase, *The Emergence of the Presidential Nominating Convention, 1789–1832* (Urbana: University of Illinois Press, 1973), but the democratic purposes of those who defended the congressional caucus in 1824 are brought out by Thomas M. Coens, "The Formation of the Jackson Party, 1822–1825" (Ph.D. diss., Harvard University, 2004).

The House election is frequently described, but not always well. Both Dangerfield, *Era of Good Feelings,* and Samuel F. Bemis, *John Quincy Adams and the Union* (New York: Knopf, 1956), describe Adams's agonies as he is compelled to enter into deals contrary to his inclinations but necessary for his success. Alan S. Weiner, "John Scott, Thomas Hart Benton, David Barton, and the Presidential Election of 1824: A Case Study in Pressure Politics," *Missouri Historical Review* 60 (1965–1966): 460–494, offers the best study of the pressures behind a single vote in the House election. On the Van Rensselaer story, see William B. Fink, "Stephen Van Rensselaer and the House Election of 1825," *New York History* 32 (1951): 323–330. Jeffery J. Jenkins and Brian R. Sala, "The Spatial Theory of Voting and the Presidential Election of 1824," *American Journal of Political Science* 42 (1998): 1157–1179, uses the spatial theory of voting and the notion of electoral connection to contradict the corrupt bargain charge by arguing that in the House election congressmen voted for the candidate closest to them ideologically. One does not have to accept Richard R. Stenberg's character assassination of Jackson in his "Jackson, Buchanan, and the 'Corrupt Bargain' Calumny," *Pennsylvania Magazine of History and Biography* 58 (1934): 61–85, to appreciate his demonstration of the thinness of the evidence for the "bargain and corruption" charge.

For the Adams administration, see Mary W. M. Hargreaves, *The Presidency of John Quincy Adams* (Lawrence: University Press of Kansas, 1985). In "Assessing the Electoral Connection: Evidence from the Early United States," *American Journal of Political Science* 49 (2005): 746–757, Jamie L. Carson and Erik J. Engstrom demonstrate that in the elections of 1826–1827, individual congressmen were punished for having voted against the presidential preference previously expressed by their constituents' wishes, but most survived the contest. The best recent book on the 1828 election is Donald B. Cole, *Vindicating Andrew Jackson: The 1828 Election and the Rise of the Two-Party System* (Lawrence: University Press of Kansas, 2009). Lynn Hudson Parsons, *The Birth of Modern Politics: Andrew Jackson, John Quincy Adams, and the Election of 1828* (New York: Oxford University Press, 2009), emphasizes the personal rivalry between its two protagonists but adds little to our understanding. Robert V. Remini, *The Election of Andrew Jackson* (Philadelphia: Lippincott, 1963), remains a lively and rewarding read.

McCormick's *Second American Party System* demonstrated the value of state-level studies and provides useful introductions to the constitutional and political structures on each state at this time. However, state-level study of this election remains patchy. The rich historiography of New England is disappointingly thin or unhelpful in this instance; the main exception is Donald B. Cole, *Jacksonian Democracy in New Hampshire, 1800–1851* (Cambridge, Mass.: Harvard University Press, 1970). The South, with the exception of North Carolina is also thinly served, though it can boast the best brief regional survey of the 1824 election in Charles S. Sydnor's *The Development of Southern Sectionalism, 1819–1848* (Baton Rouge: Louisiana State University Press, 1948), 157–176. William J. Cooper Jr., *Liberty and Slavery: Southern Politics to 1860* (New York: Knopf, 1983), offers a useful summary. Neither makes the mistake of thinking that state and local concerns took priority over the perception of national contests.

New York has rightly attracted the most attention, though it was a most untypical state politically. The masterly account is Jabez D. Hammond, *The History of Political Parties in the State of New York, From the Ratification of the Constitution to December, 1840*, 2 vols. (Albany: printed by C. Van Benthuysen, 1842), which is remarkable for the sympathetic analytical balance maintained by an author who was himself an active Clintonian. Dixon Ryan Fox, *The Decline of Aristocracy in the Politics of New York, 1801–1840* (1919; reprint, New York: Harper & Row, 1965) is the classic Progressive account and remains far more revealing on the 1820s than Lee Benson's hit-and-miss but stimulating *The Concept of Jacksonian Democracy: New York as a Test Case* (Princeton, N.J.: Princeton University Press, 1961). Alvin Kass presents a skeptical look at *Politics in New York State, 1800–1830* (Syracuse, N.Y.: Syracuse University Press, 1965), in the spirit of Richard P. McCormick, but the analysis suffers from a failure to consider change over time during the period.

The significance of the presidential contest as the origin of New York's political crisis of 1824 did not escape C. H. Rammelkamp in his still useful "The Campaign of 1824 in New York," *Annual Report of the American Historical Association for the Year 1904* (Washington, D.C., 1905), 177–201. Remini's lively *Martin Van Buren and the Making of the Democratic Party* remains most useful, although it occasionally oversimplifies Van Buren's policy and maneuverings. Remini's earlier "The Albany Regency," *New York History* 39 (1958): 341–355, is a useful summary but underestimates the extent of party organization and the centralized use of patronage before 1821. Michael Wallace, "Changing Concepts of Party in the United States: New York, 1815–1828," *American Historical Review* 74 (1968): 453–491, is an important study of the ideology of the Van Burenites but underplays its earlier development and dissociates the analysis of ideas from the electoral situation in which they were uttered. Jerome Mushkat, *Tammany: The Evolution of a Political Machine, 1789–1865* (Syracuse, N.Y.: Syracuse University Press, 1971), provides the essential city perspective on the early Democrats.

The confusions of Pennsylvania's politics are explained in Philip Shriver Klein's rewarding *Pennsylvania Politics, 1817–1832: A Game without Rules* (Philadelphia: Historical Society of Pennsylvania, 1940), though there were "rules" that the attentive reader can decipher. Kim Phillips's brilliantly perceptive "The

Pennsylvania Origins of the Jackson Movement" (1976) is a little too focused on urban politics and exaggerates the significance of the Old School Democratic Republicans in the Jackson coalition. Her dissertation, published as Kim Tousley Phillips, ed., *William Duane, Radical Journalist in the Age of Jackson* (New York: Garland, 1989), is essential reading, especially for the Jacksonian revolution of January 1824 in Philadelphia.

The key works for New Jersey are Herbert Ershkowitz, *The Origin of the Whig and Democratic Parties: New Jersey Politics, 1820–1837* (Washington, D.C.: University Press of America, 1982), and Michael J. Birkner and Herbert Ershkowitz, "'Men and Measures': The Creation of the Second Party System in New Jersey," *New Jersey History* 107 (1989): 41–59. The election in Maryland is surveyed in Mark H. Haller, "The Rise of the Jackson Party in Maryland, 1820–1829," *Journal of Southern History* 28 (1962), 307–326, but the subject is best approached through biographies of two men: Carl Brent Swisher, *Roger B. Taney* (New York: Macmillan, 1935), and John S. Pancake, *Samuel Smith and the Politics of Business, 1752–1839* (Tuscaloosa: University of Alabama Press, 1972), which is a little wild in its timings and therefore some explanations. For the metropolis, see Gary Lawson Browne, *Baltimore in the Nation, 1789–1861* (Chapel Hill: University of North Carolina Press, 1980).

Virginia has been surprisingly neglected despite its importance in 1824. The most revealing book is Norman Risjord's *The Old Republicans* (1965). William G. Shade, *Democratizing the Old Dominion: Virginia and the Second Party System, 1824–1861* (Charlottesville: University of Virginia Press, 1996), provides essential context, while Harry Ammon, "The Richmond Junto, 1800–1824," *Virginia Magazine of History and Biography* 61 (1953): 395–418, describes the inner body controlling the state's politics at this time. For the argument that the Junto did not actually exist, see the articles by T. F. Miller in the *Virginia Magazine of History and Biography* 61 (1953): 395–418 and 99 (1991): 63–80, balanced by Trenton E. Hizer, "Virginia Is Now Divided: Politics in the Old Dominion, 1820–1833" (Ph.D. diss., University of South Carolina, 1997).

North Carolina is unique in the range and quality of its published primary materials and secondary work relating to this election. Albert Ray Newsome, *The Presidential Election in 1824 in North Carolina* (Chapel Hill: University of North Carolina Press, 1939), remains the essential study, while Thomas E. Jeffrey, *State Parties and National Politics: North Carolina, 1815–1861* (Athens: University of Georgia Press, 1989) emphasizes the importance of the old Federalist vote in the opposition to Crawford. Of the many published collections of correspondence, see in particular *The Papers of Willie Person Mangum*, ed. Henry Thomas Shanks, 5 vols. (Raleigh, N.C.: State Department of Archives and History, 1950), vol. 1, together with *The Papers of Thomas Ruffin*, ed., J. G. DeRoulac Hamilton, 4 vols. (Raleigh: North Carolina Historical Commission, 1918–1920), and *The Papers of Archibald D. Murphy*, ed. William Henry Hoyt (Raleigh: North Carolina Historical Commission, 1914), 1:289–299.

Most studies of politics in other Southern states are too focused on later periods to be useful for this election. Some classics remain essential, notably Ulrich

B. Phillips, *Georgia and States Rights* (1902; reprint, Antioch Press, 1968), and Thomas P. Abernethy, *The Formative Period in Alabama, 1815–1828* (Montgomery, Ala.: Brown Printing, 1922), as well as William W. Freehling's exciting *Prelude to Civil War: The Nullification Controversy in South Carolina, 1816–1836* (New York: Harper & Row, 1966). For a delightful analysis of Louisiana and its politics, see Joseph G. Tregle Jr., *Louisiana in the Age of Jackson: A Clash of Cultures and Personalities* (Baton Rouge: Louisiana State University Press, 1999), which should be supplemented by John M. Sacher, *A Perfect War of Politics: Parties, Politicians, and Democracy in Louisiana, 1824–1861* (Baton Rouge: Louisiana State University Press, 2003).

In the upper southwest, Tennessee has benefited from insightful studies by Charles Sellers, notably, for this election, his classic "Jackson Men with Feet of Clay," *American Historical Review* 62 (1957): 537–551. See also "Banking and Politics in Jackson's Tennessee," *Mississippi Valley Historical Review* 14 (1927): 311–325, and the stunning *James K. Polk, Jacksonian, 1795–1843* (Princeton, N.J.: Princeton University Press, 1957). The fullest account of Kentucky's internal politics are to be found in Arndt M. Stickles, *The Critical Court Struggle in Kentucky, 1819–1829* (Bloomington: Indiana University, 1929), but Donald B. Cole, *A Jackson Man: Amos Kendall and the Rise of American Democracy* (Baton Rouge: Louisiana State University Press, 2004), offers insights into the Relief and New Court movements and the rise of Jacksonism, especially after 1824.

In the Old Northwest, the Ohio election received closely detailed attention in Harry R. Stevens, *The Early Jackson Party in Ohio* (Durham, N.C.: Duke University Press, 1955), which argued that personal connections were the key to party formation. A broader interpretation was suggested in Donald J. Ratcliffe's critical "The Role of Voters and Issues in Party Formation: Ohio, 1824," *Journal of American History* 59 (1973): 847–870, which itself prompted a debate in the pages of *Ohio History* 86 (1977): 155–170, 88 (1979): 5–36, 100 (1991): 89–90, and was followed by a fuller analysis in the context of the whole process of party formation in my *Politics of Long Division* (2000). The most useful studies of Indiana are Thomas W. Howard, "Indiana Newspapers and the Presidential Election of 1824," *Indiana Magazine of History* 63 (1967): 177–206, and Donald F. Carmony, *Indiana, 1816–1850: The Pioneer Era* (Indianapolis: Indiana Historical Society, 1998), esp. 467–484.

Illinois has attracted much interesting writing in recent years because of the critical antislavery struggle of 1823–1824. I found James Simeone's *Democracy and Slavery in Frontier Illinois: The Bottomland Republic* (DeKalb: Northern Illinois University Press, 2000), highly informative about the political context, though its interpretations are overly generalized and dichotomized; David Ress's *Governor Edward Coles and the Vote to Forbid Slavery in Illinois, 1823–1824* (Jefferson, N.C.: McFarland, 2006) helpful on the politics; and Suzanne Cooper Guasco, *Confronting Slavery: Edward Coles and the Rise of Antislavery Politics in Nineteenth-Century America* (DeKalb: Northern Illinois University Press, 2013), persuasive in its interpretation of the antislavery campaigns. Gerard Leonard, *The Invention of Party Politics: Federalism, Popular Sovereignty, and Constitutional*

*Development in Jacksonian Illinois* (Chapel Hill: University of North Carolina Press, 2002), and Daniel Peart, *Era of Experimentation* (2014), 47–72, both establish the power of antipartyism in frontier Illinois but, like other works, seem unwilling to make connections between the various election campaigns of 1824. Thus Theodore Pease, *The Frontier State, 1818–1848* (Springfield: Illinois Centennial Commission, 1918), and Karl E. Leichtle, "The Rise of Jacksonian Politics in Illinois," *Illinois Historical Journal* 82 (1989): 93–107, remain invaluable.

Highly regrettable is the comparative lack of modern writing on the 1824 election. Robin Kolodny, "The Several Elections of 1824," *Congress and the Presidency* 23 (1996): 139–164, emphasizes the role of issues but is too schematized and unreliable in detailed comment. Andrew Burstein's lively *America's Jubilee* (New York: Alfred A. Knopf, 2001), captures the atmosphere of American life and thought in the mid-1820s but throws little light directly on the election. James H. Rigali, "Restoring the Republic of Virtue: The Presidential Election of 1824" (Ph.D. diss., University of Washington, 2004), examines how republican concepts of virtue, honor, and manhood shaped the behavior and campaigns of the candidates. Thomas M. Coens, "The Formation of the Jackson Party, 1822–1825" (Ph.D. diss., Harvard University, 2004), effectively bludgeons those who believe the early Jackson movement was a radical democratizing force, stressing instead practical and historic pressures. Like Coens, Joseph Clinton Clifft's "The Politics of Transition: Virginia and North Carolina and the Presidential Election of 1824" (Ph.D. diss., University of Tennessee, 1999) stresses the building of the Jacksonian coalition after March 1825. Sean Patrick Adams, ed., *A Companion to the Era of Andrew Jackson* (Chichester, U.K.: Wiley-Blackwell, 2013), including essays on 1824 by Coens, Sharon Ann Murphy, and John M. Sacher, appeared too recently to help with this volume.

# INDEX

128–129, 176, 180, 184, 200, 265

Old Republicans, 29, 295n41
  meaning Democratic Republican loyalists, 40–44, 48, 134, 275, 276
  meaning Southern conservatives (*see* neo-Antifederalists)

Otis, Harrison Gray, 57, 67–68, 69

Overton, John, 116, 117

*Painesville Telegraph*, Ohio, 175

pamphlets, 91, 130, 176, 178, 181, 192, 205

Panic of 1819, 5, 14–17, 99–100, 121, 188, 256–257, 275

parties, political
  persistence of party loyalties, 11–12, 43–44, 77–78, 84, 227, 272–273, 275–276
  proper role of, 4–5, 11–13, 39–44, 218
  source of national unity, 57, 76–78, 80
  *See also* caucus, congressional

Parton, James, 219, 328

Patchell, Edward, 125

"Patriot King," 129–133, 256, 276

Pennsylvania, 53, 100, 105–106, 119–128, 171–172
  appeal of American System, 103–104, 105, 156–157, 162
  Calhoun's initiative, 36, 151–152
  Clinton's appeal, 72, 73, 90
  Democratic factions, 36, 120–128
  earlier electoral experience, 12, 49, 121, 262
  Family Party, 36, 120, 121–126
  House election, 235, 258–259
  Independent Republican coalition, 120–123, 125–126
  Jacksonian coup, 116, 119–120, 122–124, 127, 162
  Jacksonism, sources of, 125–128, 128–133

New School Democrats, 120–121, 124, 125

old party appeal, 42, 43–44, 150, 154, 157, 165, 167

Old School Democrats, 120–122, 126–128

Pennsylvania Dutch. *See* Germans

People's Party (New York), 75, 86–89, 92, 105, 216–223

People's Ticket (North Carolina), 191–195

Philadelphia, 12, 75, 123–124, 126–127, 254, 258
  business politics, 36, 103, 105, 120, 124, 125
  Federalist plurality, 44, 106, 120, 124, 127, 171
  immigrant community, 55, 127–128, 165–167

*Philadelphia Sentinel*, 87, 88

Pickering, Timothy, 69

Pittsburgh, 111, 122, 125, 129

Plumer, William
  neo-Federalists, 31, 35, 153, 155
  Northern man, 49, 62, 70, 133, 222–223, 235–236
  quoted, 94–95, 120, 219, 240, 241–242, 249

polling stations, 199–200

Polk, William, 191–192

popular interest in election, 7, 20, 21–22, 144, 179, 194, 230, 253, 272

Porter, Peter B., 85, 222, 224, 226

*Portland Argus*, Maine, 88

post offices, 39, 80

Presbyterians, 58, 108, 125, 133, 175, 211

press, role of
  interchange of news, 19, 35, 39, 80, 102, 130
  local press, 174, 176, 199, 214–215, 261, 264–265
  metropolitan press, 61–62, 105, 137, 165–167, 261
  *See also individual titles*